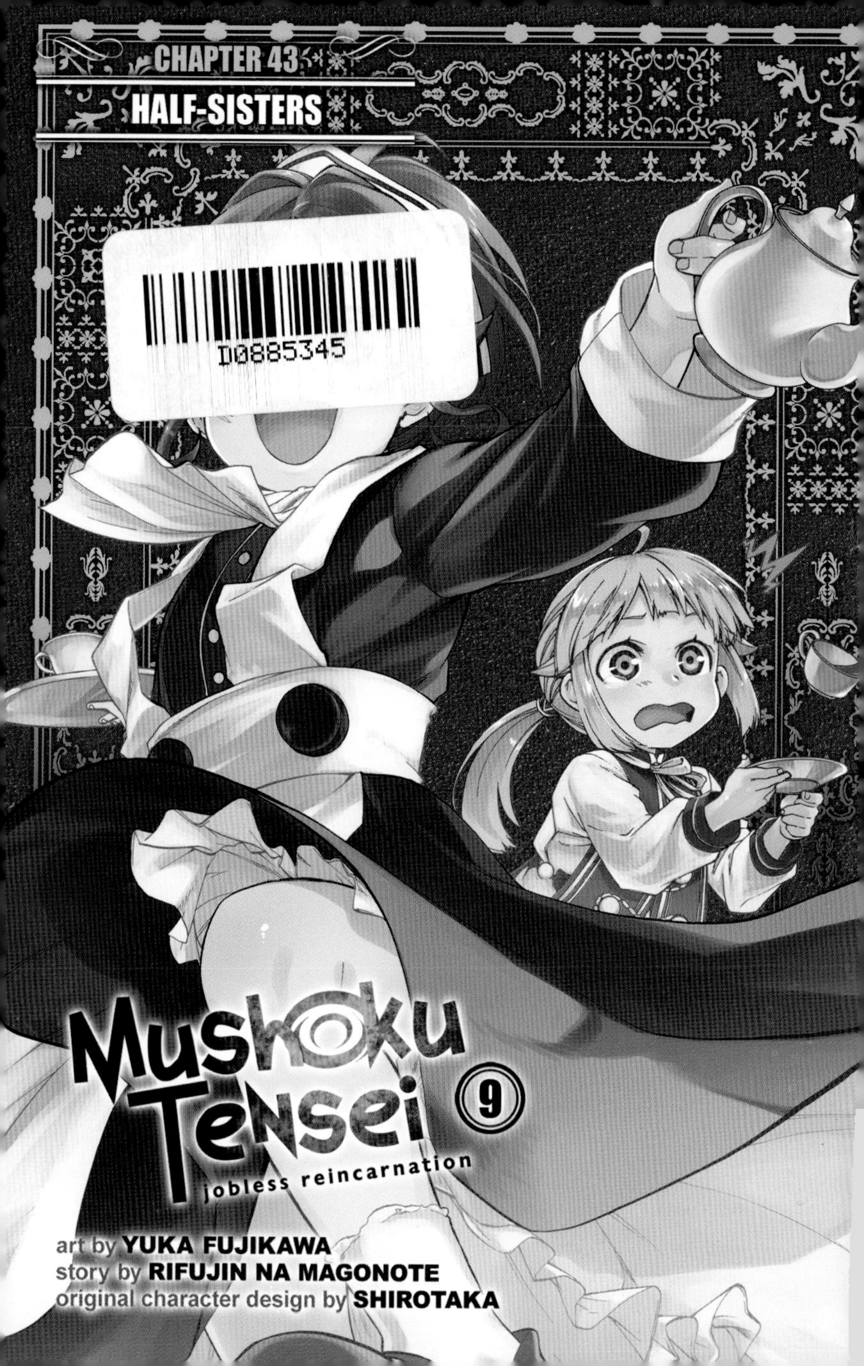
CHAPTER 43
HALF-SISTERS
Mushoku Tensei
9
jobless reincarnation
art by YUKA FUJIKAWA
story by RIFUJIN NA MAGONOTE
original character design by SHIROTAKA

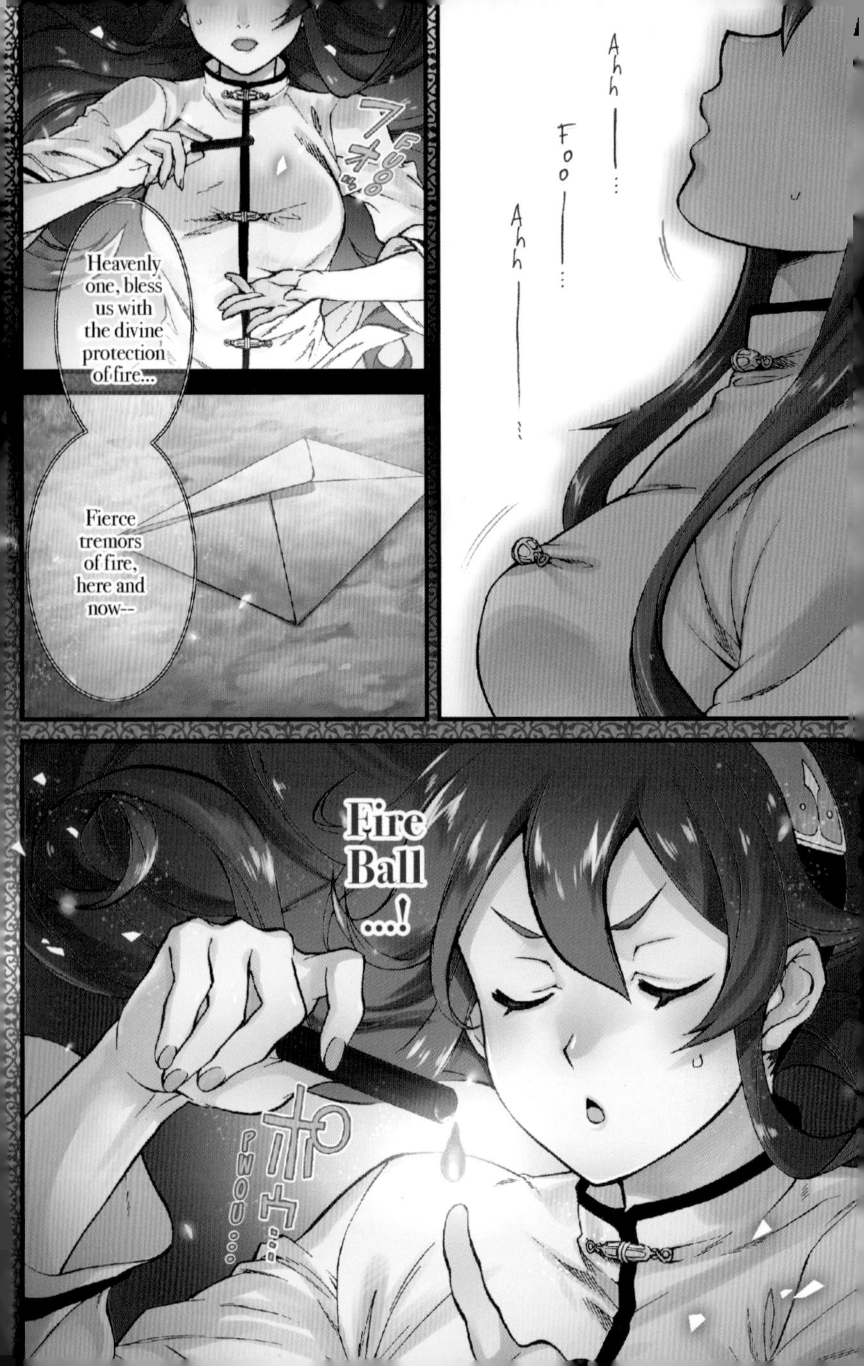
Ahh—...
Foo—...
Ahh—...
FUOO
Heavenly one, bless us with the divine protection of fire...
Fierce tremors of fire, here and now--
Fire Ball ...!
PWOU...

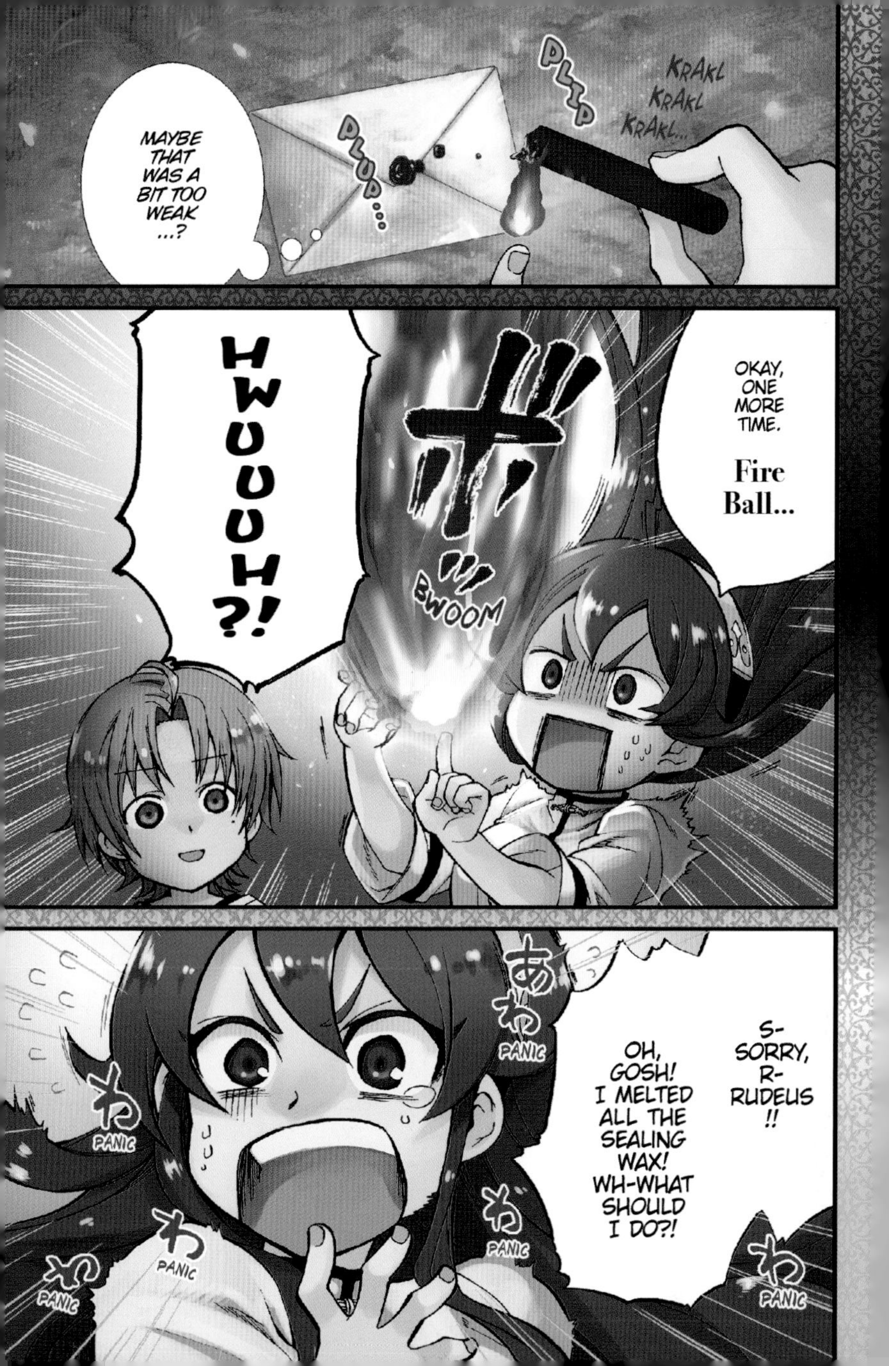
KRAKL KRAKL KRAKL...
PLIP
PLUP...
MAYBE THAT WAS A BIT TOO WEAK ...?
OKAY, ONE MORE TIME.
Fire Ball...
BWOOM
HWUUUUH?!
S-SORRY, R-RUDEUS!!
OH, GOSH! I MELTED ALL THE SEALING WAX! WH-WHAT SHOULD I DO?!
あわ
PANIC
わ
PANIC
わ
PANIC
わ
PANIC
わ
PANIC
わ
PANIC

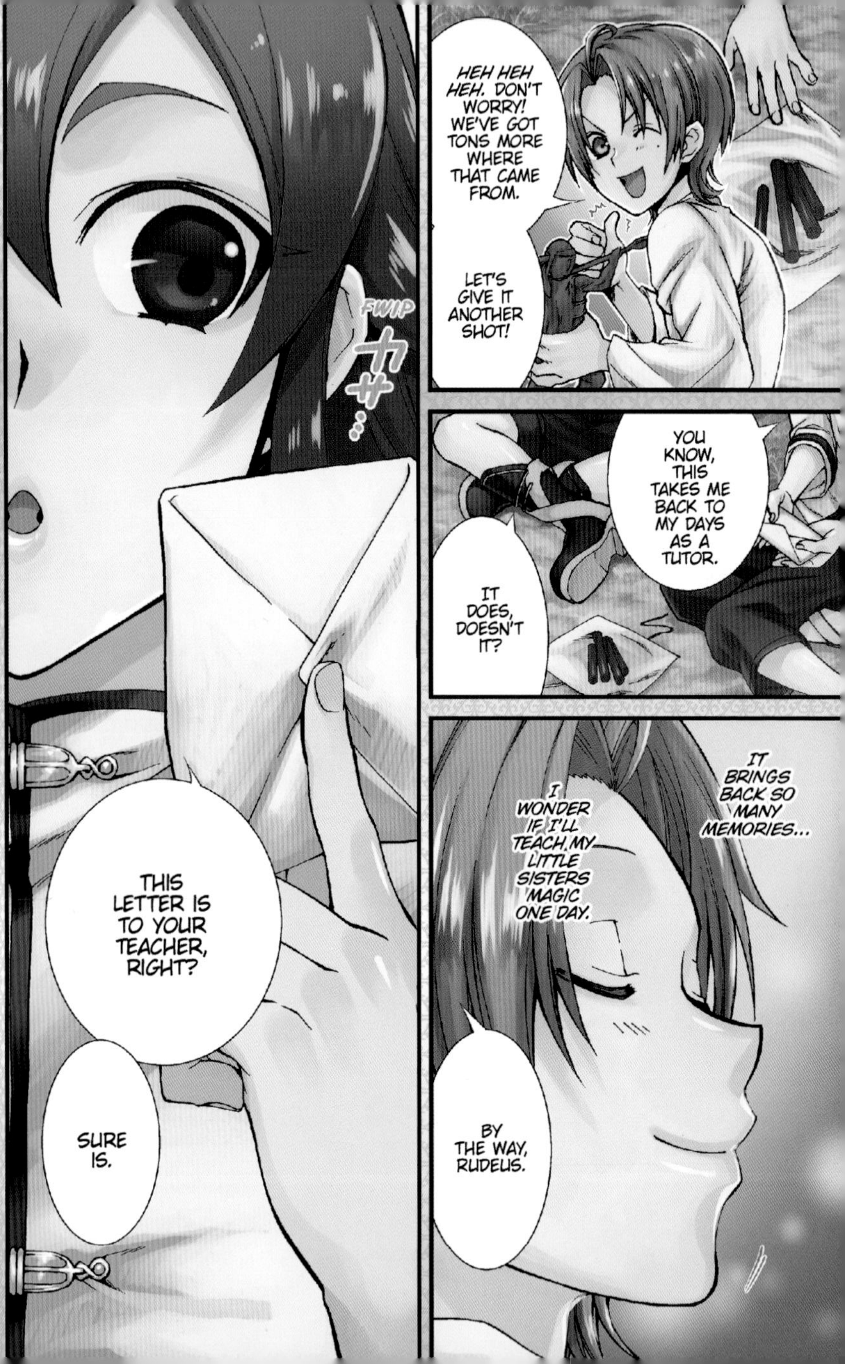
HEH HEH HEH. DON'T WORRY! WE'VE GOT TONS MORE WHERE THAT CAME FROM.
LET'S GIVE IT ANOTHER SHOT!
YOU KNOW, THIS TAKES ME BACK TO MY DAYS AS A TUTOR.
IT DOES, DOESN'T IT?
IT BRINGS BACK SO MANY MEMORIES...
I WONDER IF I'LL TEACH MY LITTLE SISTERS MAGIC ONE DAY.
BY THE WAY, RUDEUS.
FWIP
THIS LETTER IS TO YOUR TEACHER, RIGHT?
SURE IS.

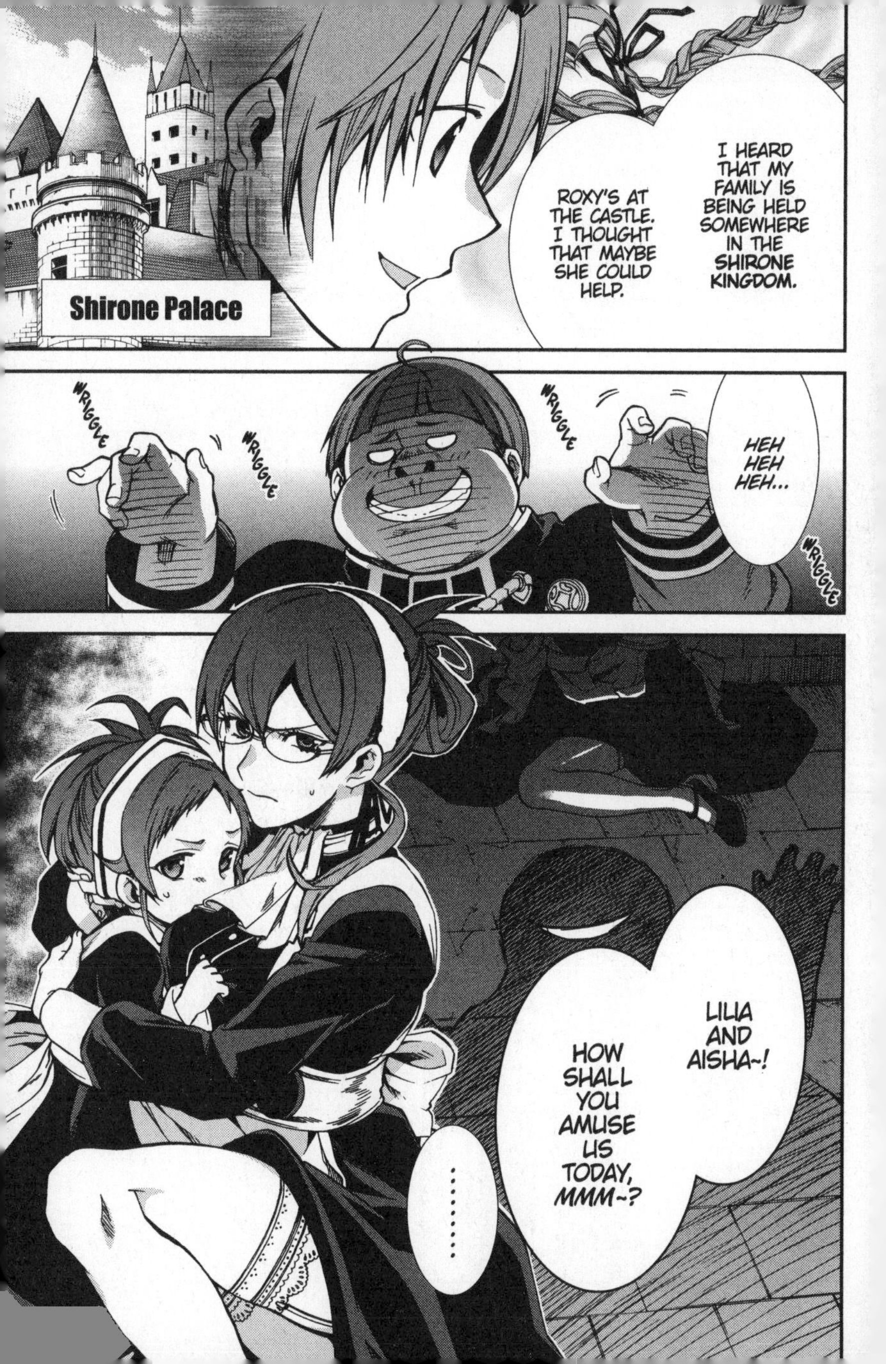
I HEARD THAT MY FAMILY IS BEING HELD SOMEWHERE IN THE SHIRONE KINGDOM.
ROXY'S AT THE CASTLE. I THOUGHT THAT MAYBE SHE COULD HELP.
Shirone Palace
HEH HEH HEH...
WRIGGLE
WRIGGLE
WRIGGLE
WRIGGLE
LILIA AND AISHA~!
HOW SHALL YOU AMUSE US TODAY, MMM~?
......

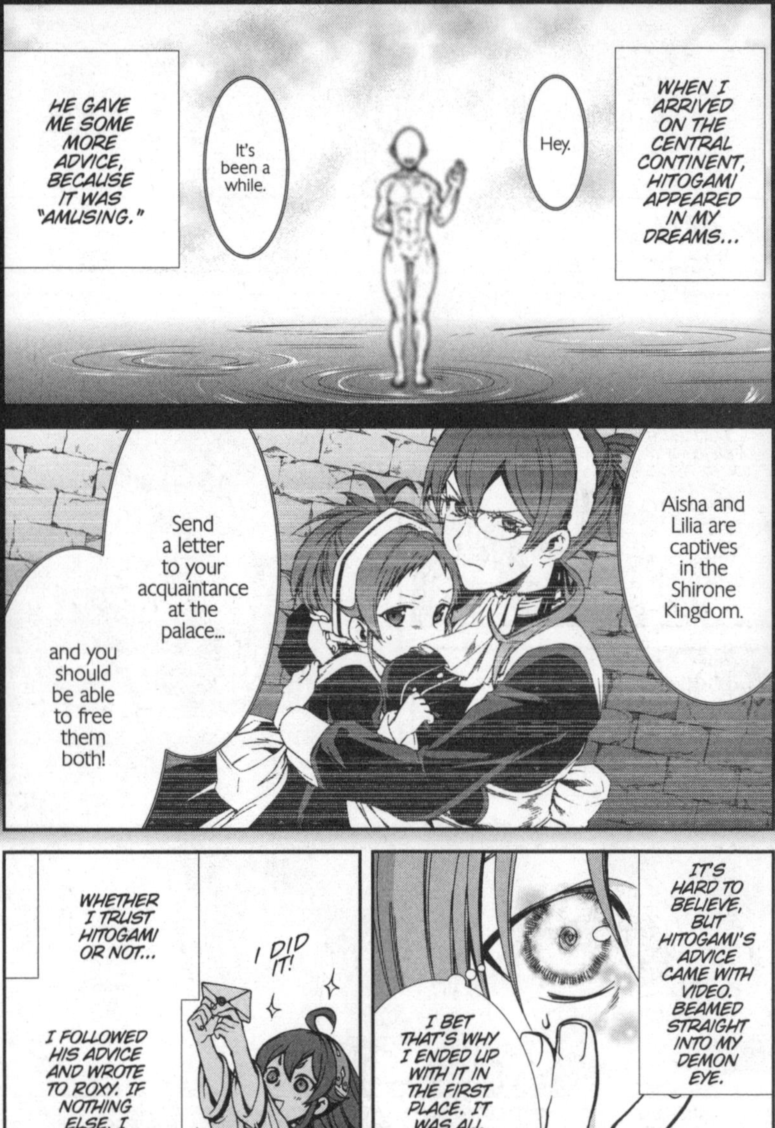
WHEN I ARRIVED ON THE CENTRAL CONTINENT, HITOGAMI APPEARED IN MY DREAMS...
Hey.
It's been a while.
HE GAVE ME SOME MORE ADVICE, BECAUSE IT WAS "AMUSING."
Aisha and Lilia are captives in the Shirone Kingdom.
Send a letter to your acquaintance at the palace...
and you should be able to free them both!
IT'S HARD TO BELIEVE, BUT HITOGAMI'S ADVICE CAME WITH VIDEO. BEAMED STRAIGHT INTO MY DEMON EYE.
I BET THAT'S WHY I ENDED UP WITH IT IN THE FIRST PLACE. IT WAS ALL PART OF HITOGAMI'S PLAN...
WHETHER I TRUST HITOGAMI OR NOT...
I DID IT!
I FOLLOWED HIS ADVICE AND WROTE TO ROXY. IF NOTHING ELSE, I WANTED TO SEE HER.

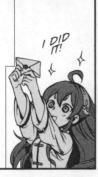

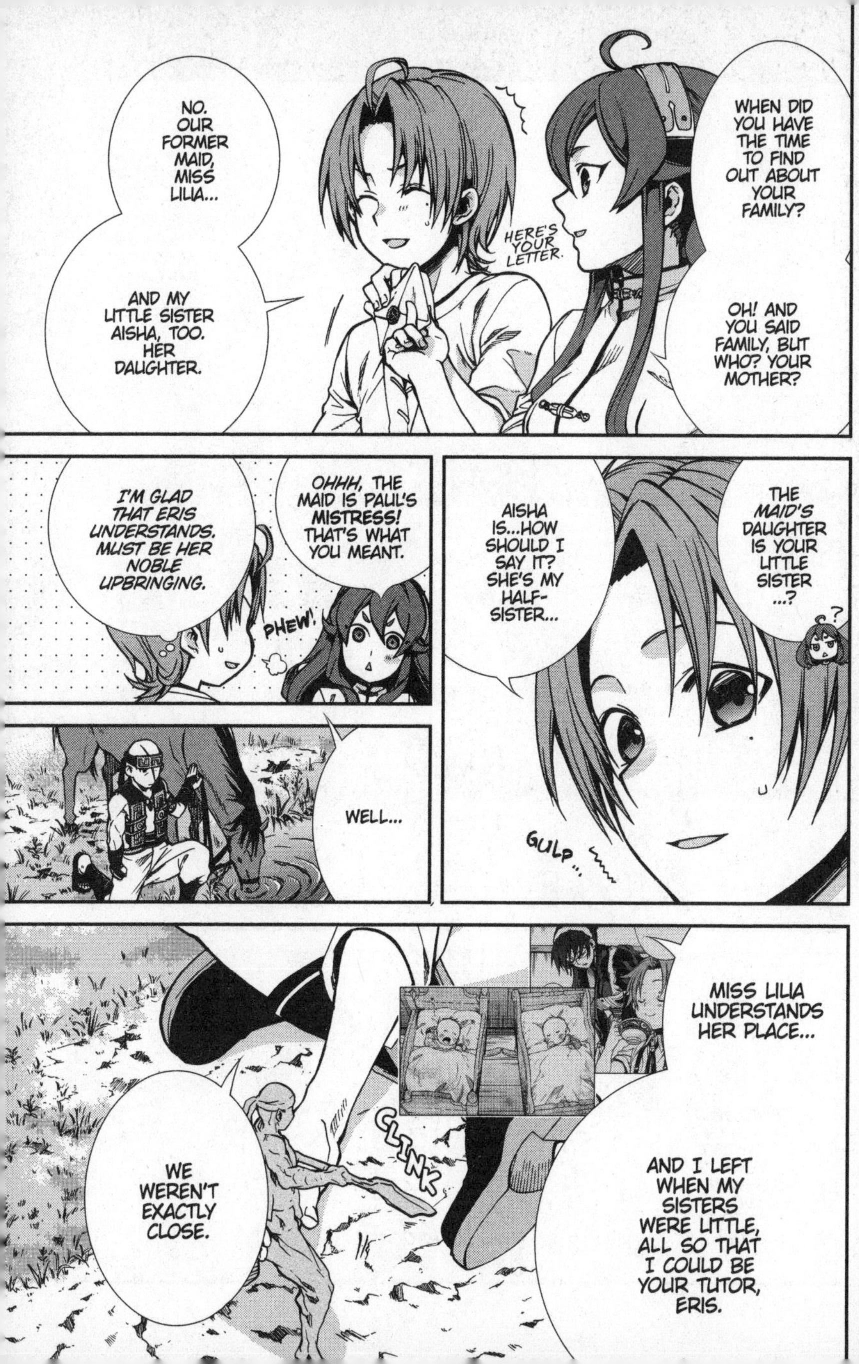
WHEN DID YOU HAVE THE TIME TO FIND OUT ABOUT YOUR FAMILY?
OH! AND YOU SAID FAMILY, BUT WHO? YOUR MOTHER?
HERE'S YOUR LETTER.
NO. OUR FORMER MAID, MISS LILIA...
AND MY LITTLE SISTER AISHA, TOO. HER DAUGHTER.
THE *MAID'S* DAUGHTER IS YOUR LITTLE SISTER ...?
?
AISHA IS...HOW SHOULD I SAY IT? SHE'S MY HALF-SISTER...
GULP...
OHHH, THE MAID IS PAUL'S MISTRESS! THAT'S WHAT YOU MEANT.
PHEW!
I'M GLAD THAT ERIS UNDERSTANDS. MUST BE HER NOBLE UPBRINGING.
WELL...
MISS LILIA UNDERSTANDS HER PLACE...
AND I LEFT WHEN MY SISTERS WERE LITTLE, ALL SO THAT I COULD BE YOUR TUTOR, ERIS.
CLINK
WE WEREN'T EXACTLY CLOSE.

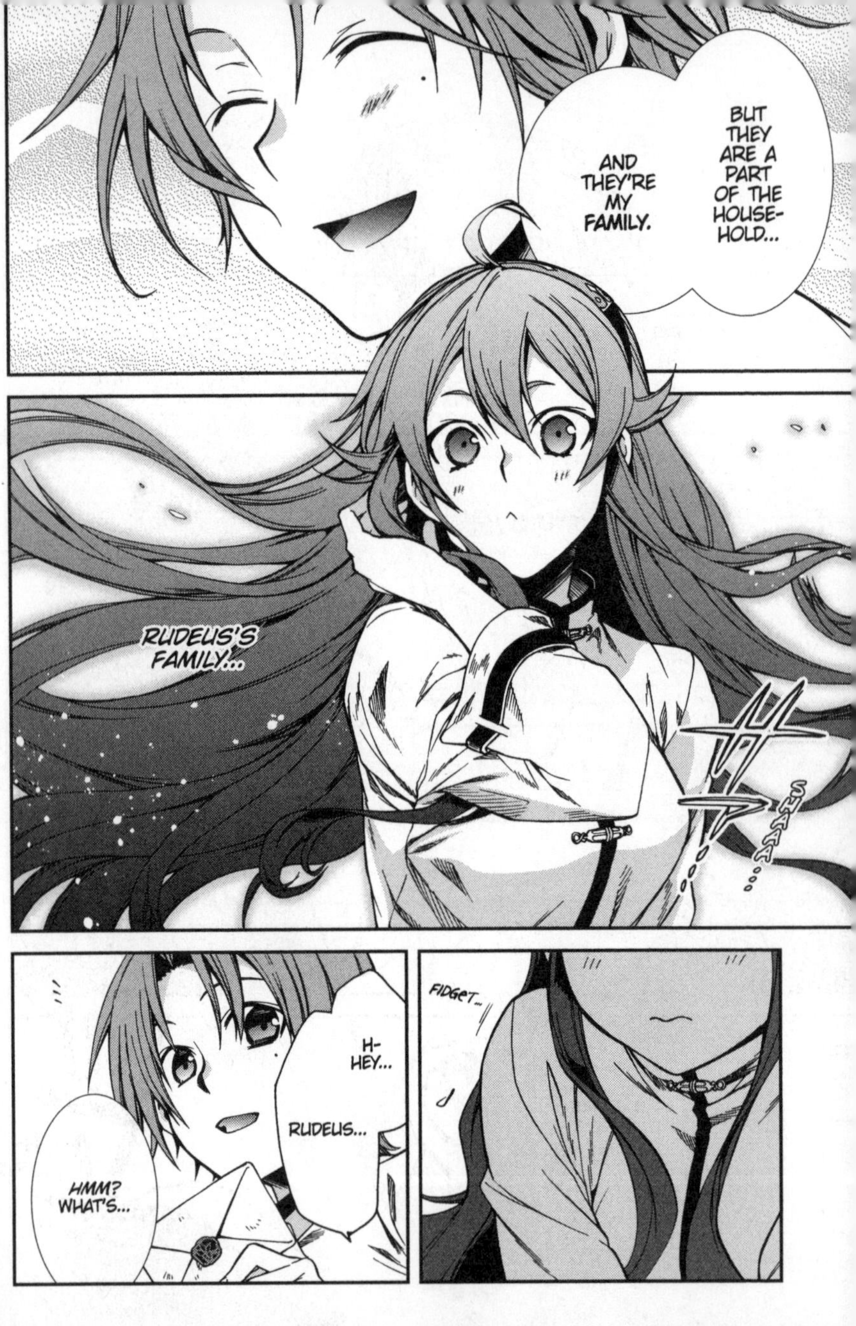
BUT THEY ARE A PART OF THE HOUSE-HOLD...
AND THEY'RE MY FAMILY.
RUDEUS'S FAMILY...
SHAAA...
FIDGET...
H-HEY...
RUDEUS...
HMM? WHAT'S...

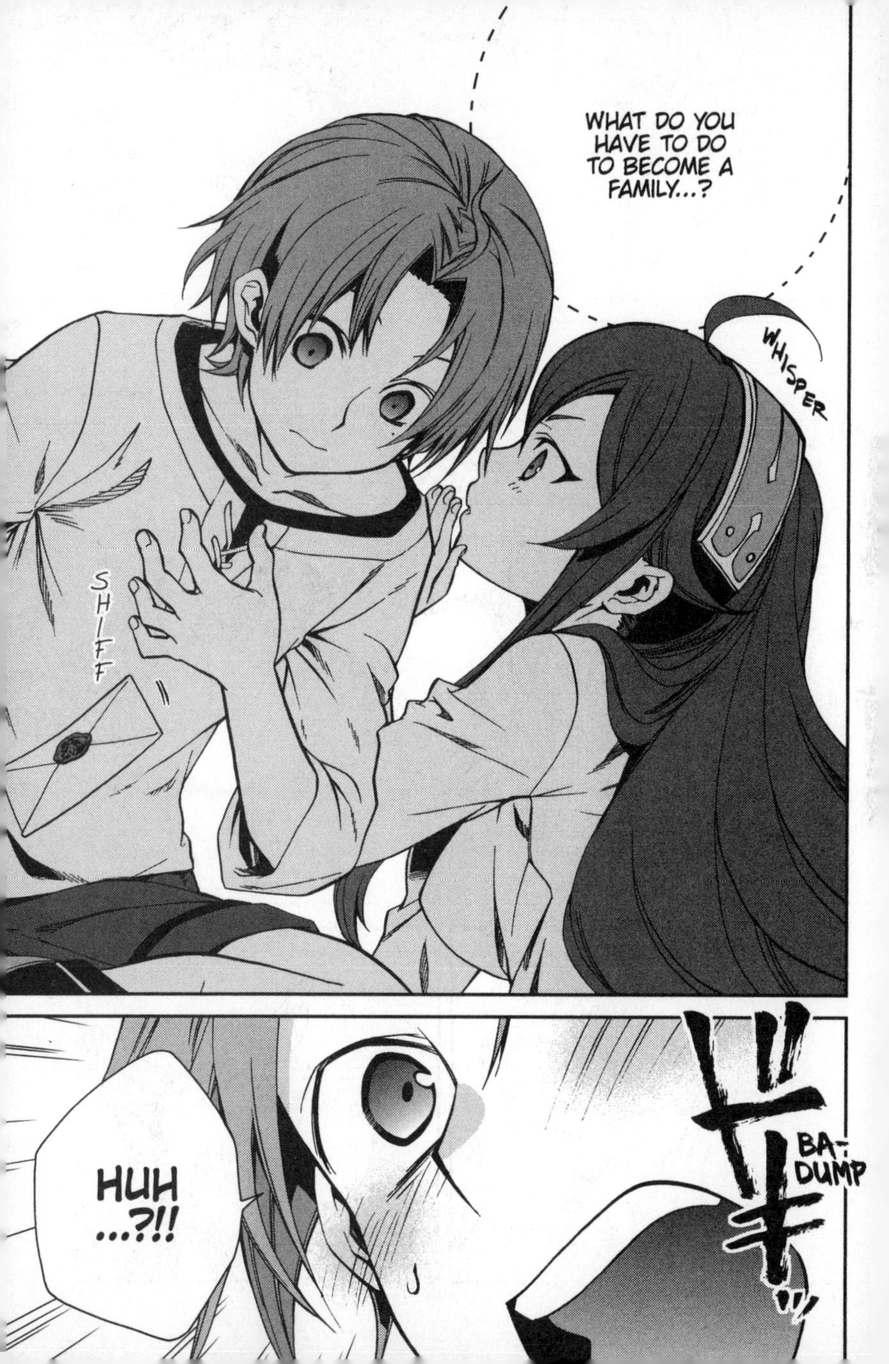
WHAT DO YOU HAVE TO DO TO BECOME A FAMILY...?
WHISPER
SHIFF
BA-DUMP
HUH ...?!!

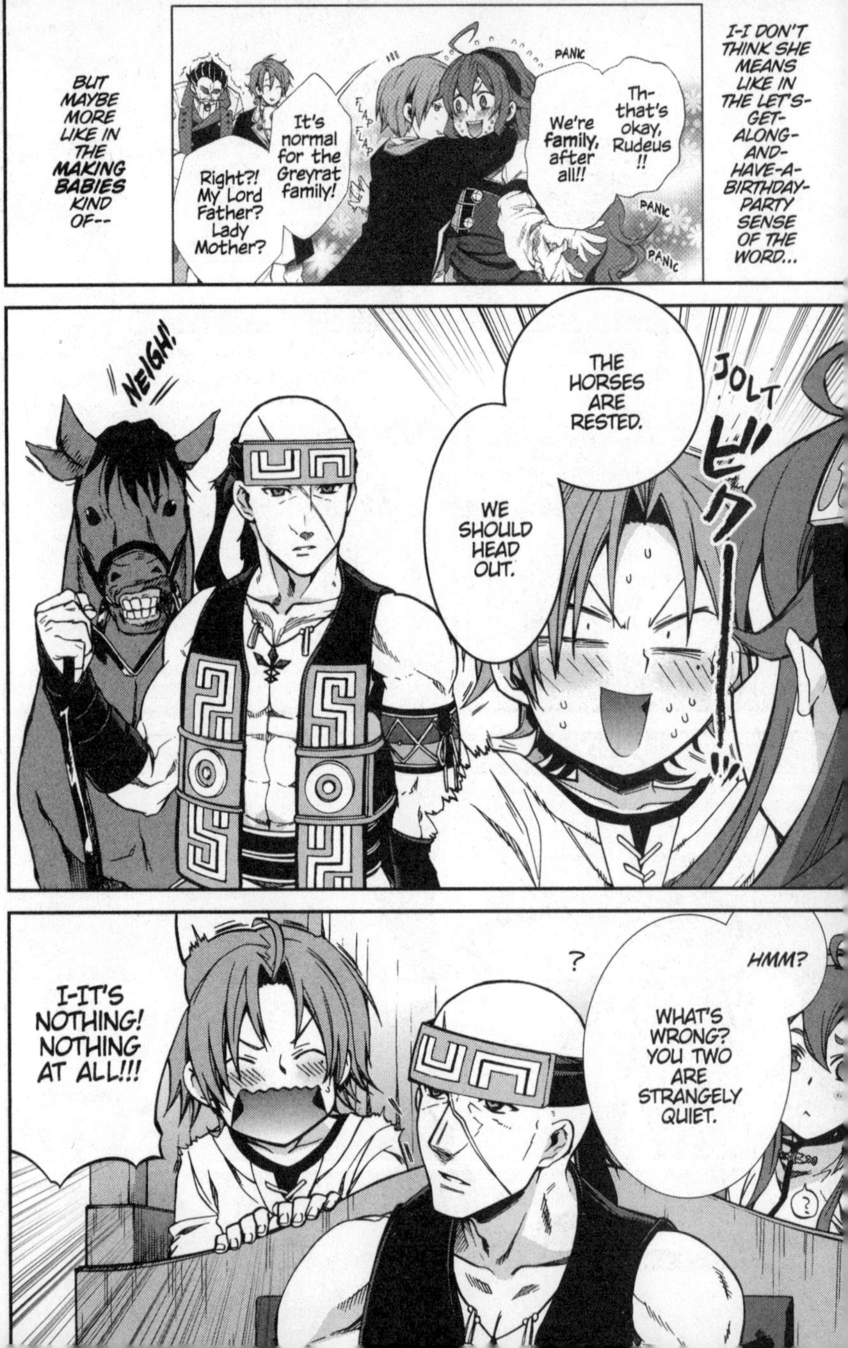
I-I DON'T THINK SHE MEANS LIKE IN THE LET'S-GET-ALONG-AND-HAVE-A-BIRTHDAY-PARTY SENSE OF THE WORD...
PANIC
Th-that's okay, Rudeus!!
We're family, after all!!
PANIC
PANIC
FLAP FLAP
It's normal for the Greyrat family!
Right?! My Lord Father? Lady Mother?
BUT MAYBE MORE LIKE IN THE MAKING BABIES KIND OF--
JOLT
THE HORSES ARE RESTED.
WE SHOULD HEAD OUT.
NEIGH!
HMM?
WHAT'S WRONG? YOU TWO ARE STRANGELY QUIET.
?
I-IT'S NOTHING! NOTHING AT ALL!!!

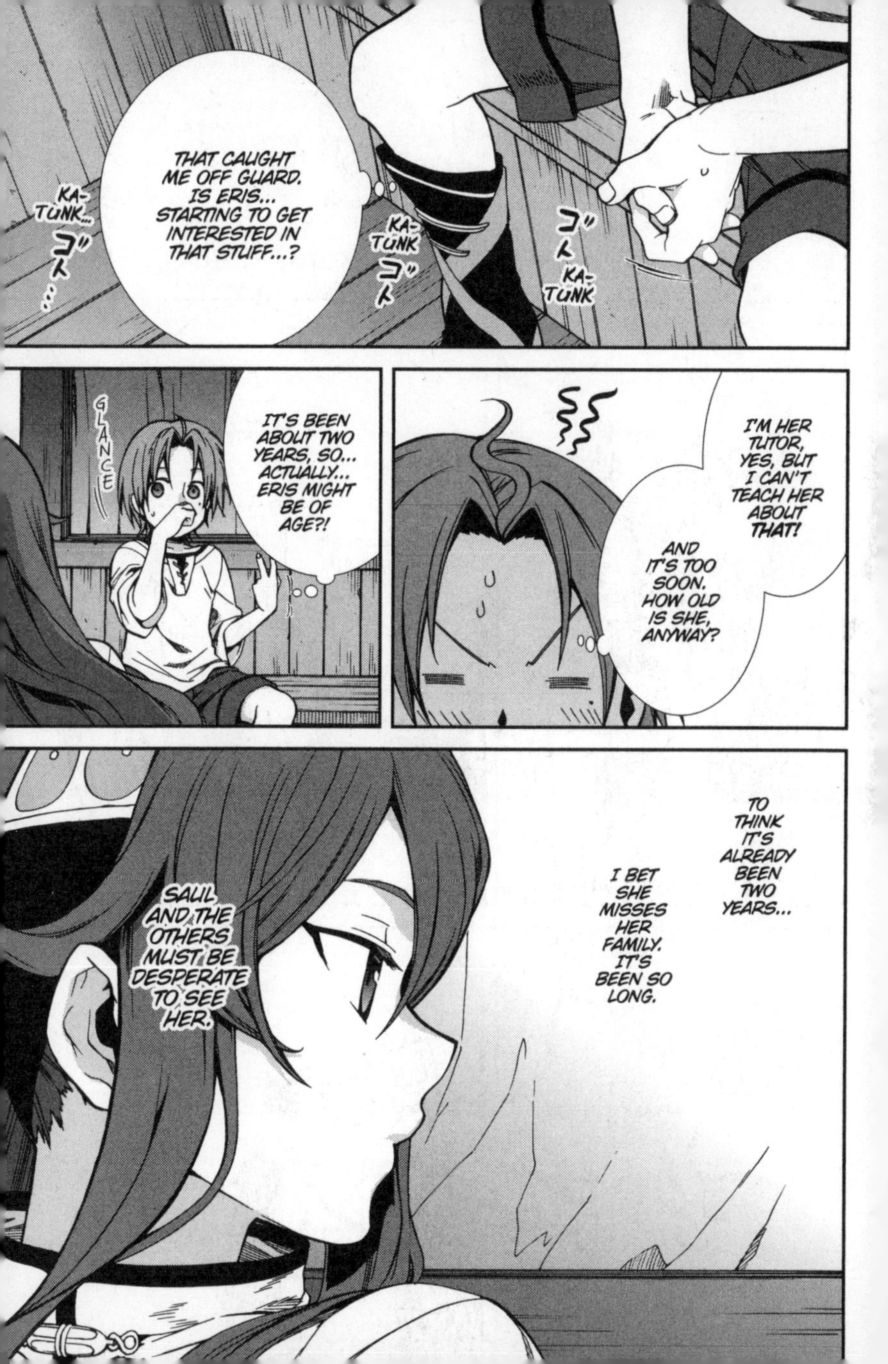
ゴト KA-TUNK
KA-TUNK ゴト
THAT CAUGHT ME OFF GUARD. IS ERIS... STARTING TO GET INTERESTED IN THAT STUFF...?
KA-TUNK... ゴト...
I'M HER TUTOR, YES, BUT I CAN'T TEACH HER ABOUT THAT!
AND IT'S TOO SOON. HOW OLD IS SHE, ANYWAY?
IT'S BEEN ABOUT TWO YEARS, SO... ACTUALLY... ERIS MIGHT BE OF AGE?!
GLANCE
TO THINK IT'S ALREADY BEEN TWO YEARS...
I BET SHE MISSES HER FAMILY. IT'S BEEN SO LONG.
SAUL AND THE OTHERS MUST BE DESPERATE TO SEE HER.

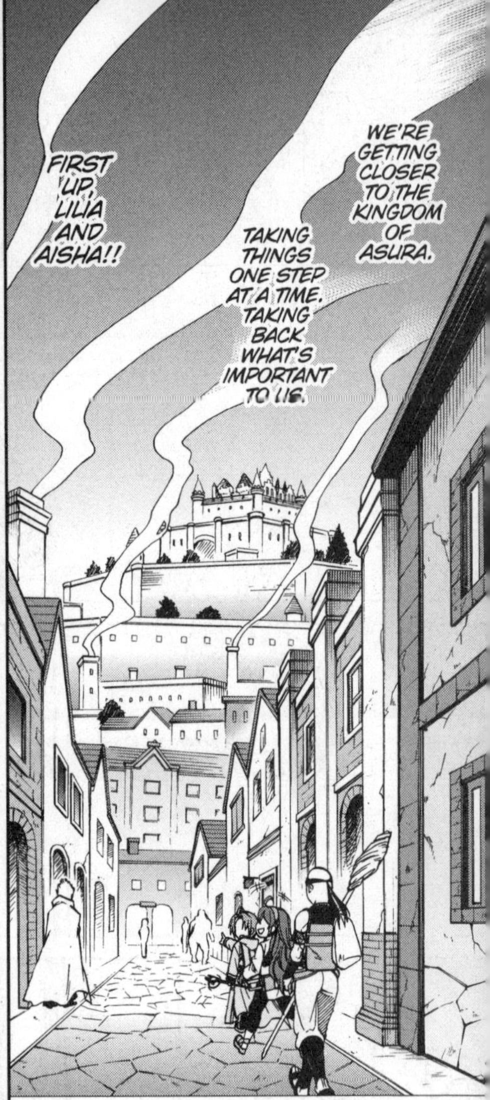
WE'RE GETTING CLOSER TO THE KINGDOM OF ASURA.
TAKING THINGS ONE STEP AT A TIME. TAKING BACK WHAT'S IMPORTANT TO US.
FIRST UP, LILIA AND AISHA!!

Central Continent

Shirone Kingdom: Latakia, the Capital City

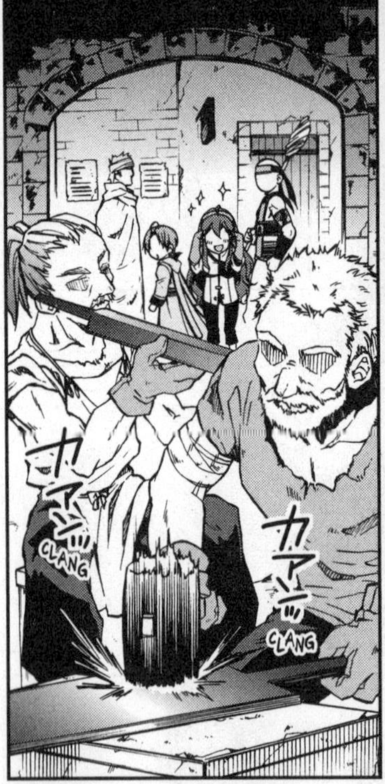
CLANG
CLANG

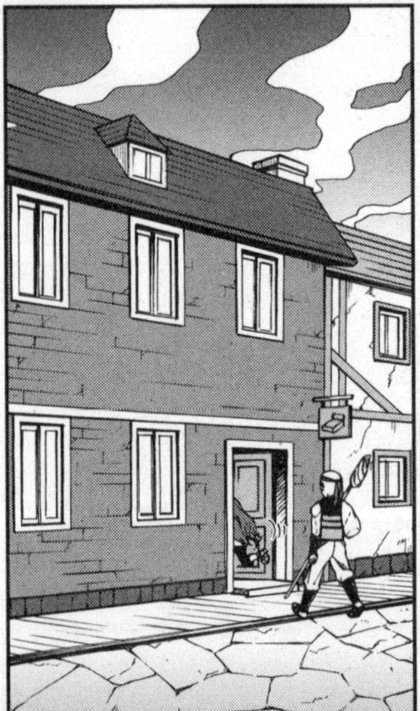

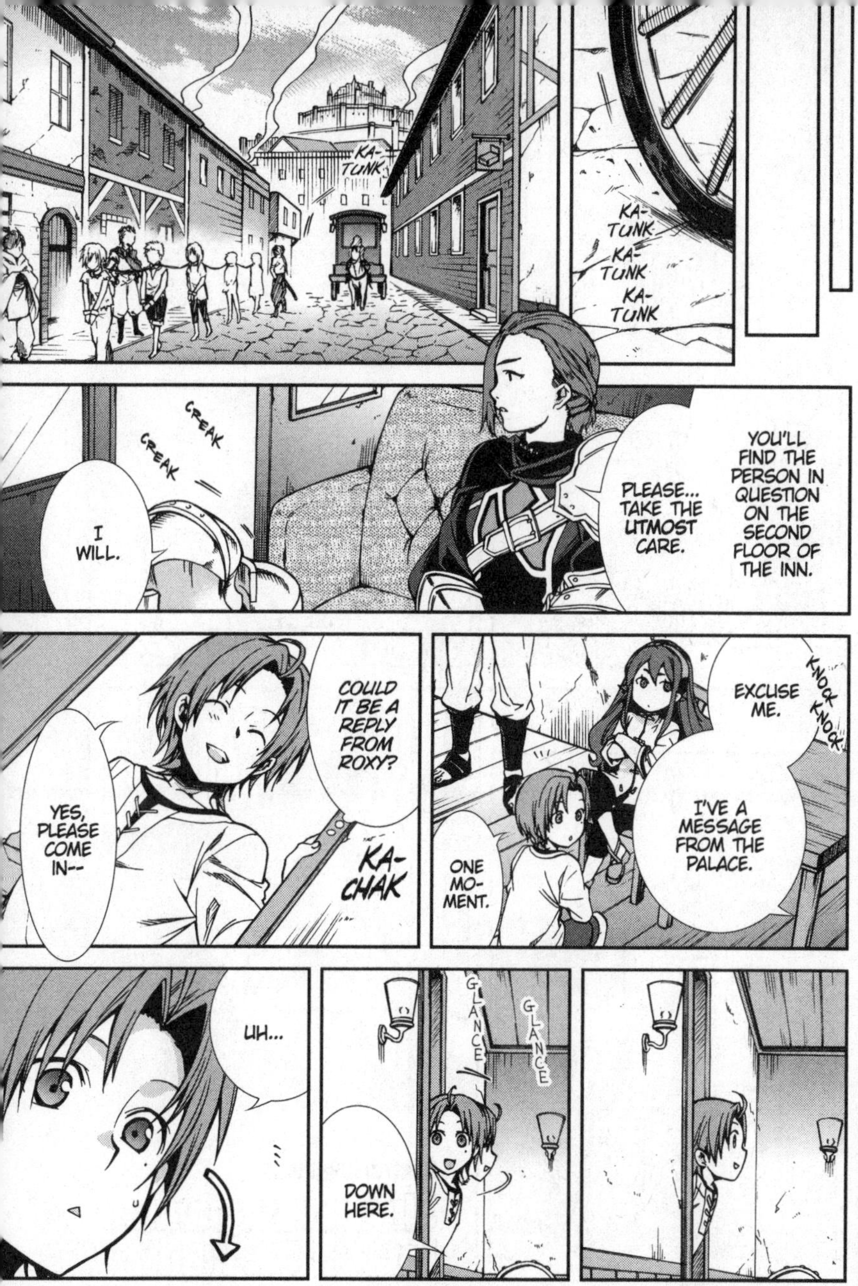
KA-TUNK
KA-TUNK
KA-TUNK
KA-TUNK
YOU'LL FIND THE PERSON IN QUESTION ON THE SECOND FLOOR OF THE INN.
PLEASE... TAKE THE UTMOST CARE.
CREAK
CREAK
I WILL.
KNOCK KNOCK
EXCUSE ME.
I'VE A MESSAGE FROM THE PALACE.
ONE MO-MENT.
COULD IT BE A REPLY FROM ROXY?
KA-CHAK
YES, PLEASE COME IN--
GLANCE
GLANCE
DOWN HERE.
UH...

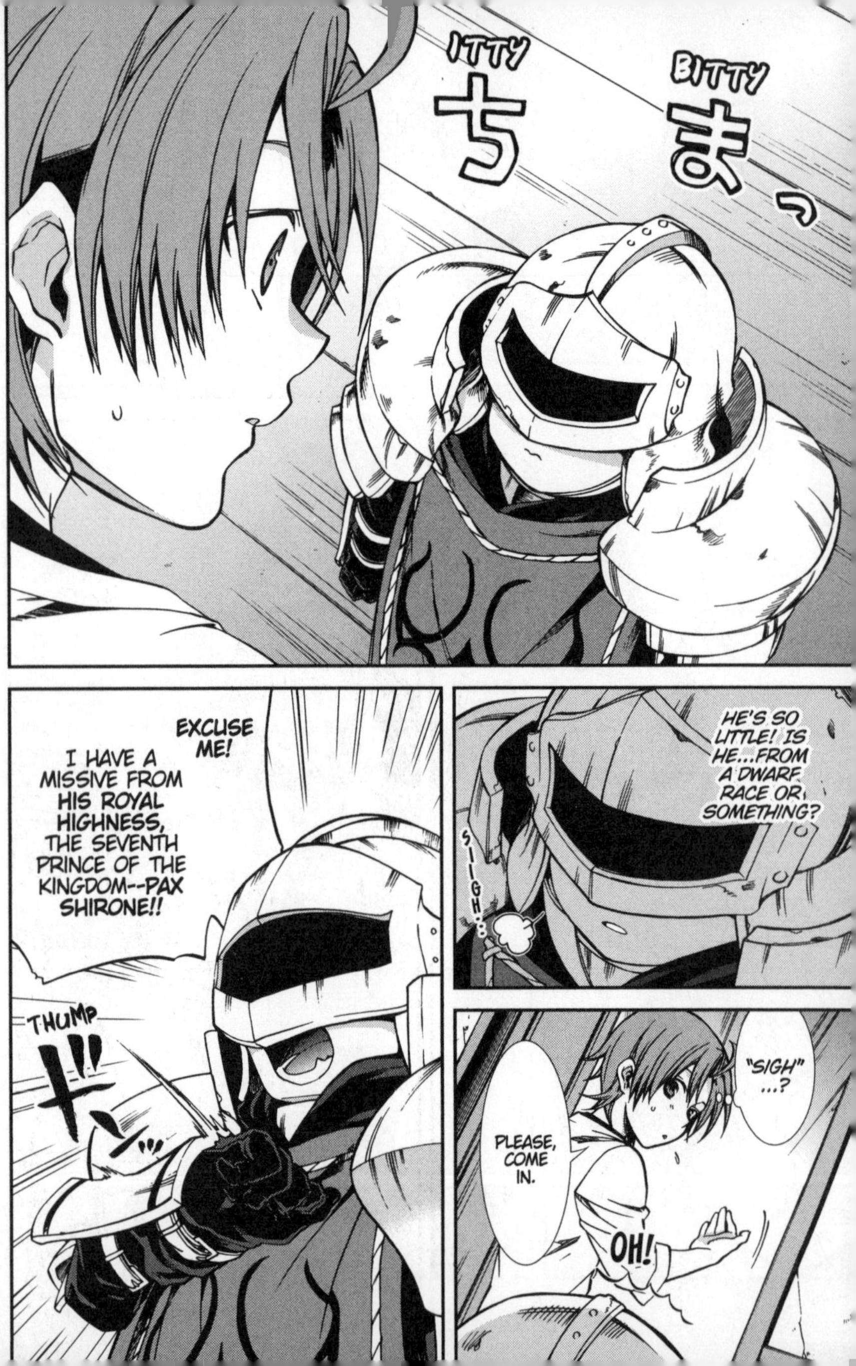
ITTY BITTY
ちまっ
HE'S SO LITTLE! IS HE...FROM A DWARF RACE OR SOMETHING?
SIIGH...
"SIGH" ...?
PLEASE, COME IN.
OH!
EXCUSE ME!
I HAVE A MISSIVE FROM HIS ROYAL HIGHNESS, THE SEVENTH PRINCE OF THE KINGDOM--PAX SHIRONE!!
THUMP
ドン!!

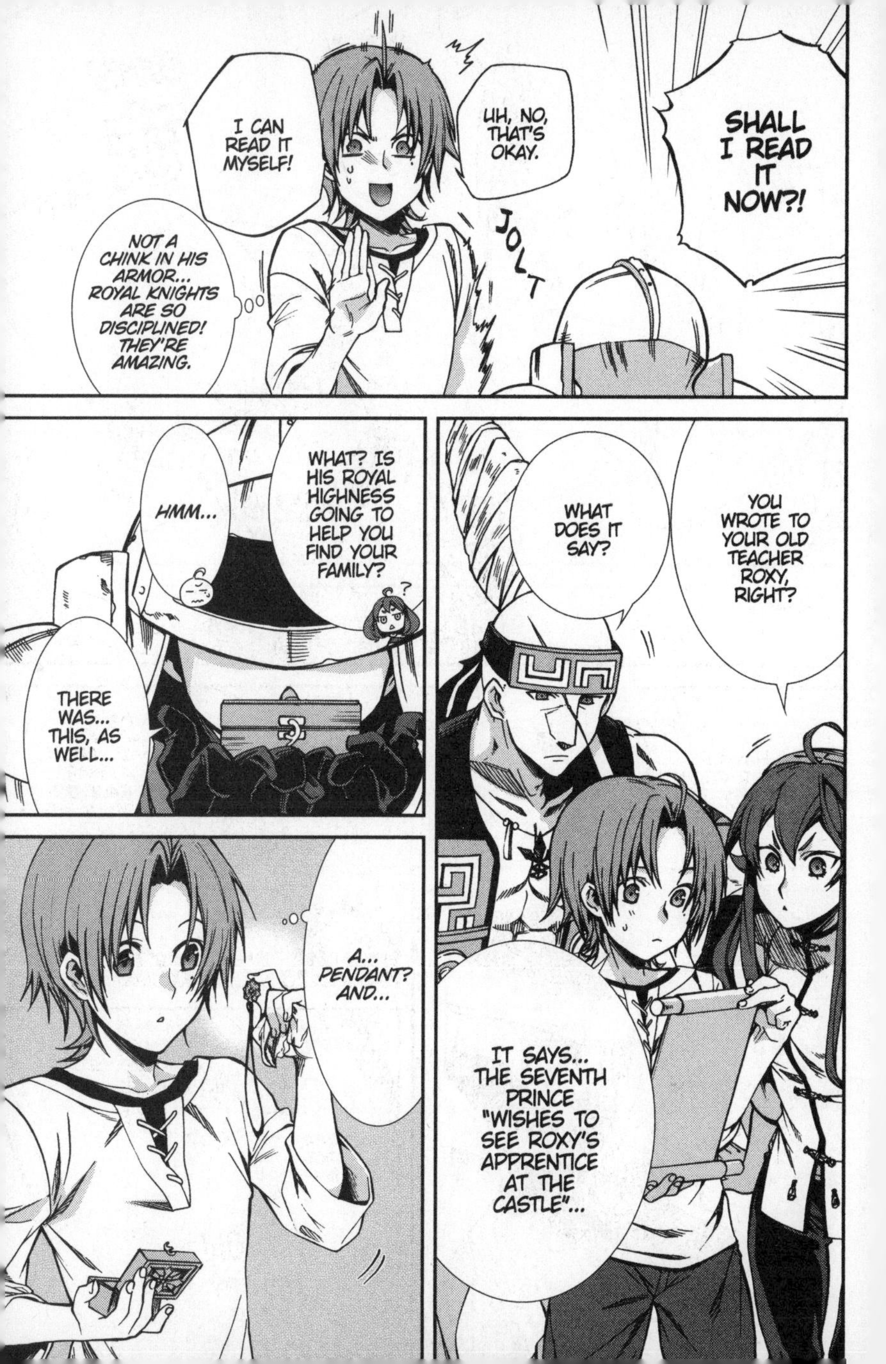
SHALL I READ IT NOW?!
JOLT
UH, NO, THAT'S OKAY.
I CAN READ IT MYSELF!
NOT A CHINK IN HIS ARMOR... ROYAL KNIGHTS ARE SO DISCIPLINED! THEY'RE AMAZING.
YOU WROTE TO YOUR OLD TEACHER ROXY, RIGHT?
WHAT DOES IT SAY?
IT SAYS... THE SEVENTH PRINCE "WISHES TO SEE ROXY'S APPRENTICE AT THE CASTLE"...
WHAT? IS HIS ROYAL HIGHNESS GOING TO HELP YOU FIND YOUR FAMILY?
HMM...
THERE WAS... THIS, AS WELL...
A... PENDANT? AND...

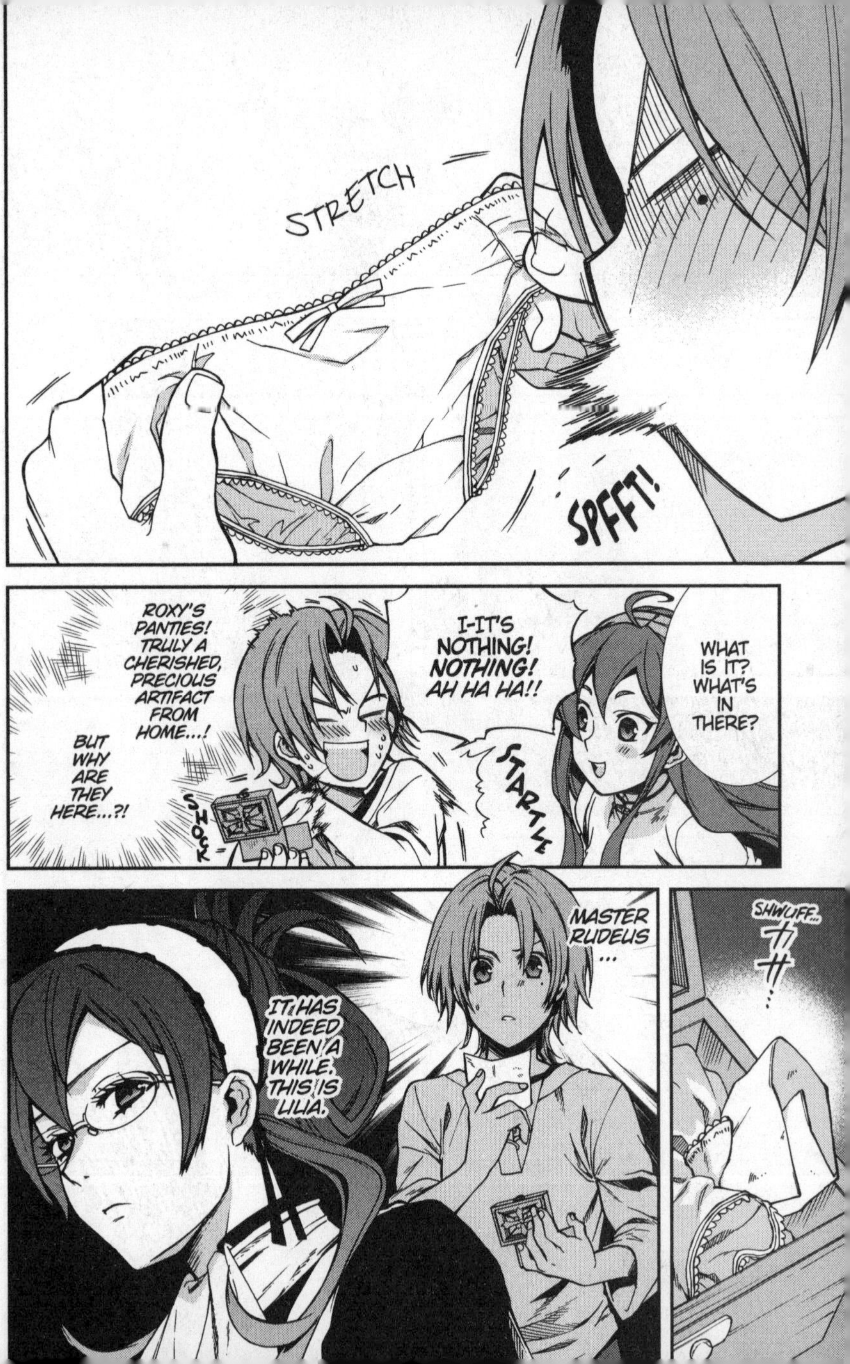
STRETCH
SPFFT!
WHAT IS IT? WHAT'S IN THERE?
STARTLE
I-IT'S NOTHING! NOTHING! AH HA HA!!
ROXY'S PANTIES! TRULY A CHERISHED, PRECIOUS ARTIFACT FROM HOME...!
BUT WHY ARE THEY HERE...?!
SHOCK
SHWUFF...
MASTER RUDEUS ...
IT HAS INDEED BEEN A WHILE. THIS IS LILIA.

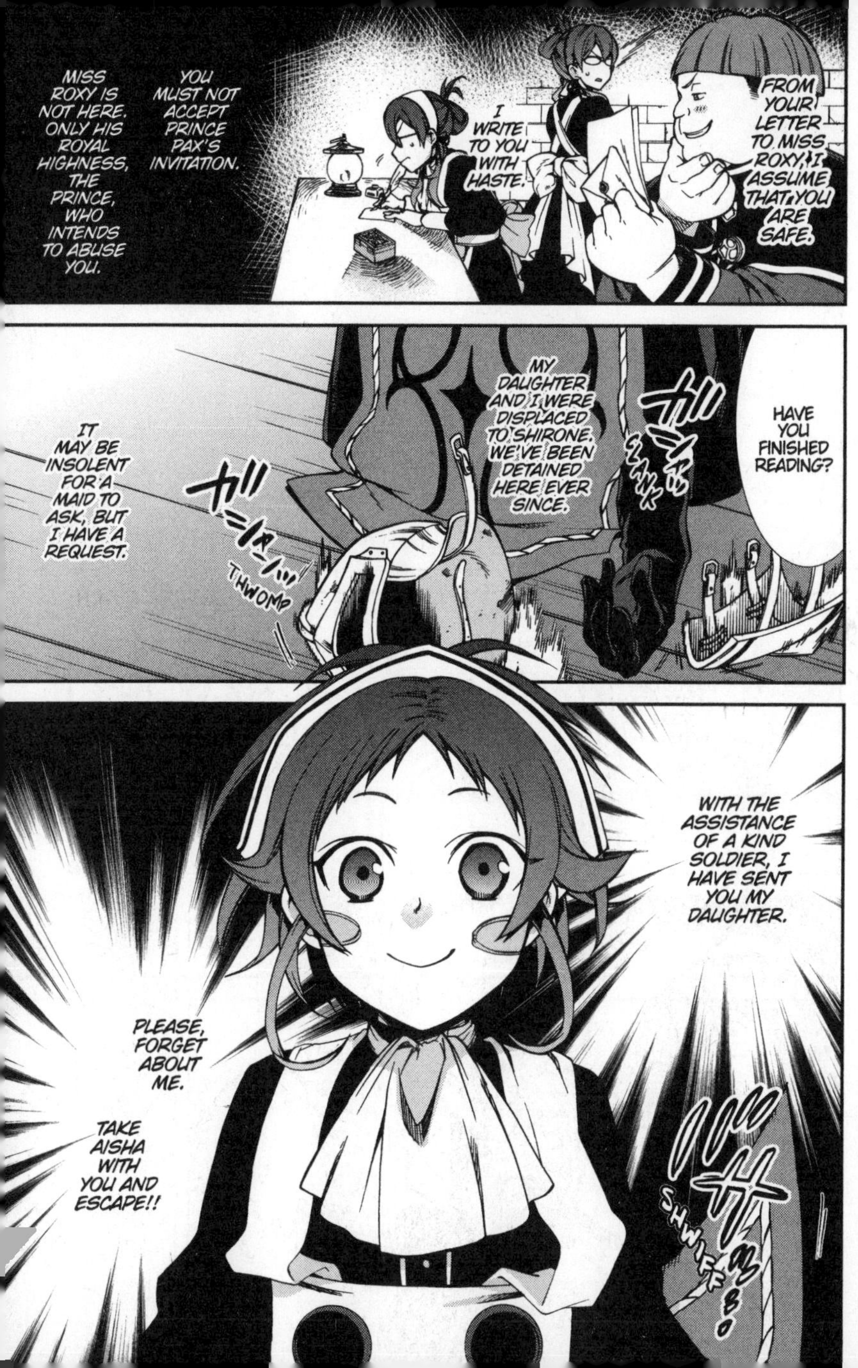
FROM YOUR LETTER TO MISS ROXY, I ASSUME THAT YOU ARE SAFE.
I WRITE TO YOU WITH HASTE.
YOU MUST NOT ACCEPT PRINCE PAX'S INVITATION.
MISS ROXY IS NOT HERE. ONLY HIS ROYAL HIGHNESS, THE PRINCE, WHO INTENDS TO ABUSE YOU.
HAVE YOU FINISHED READING?
CLANK
MY DAUGHTER AND I WERE DISPLACED TO SHIRONE. WE'VE BEEN DETAINED HERE EVER SINCE.
THWOMP
IT MAY BE INSOLENT FOR A MAID TO ASK, BUT I HAVE A REQUEST.
WITH THE ASSISTANCE OF A KIND SOLDIER, I HAVE SENT YOU MY DAUGHTER.
SHWIFF
PLEASE, FORGET ABOUT ME.
TAKE AISHA WITH YOU AND ESCAPE!!

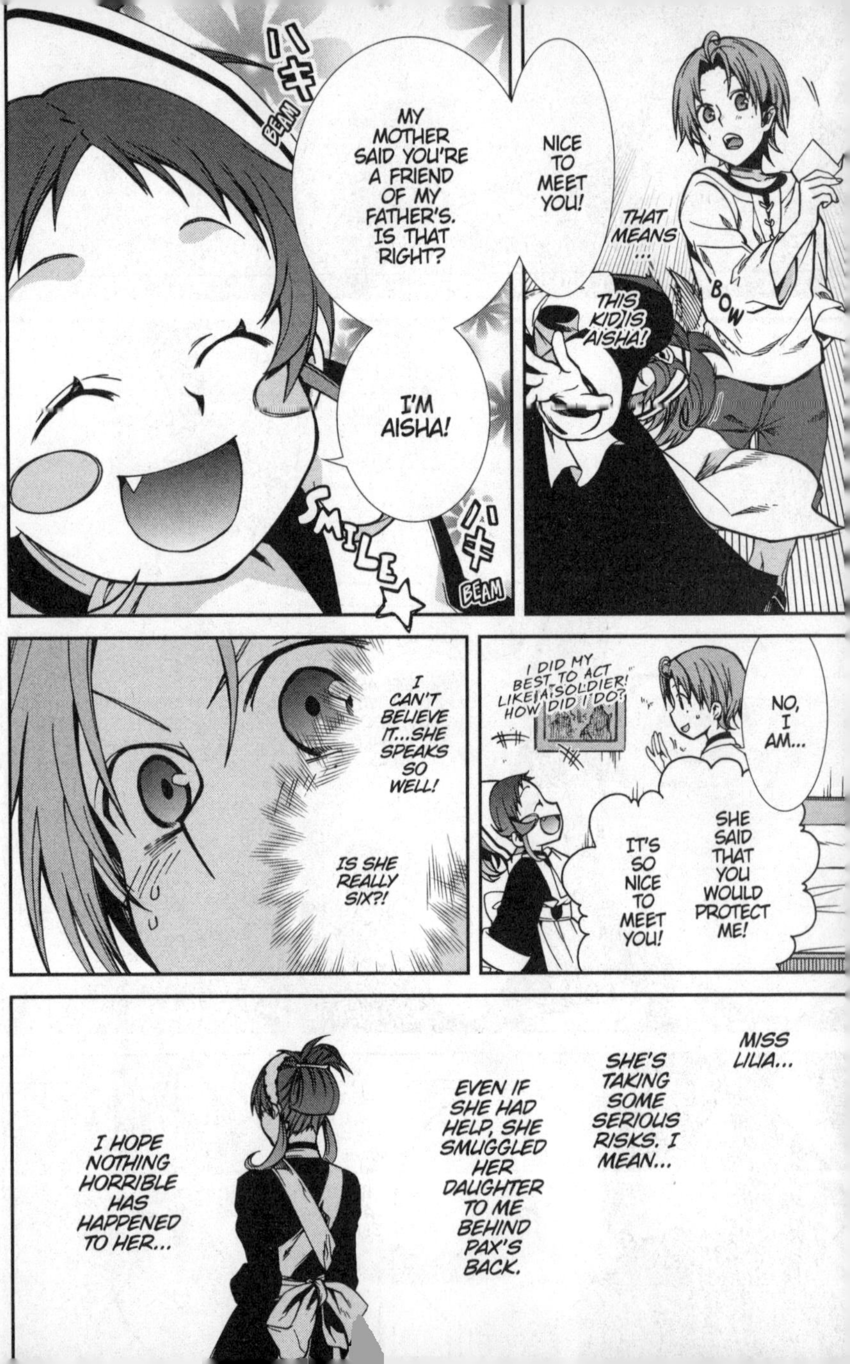
THAT MEANS ...
THIS KID IS AISHA!
BOW
NICE TO MEET YOU!
MY MOTHER SAID YOU'RE A FRIEND OF MY FATHER'S. IS THAT RIGHT?
BEAM
I'M AISHA!
SMILE
BEAM
NO, I AM...
SHE SAID THAT YOU WOULD PROTECT ME!
IT'S SO NICE TO MEET YOU!
I DID MY BEST TO ACT LIKE A SOLDIER! HOW DID I DO?
I CAN'T BELIEVE IT...SHE SPEAKS SO WELL!
IS SHE REALLY SIX?!
MISS LILIA...
SHE'S TAKING SOME SERIOUS RISKS. I MEAN...
EVEN IF SHE HAD HELP, SHE SMUGGLED HER DAUGHTER TO ME BEHIND PAX'S BACK.
I HOPE NOTHING HORRIBLE HAS HAPPENED TO HER...

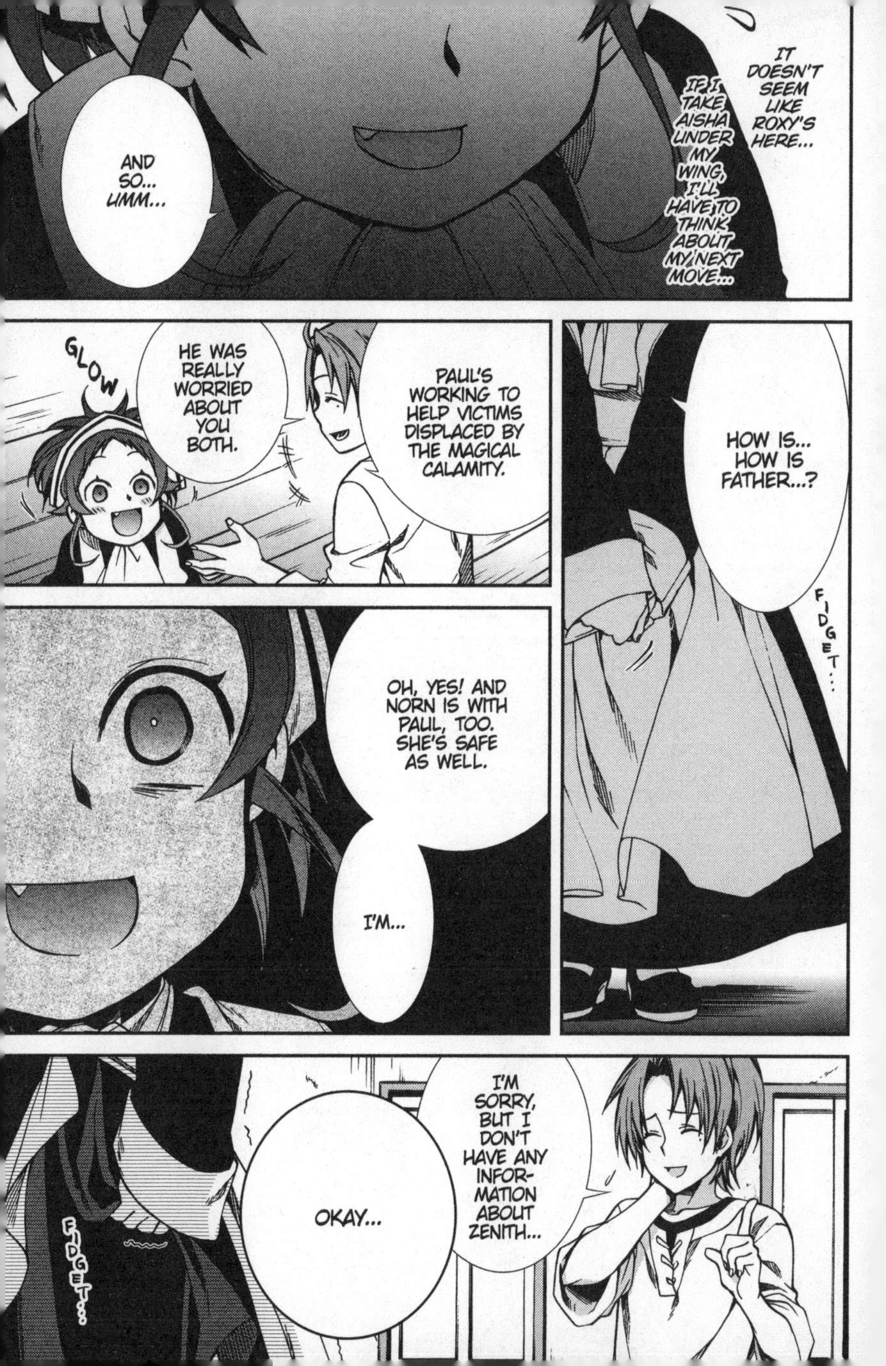
IT DOESN'T SEEM LIKE ROXY'S HERE...
IF I TAKE AISHA UNDER MY WING, I'LL HAVE TO THINK ABOUT MY NEXT MOVE...
AND SO... UMM...
HOW IS... HOW IS FATHER...?
FIDGET...
PAUL'S WORKING TO HELP VICTIMS DISPLACED BY THE MAGICAL CALAMITY.
HE WAS REALLY WORRIED ABOUT YOU BOTH.
GLOW
OH, YES! AND NORN IS WITH PAUL, TOO. SHE'S SAFE AS WELL.
I'M...
I'M SORRY, BUT I DON'T HAVE ANY INFOR-MATION ABOUT ZENITH...
OKAY...
FIDGET...

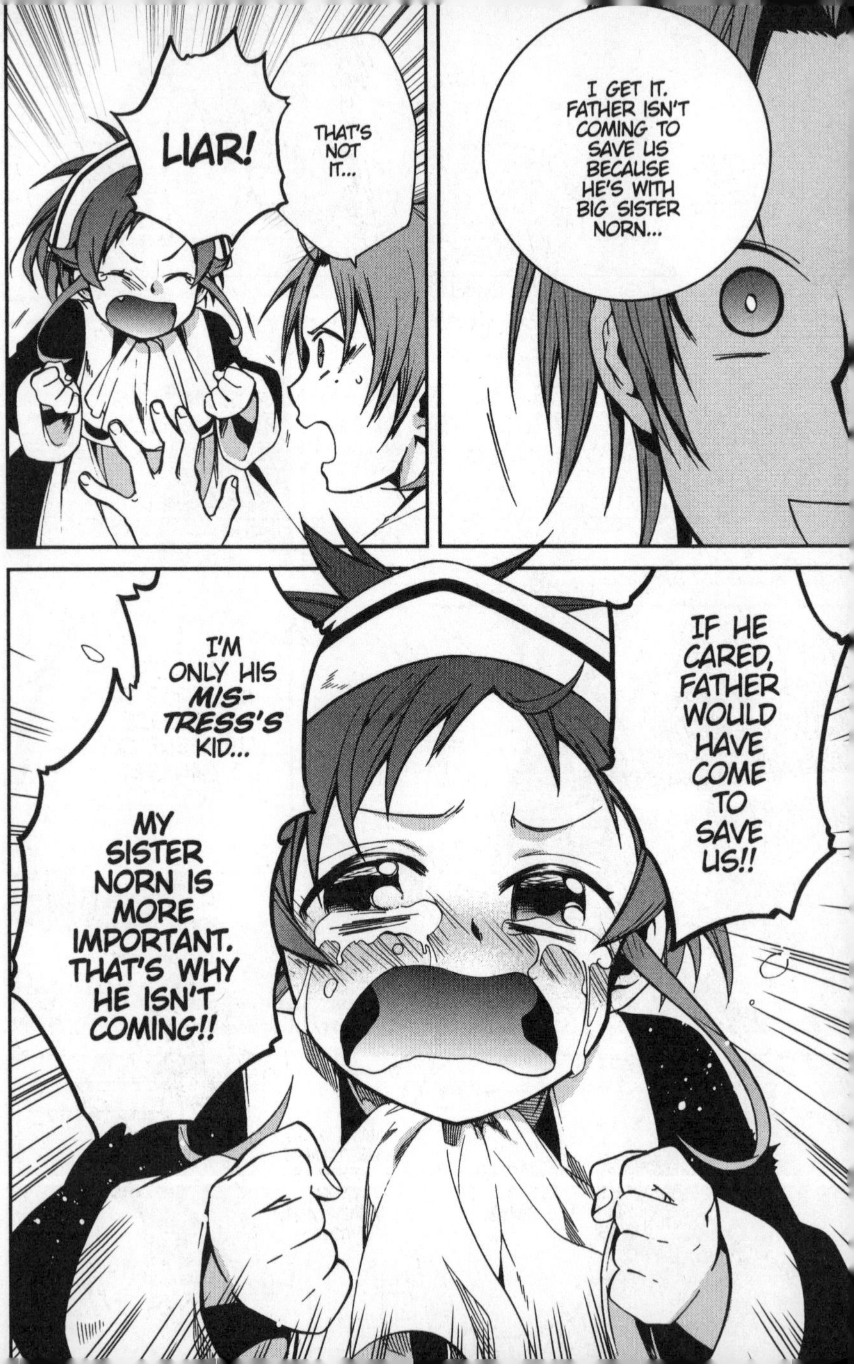
I GET IT. FATHER ISN'T COMING TO SAVE US BECAUSE HE'S WITH BIG SISTER NORN...
THAT'S NOT IT...
LIAR!
IF HE CARED, FATHER WOULD HAVE COME TO SAVE US!!
I'M ONLY HIS *MIS-TRESS'S* KID...
MY SISTER NORN IS MORE IMPORTANT. THAT'S WHY HE ISN'T COMING!!

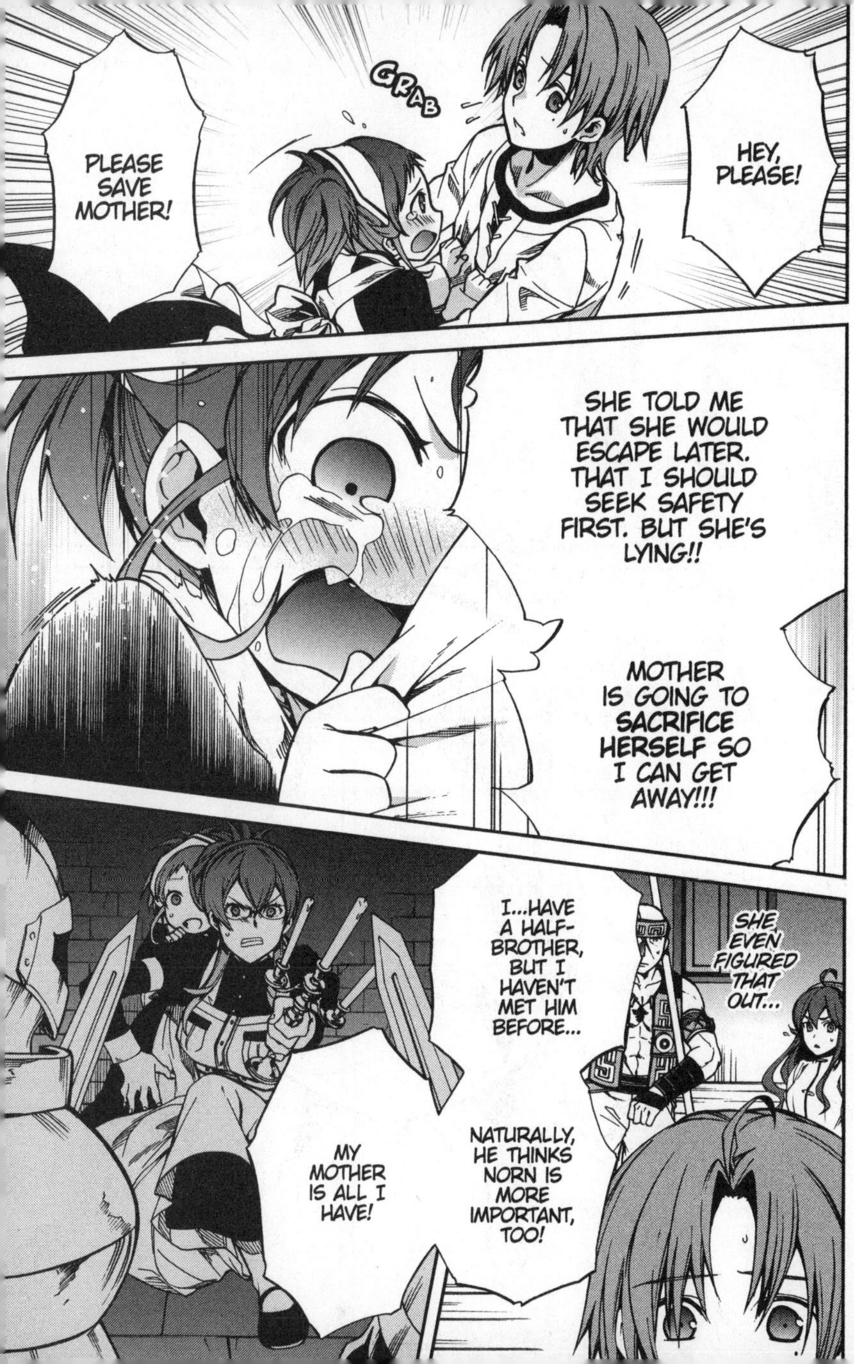
HEY, PLEASE!
GRAB
PLEASE SAVE MOTHER!
SHE TOLD ME THAT SHE WOULD ESCAPE LATER. THAT I SHOULD SEEK SAFETY FIRST. BUT SHE'S LYING!!
MOTHER IS GOING TO SACRIFICE HERSELF SO I CAN GET AWAY!!!
SHE EVEN FIGURED THAT OUT...
I...HAVE A HALF-BROTHER, BUT I HAVEN'T MET HIM BEFORE...
NATURALLY, HE THINKS NORN IS MORE IMPORTANT, TOO!
MY MOTHER IS ALL I HAVE!

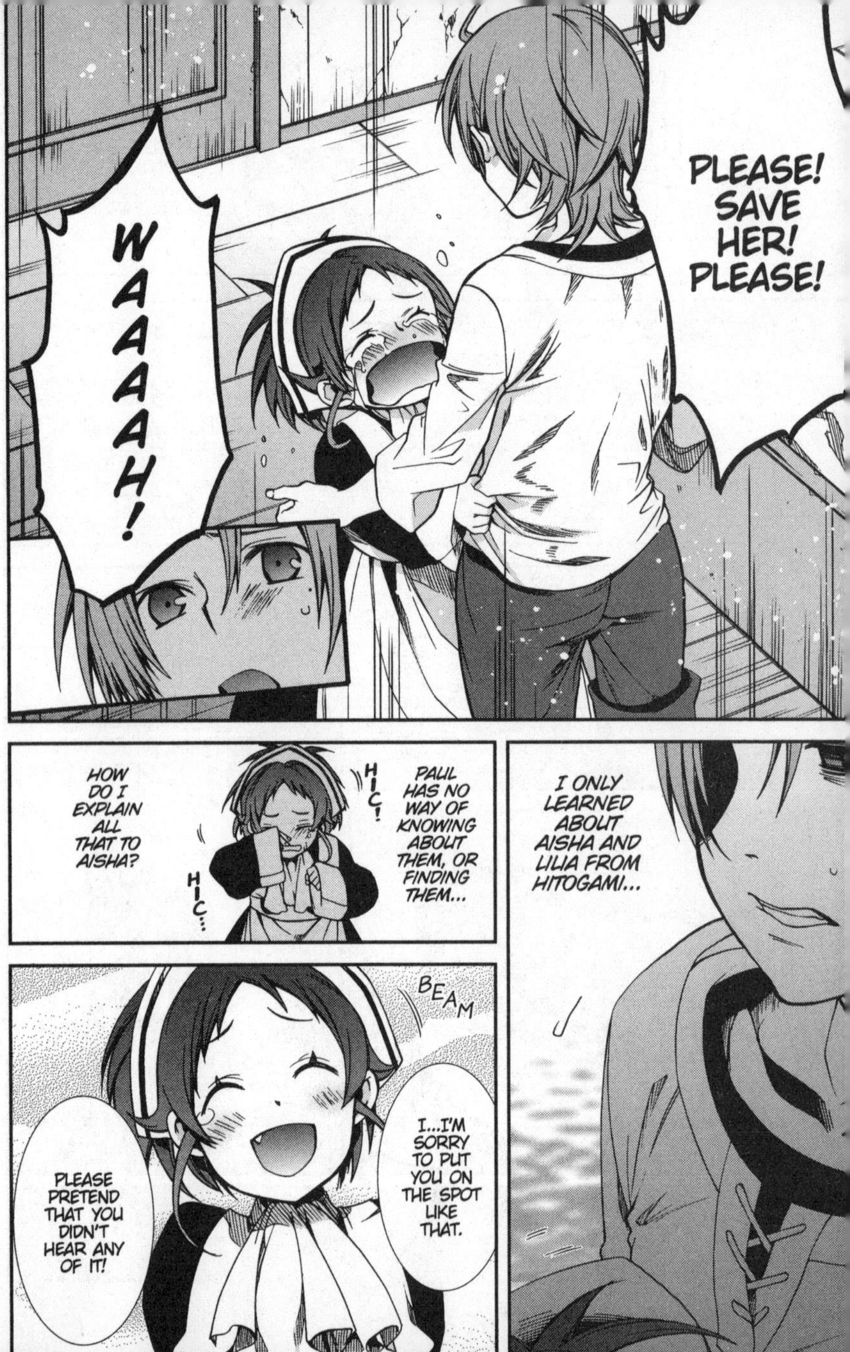
PLEASE! SAVE HER! PLEASE!
WAAAAAH!
I ONLY LEARNED ABOUT AISHA AND LILIA FROM HITOGAMI...
PAUL HAS NO WAY OF KNOWING ABOUT THEM, OR FINDING THEM...
HIC!
HOW DO I EXPLAIN ALL THAT TO AISHA?
HIC...
BEAM
I...I'M SORRY TO PUT YOU ON THE SPOT LIKE THAT.
PLEASE PRETEND THAT YOU DIDN'T HEAR ANY OF IT!

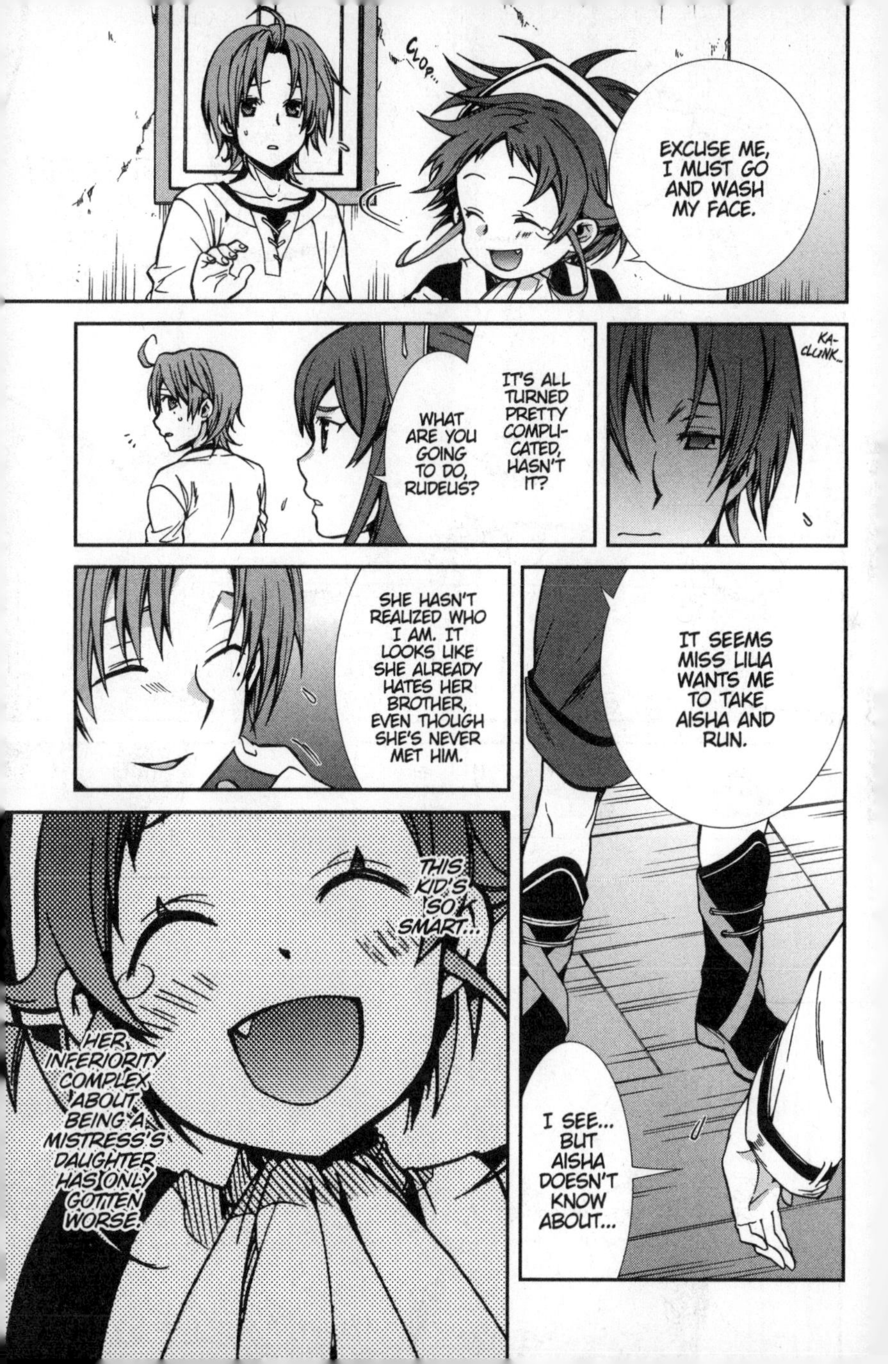
CLOP...
EXCUSE ME, I MUST GO AND WASH MY FACE.
KA-CLUNK...
IT'S ALL TURNED PRETTY COMPLICATED, HASN'T IT?
WHAT ARE YOU GOING TO DO, RUDEUS?
IT SEEMS MISS LILIA WANTS ME TO TAKE AISHA AND RUN.
I SEE... BUT AISHA DOESN'T KNOW ABOUT...
SHE HASN'T REALIZED WHO I AM. IT LOOKS LIKE SHE ALREADY HATES HER BROTHER, EVEN THOUGH SHE'S NEVER MET HIM.
THIS KID'S SO SMART...
HER INFERIORITY COMPLEX ABOUT BEING A MISTRESS'S DAUGHTER HAS ONLY GOTTEN WORSE.

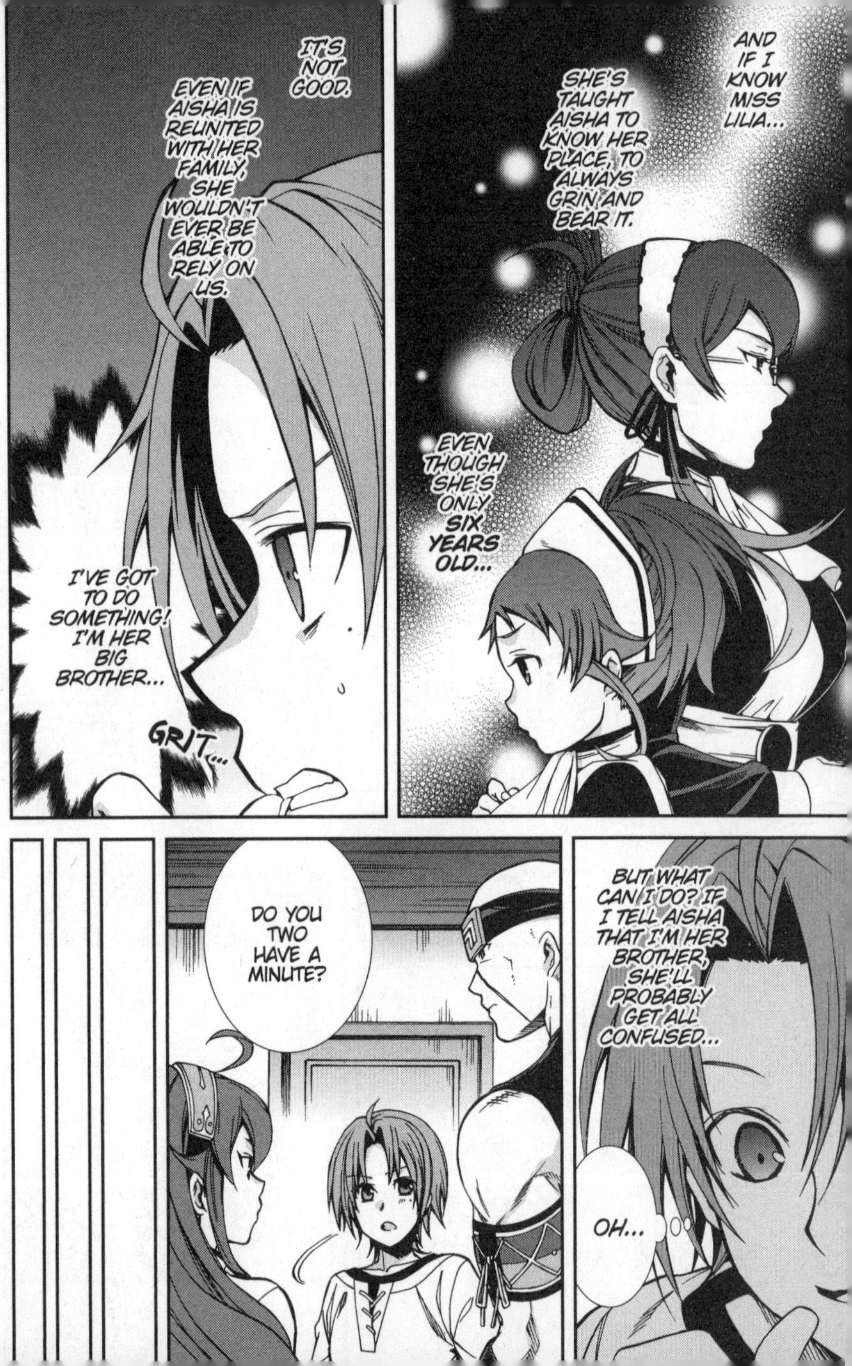
AND IF I KNOW MISS LILIA...
SHE'S TAUGHT AISHA TO KNOW HER PLACE, TO ALWAYS GRIN AND BEAR IT.
EVEN THOUGH SHE'S ONLY SIX YEARS OLD...
IT'S NOT GOOD.
EVEN IF AISHA IS REUNITED WITH HER FAMILY, SHE WOULDN'T EVER BE ABLE TO RELY ON US.
I'VE GOT TO DO SOMETHING! I'M HER BIG BROTHER...
GRIT...
BUT WHAT CAN I DO? IF I TELL AISHA THAT I'M HER BROTHER, SHE'LL PROBABLY GET ALL CONFUSED...
OH...
DO YOU TWO HAVE A MINUTE?

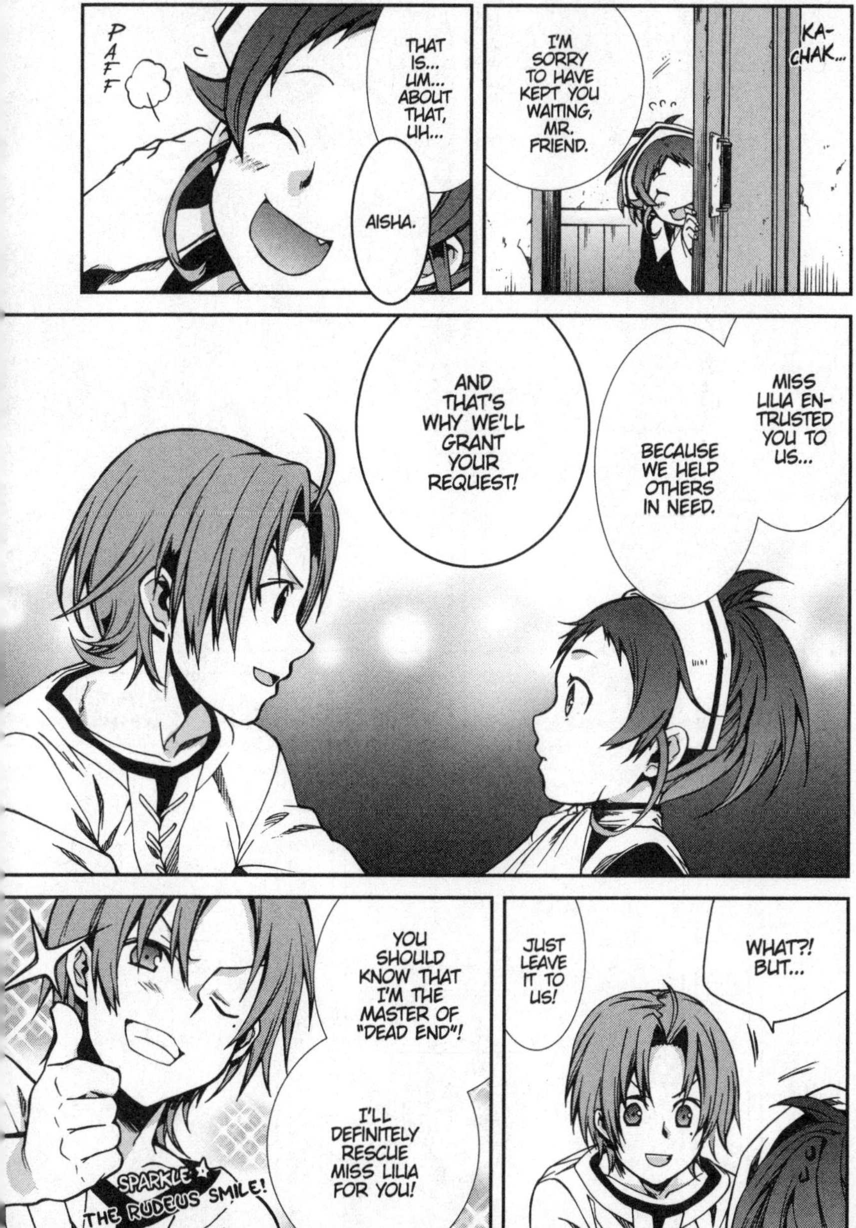
KA-CHAK...
I'M SORRY TO HAVE KEPT YOU WAITING, MR. FRIEND.
THAT IS... UM... ABOUT THAT, UH...
AISHA.
PAFF
MISS LILIA EN-TRUSTED YOU TO US...
BECAUSE WE HELP OTHERS IN NEED.
AND THAT'S WHY WE'LL GRANT YOUR REQUEST!
WHAT?! BUT...
JUST LEAVE IT TO US!
YOU SHOULD KNOW THAT I'M THE MASTER OF "DEAD END"!
I'LL DEFINITELY RESCUE MISS LILIA FOR YOU!
SPARKLE ☆ THE RUDEUS SMILE!

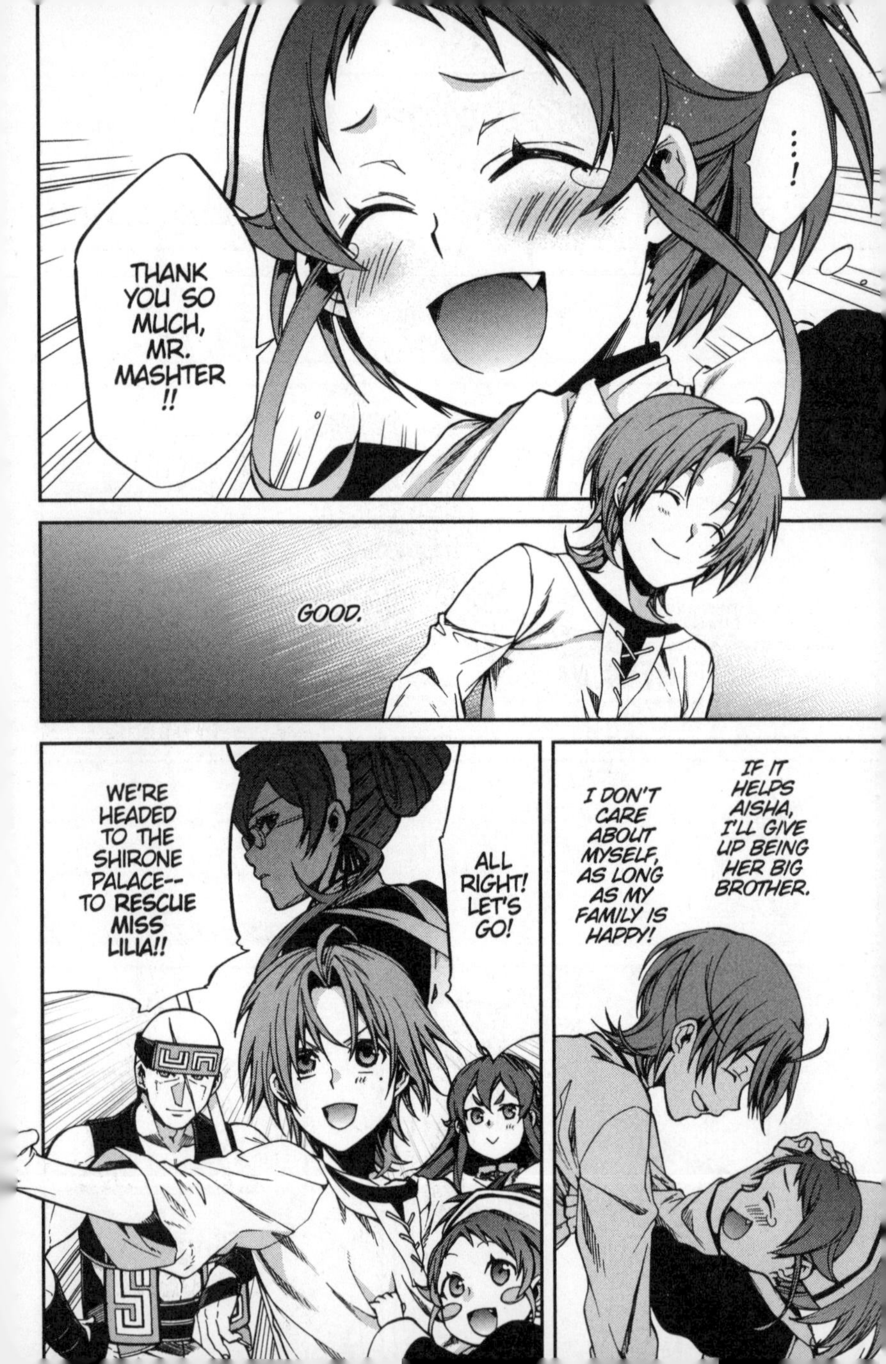
...!
THANK YOU SO MUCH, MR. MASHTER!!
GOOD.
IF IT HELPS AISHA, I'LL GIVE UP BEING HER BIG BROTHER.
I DON'T CARE ABOUT MYSELF, AS LONG AS MY FAMILY IS HAPPY!
ALL RIGHT! LET'S GO!
WE'RE HEADED TO THE SHIRONE PALACE-- TO RESCUE MISS LILIA!!

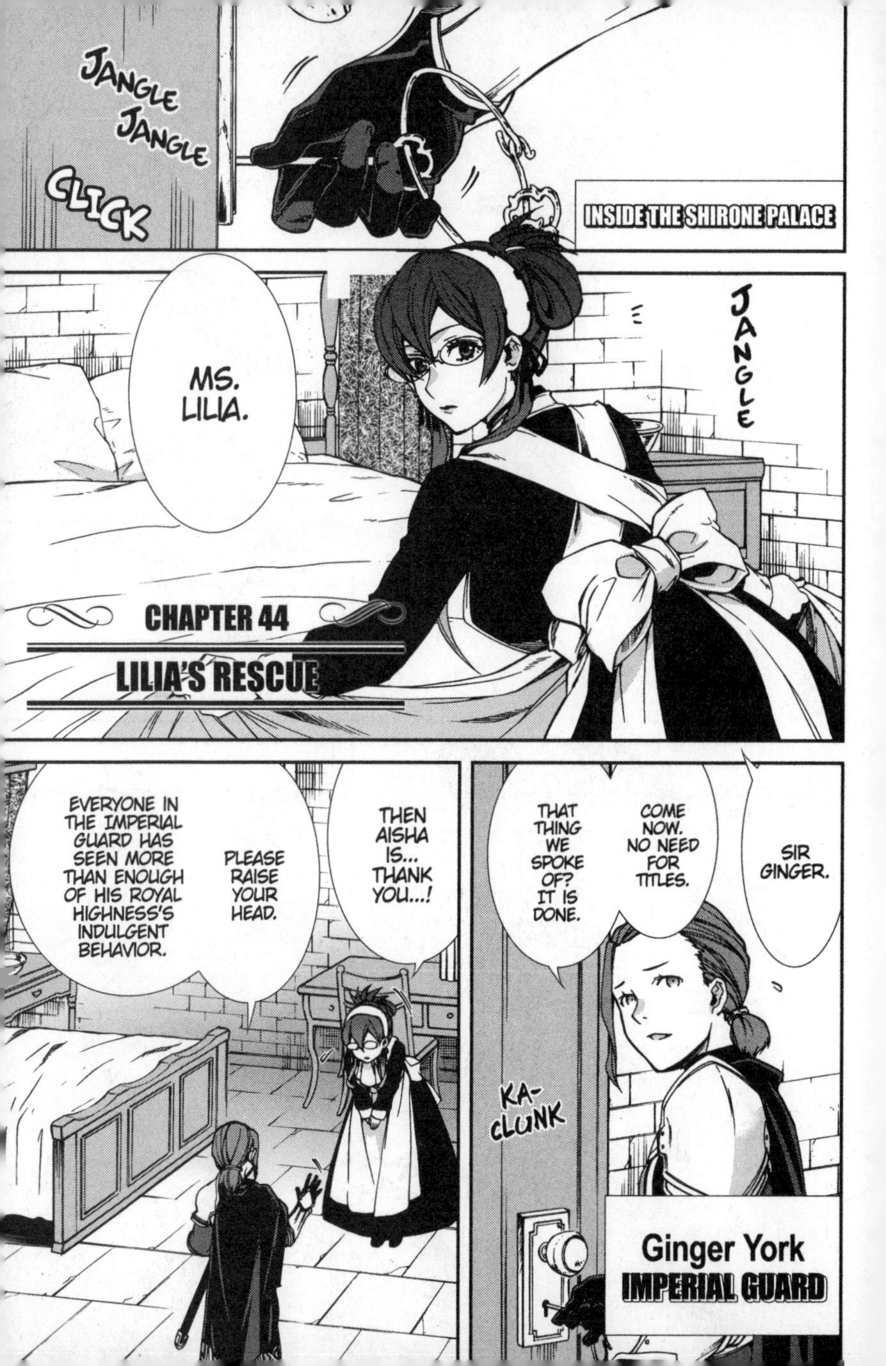

INSIDE THE SHIRONE PALACE
JANGLE JANGLE
CLICK
JANGLE
MS. LILIA.
CHAPTER 44
LILIA'S RESCUE
SIR GINGER.
COME NOW. NO NEED FOR TITLES.
THAT THING WE SPOKE OF? IT IS DONE.
KA-CLUNK
Ginger York
IMPERIAL GUARD
THEN AISHA IS... THANK YOU...!
PLEASE RAISE YOUR HEAD.
EVERYONE IN THE IMPERIAL GUARD HAS SEEN MORE THAN ENOUGH OF HIS ROYAL HIGHNESS'S INDULGENT BEHAVIOR.

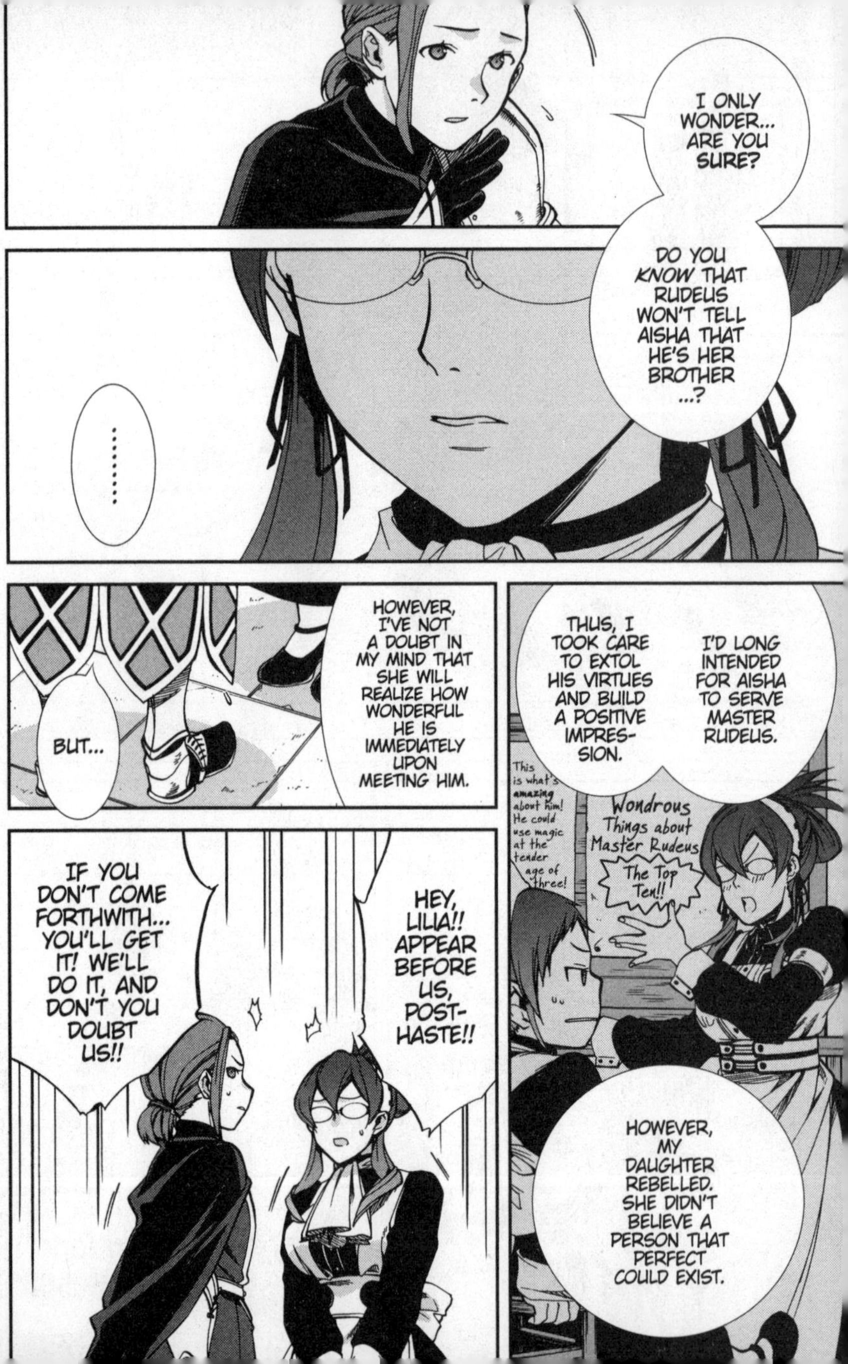
I ONLY WONDER... ARE YOU SURE?
DO YOU KNOW THAT RUDEUS WON'T TELL AISHA THAT HE'S HER BROTHER ...?
......
I'D LONG INTENDED FOR AISHA TO SERVE MASTER RUDEUS.
THUS, I TOOK CARE TO EXTOL HIS VIRTUES AND BUILD A POSITIVE IMPRES-SION.
Wondrous Things about Master Rudeus
The Top Ten!!
This is what's amazing about him! He could use magic at the tender age of three!
HOWEVER, MY DAUGHTER REBELLED. SHE DIDN'T BELIEVE A PERSON THAT PERFECT COULD EXIST.
HOWEVER, I'VE NOT A DOUBT IN MY MIND THAT SHE WILL REALIZE HOW WONDERFUL HE IS IMMEDIATELY UPON MEETING HIM.
BUT...
HEY, LILIA!! APPEAR BEFORE US, POST-HASTE!!
IF YOU DON'T COME FORTHWITH... YOU'LL GET IT! WE'LL DO IT, AND DON'T YOU DOUBT US!!

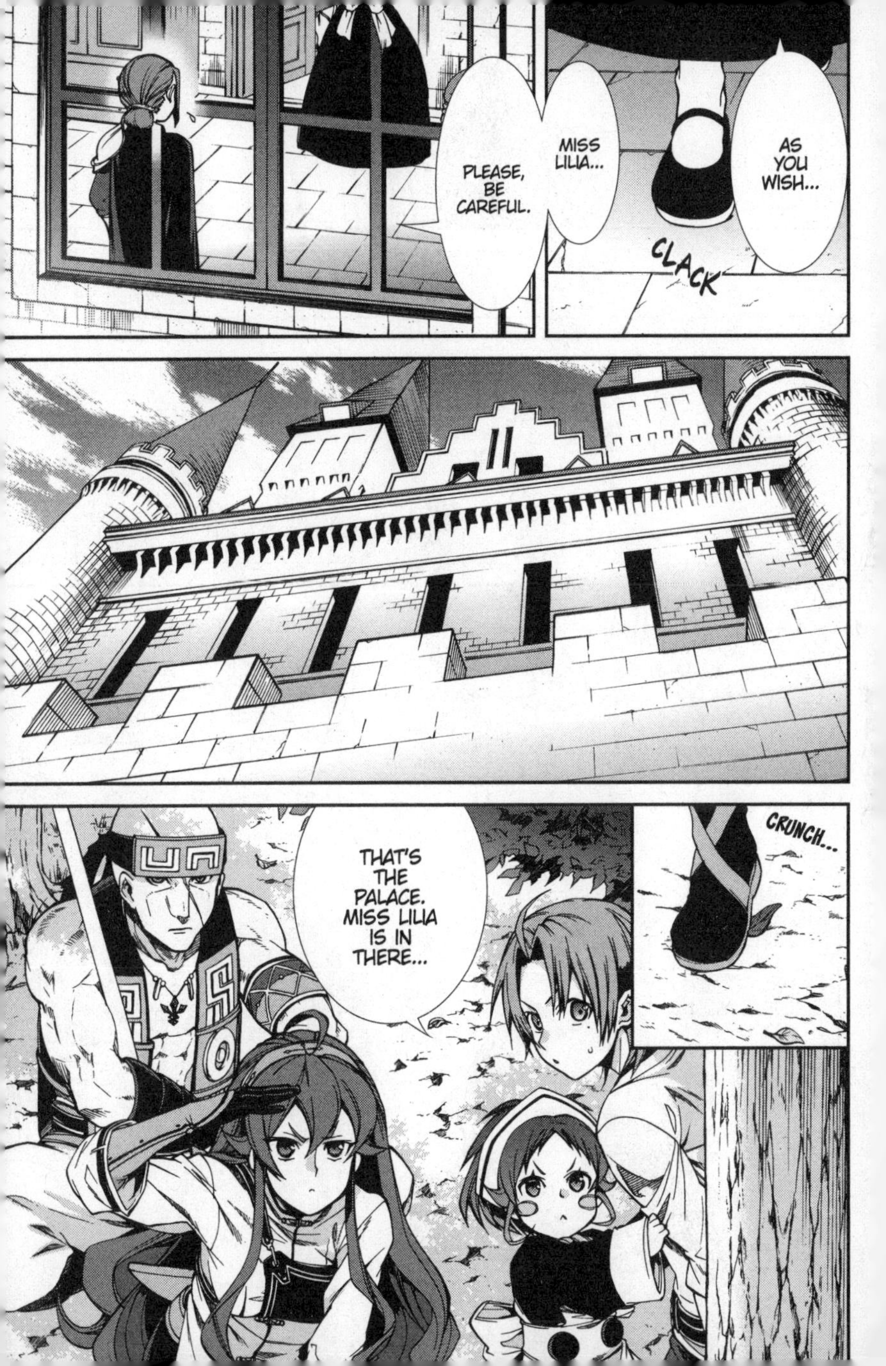
AS YOU WISH...
CLACK
MISS LILIA...
PLEASE, BE CAREFUL.
CRUNCH...
THAT'S THE PALACE. MISS LILIA IS IN THERE...

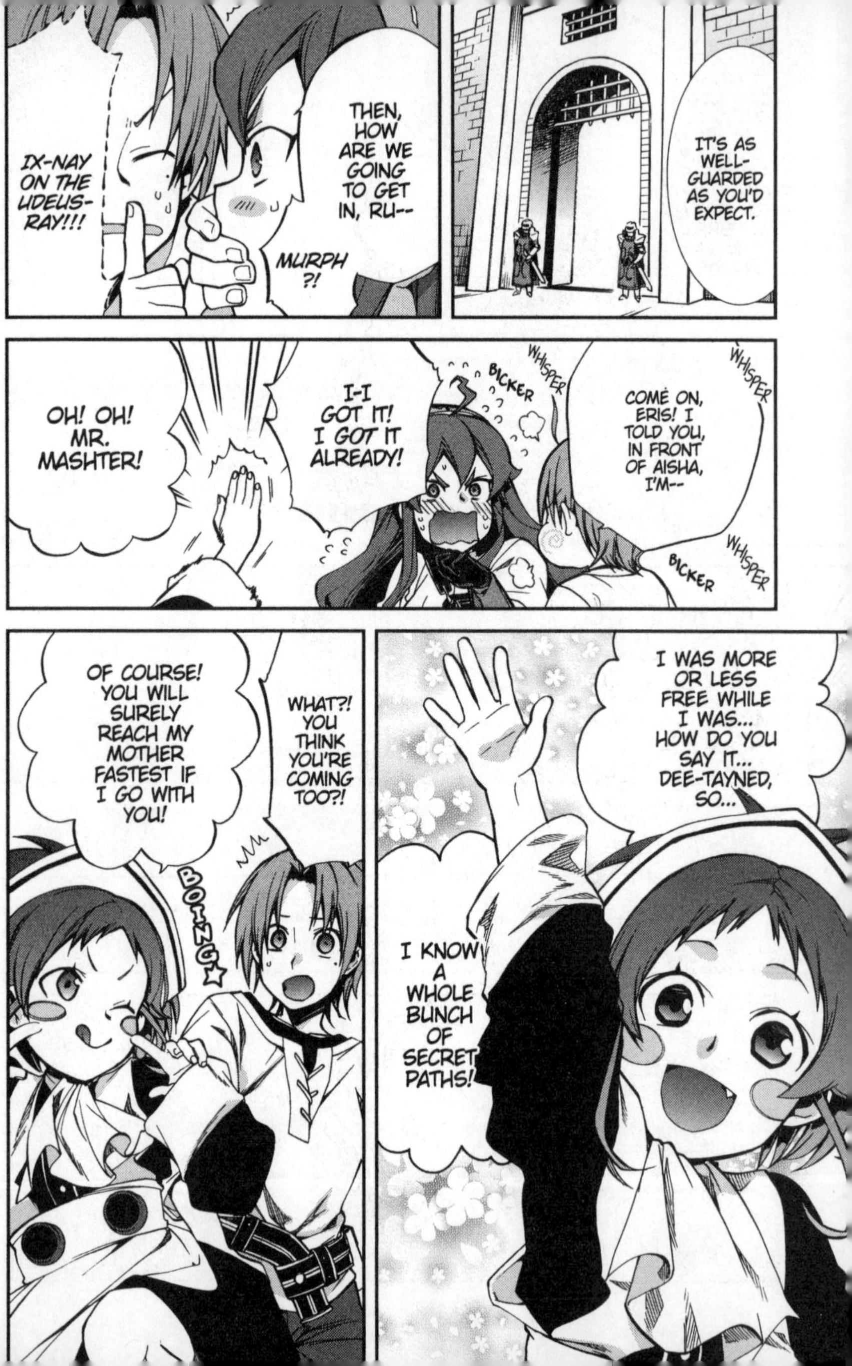
IT'S AS WELL-GUARDED AS YOU'D EXPECT.
THEN, HOW ARE WE GOING TO GET IN, RU--
MURPH ?!
IX-NAY ON THE UDEUS-RAY!!!
COME ON, ERIS! I TOLD YOU, IN FRONT OF AISHA, I'M--
WHISPER
BICKER
WHISPER
BICKER
I-I GOT IT! I GOT IT ALREADY!
OH! OH! MR. MASHTER!
I WAS MORE OR LESS FREE WHILE I WAS... HOW DO YOU SAY IT... DEE-TAYNED, SO...
I KNOW A WHOLE BUNCH OF SECRET PATHS!
WHAT?! YOU THINK YOU'RE COMING TOO?!
OF COURSE! YOU WILL SURELY REACH MY MOTHER FASTEST IF I GO WITH YOU!
BOING☆

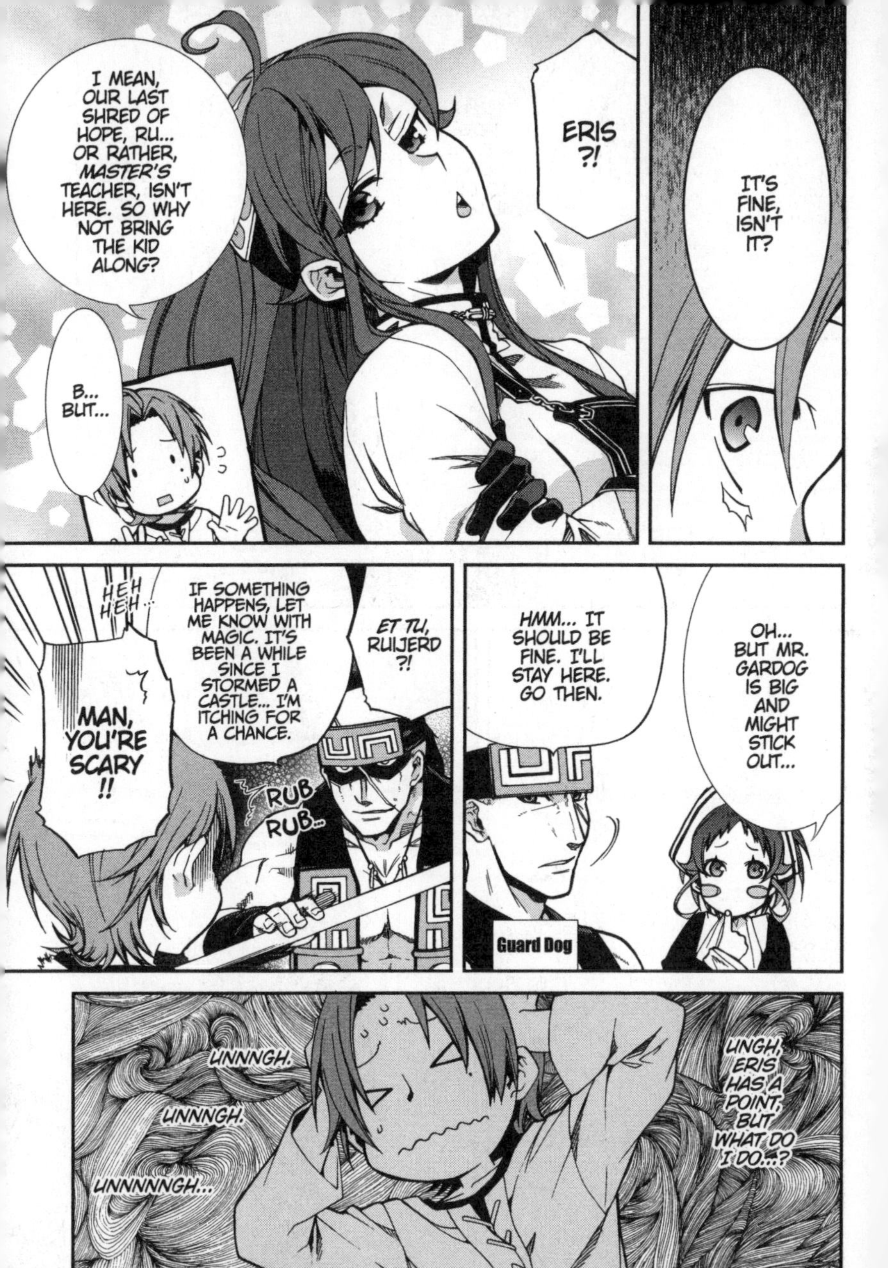
IT'S FINE, ISN'T IT?
ERIS ?!
I MEAN, OUR LAST SHRED OF HOPE, RU... OR RATHER, *MASTER'S* TEACHER, ISN'T HERE. SO WHY NOT BRING THE KID ALONG?
B... BUT...
OH... BUT MR. GARDOG IS BIG AND MIGHT STICK OUT...
HMM... IT SHOULD BE FINE. I'LL STAY HERE. GO THEN.
Guard Dog
ET TU, RUIJERD ?!
IF SOMETHING HAPPENS, LET ME KNOW WITH MAGIC. IT'S BEEN A WHILE SINCE I STORMED A CASTLE... I'M ITCHING FOR A CHANCE.
HEH HEH...
MAN, YOU'RE SCARY !!
RUB RUB...
UNGH, ERIS HAS A POINT, BUT WHAT DO I DO...?
UNNNGH.
UNNNGH.
UNNNNNGH...

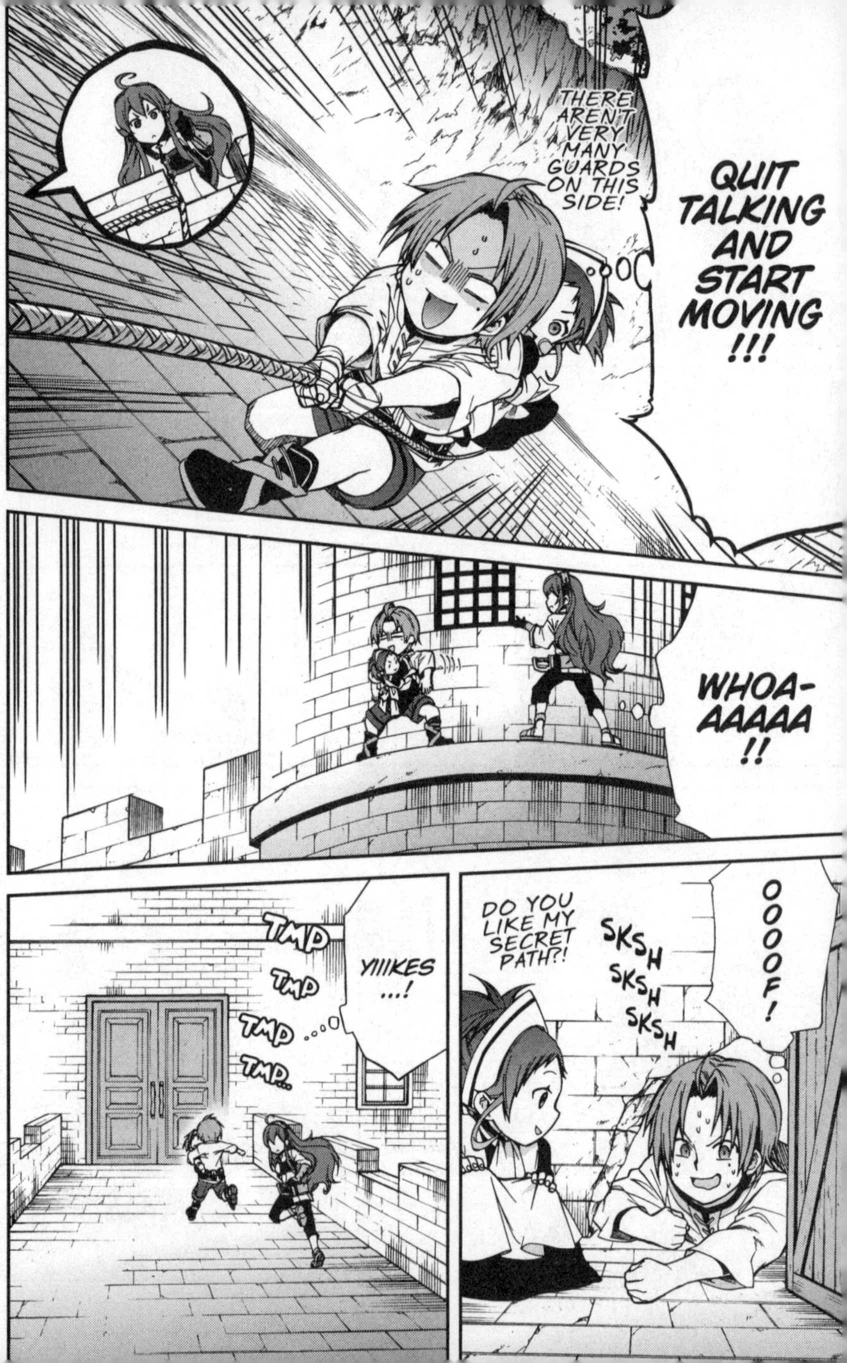
THERE AREN'T VERY MANY GUARDS ON THIS SIDE!
QUIT TALKING AND START MOVING!!!
WHOA-AAAAA!!
OOOOF!
SKSH SKSH SKSH
DO YOU LIKE MY SECRET PATH?!
YIIIKES...!
TMP TMP TMP TMP...

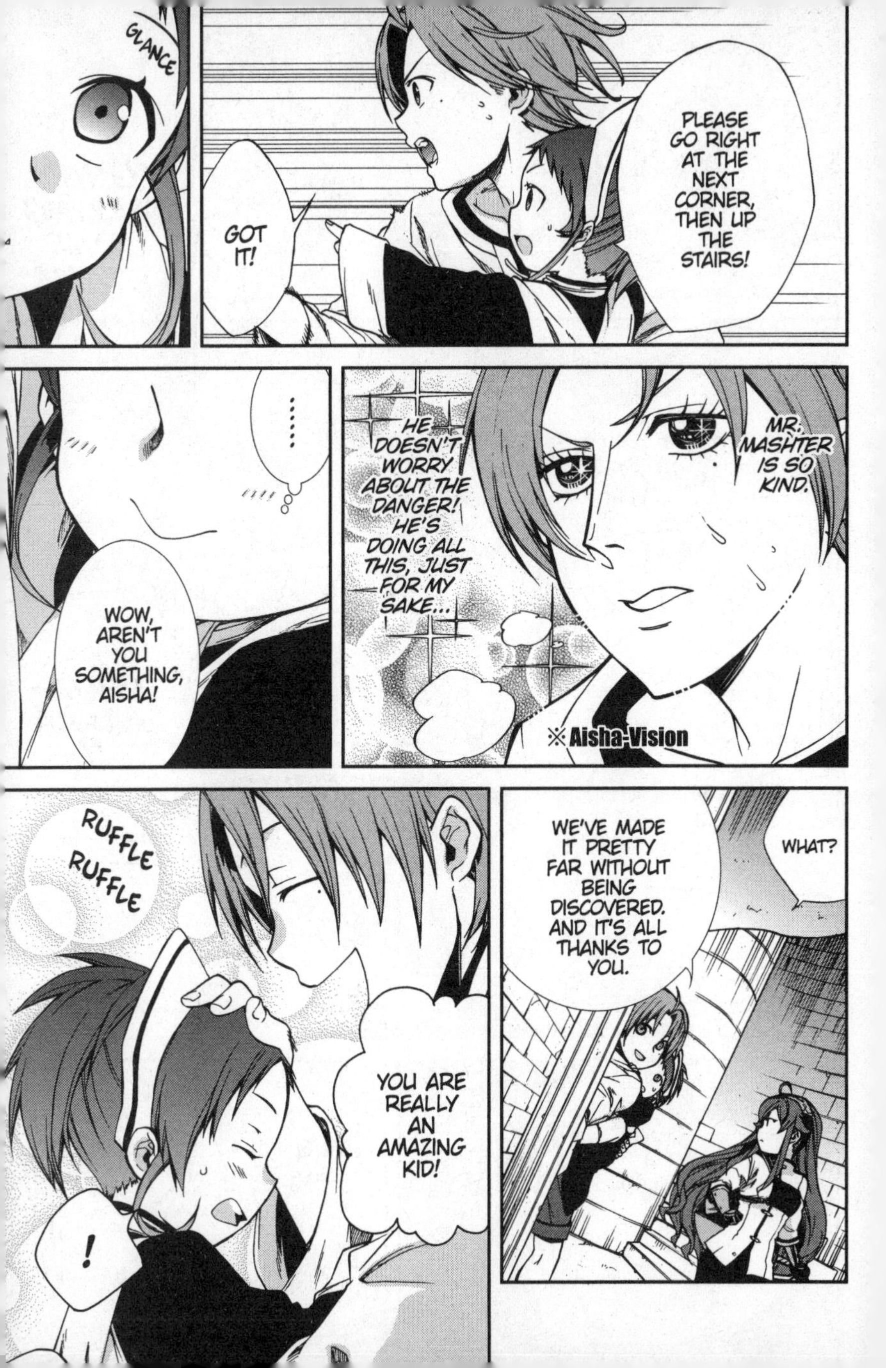
PLEASE GO RIGHT AT THE NEXT CORNER, THEN UP THE STAIRS!
GOT IT!
GLANCE
MR. MASHTER IS SO KIND.
HE DOESN'T WORRY ABOUT THE DANGER! HE'S DOING ALL THIS, JUST FOR MY SAKE...
※Aisha-Vision
......
WOW, AREN'T YOU SOMETHING, AISHA!
WHAT?
WE'VE MADE IT PRETTY FAR WITHOUT BEING DISCOVERED. AND IT'S ALL THANKS TO YOU.
RUFFLE RUFFLE
YOU ARE REALLY AN AMAZING KID!
!

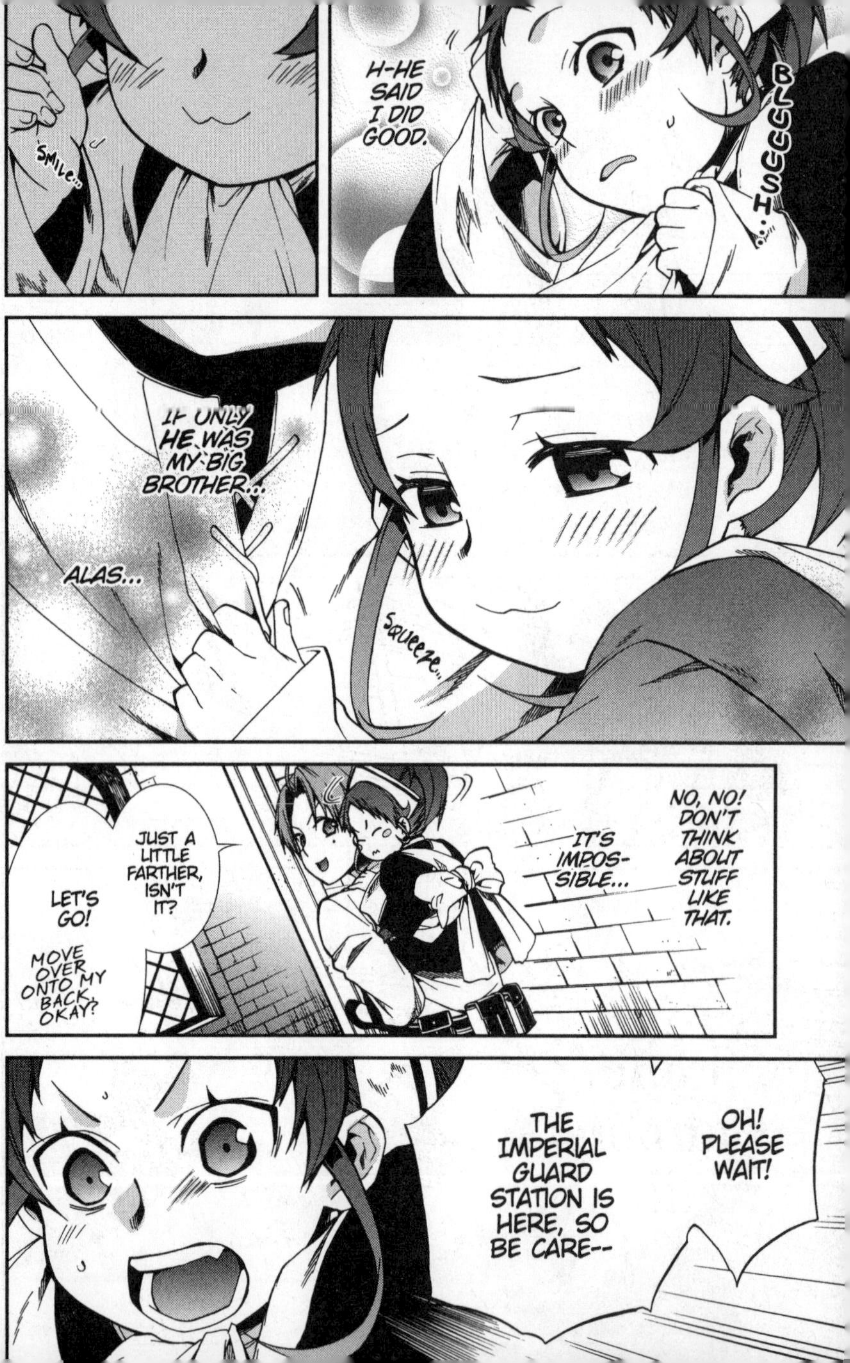
BLUUUSH...
H-HE SAID I DID GOOD.
Smile...
IF ONLY HE WAS MY BIG BROTHER...
ALAS...
Squeeze...
NO, NO! DON'T THINK ABOUT STUFF LIKE THAT.
IT'S IMPOS-SIBLE...
JUST A LITTLE FARTHER, ISN'T IT?
LET'S GO!
MOVE OVER ONTO MY BACK, OKAY?
OH! PLEASE WAIT!
THE IMPERIAL GUARD STATION IS HERE, SO BE CARE--

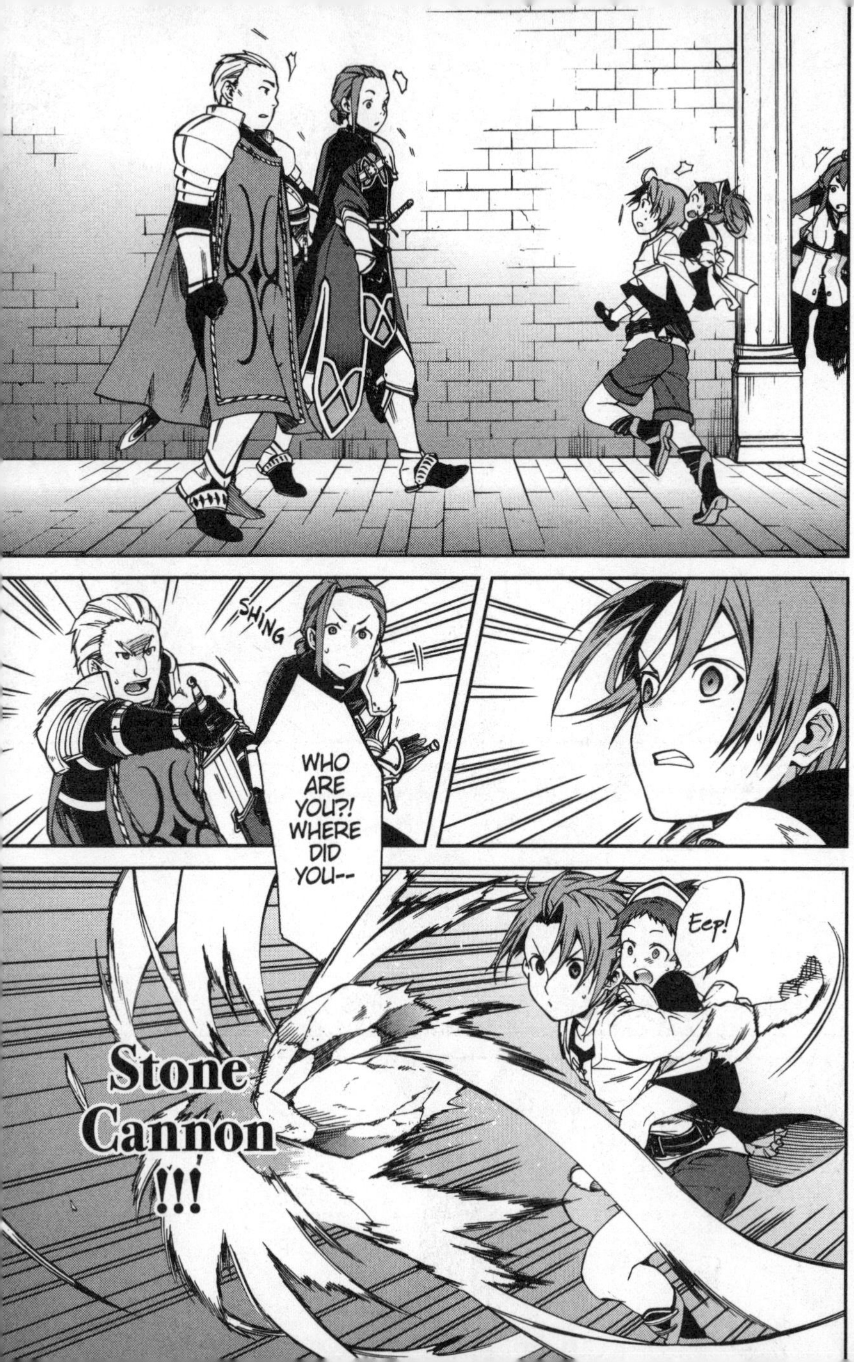
SHING
WHO ARE YOU?! WHERE DID YOU--
Eep!
Stone Cannon!!!

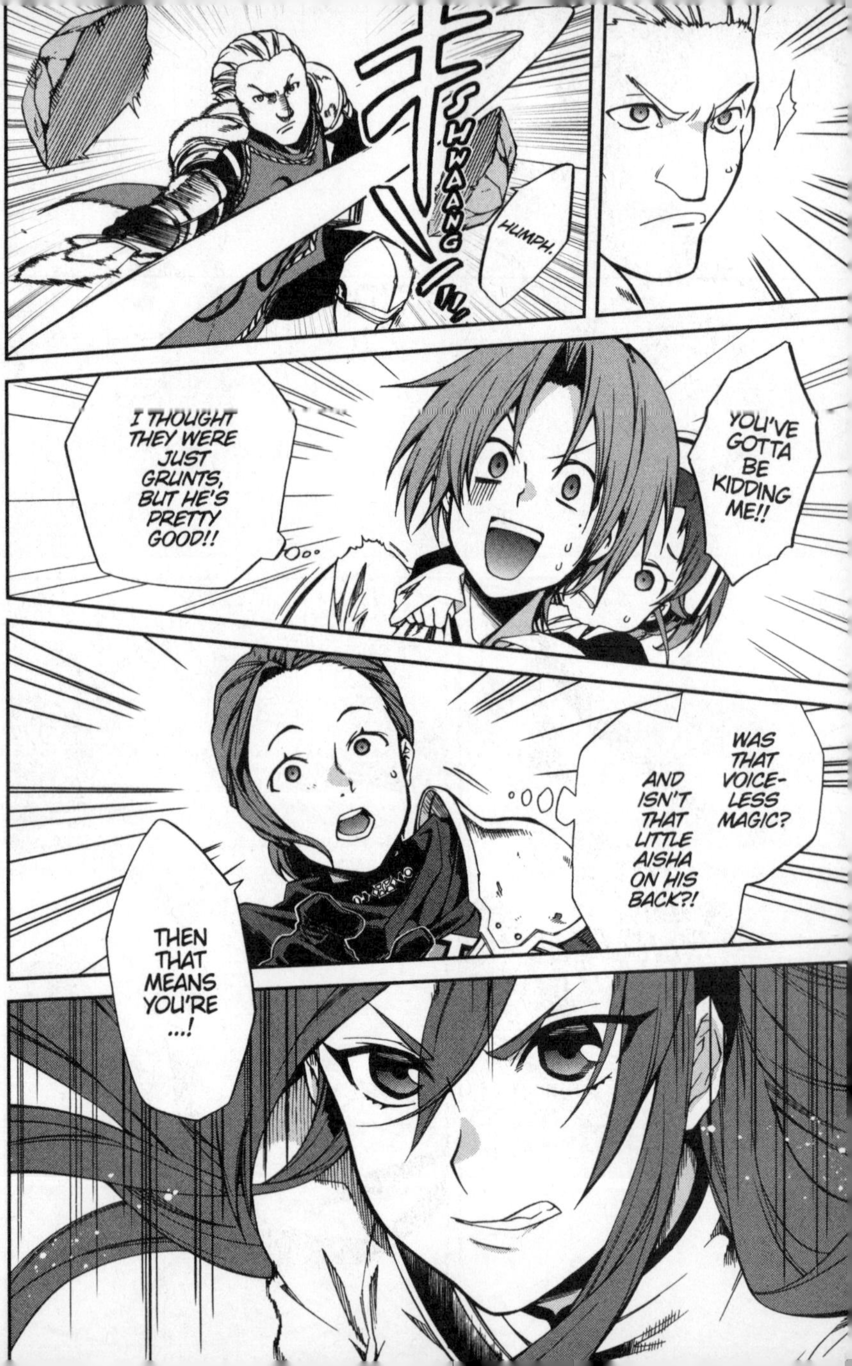
HUMPH.
SHWAANG
YOU'VE GOTTA BE KIDDING ME!!
I THOUGHT THEY WERE JUST GRUNTS, BUT HE'S PRETTY GOOD!!
WAS THAT VOICELESS MAGIC?
AND ISN'T THAT LITTLE AISHA ON HIS BACK?!
THEN THAT MEANS YOU'RE ...!

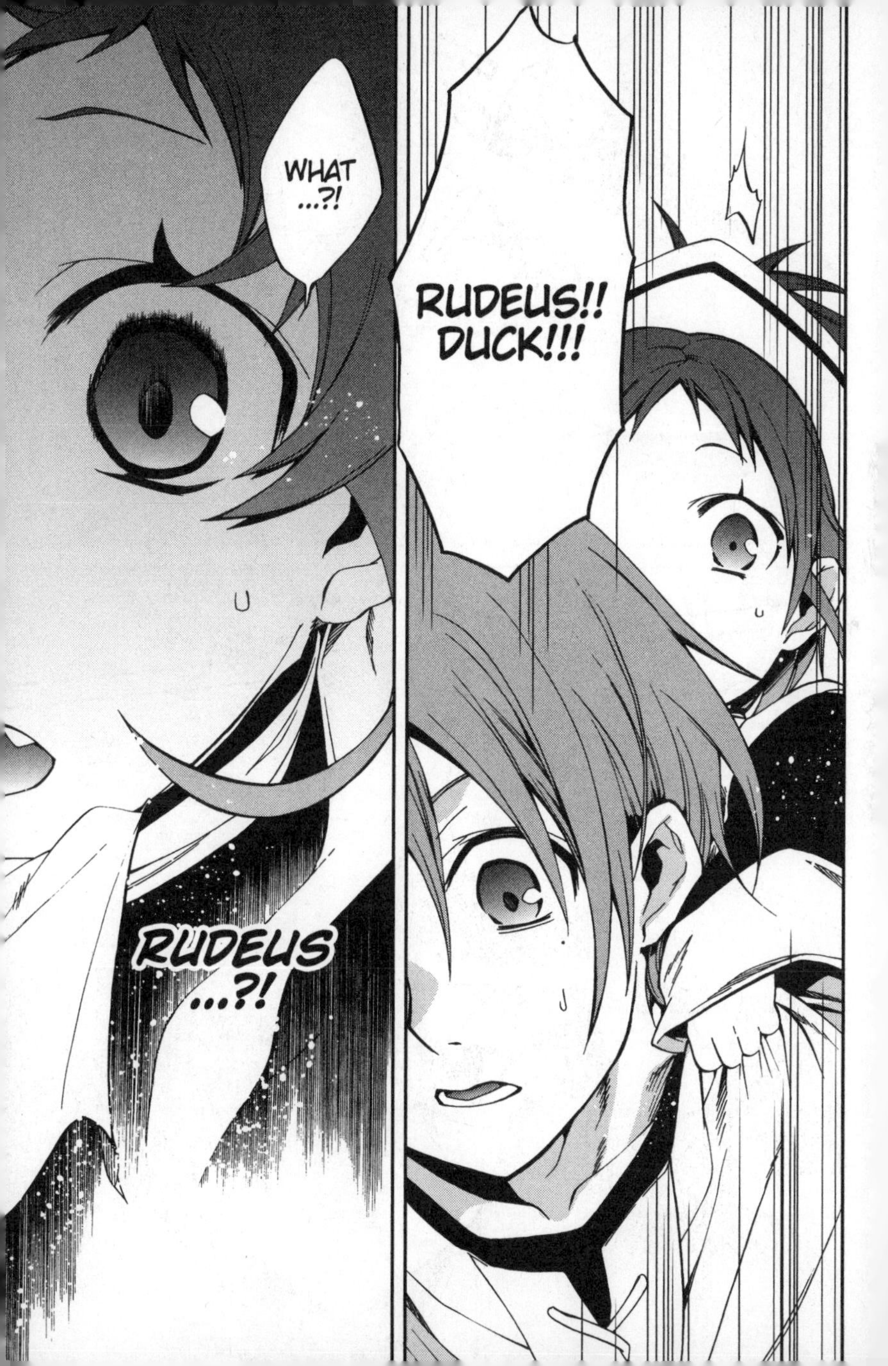
RUDEUS!! DUCK!!!
WHAT ...?!
RUDEUS ...?!

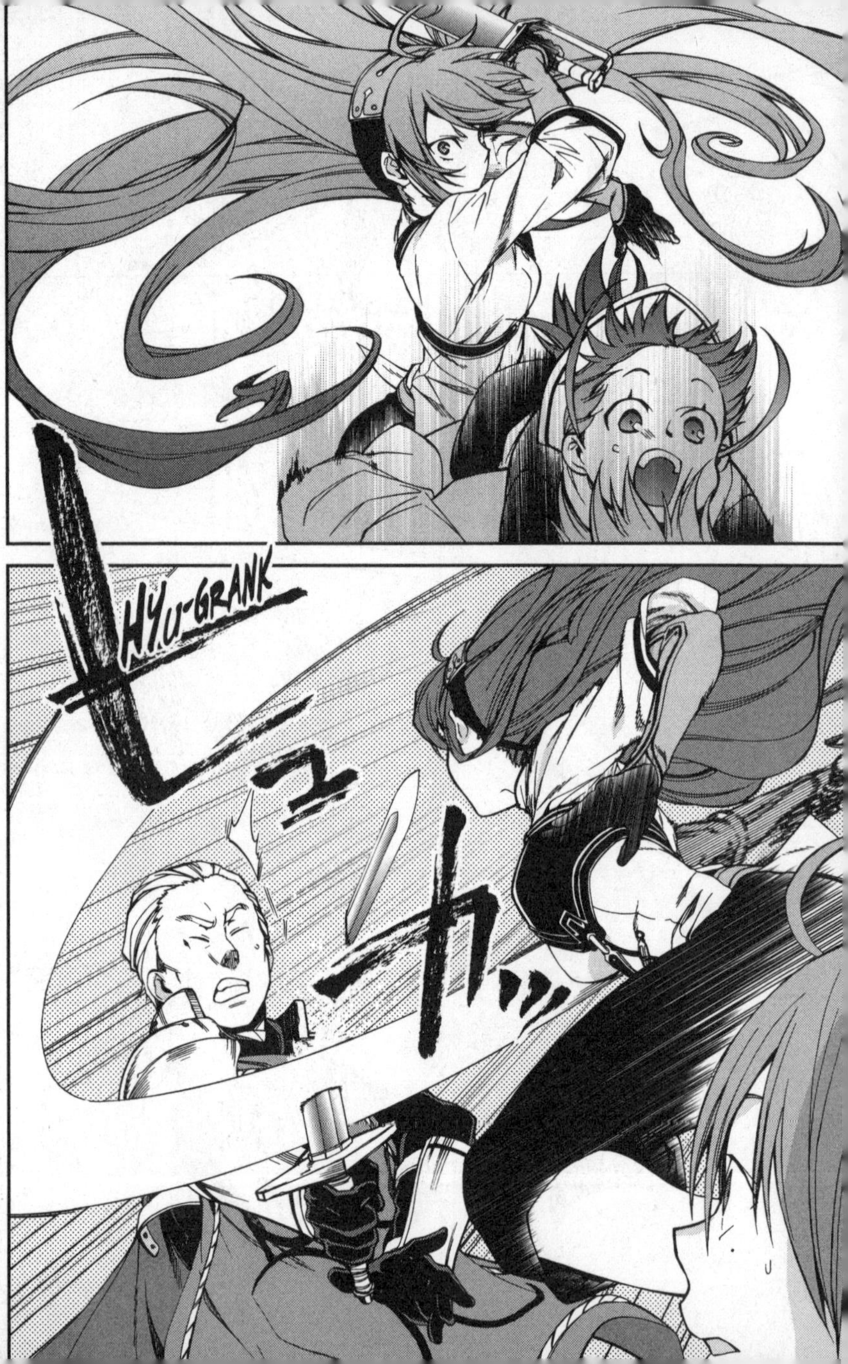
HYU-GRANK
ヒュ
ーカッ

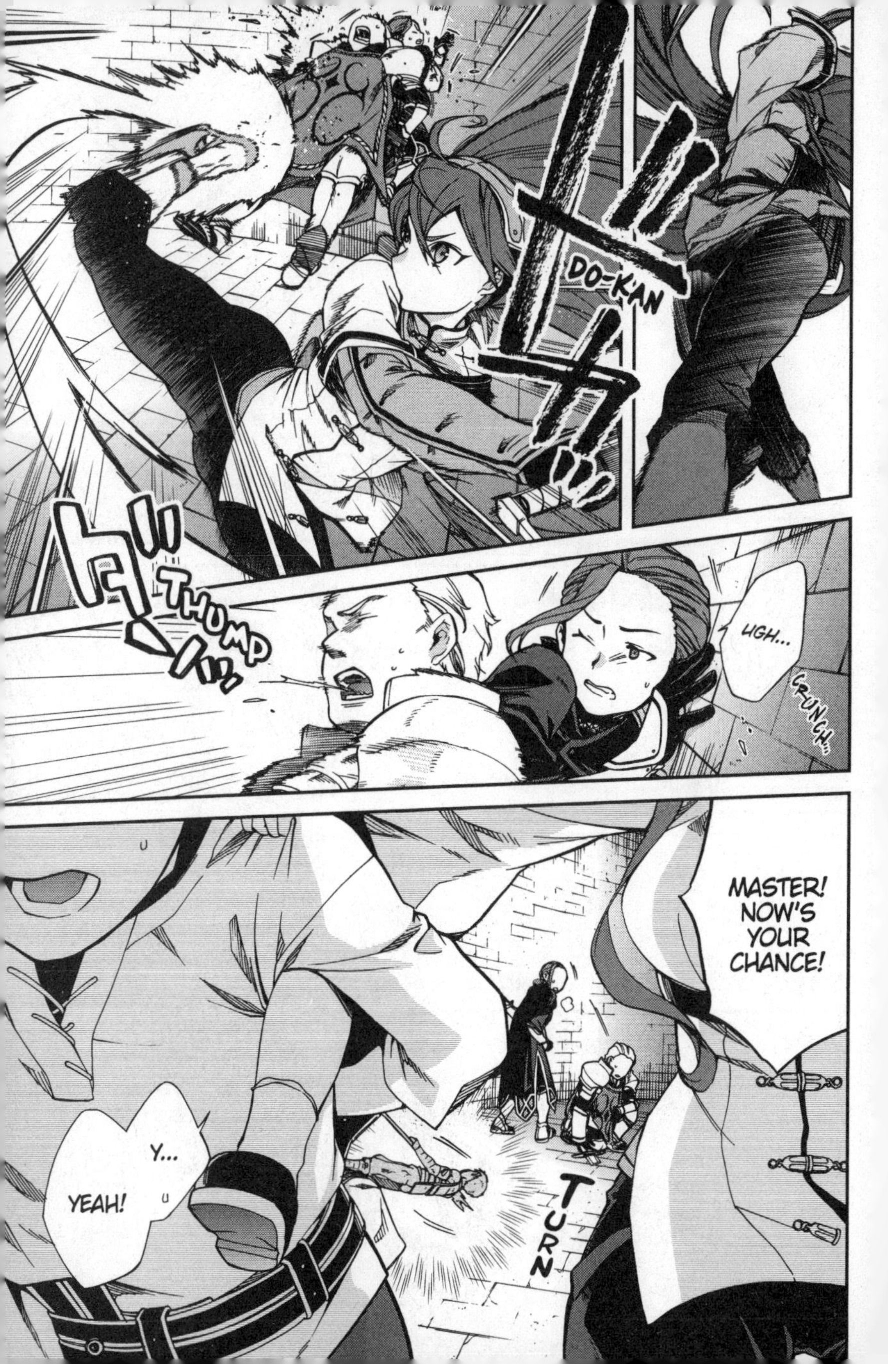
DO-KAN
UGH...
CRUNCH...
THUMP
MASTER! NOW'S YOUR CHANCE!
TURN
Y...
YEAH!

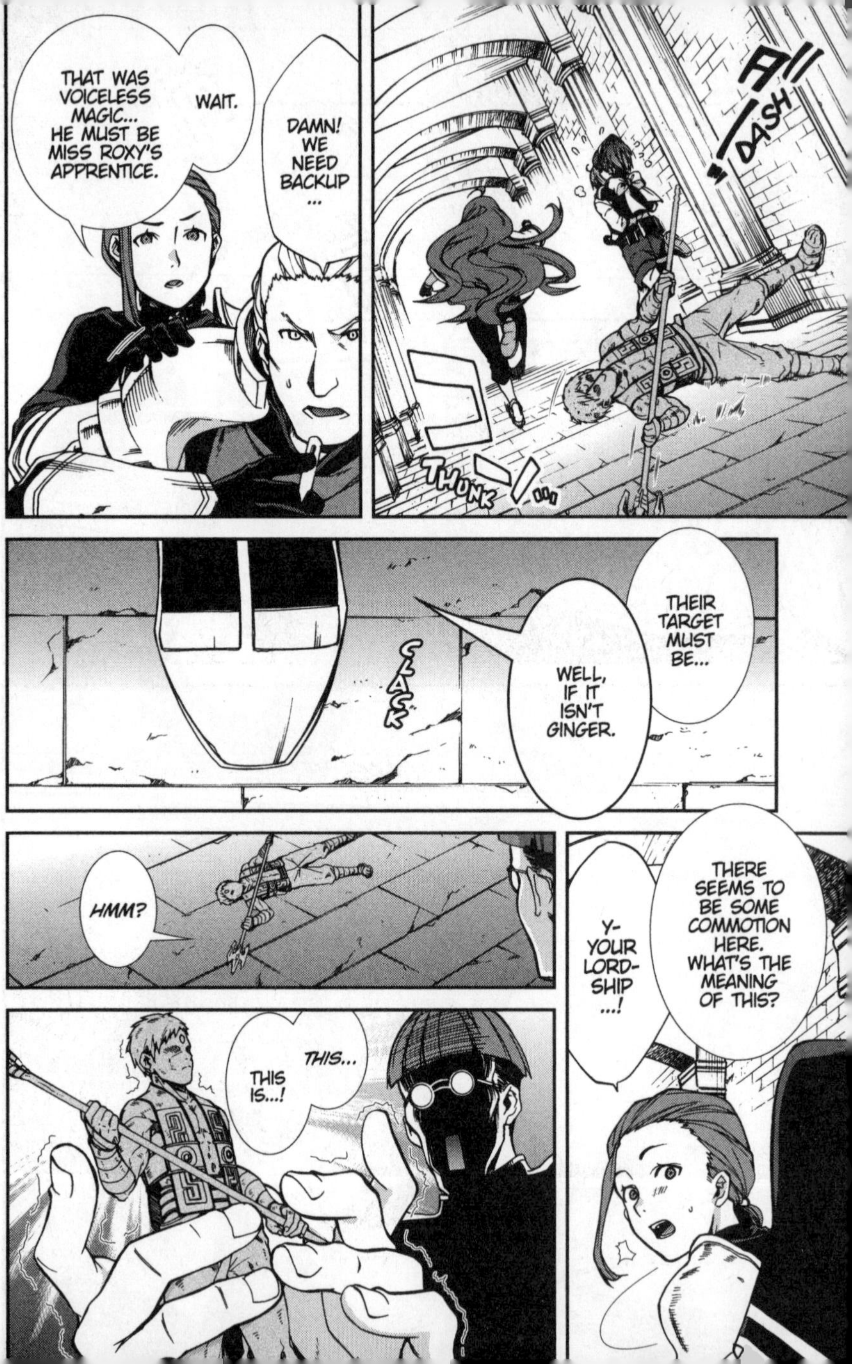
DASH
THUNK
DAMN! WE NEED BACKUP...
WAIT.
THAT WAS VOICELESS MAGIC... HE MUST BE MISS ROXY'S APPRENTICE.
THEIR TARGET MUST BE...
WELL, IF IT ISN'T GINGER.
CLACK
THERE SEEMS TO BE SOME COMMOTION HERE. WHAT'S THE MEANING OF THIS?
Y-YOUR LORDSHIP...!
HMM?
THIS...
THIS IS...!

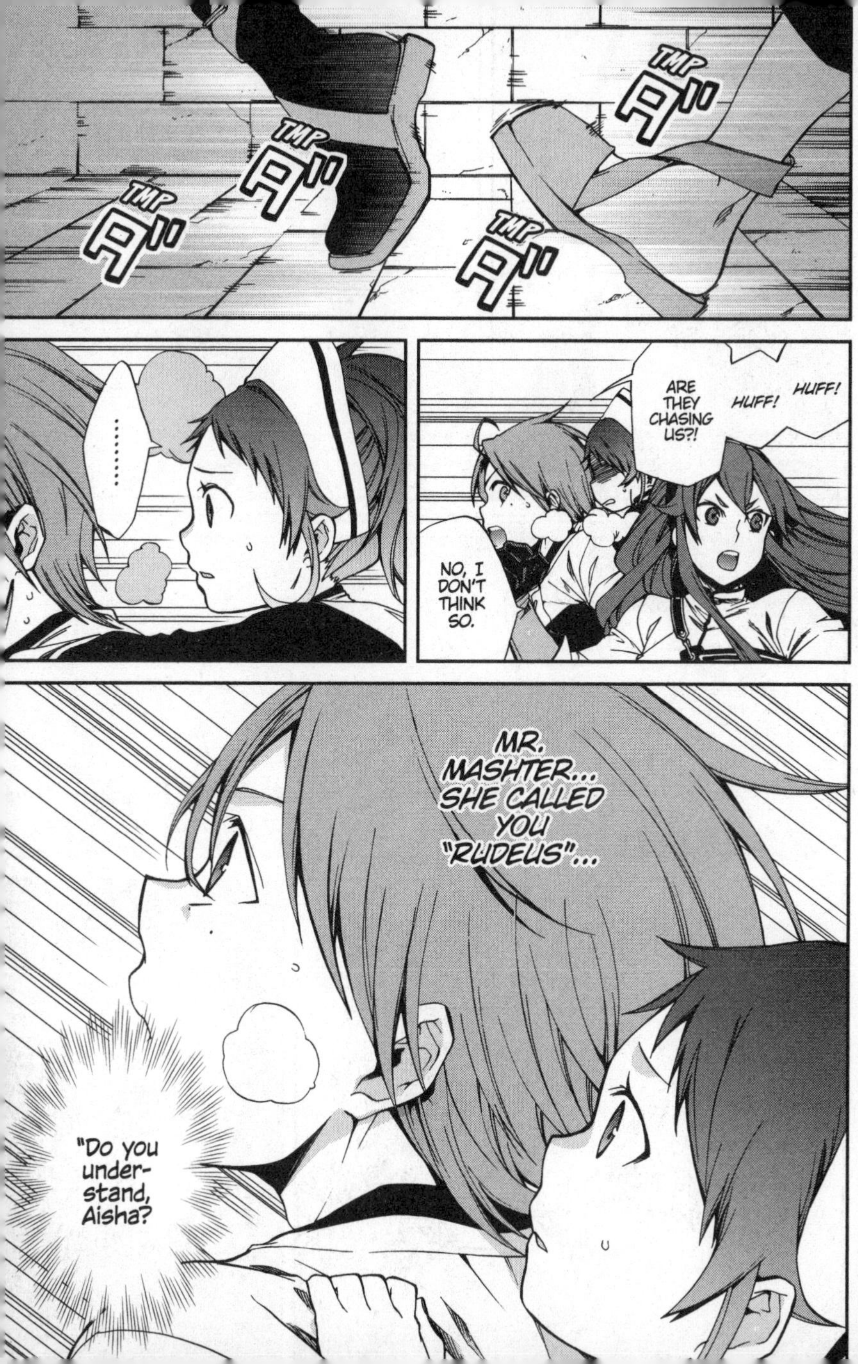
TMP
TMP
TMP
TMP
ARE THEY CHASING US?!
HUFF! HUFF!
NO, I DON'T THINK SO.
......
MR. MASHTER... SHE CALLED YOU "RUDEUS"...
"Do you under-stand, Aisha?

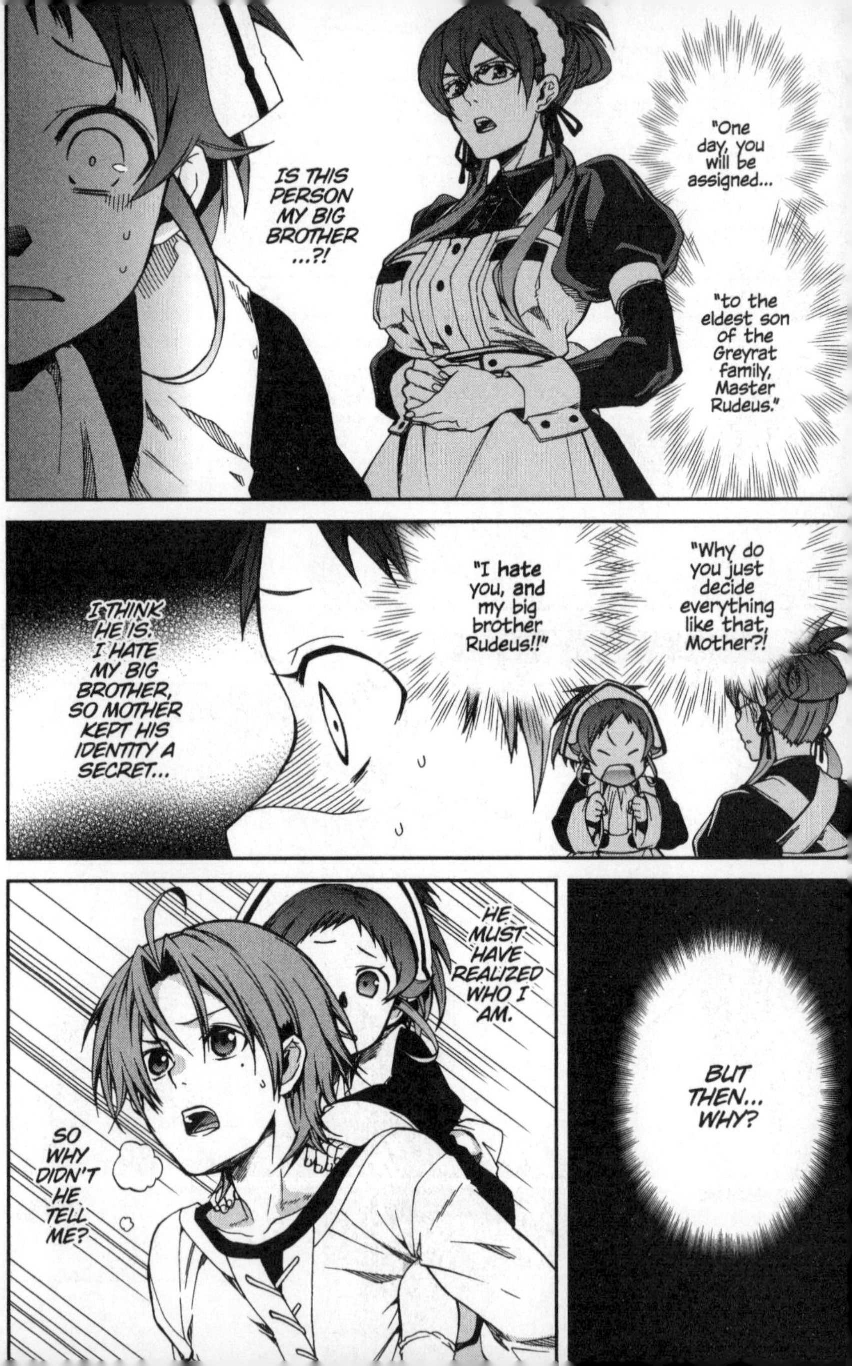
"One day, you will be assigned...
"to the eldest son of the Greyrat family, Master Rudeus."
IS THIS PERSON MY BIG BROTHER ...?!
"Why do you just decide everything like that, Mother?!
"I hate you, and my big brother Rudeus!!"
I THINK HE IS. I HATE MY BIG BROTHER, SO MOTHER KEPT HIS IDENTITY A SECRET...
BUT THEN... WHY?
HE MUST HAVE REALIZED WHO I AM.
SO WHY DIDN'T HE TELL ME?

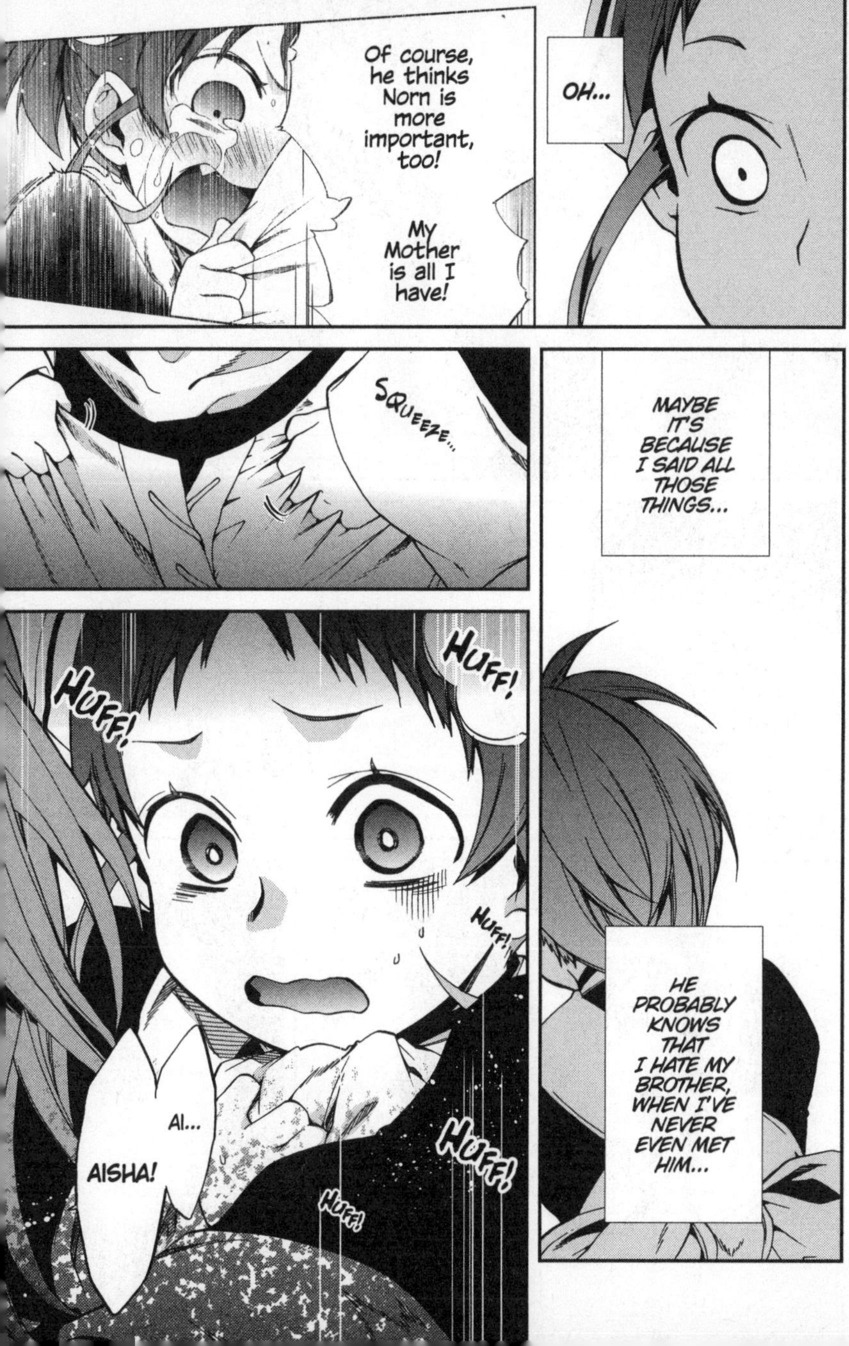
OH...
Of course, he thinks Norn is more important, too!
My Mother is all I have!
MAYBE IT'S BECAUSE I SAID ALL THOSE THINGS...
HE PROBABLY KNOWS THAT I HATE MY BROTHER, WHEN I'VE NEVER EVEN MET HIM...
SQUEEZE...
HUFF!
HUFF!
HUFF!
AI...
AISHA!
HUFF!
HUFF!

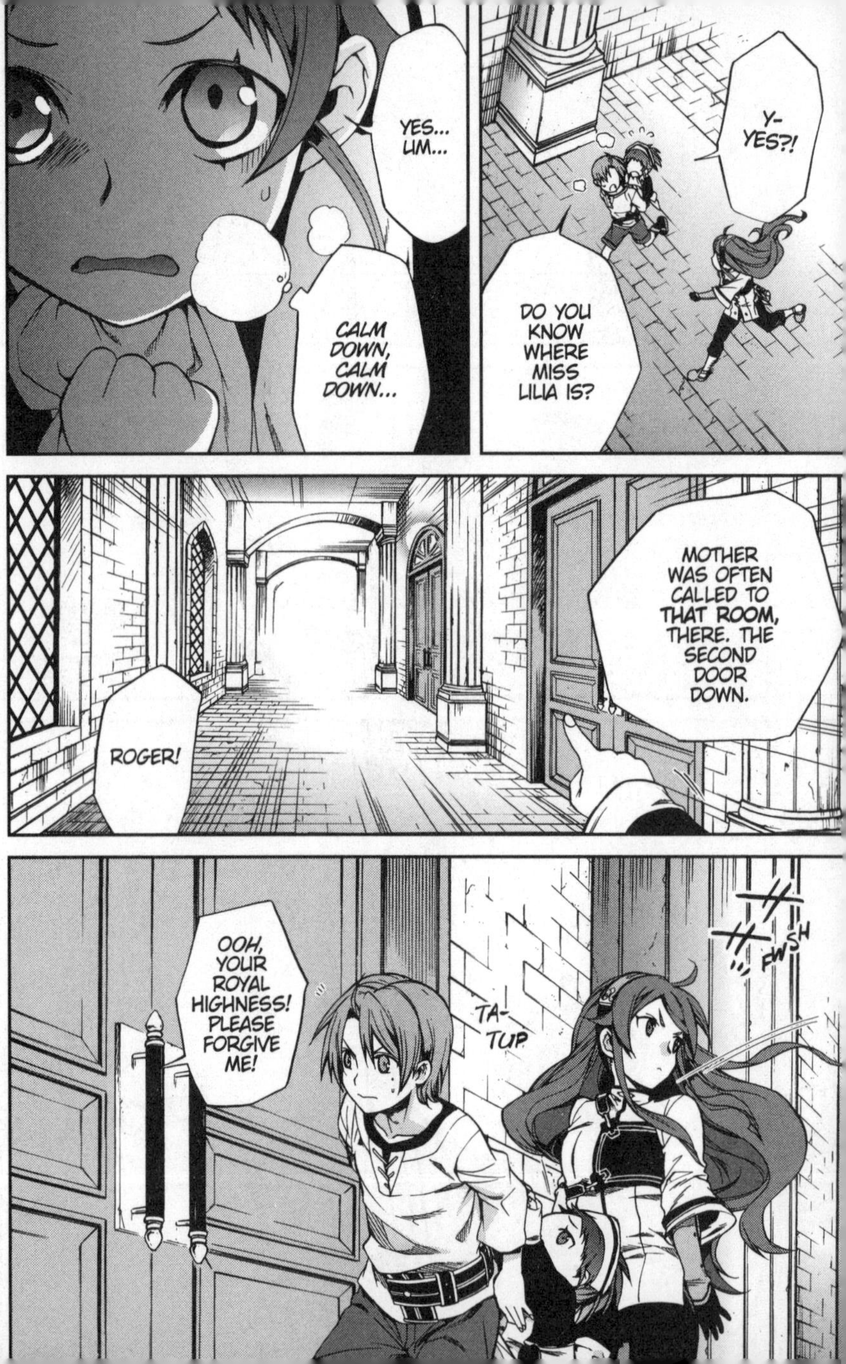
Y-YES?!
DO YOU KNOW WHERE MISS LILIA IS?
YES... UM...
CALM DOWN, CALM DOWN...
MOTHER WAS OFTEN CALLED TO THAT ROOM, THERE. THE SECOND DOOR DOWN.
ROGER!
FWSH
TA-TUP
OOH, YOUR ROYAL HIGHNESS! PLEASE FORGIVE ME!

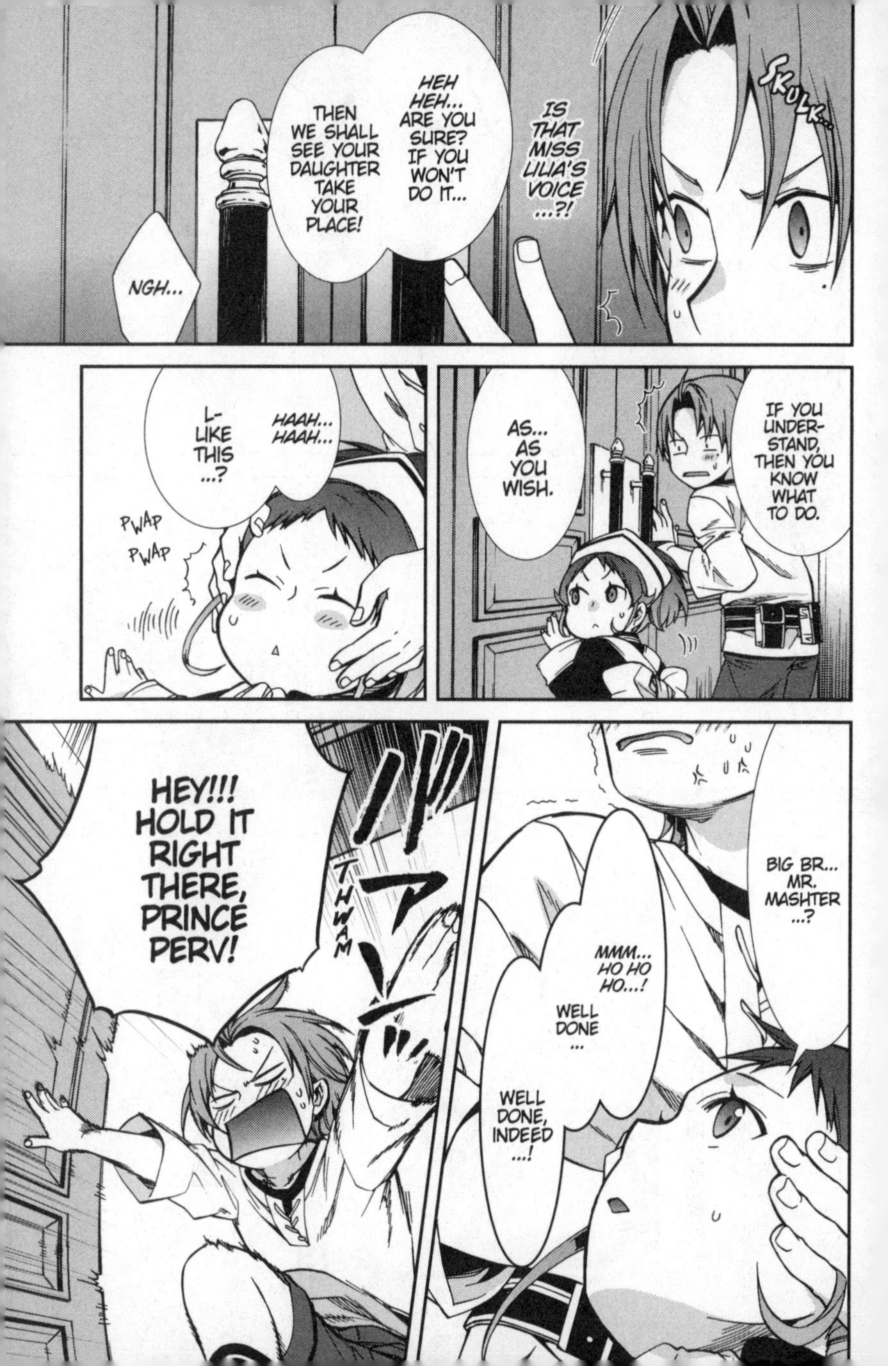
SKULK...
IS THAT MISS LILIA'S VOICE ...?!
HEH HEH... ARE YOU SURE? IF YOU WON'T DO IT...
THEN WE SHALL SEE YOUR DAUGHTER TAKE YOUR PLACE!
NGH...
IF YOU UNDER-STAND, THEN YOU KNOW WHAT TO DO.
AS... AS YOU WISH.
HAAH... HAAH...
L-LIKE THIS ...?
PWAP PWAP
BIG BR... MR. MASHTER ...?
MMM... HO HO HO...!
WELL DONE ...
WELL DONE, INDEED ...!
THWAM
HEY!!! HOLD IT RIGHT THERE, PRINCE PERV!

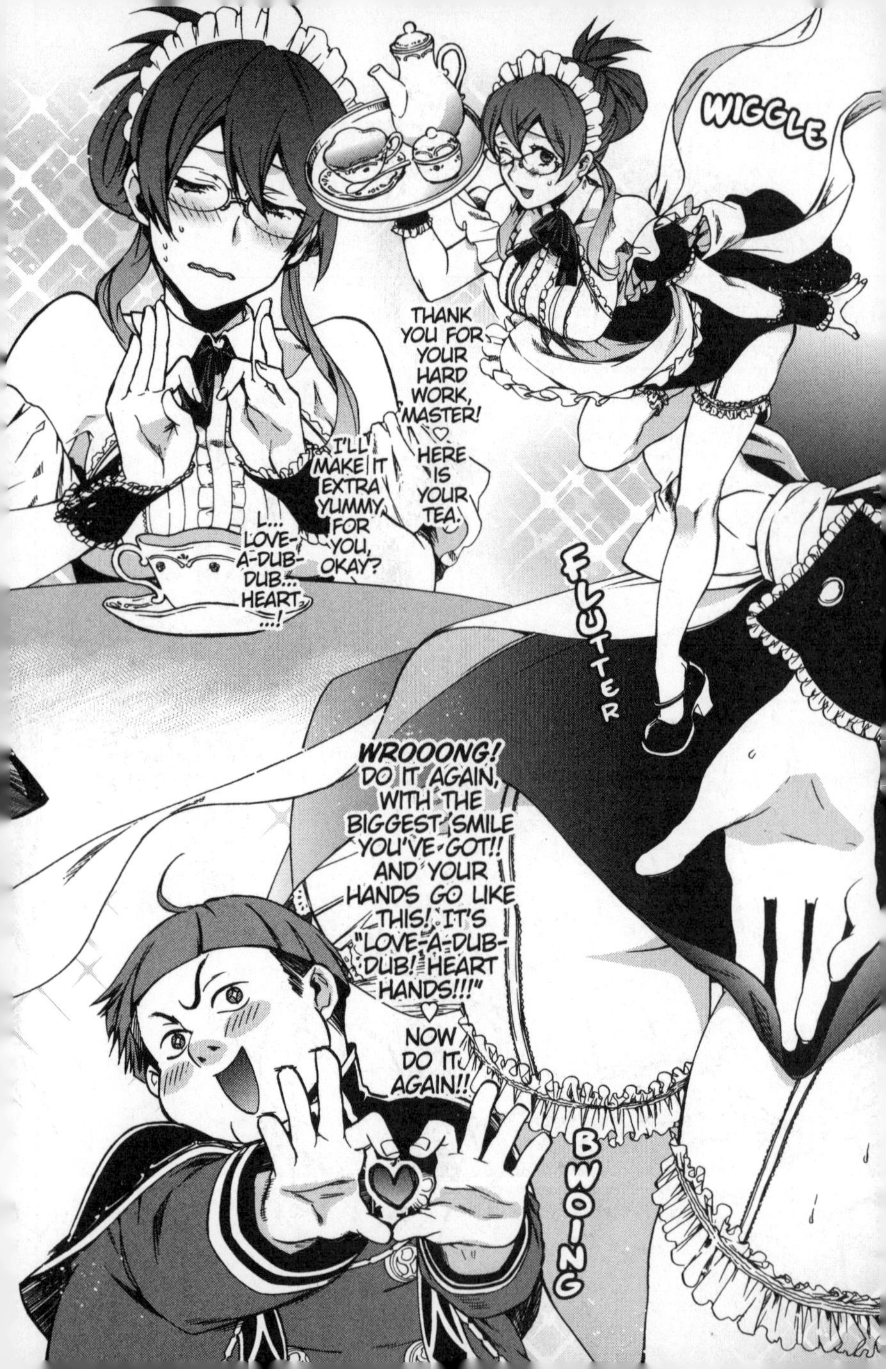
WIGGLE
THANK YOU FOR YOUR HARD WORK, MASTER! ♡
HERE IS YOUR TEA.
I'LL MAKE IT EXTRA YUMMY FOR YOU, OKAY?
FLUTTER
L... LOVE-A-DUB-DUB... HEART...!
BWOING
WROOONG! DO IT AGAIN, WITH THE BIGGEST SMILE YOU'VE GOT!! AND YOUR HANDS GO LIKE THIS! IT'S "LOVE-A-DUB-DUB! HEART HANDS!!!" ♡
NOW DO IT AGAIN!!

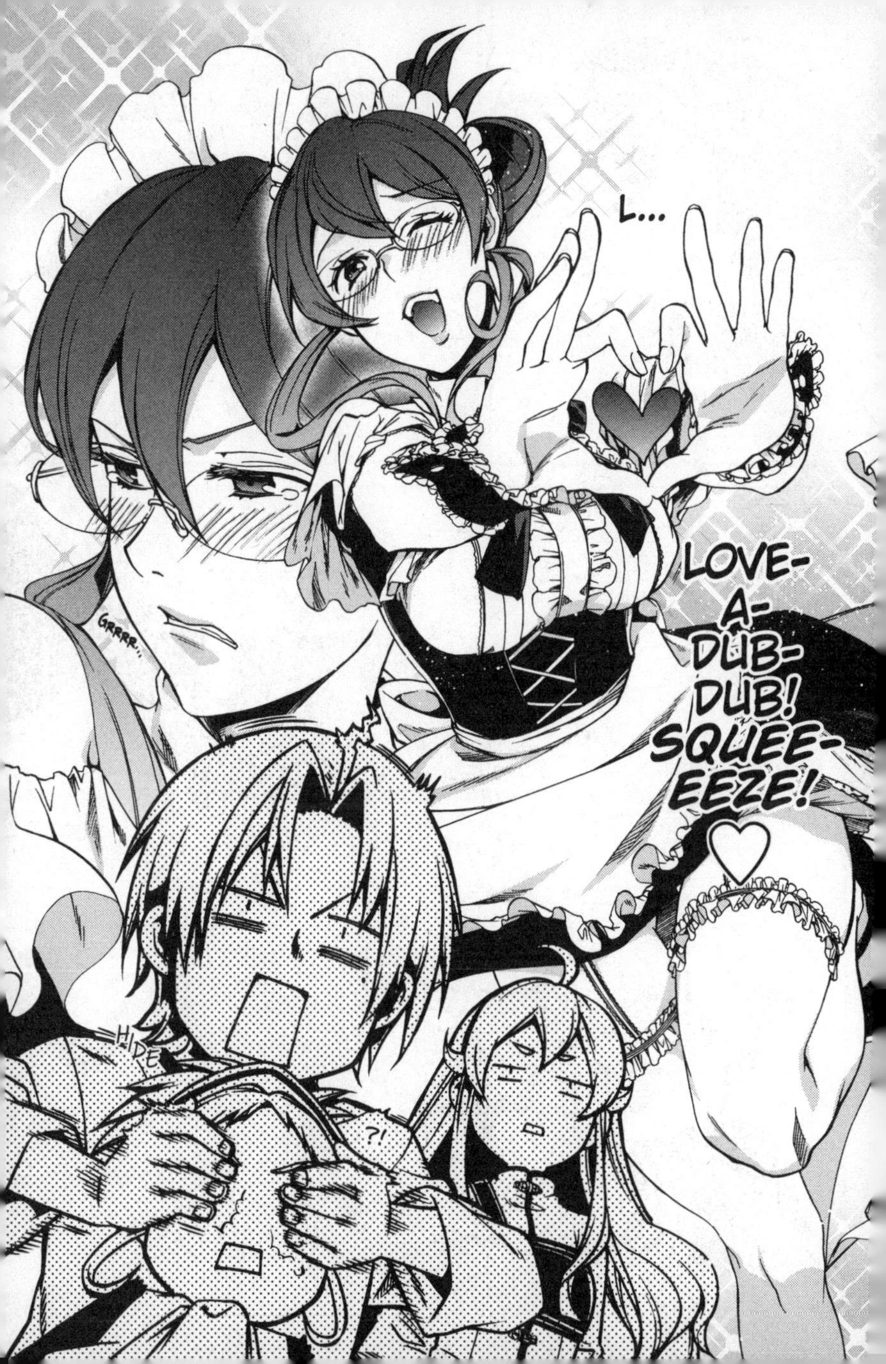
L...
LOVE-A-DUB-DUB! SQUEEE-EEZE! ♥
GRRRR..
HIDE
?!

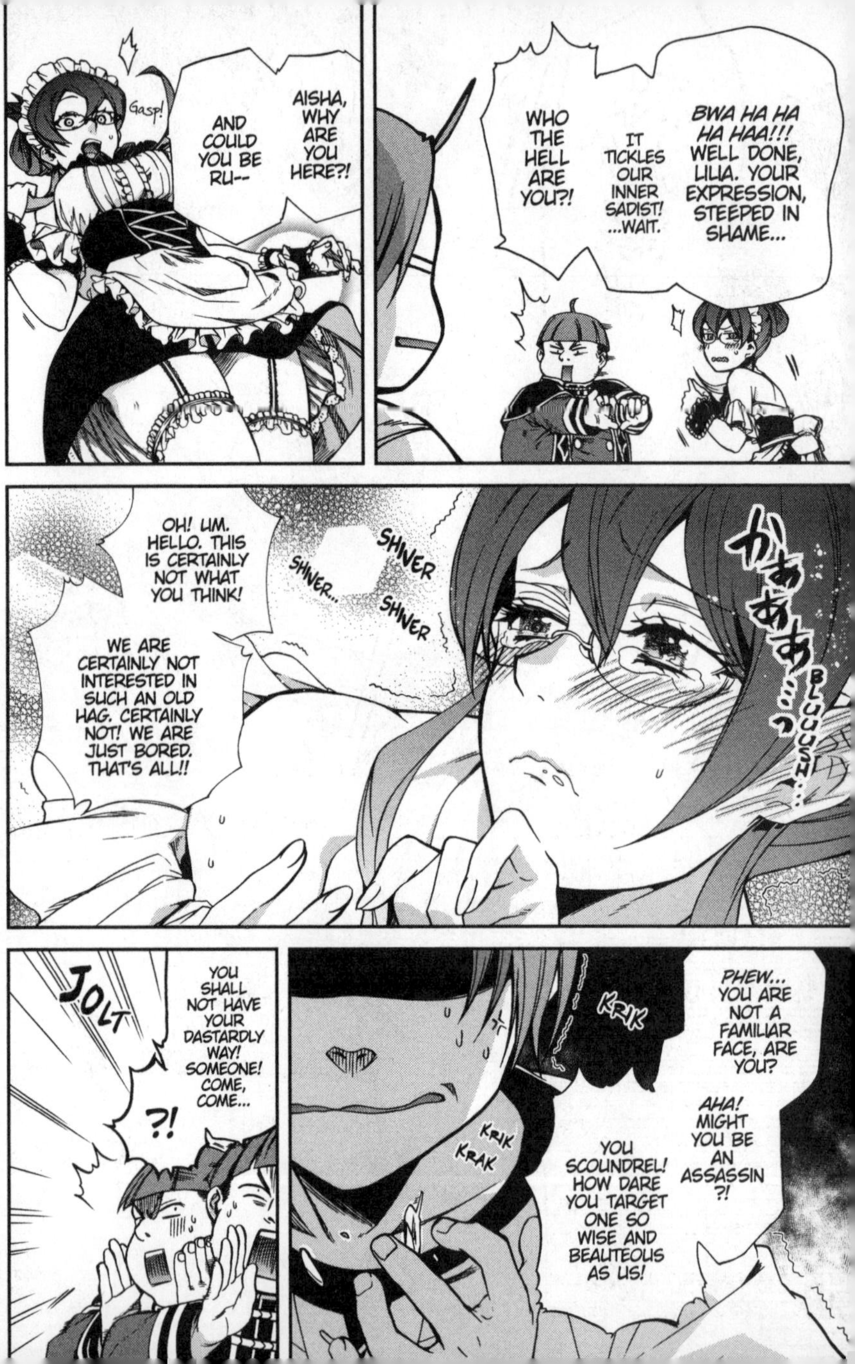
BWA HA HA HA HAA!!! WELL DONE, LILIA. YOUR EXPRESSION, STEEPED IN SHAME...
IT TICKLES OUR INNER SADIST! ...WAIT.
WHO THE HELL ARE YOU?!
AISHA, WHY ARE YOU HERE?!
AND COULD YOU BE RU--
Gasp!
かあああ…っ
BLUUUSH...
SHIVER
SHIVER
SHIVER...
OH! UM. HELLO. THIS IS CERTAINLY NOT WHAT YOU THINK!
WE ARE CERTAINLY NOT INTERESTED IN SUCH AN OLD HAG. CERTAINLY NOT! WE ARE JUST BORED. THAT'S ALL!!
PHEW... YOU ARE NOT A FAMILIAR FACE, ARE YOU?
KRIK
AHA! MIGHT YOU BE AN ASSASSIN?!
YOU SCOUNDREL! HOW DARE YOU TARGET ONE SO WISE AND BEAUTEOUS AS US!
KRIK
KRAK
JOLT
YOU SHALL NOT HAVE YOUR DASTARDLY WAY! SOMEONE! COME, COME...
?!

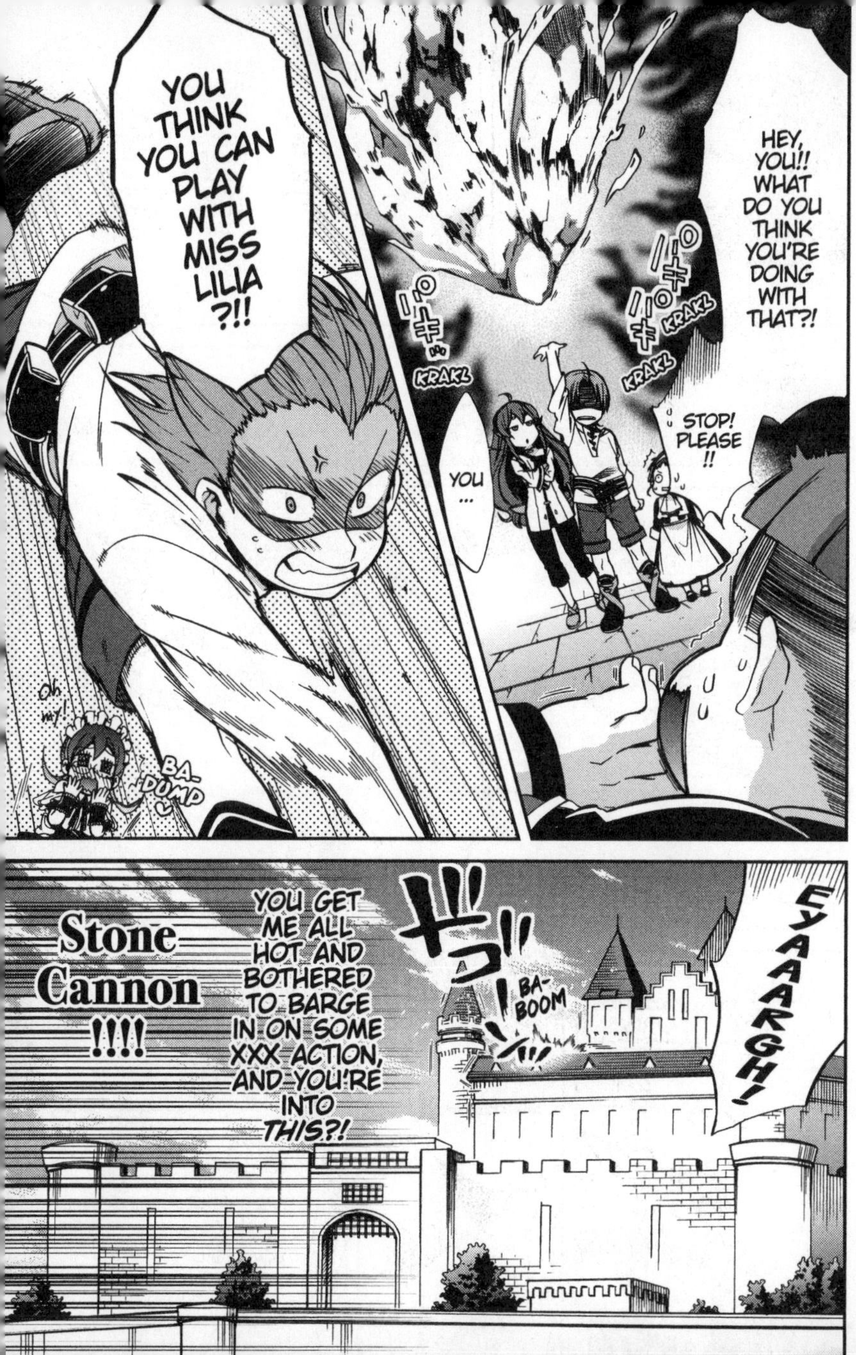
HEY, YOU!! WHAT DO YOU THINK YOU'RE DOING WITH THAT?!
KRAKL
KRAKL
KRAKL
STOP! PLEASE !!
YOU ...
YOU THINK YOU CAN PLAY WITH MISS LILIA ?!!
Oh my!
BA-DUMP
EYAAAARGH!
BA-BOOM
YOU GET ME ALL HOT AND BOTHERED TO BARGE IN ON SOME XXX ACTION, AND YOU'RE INTO THIS?!
Stone Cannon !!!!

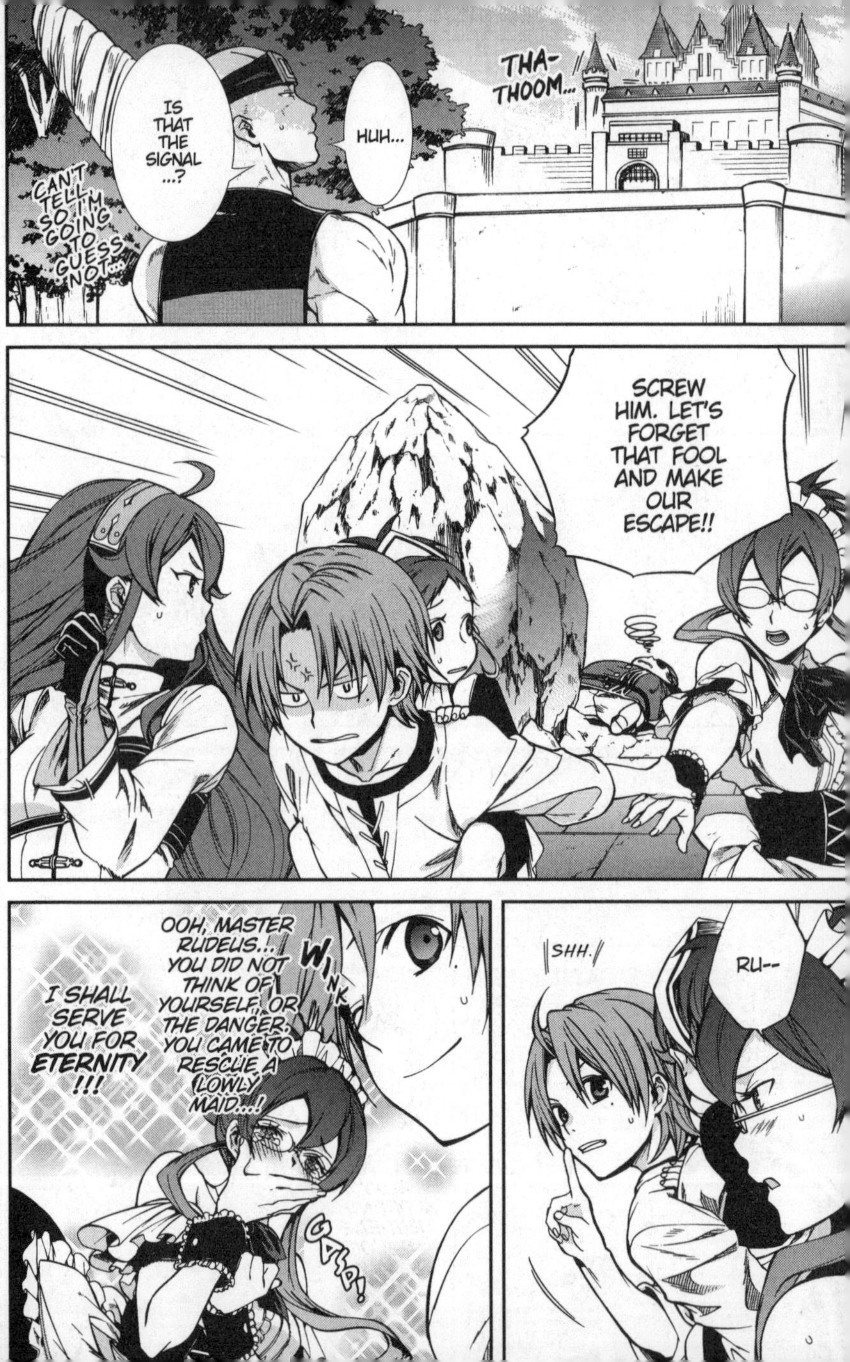
THA-THOOM...
HUH...
IS THAT THE SIGNAL...?
CAN'T TELL SO I'M GOING TO GUESS NOT...
SCREW HIM. LET'S FORGET THAT FOOL AND MAKE OUR ESCAPE!!
RU--
SHH.
WINK
OOH, MASTER RUDEUS... YOU DID NOT THINK OF YOURSELF, OR THE DANGER. YOU CAME TO RESCUE A LOWLY MAID...!
I SHALL SERVE YOU FOR ETERNITY!!!
GASP!

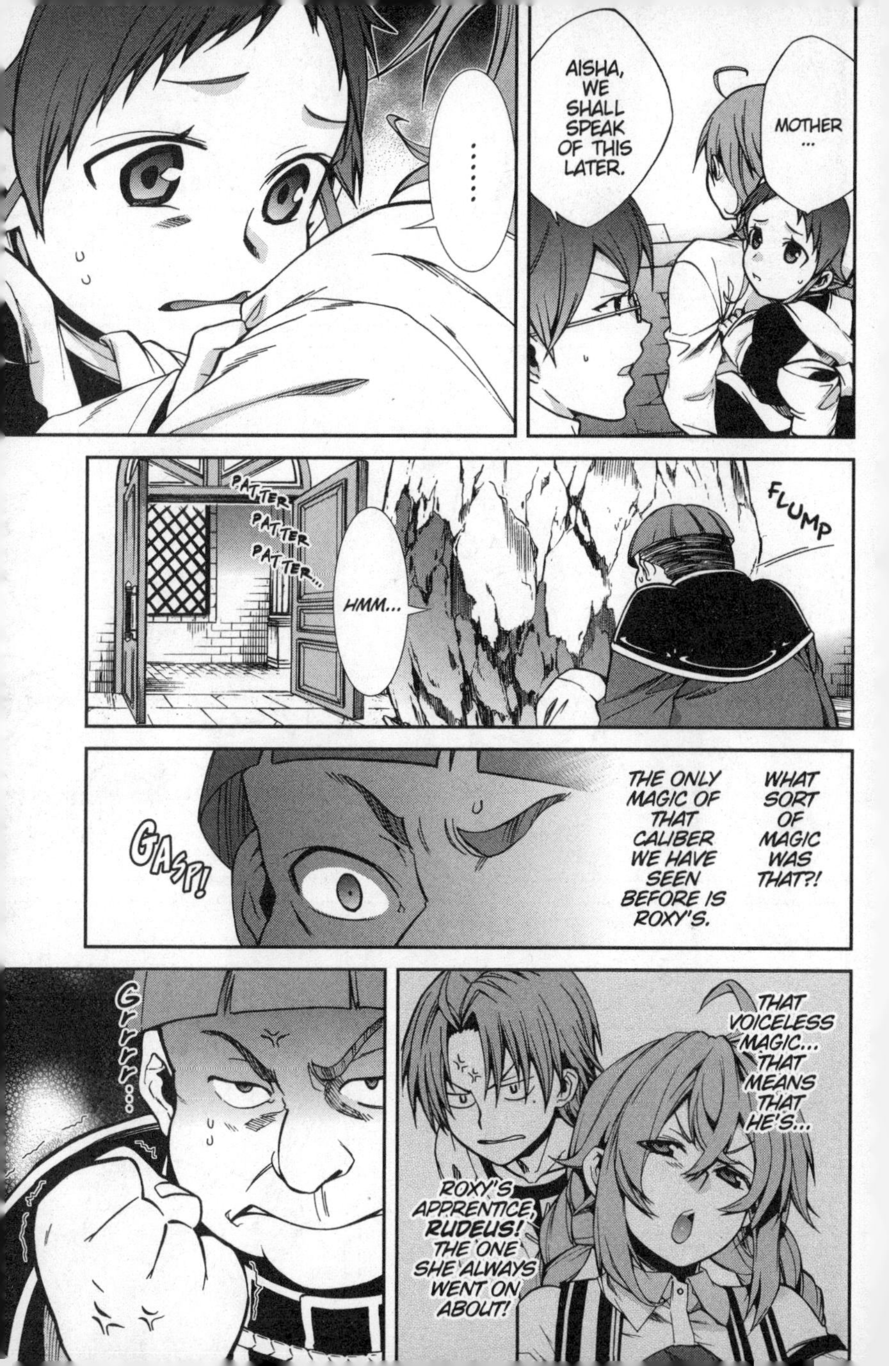
MOTHER ...
AISHA, WE SHALL SPEAK OF THIS LATER.
......
FLUMP
HMM...
PATTER PATTER PATTER...
WHAT SORT OF MAGIC WAS THAT?!
THE ONLY MAGIC OF THAT CALIBER WE HAVE SEEN BEFORE IS ROXY'S.
GASP!
THAT VOICELESS MAGIC... THAT MEANS THAT HE'S...
ROXY'S APPRENTICE, RUDEUS! THE ONE SHE ALWAYS WENT ON ABOUT!
Grrrr...

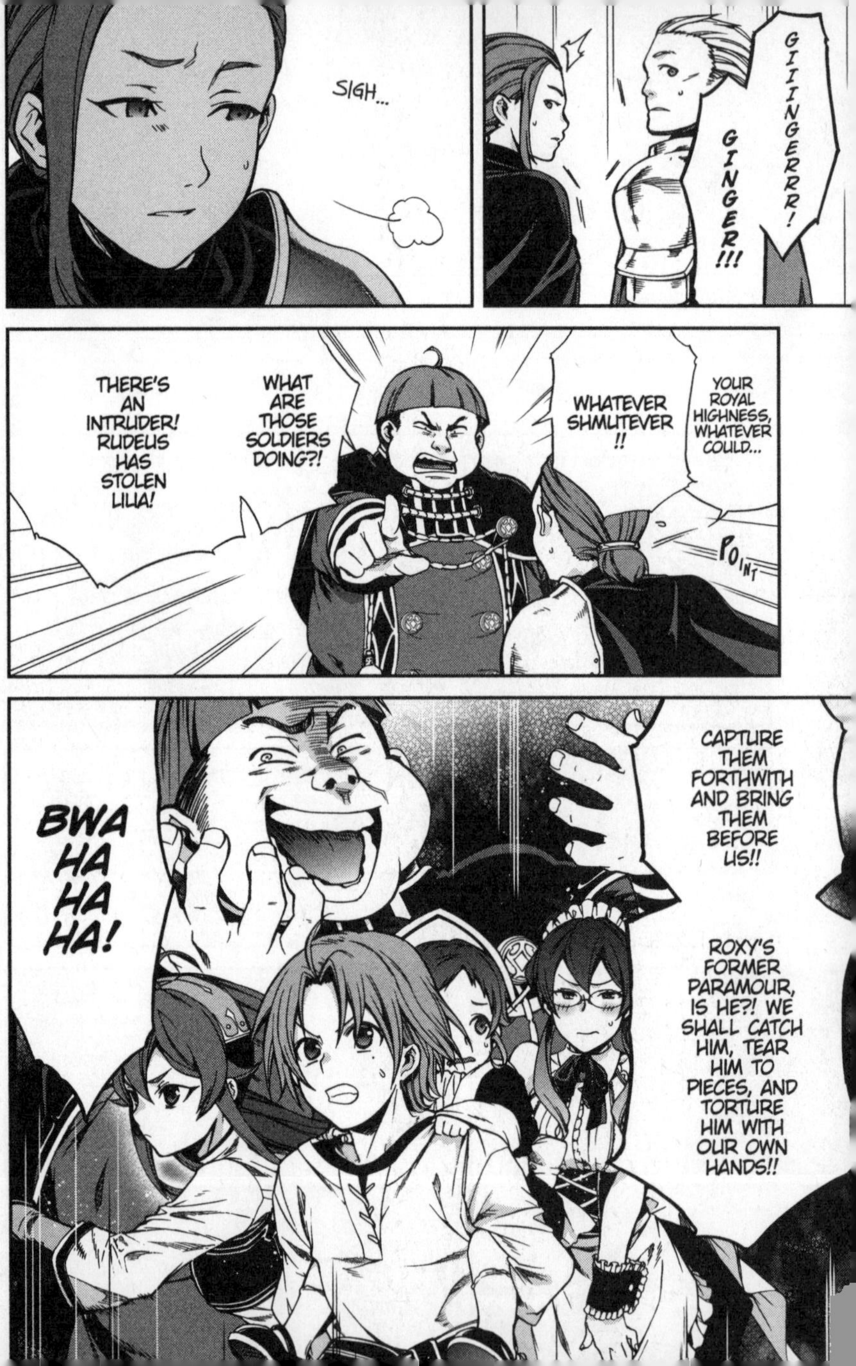
GIIINGERRR!
GINGER!!!
SIGH...
YOUR ROYAL HIGHNESS, WHATEVER COULD...
POINT
WHATEVER SHMUTEVER !!
WHAT ARE THOSE SOLDIERS DOING?!
THERE'S AN INTRUDER! RUDEUS HAS STOLEN LILIA!
CAPTURE THEM FORTHWITH AND BRING THEM BEFORE US!!
ROXY'S FORMER PARAMOUR, IS HE?! WE SHALL CATCH HIM, TEAR HIM TO PIECES, AND TORTURE HIM WITH OUR OWN HANDS!!
BWA HA HA HA HA!

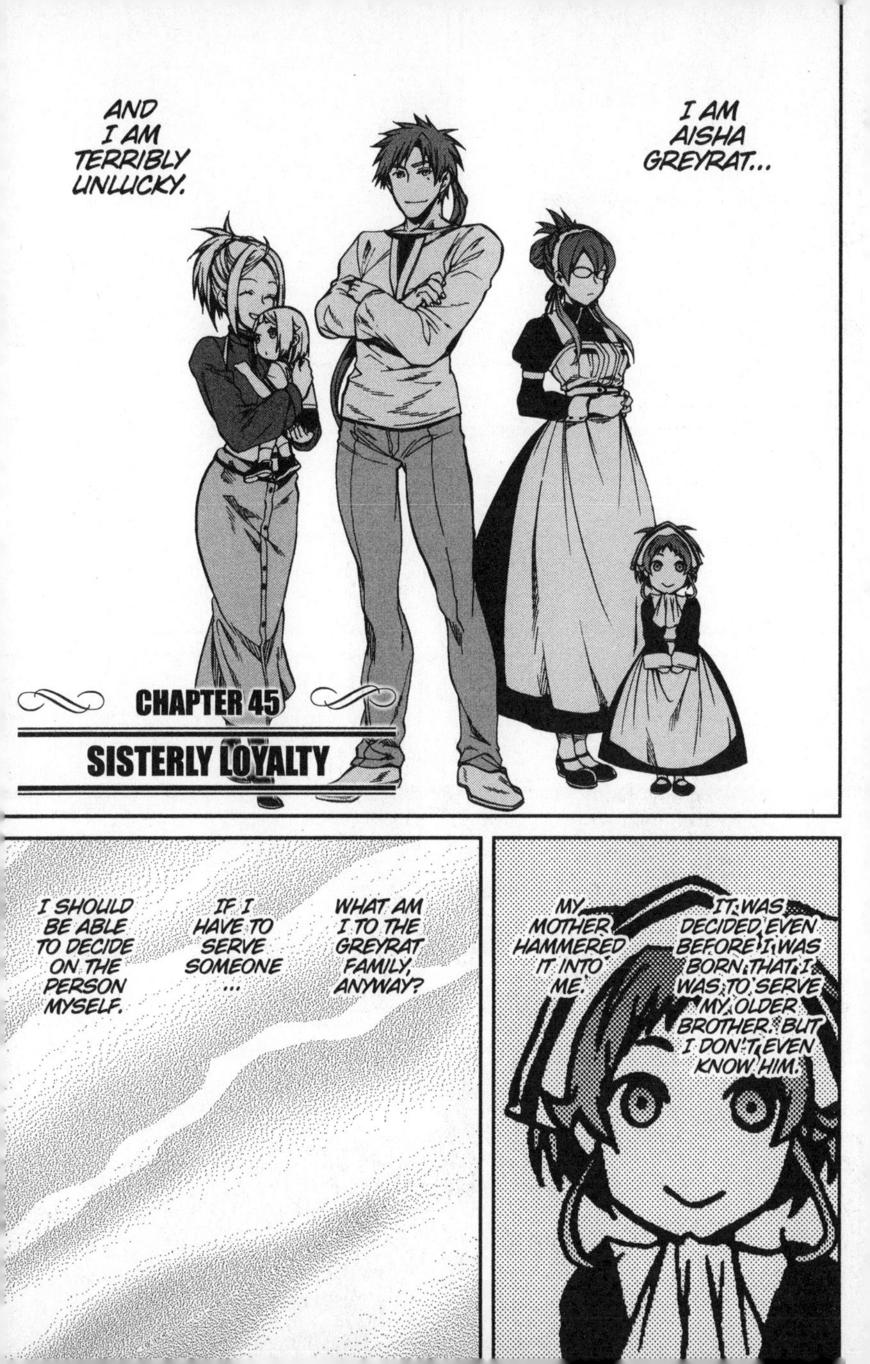
I AM AISHA GREYRAT...
AND I AM TERRIBLY UNLUCKY.
CHAPTER 45
SISTERLY LOYALTY
IT WAS DECIDED EVEN BEFORE I WAS BORN THAT I WAS TO SERVE MY OLDER BROTHER. BUT I DON'T EVEN KNOW HIM.
MY MOTHER HAMMERED IT INTO ME.
WHAT AM I TO THE GREYRAT FAMILY, ANYWAY?
IF I HAVE TO SERVE SOMEONE...
I SHOULD BE ABLE TO DECIDE ON THE PERSON MYSELF.

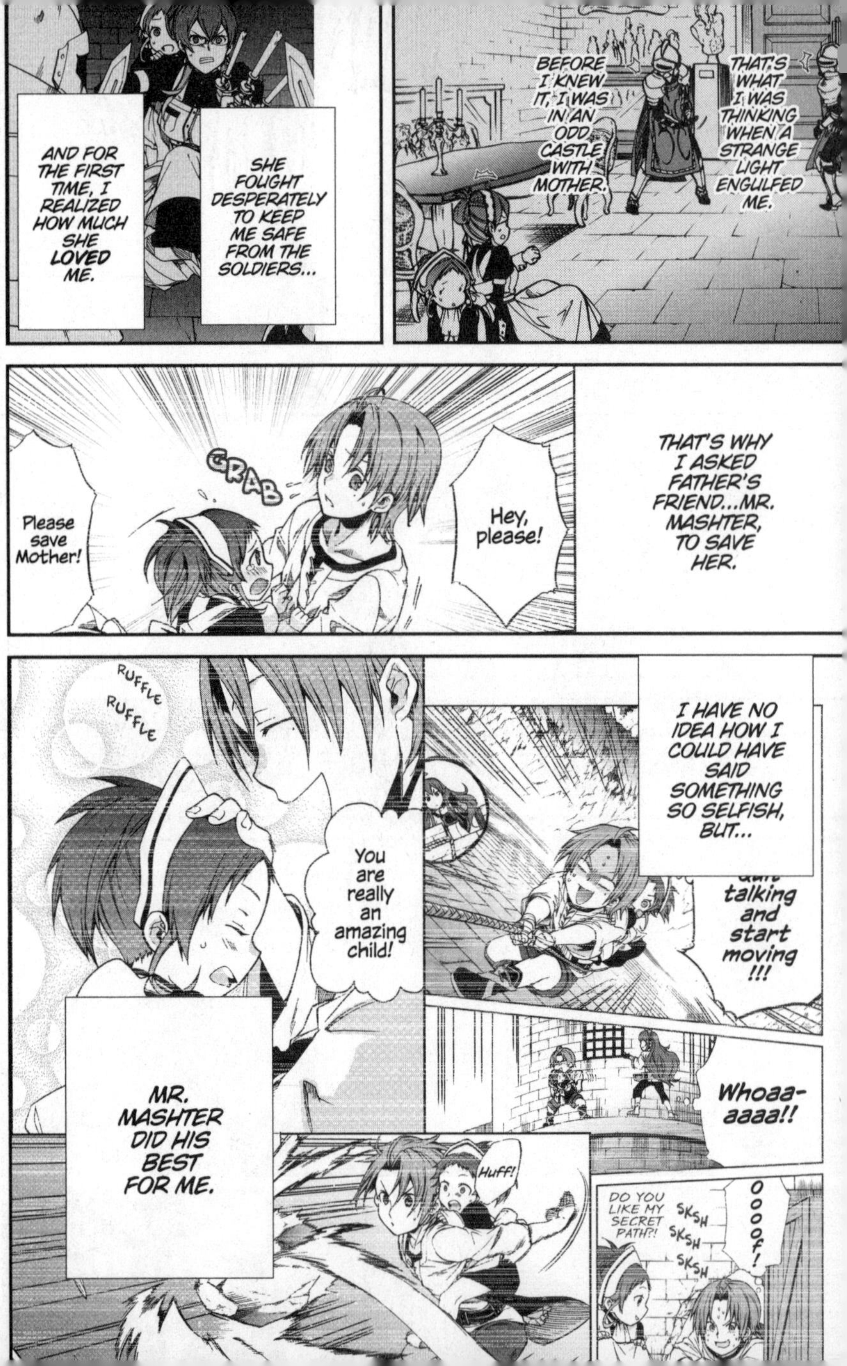
THAT'S WHAT I WAS THINKING WHEN A STRANGE LIGHT ENGULFED ME.
BEFORE I KNEW IT, I WAS IN AN ODD CASTLE WITH MOTHER.
SHE FOUGHT DESPERATELY TO KEEP ME SAFE FROM THE SOLDIERS...
AND FOR THE FIRST TIME, I REALIZED HOW MUCH SHE LOVED ME.
THAT'S WHY I ASKED FATHER'S FRIEND...MR. MASHTER, TO SAVE HER.
Hey, please!
GRAB
Please save Mother!
I HAVE NO IDEA HOW I COULD HAVE SAID SOMETHING SO SELFISH, BUT...
talking and start moving!!!
Whoaa-aaaa!!
Ooooof!
SKSH SKSH SKSH
DO YOU LIKE MY SECRET PATH?!
Huff!
RUFFLE RUFFLE
You are really an amazing child!
MR. MASHTER DID HIS BEST FOR ME.

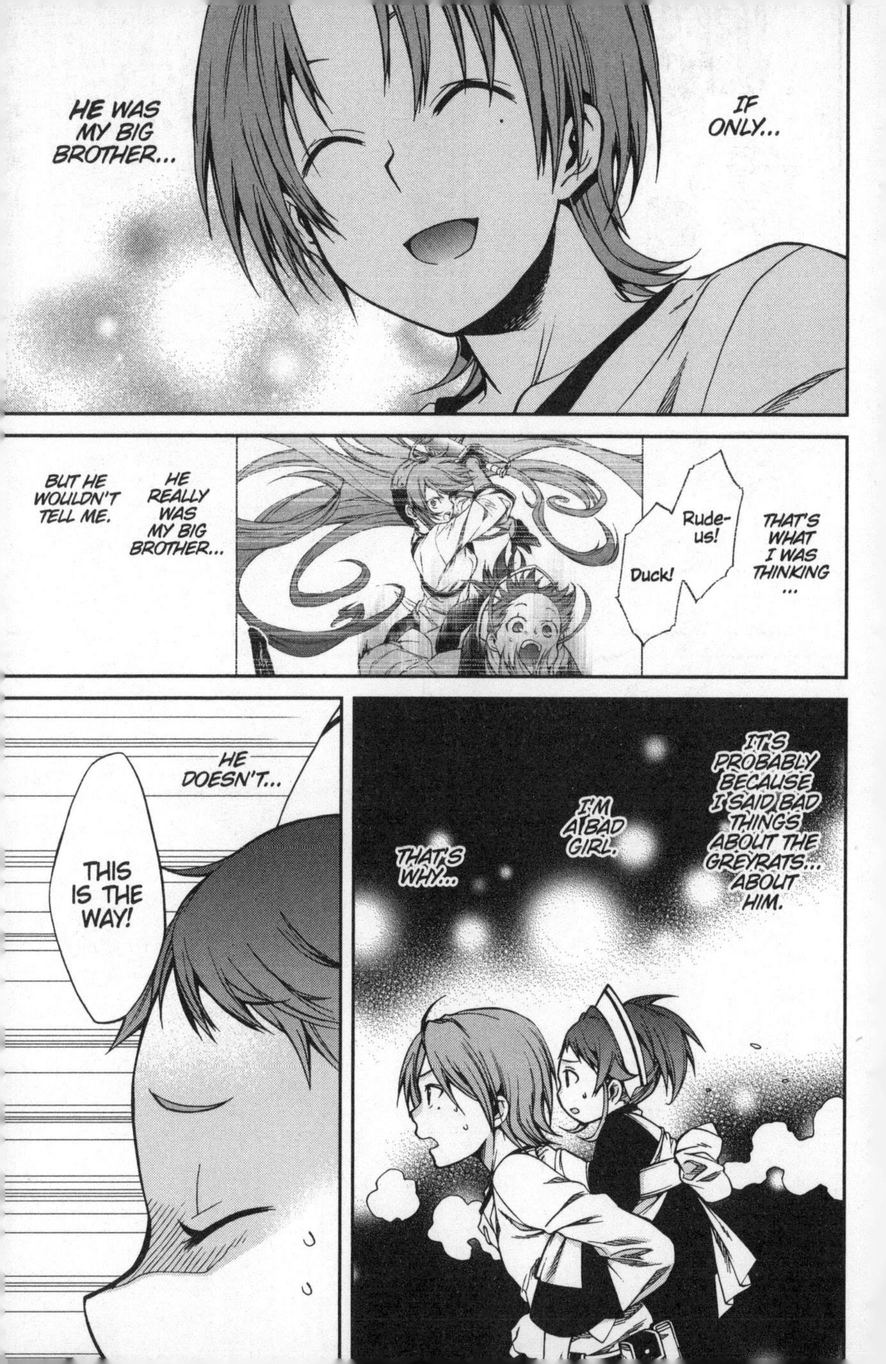
IF ONLY...
HE WAS MY BIG BROTHER...
THAT'S WHAT I WAS THINKING...
Rude-us!
Duck!
HE REALLY WAS MY BIG BROTHER...
BUT HE WOULDN'T TELL ME.
IT'S PROBABLY BECAUSE I SAID BAD THINGS ABOUT THE GREYRATS... ABOUT HIM.
I'M A BAD GIRL.
THAT'S WHY...
HE DOESN'T...
THIS IS THE WAY!

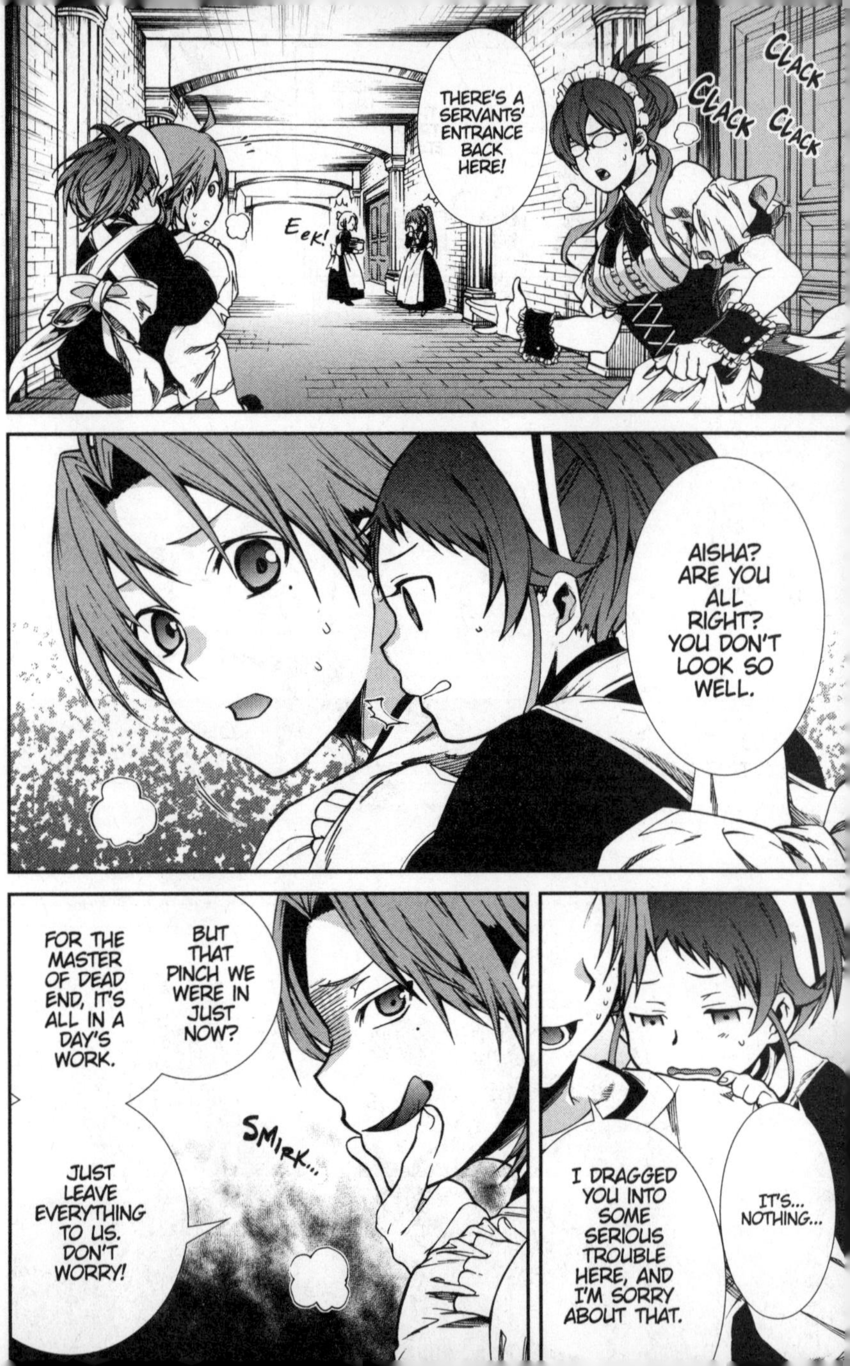
CLACK
CLACK CLACK
THERE'S A SERVANTS' ENTRANCE BACK HERE!
Eek!
AISHA? ARE YOU ALL RIGHT? YOU DON'T LOOK SO WELL.
IT'S... NOTHING...
I DRAGGED YOU INTO SOME SERIOUS TROUBLE HERE, AND I'M SORRY ABOUT THAT.
BUT THAT PINCH WE WERE IN JUST NOW?
FOR THE MASTER OF DEAD END, IT'S ALL IN A DAY'S WORK.
SMIRK...
JUST LEAVE EVERYTHING TO US. DON'T WORRY!

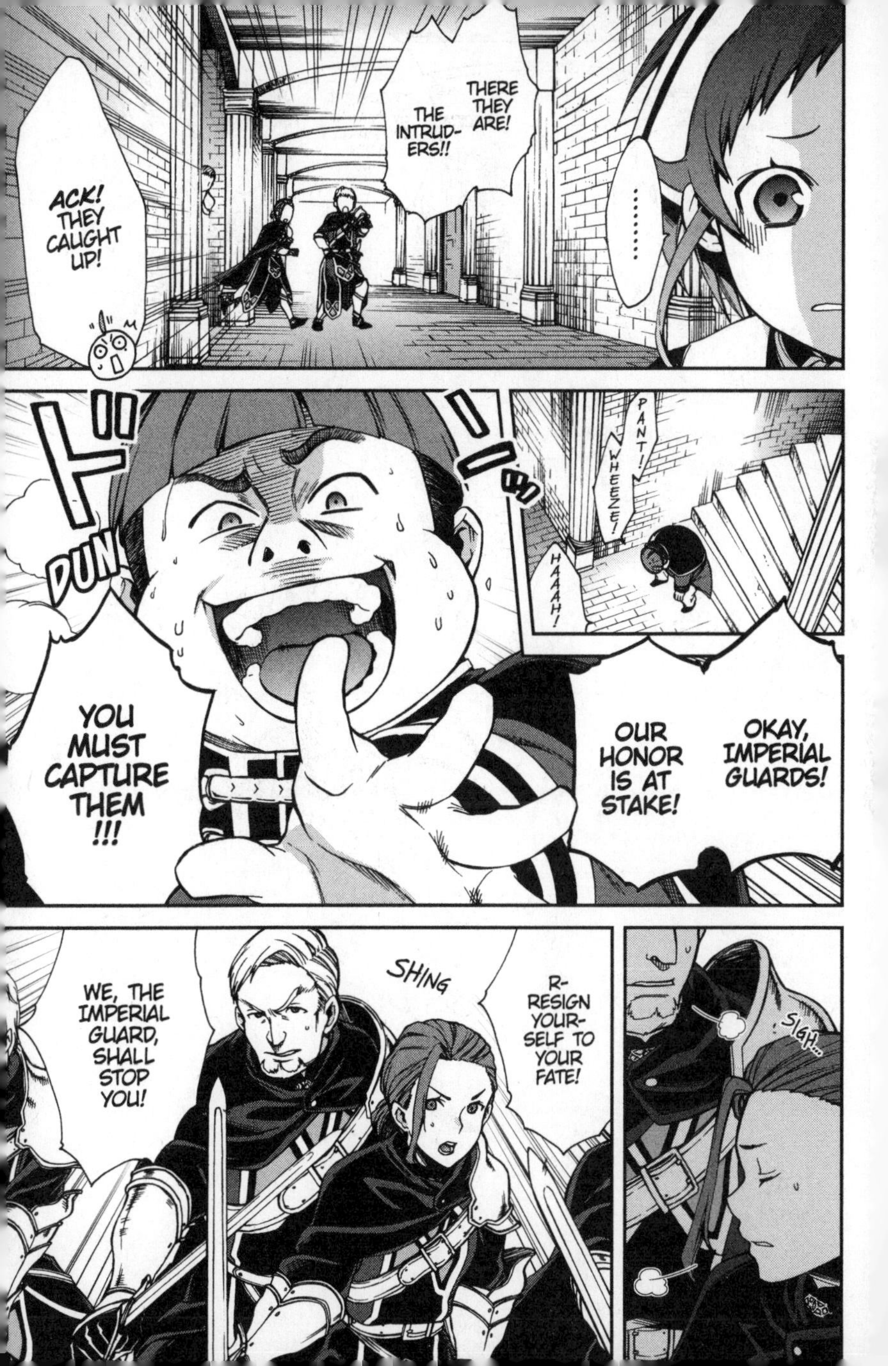
......
THERE THEY ARE!
THE INTRUDERS!!
ACK! THEY CAUGHT UP!
PANT! WHEEZE!
HAAAAH!
DUN
OKAY, IMPERIAL GUARDS!
OUR HONOR IS AT STAKE!
YOU MUST CAPTURE THEM!!!
SIGH...
R-RESIGN YOURSELF TO YOUR FATE!
SHING
WE, THE IMPERIAL GUARD, SHALL STOP YOU!

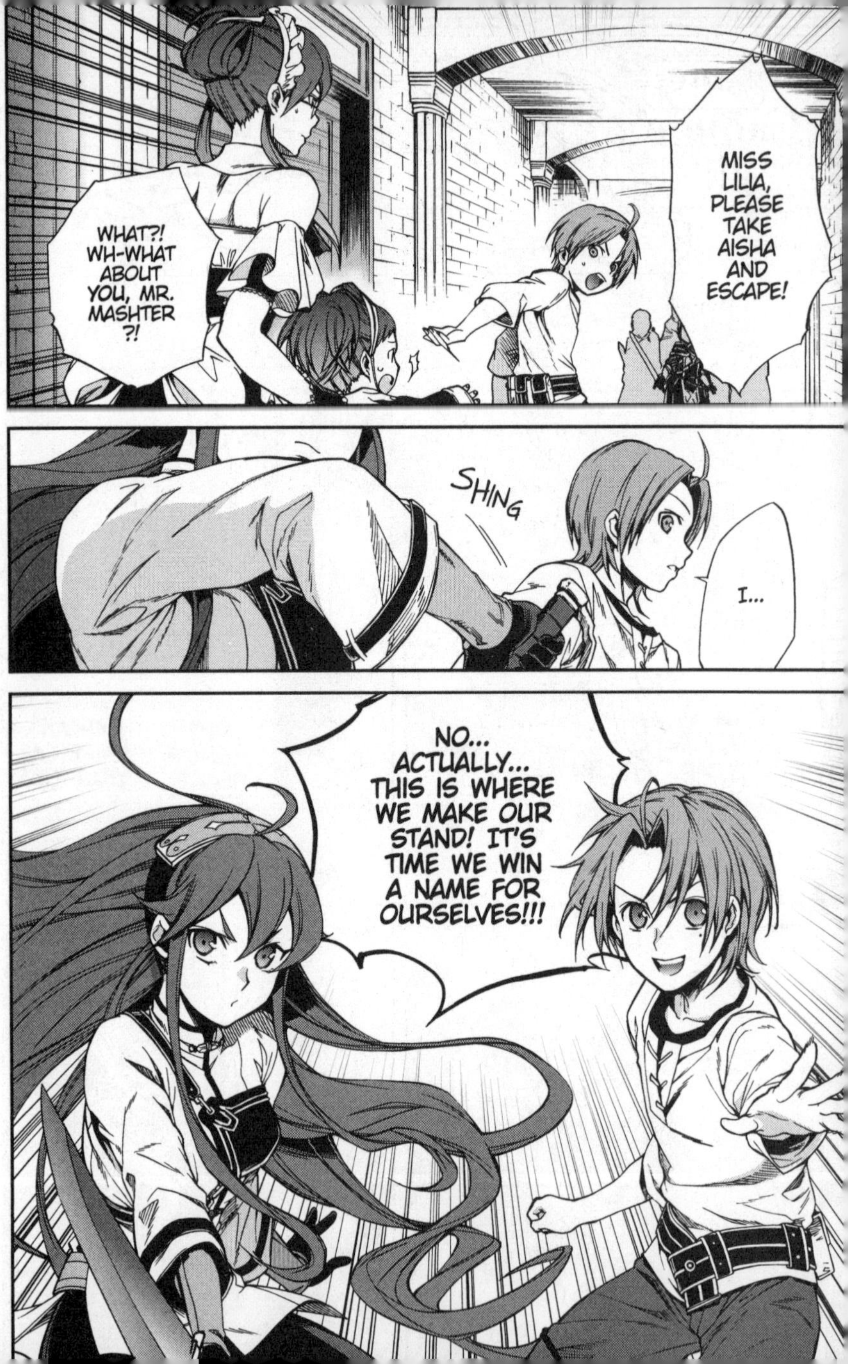
MISS LILIA, PLEASE TAKE AISHA AND ESCAPE!
WHAT?! WH-WHAT ABOUT YOU, MR. MASHTER?!
I...
SHING
NO... ACTUALLY... THIS IS WHERE WE MAKE OUR STAND! IT'S TIME WE WIN A NAME FOR OURSELVES!!!

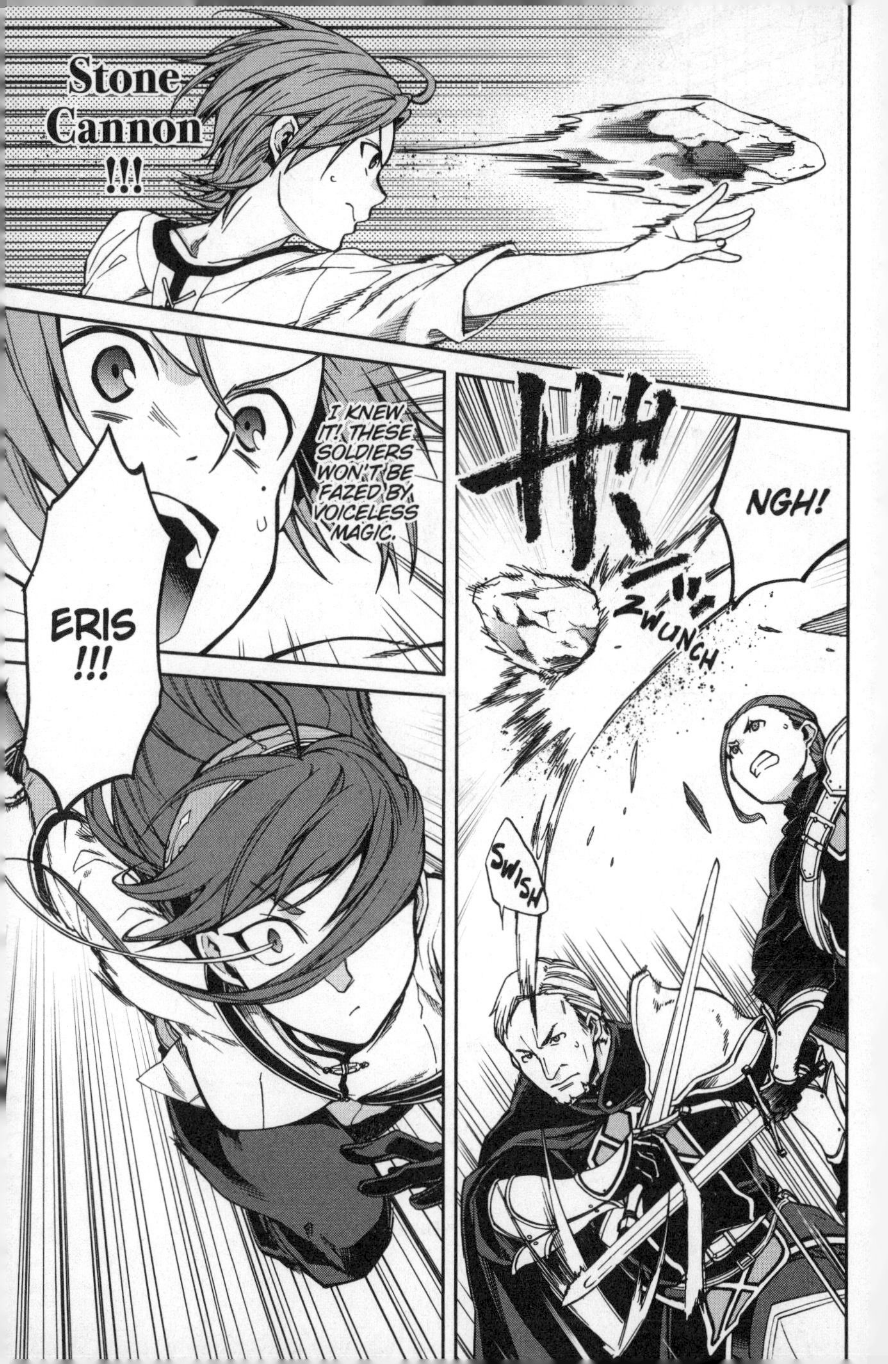
Stone Cannon !!!
NGH!
ZWUNCH
SWISH
I KNEW IT! THESE SOLDIERS WON'T BE FAZED BY VOICELESS MAGIC.
ERIS !!!

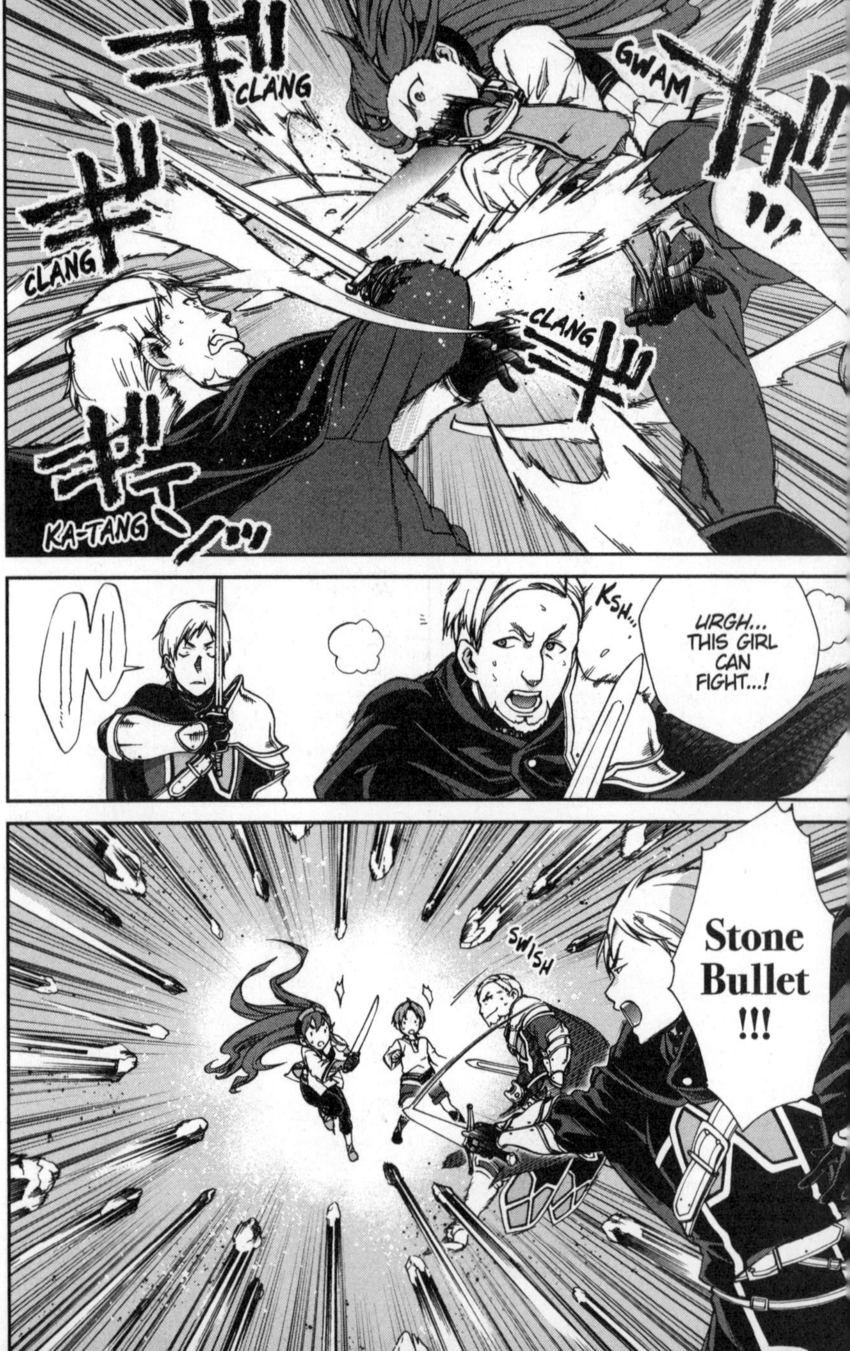
GWAM
CLANG
CLANG
CLANG
KA-TANG
URGH... THIS GIRL CAN FIGHT...!
KSH...
Stone Bullet!!!
SWISH

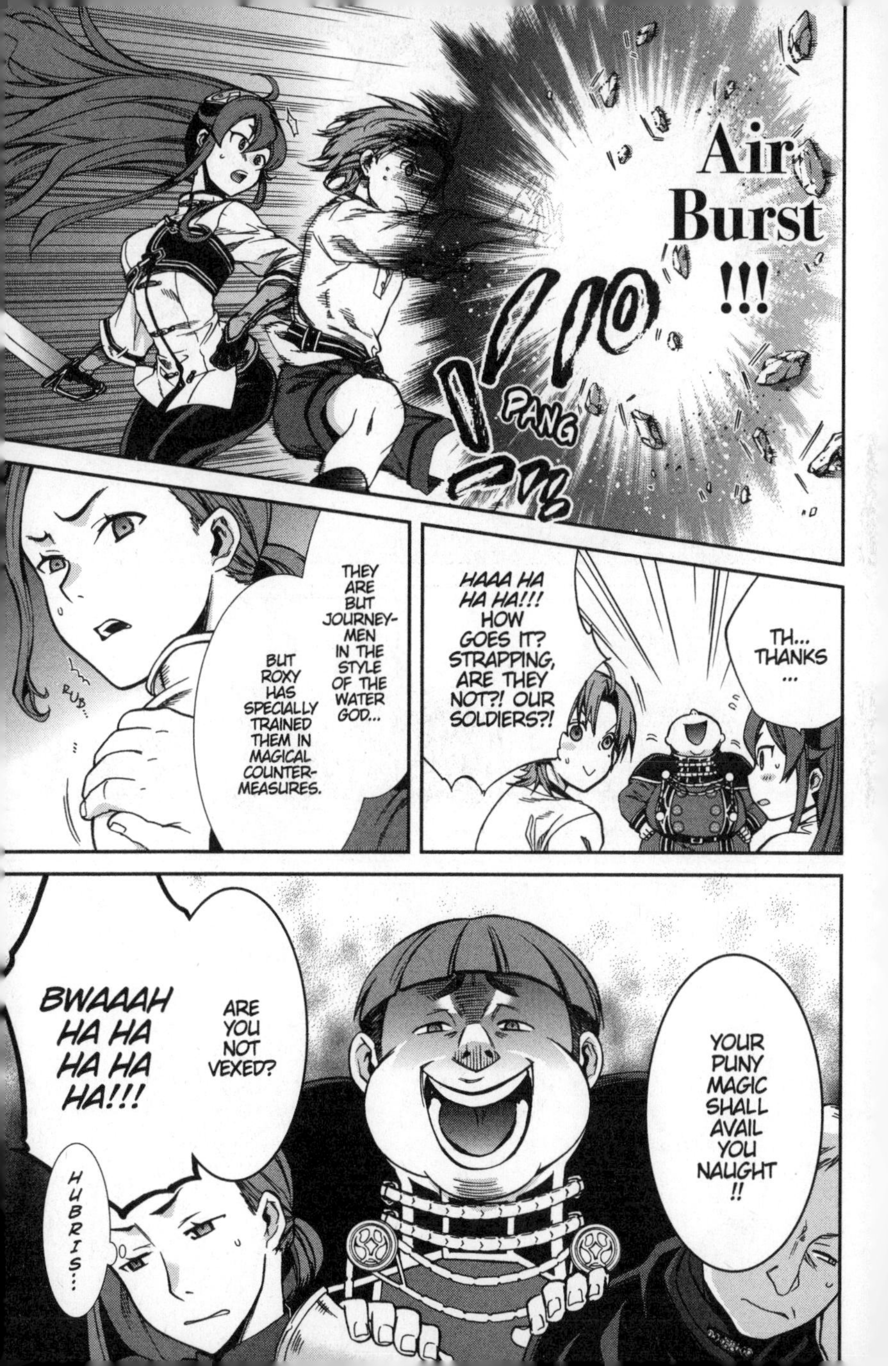
Air Burst!!!
PANG
TH... THANKS...
HAAA HA HA HA!!! HOW GOES IT? STRAPPING, ARE THEY NOT?! OUR SOLDIERS?!
THEY ARE BUT JOURNEYMEN IN THE STYLE OF THE WATER GOD...
BUT ROXY HAS SPECIALLY TRAINED THEM IN MAGICAL COUNTER-MEASURES.
RUB...
YOUR PUNY MAGIC SHALL AVAIL YOU NAUGHT!!
ARE YOU NOT VEXED?
BWAAAH HA HA HA HA HA!!!
HUBRIS...

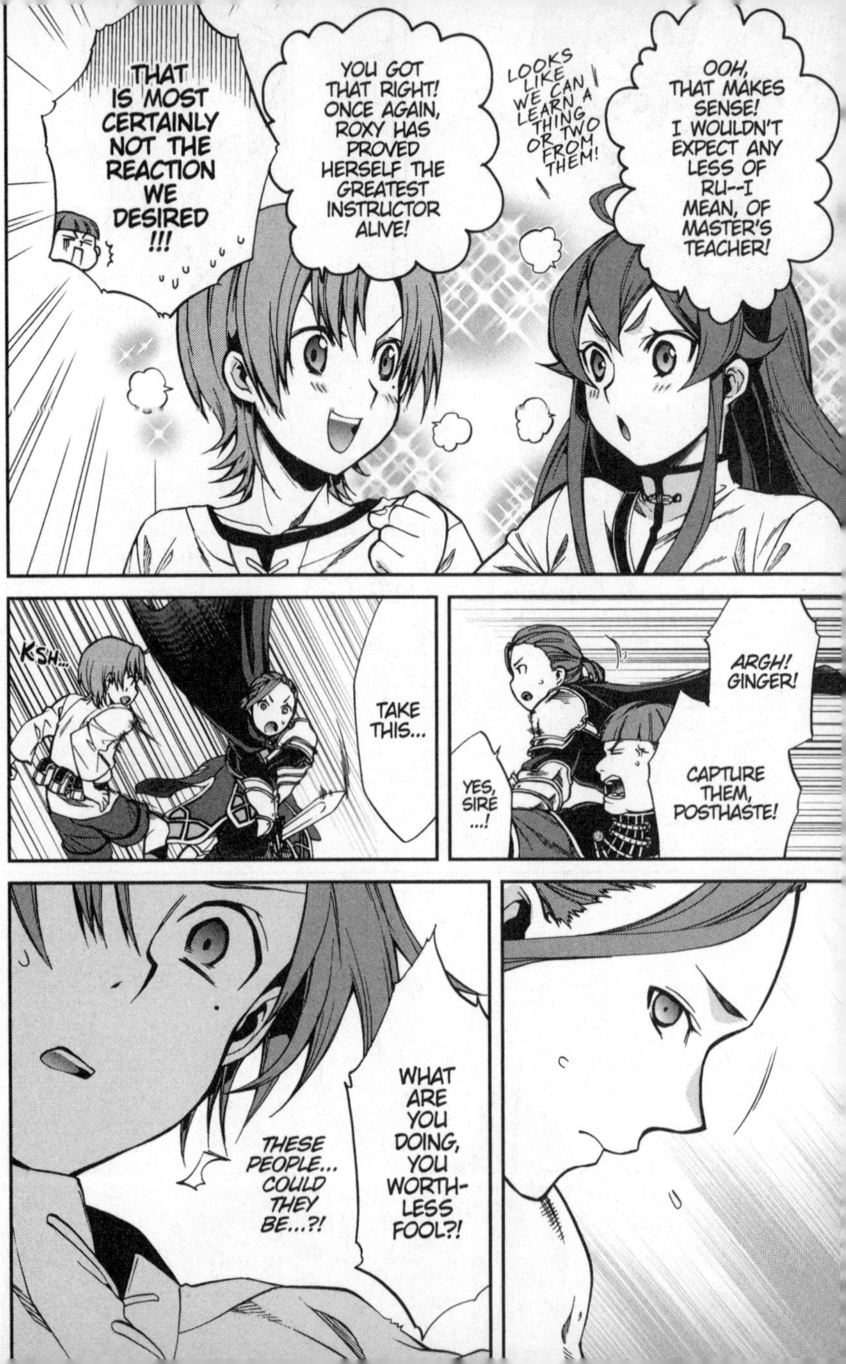
OOH, THAT MAKES SENSE! I WOULDN'T EXPECT ANY LESS OF RU--I MEAN, OF MASTER'S TEACHER!
LOOKS LIKE WE CAN LEARN A THING OR TWO FROM THEM!
YOU GOT THAT RIGHT! ONCE AGAIN, ROXY HAS PROVED HERSELF THE GREATEST INSTRUCTOR ALIVE!
THAT IS MOST CERTAINLY NOT THE REACTION WE DESIRED!!!
ARGH! GINGER!
CAPTURE THEM, POSTHASTE!
YES, SIRE...!
TAKE THIS...
K-SH...
WHAT ARE YOU DOING, YOU WORTHLESS FOOL?!
THESE PEOPLE... COULD THEY BE...?!

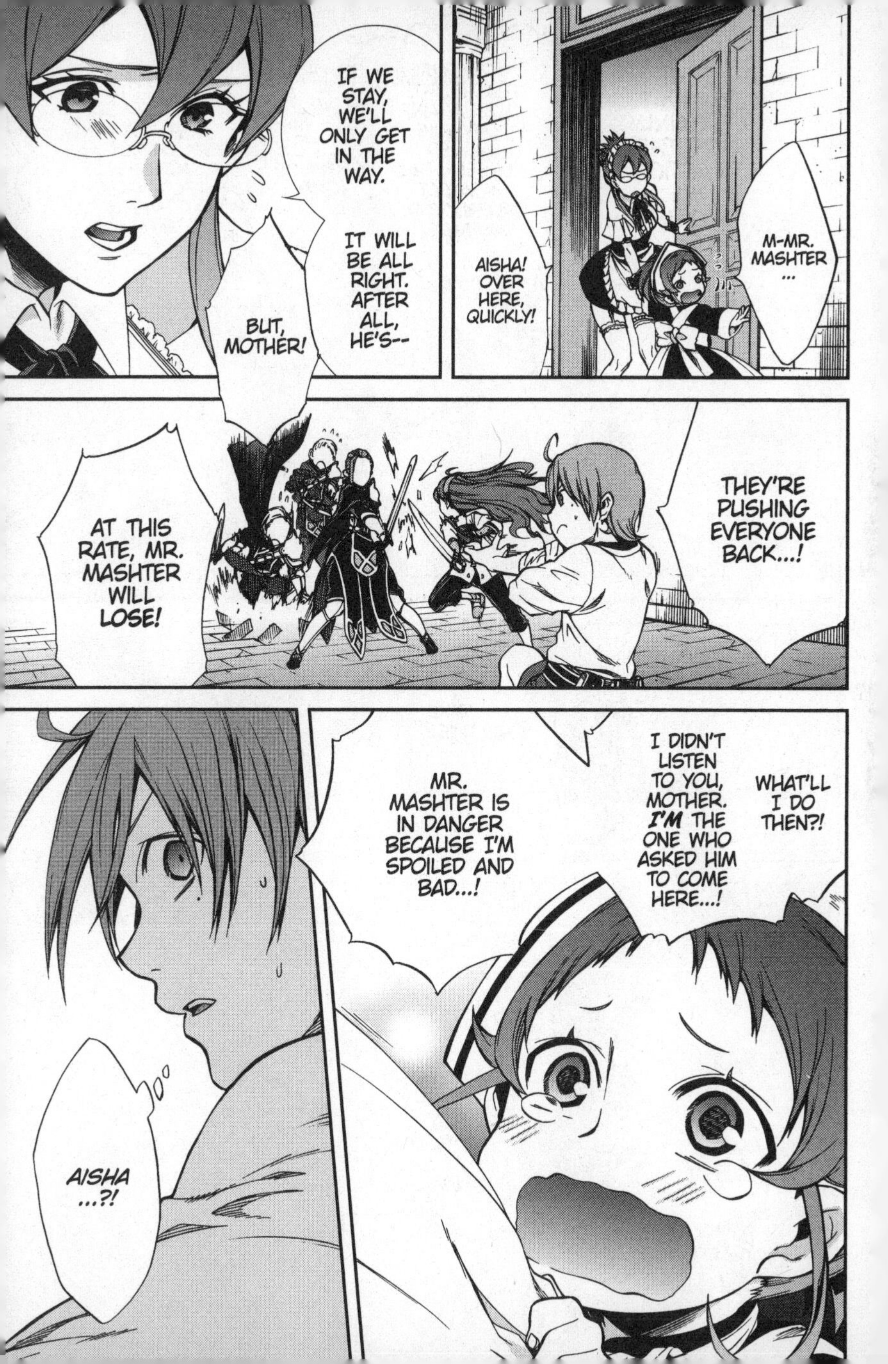
M-MR. MASHTER ...
AISHA! OVER HERE, QUICKLY!
IF WE STAY, WE'LL ONLY GET IN THE WAY.
IT WILL BE ALL RIGHT. AFTER ALL, HE'S--
BUT, MOTHER!
THEY'RE PUSHING EVERYONE BACK...!
AT THIS RATE, MR. MASHTER WILL LOSE!
WHAT'LL I DO THEN?!
I DIDN'T LISTEN TO YOU, MOTHER. *I'M* THE ONE WHO ASKED HIM TO COME HERE...!
MR. MASHTER IS IN DANGER BECAUSE I'M SPOILED AND BAD...!
AISHA ...?!

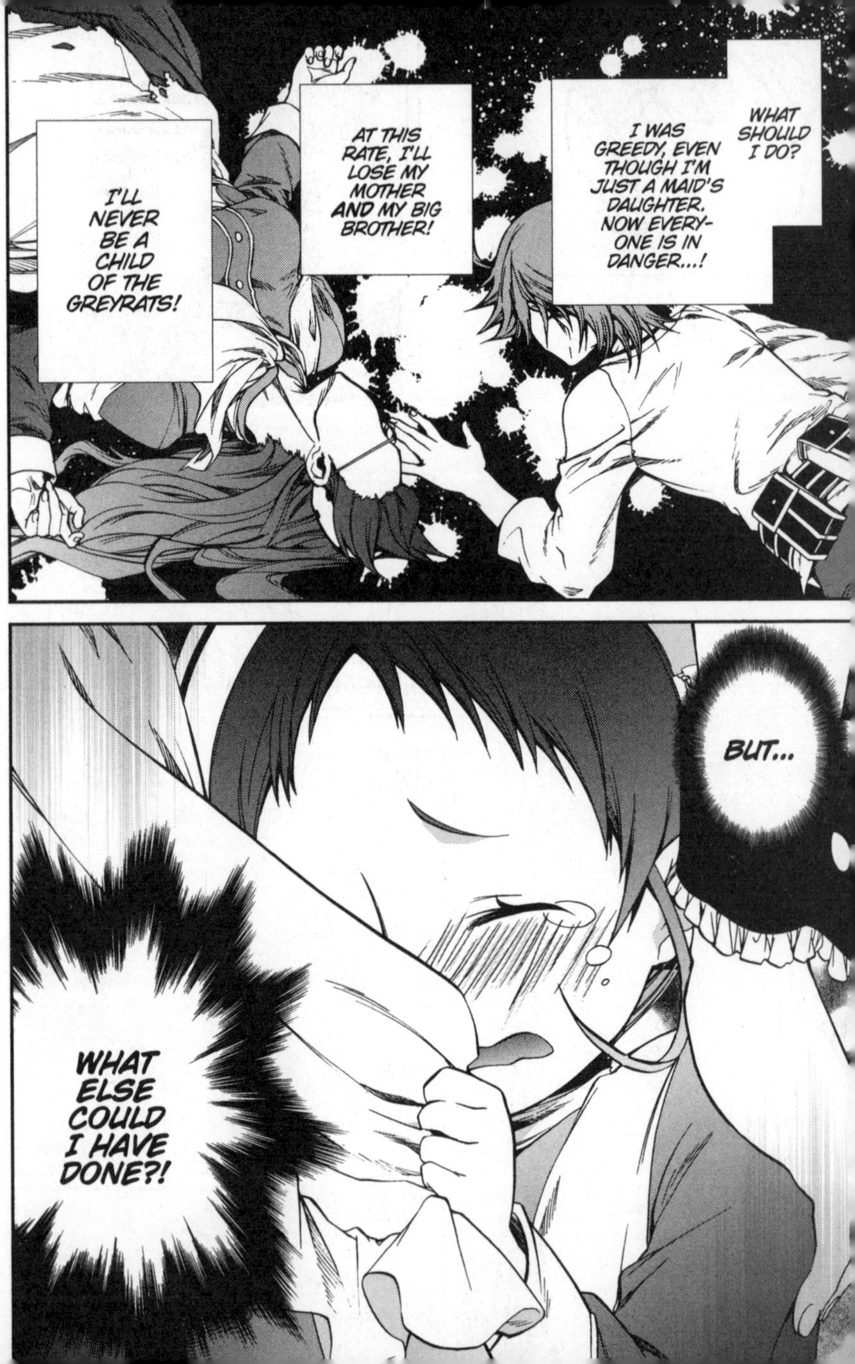
WHAT SHOULD I DO?
I WAS GREEDY, EVEN THOUGH I'M JUST A MAID'S DAUGHTER. NOW EVERY-ONE IS IN DANGER...!
AT THIS RATE, I'LL LOSE MY MOTHER AND MY BIG BROTHER!
I'LL NEVER BE A CHILD OF THE GREYRATS!
BUT...
WHAT ELSE COULD I HAVE DONE?!

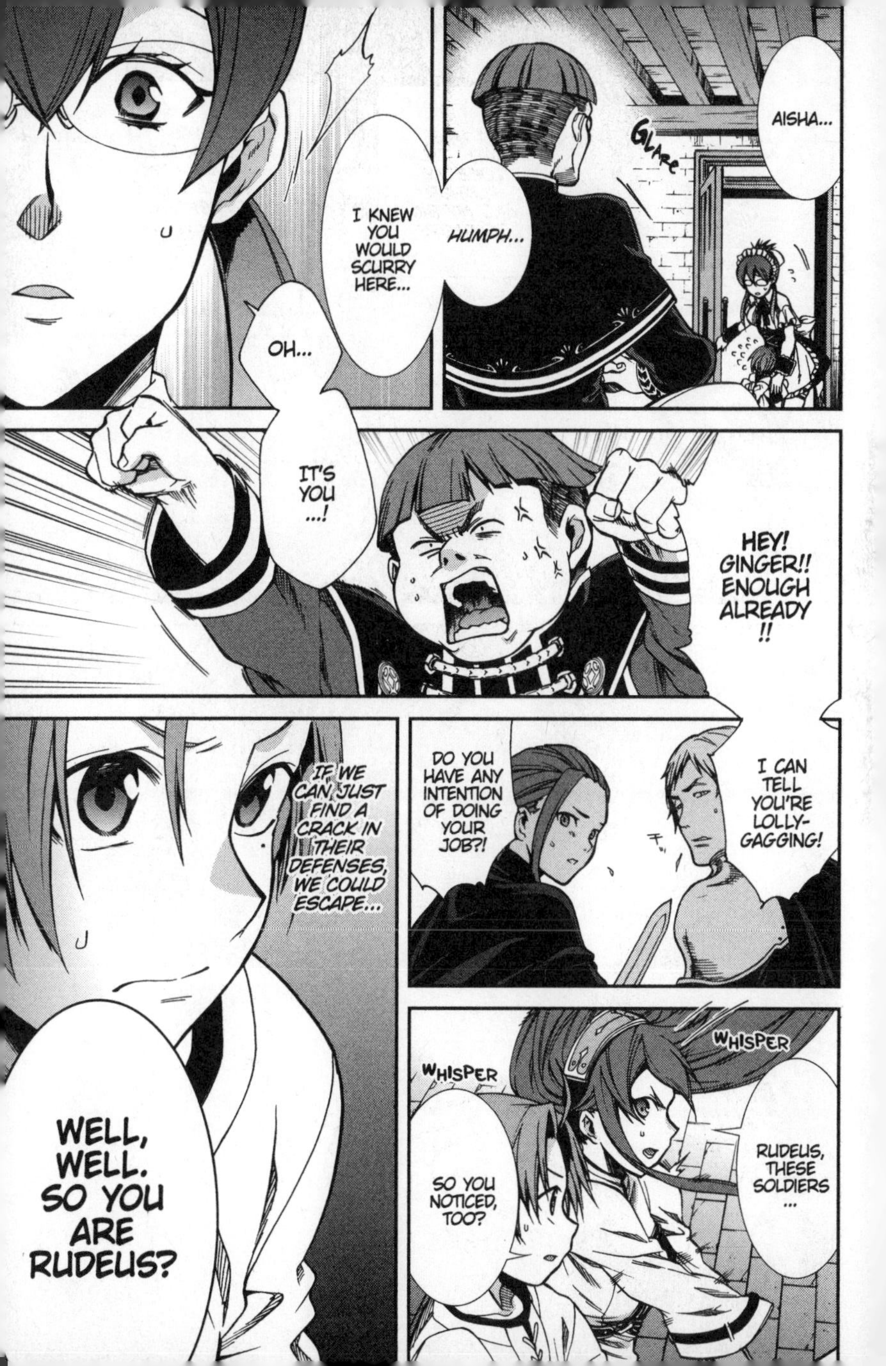
AISHA...
GLARE
HUMPH...
I KNEW YOU WOULD SCURRY HERE...
OH...
IT'S YOU ...!
HEY! GINGER!! ENOUGH ALREADY !!
I CAN TELL YOU'RE LOLLY-GAGGING!
DO YOU HAVE ANY INTENTION OF DOING YOUR JOB?!
WHISPER
RUDEUS, THESE SOLDIERS ...
WHISPER
SO YOU NOTICED, TOO?
IF WE CAN JUST FIND A CRACK IN THEIR DEFENSES, WE COULD ESCAPE...
WELL, WELL. SO YOU ARE RUDEUS?

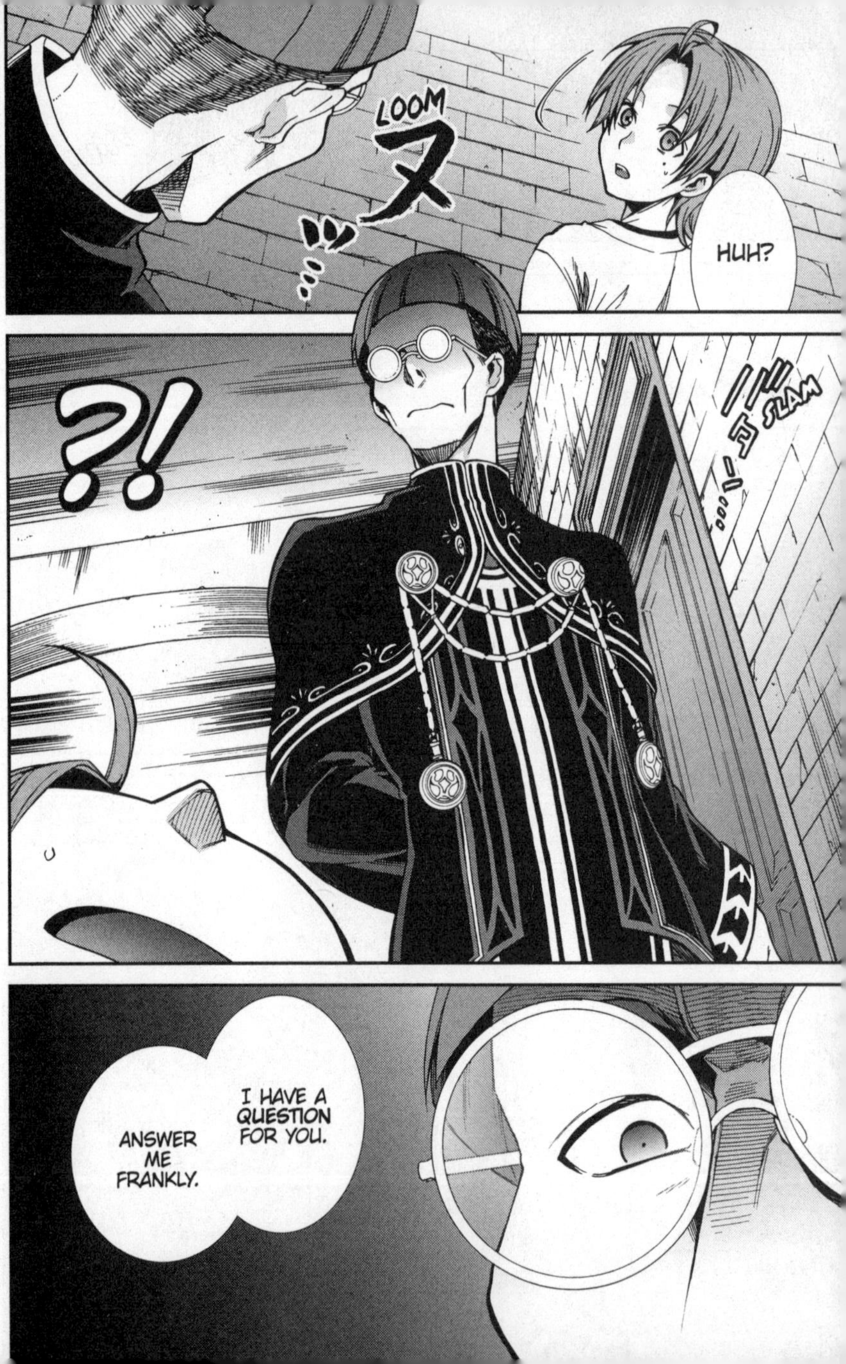
HUH?
LOOM
SLAM
?!
I HAVE A QUESTION FOR YOU.
ANSWER ME FRANKLY.

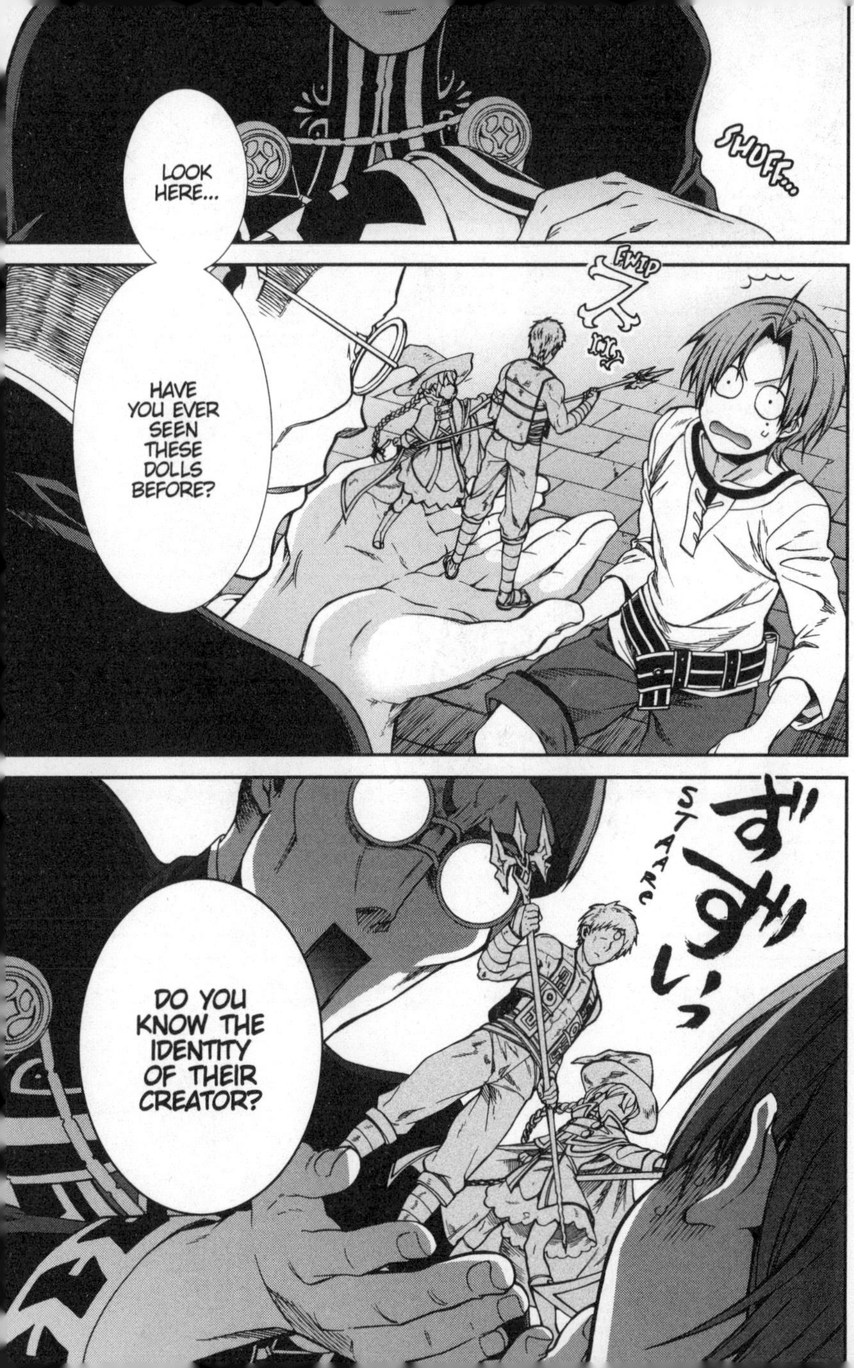
SHUFF...
LOOK HERE...
FWIP
ス
HAVE YOU EVER SEEN THESE DOLLS BEFORE?
ずずいっ
STAARE
DO YOU KNOW THE IDENTITY OF THEIR CREATOR?

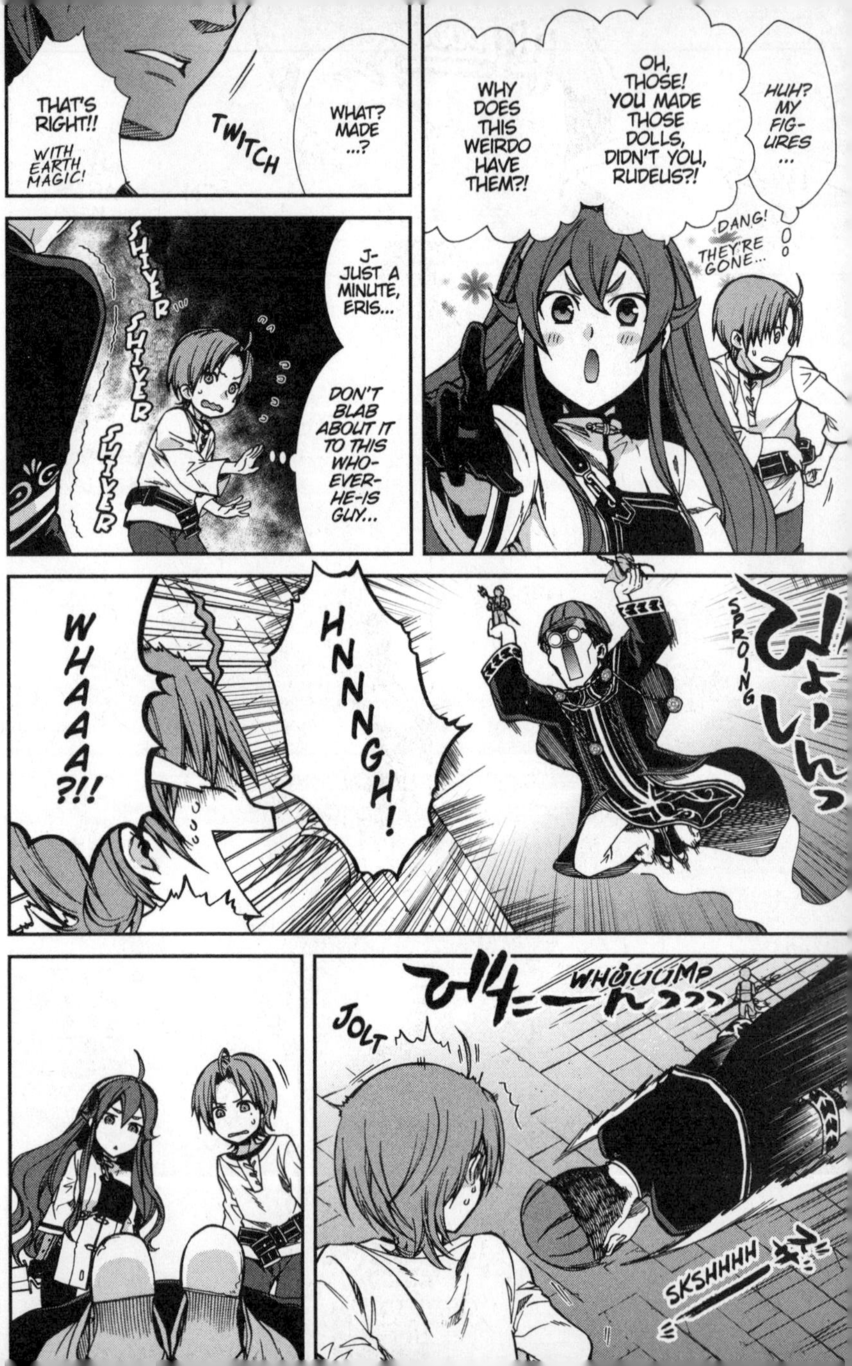
HUH? MY FIG-URES ...
OH, THOSE! YOU MADE THOSE DOLLS, DIDN'T YOU, RUDEUS?!
WHY DOES THIS WEIRDO HAVE THEM?!
DANG! THEY'RE GONE...
WHAT? MADE ...?
TWITCH
THAT'S RIGHT!!
WITH EARTH MAGIC!
J-JUST A MINUTE, ERIS...
DON'T BLAB ABOUT IT TO THIS WHO-EVER-HE-IS GUY...
SHIVER SHIVER SHIVER
SPROING
HNNNGH!
WHAAAA?!!
WHUUUMP
SKSHHHH
JOLT

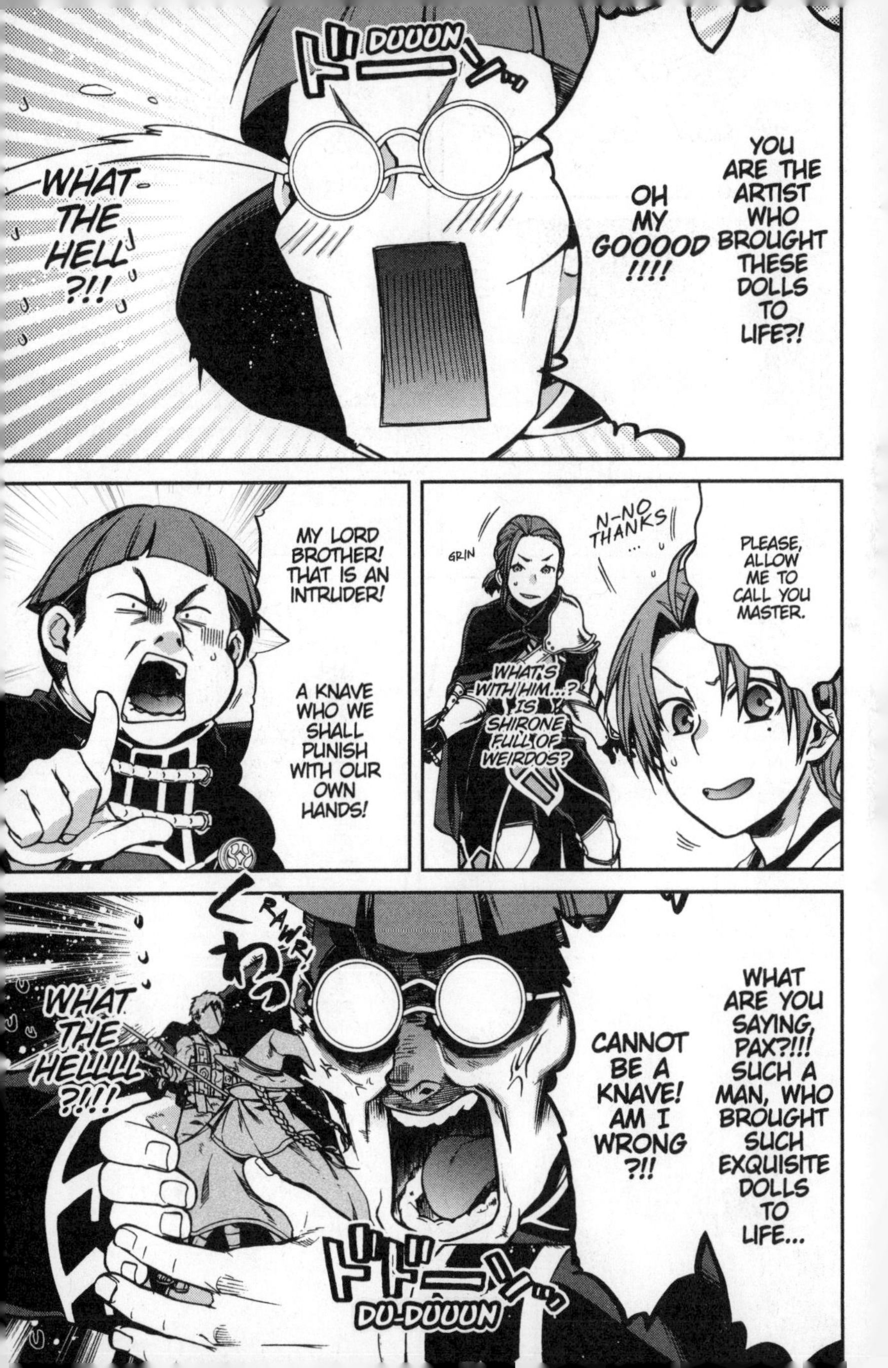
DUUUN
YOU ARE THE ARTIST WHO BROUGHT THESE DOLLS TO LIFE?!
OH MY GOOOOD !!!!
WHAT THE HELL ?!!
PLEASE, ALLOW ME TO CALL YOU MASTER.
N-NO THANKS ...
GRIN
WHAT'S WITH HIM...? IS SHIRONE FULL OF WEIRDOS?
MY LORD BROTHER! THAT IS AN INTRUDER!
A KNAVE WHO WE SHALL PUNISH WITH OUR OWN HANDS!
WHAT ARE YOU SAYING, PAX?!!! SUCH A MAN, WHO BROUGHT SUCH EXQUISITE DOLLS TO LIFE...
CANNOT BE A KNAVE! AM I WRONG ?!!
RAWR!
WHAT THE HELLLL ?!!!
DU-DUUUN

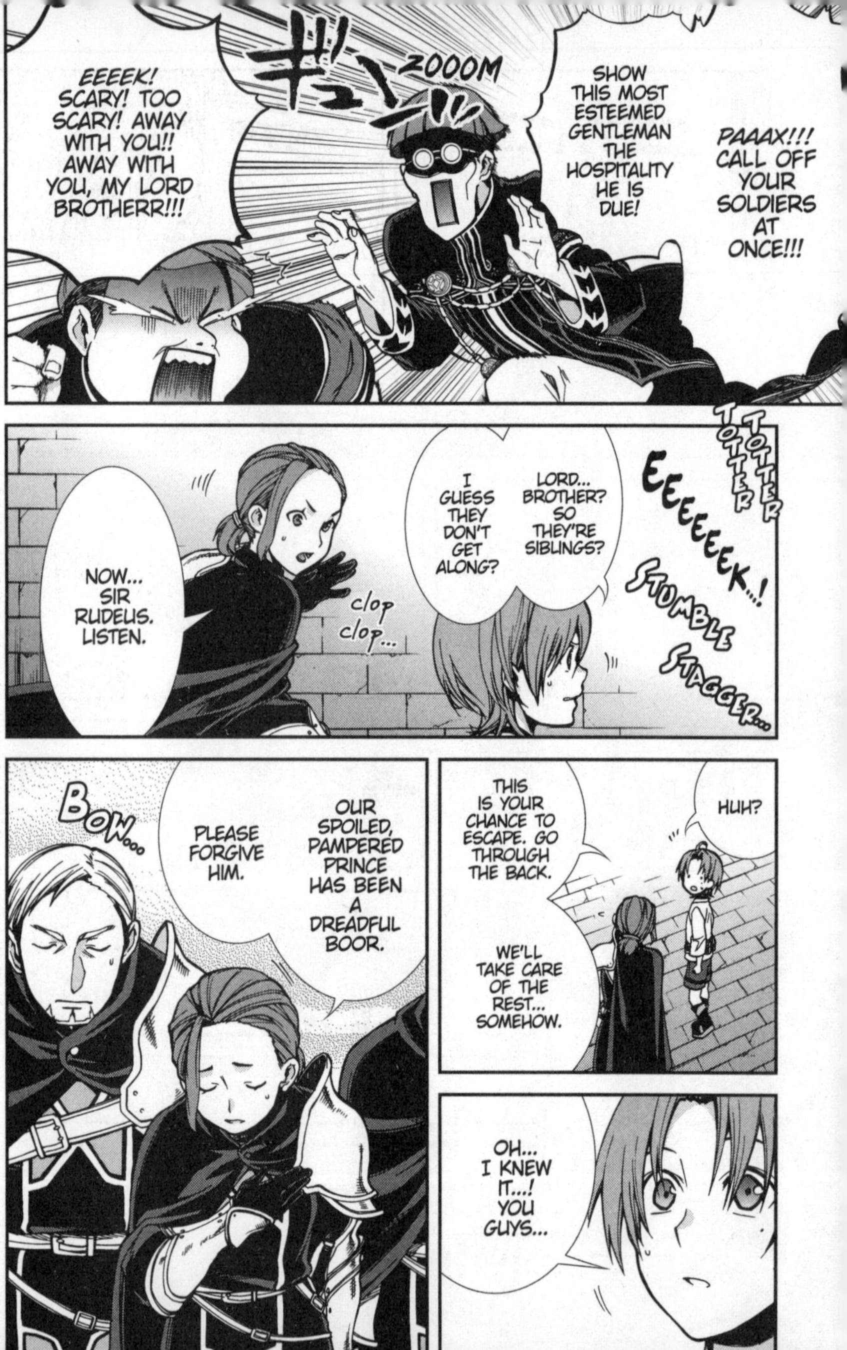

PAAAX!!! CALL OFF YOUR SOLDIERS AT ONCE!!!
SHOW THIS MOST ESTEEMED GENTLEMAN THE HOSPITALITY HE IS DUE!
ZOOOM
EEEEK! SCARY! TOO SCARY! AWAY WITH YOU!! AWAY WITH YOU, MY LORD BROTHERR!!!
TOTTER TOTTER
EEEEEEEK...!
STUMBLE STAGGER...
LORD... BROTHER? SO THEY'RE SIBLINGS?
I GUESS THEY DON'T GET ALONG?
clop clop...
NOW... SIR RUDEUS. LISTEN.
HUH?
THIS IS YOUR CHANCE TO ESCAPE. GO THROUGH THE BACK.
WE'LL TAKE CARE OF THE REST... SOMEHOW.
OH... I KNEW IT...! YOU GUYS...
OUR SPOILED, PAMPERED PRINCE HAS BEEN A DREADFUL BOOR.
PLEASE FORGIVE HIM.
BOW...

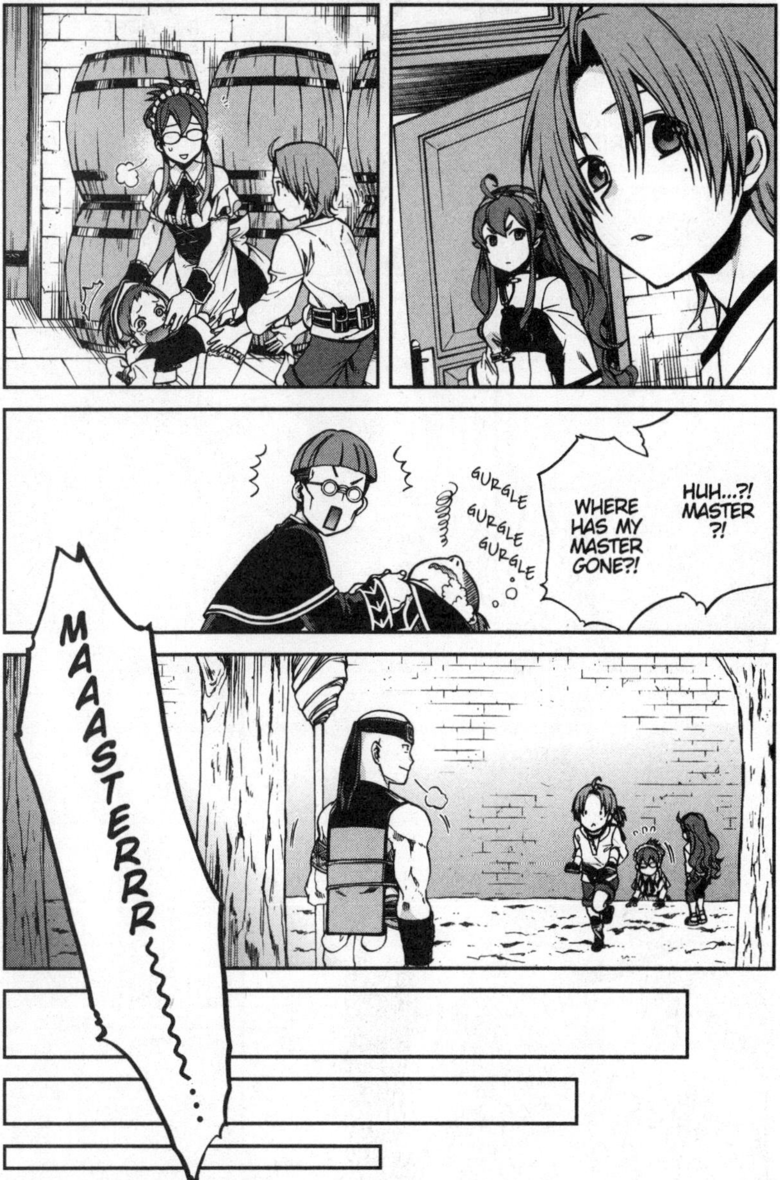
HUH...?! MASTER ?!
WHERE HAS MY MASTER GONE?!
GURGLE GURGLE GURGLE
MAAASTERRR...

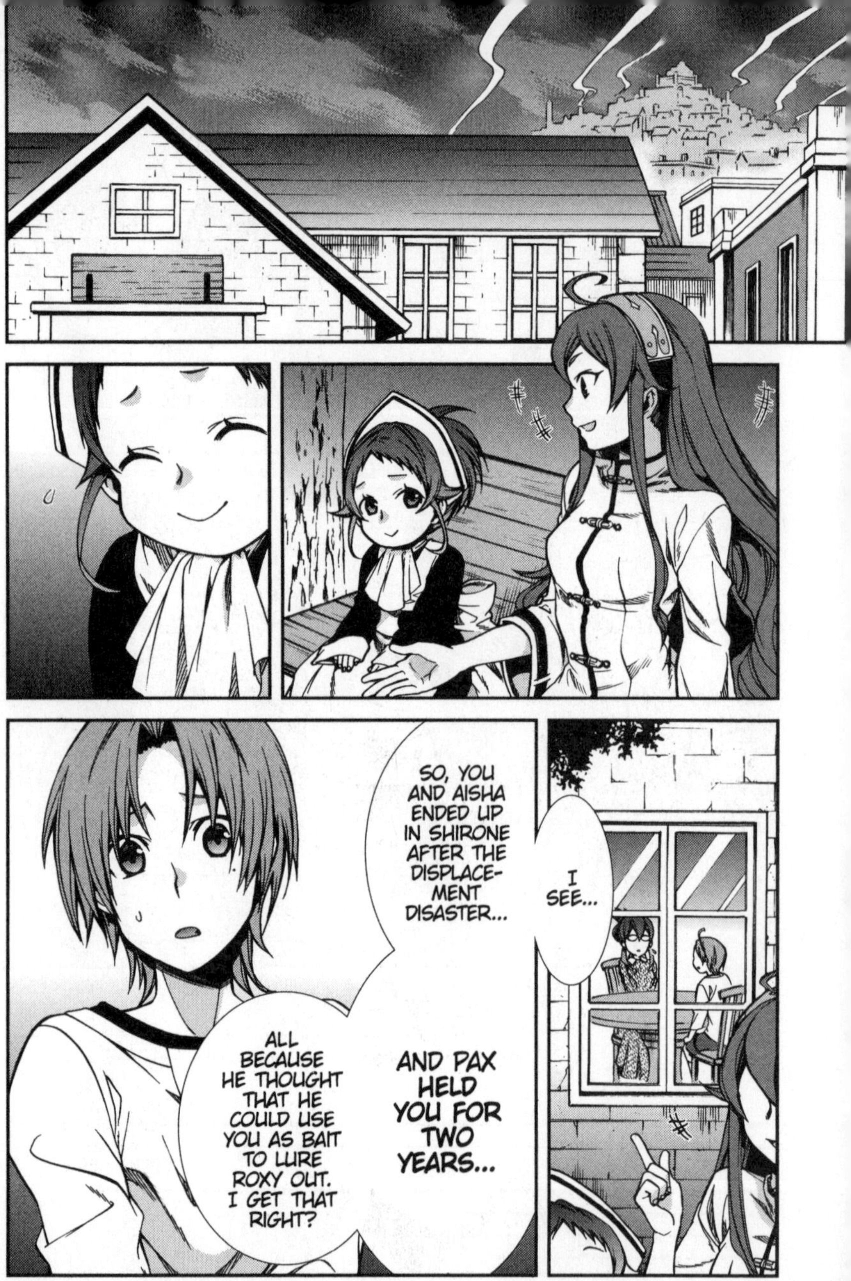

I SEE...
SO, YOU AND AISHA ENDED UP IN SHIRONE AFTER THE DISPLACEMENT DISASTER...
AND PAX HELD YOU FOR TWO YEARS...
ALL BECAUSE HE THOUGHT THAT HE COULD USE YOU AS BAIT TO LURE ROXY OUT. I GET THAT RIGHT?

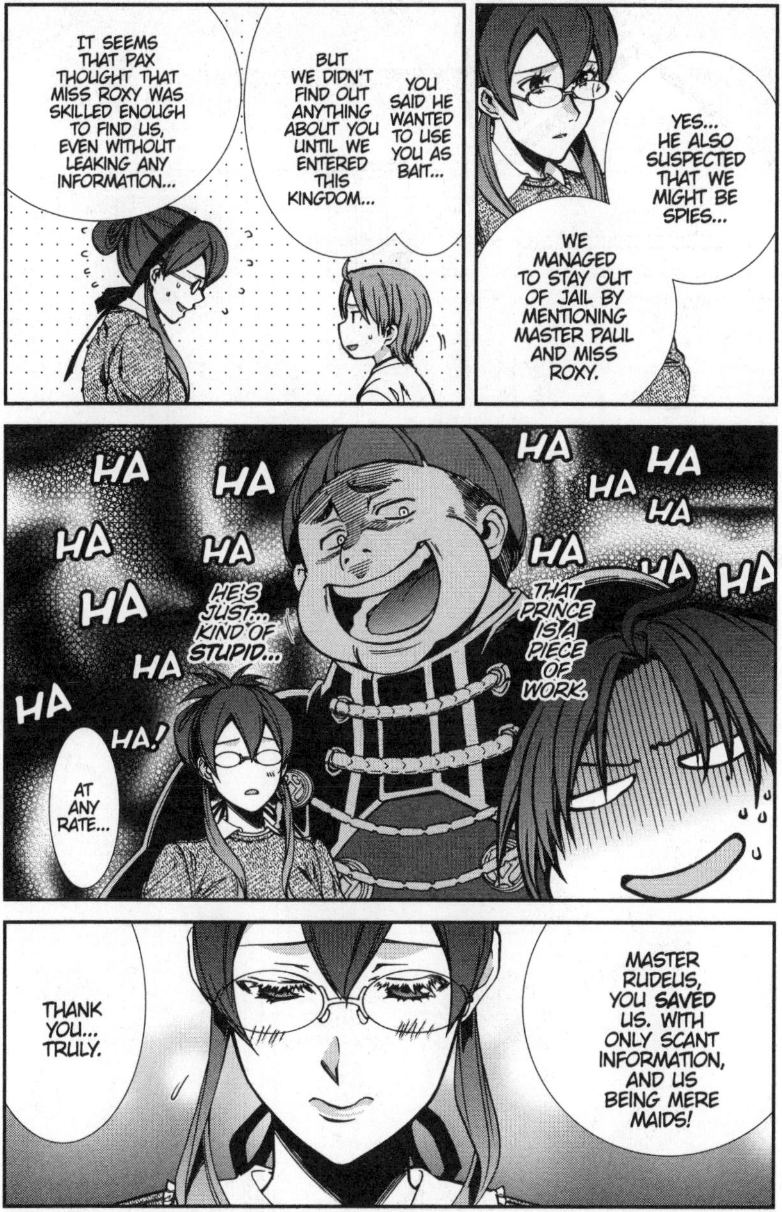
YES... HE ALSO SUSPECTED THAT WE MIGHT BE SPIES...
WE MANAGED TO STAY OUT OF JAIL BY MENTIONING MASTER PAUL AND MISS ROXY.
YOU SAID HE WANTED TO USE YOU AS BAIT...
BUT WE DIDN'T FIND OUT ANYTHING ABOUT YOU UNTIL WE ENTERED THIS KINGDOM...
IT SEEMS THAT PAX THOUGHT THAT MISS ROXY WAS SKILLED ENOUGH TO FIND US, EVEN WITHOUT LEAKING ANY INFORMATION...
HA HA HA HA HA HA HA HA HA HA HA HA HA HA HA HA HA!
THAT PRINCE IS A PIECE OF WORK.
HE'S JUST... KIND OF STUPID...
AT ANY RATE...
MASTER RUDEUS, YOU SAVED US. WITH ONLY SCANT INFORMATION, AND US BEING MERE MAIDS!
THANK YOU... TRULY.

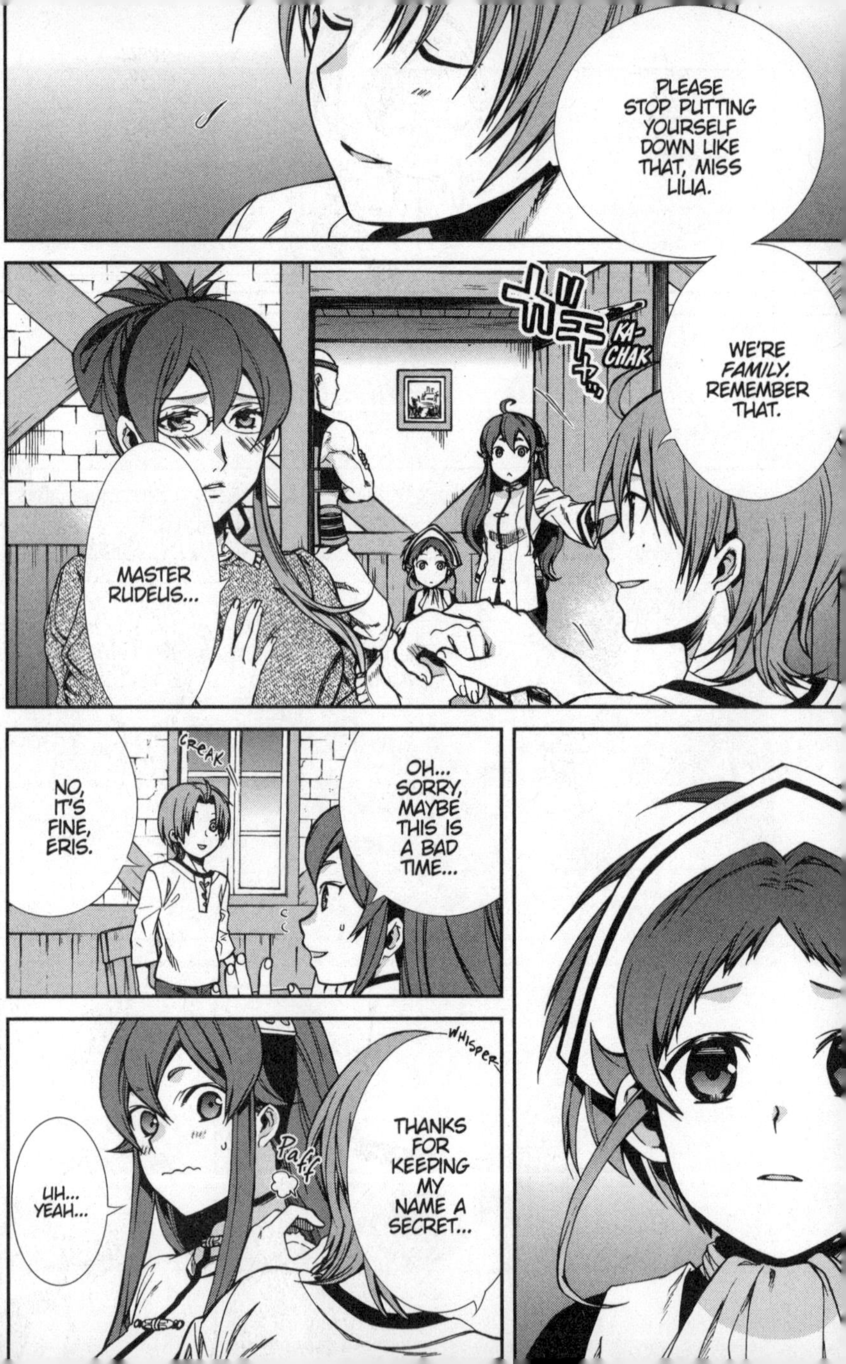
PLEASE STOP PUTTING YOURSELF DOWN LIKE THAT, MISS LILIA.
WE'RE *FAMILY.* REMEMBER THAT.
KA-CHAK
MASTER RUDEUS...
OH... SORRY, MAYBE THIS IS A BAD TIME...
CREAK
NO, IT'S FINE, ERIS.
WHISPER
THANKS FOR KEEPING MY NAME A SECRET...
Paff
UH... YEAH...

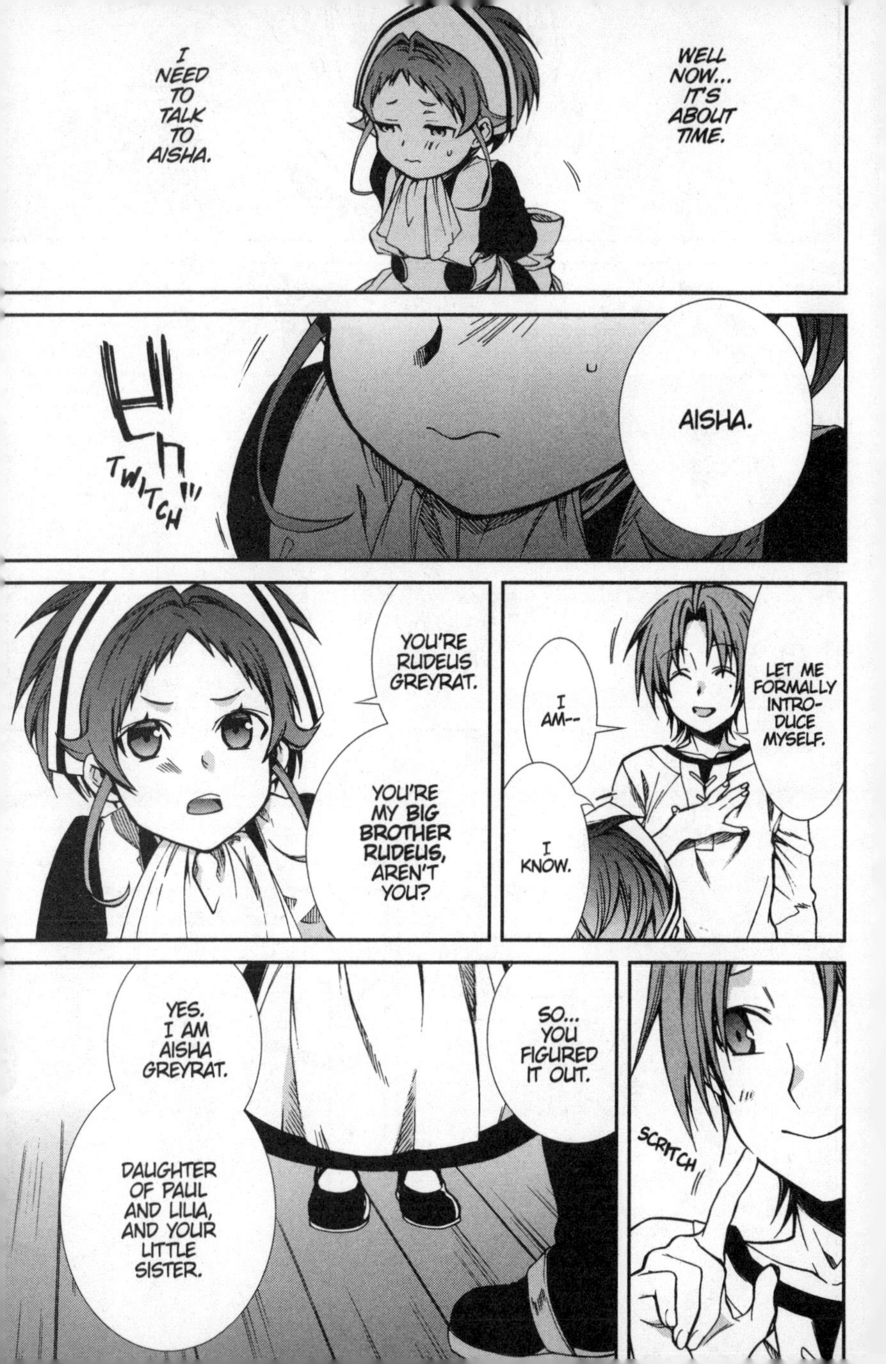

WELL NOW... IT'S ABOUT TIME.
I NEED TO TALK TO AISHA.
AISHA.
TWITCH
LET ME FORMALLY INTRO-DUCE MYSELF.
I AM--
I KNOW.
YOU'RE RUDEUS GREYRAT.
YOU'RE MY BIG BROTHER RUDEUS, AREN'T YOU?
SCRITCH
SO... YOU FIGURED IT OUT.
YES. I AM AISHA GREYRAT.
DAUGHTER OF PAUL AND LILIA, AND YOUR LITTLE SISTER.

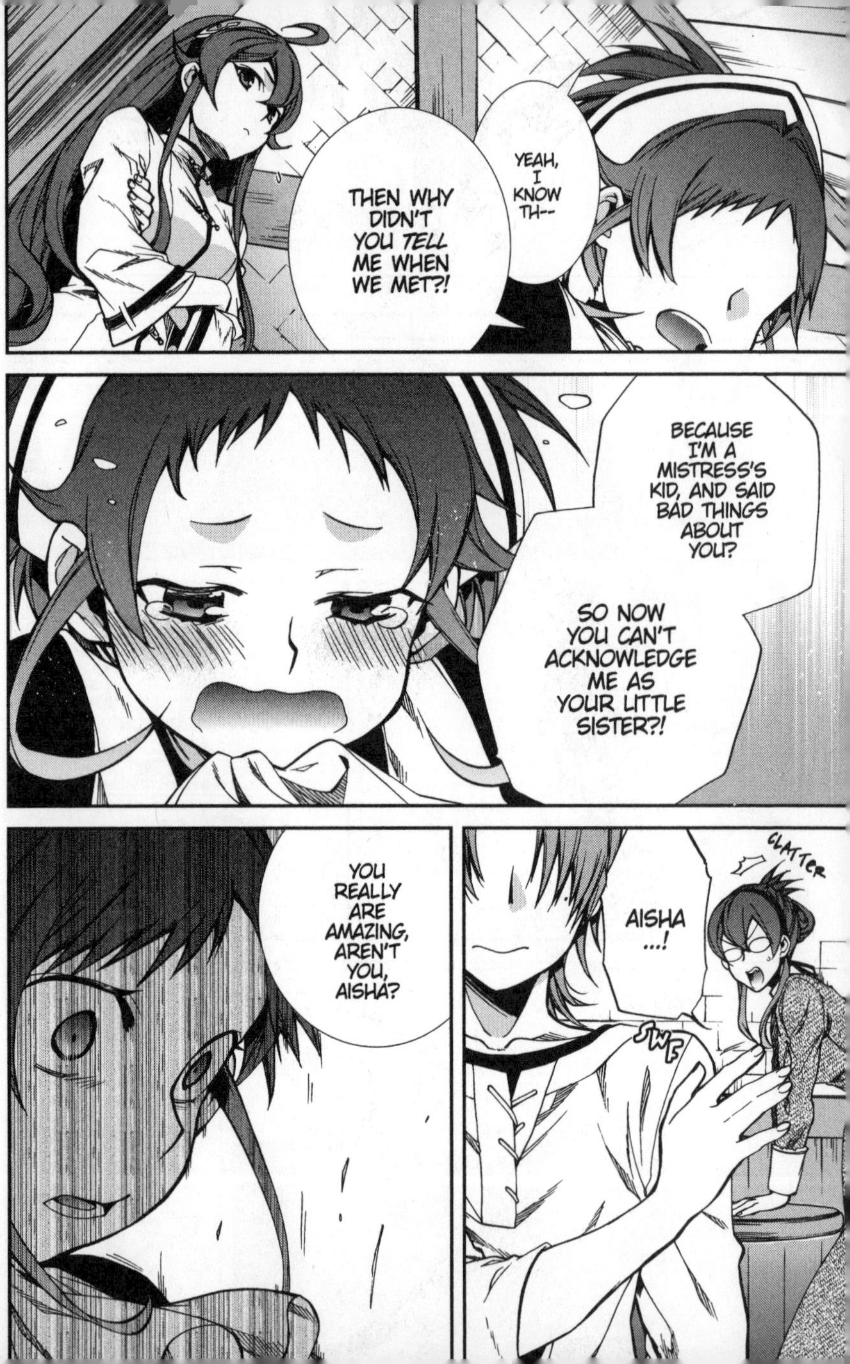
YEAH, I KNOW TH--
THEN WHY DIDN'T YOU *TELL* ME WHEN WE MET?!
BECAUSE I'M A MISTRESS'S KID, AND SAID BAD THINGS ABOUT YOU?
SO NOW YOU CAN'T ACKNOWLEDGE ME AS YOUR LITTLE SISTER?!
CLATTER
AISHA ...!
SWF
YOU REALLY ARE AMAZING, AREN'T YOU, AISHA?

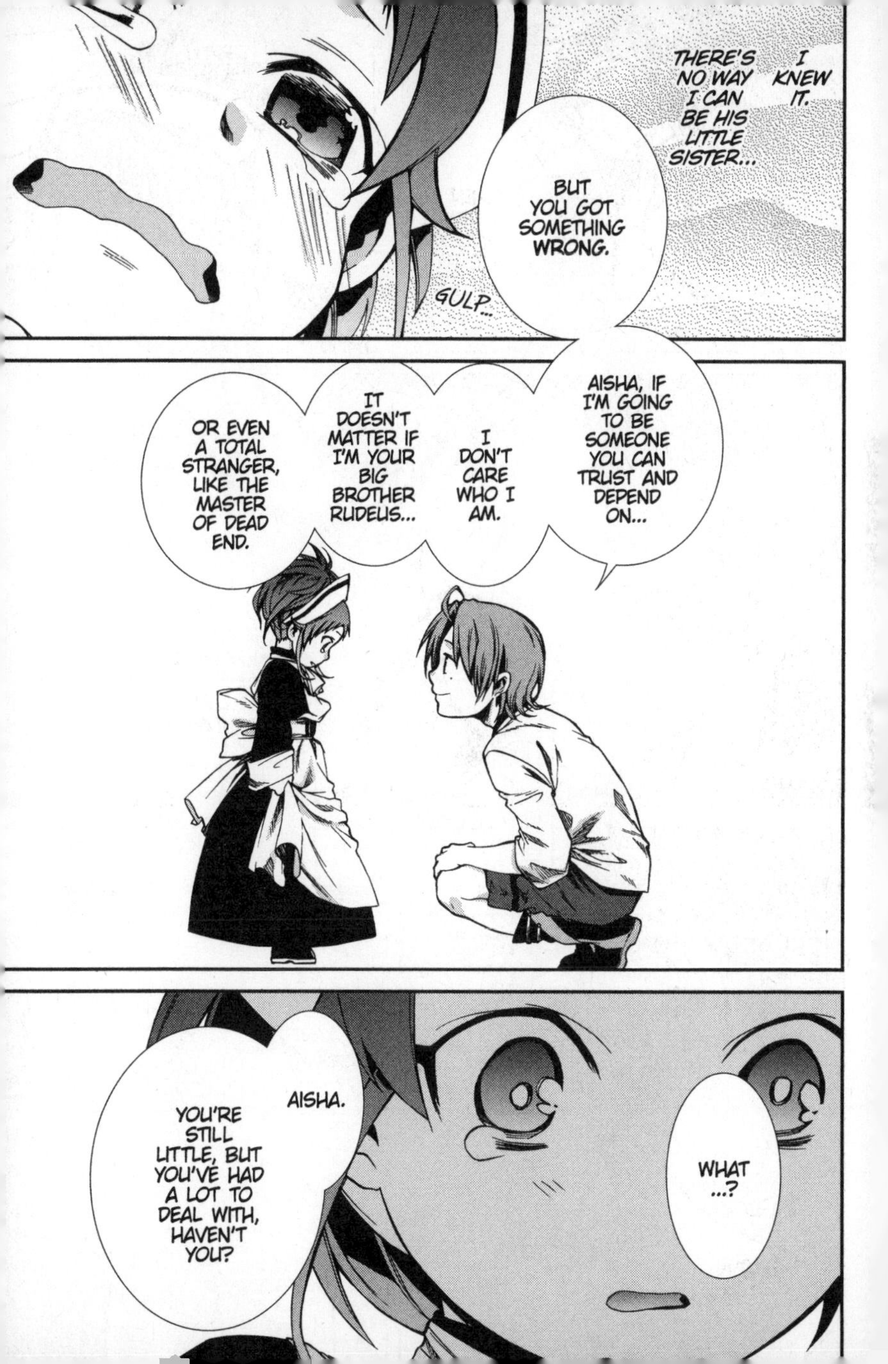
I KNEW IT.
THERE'S NO WAY I CAN BE HIS LITTLE SISTER...
BUT YOU GOT SOMETHING WRONG.
GULP...
AISHA, IF I'M GOING TO BE SOMEONE YOU CAN TRUST AND DEPEND ON...
I DON'T CARE WHO I AM.
IT DOESN'T MATTER IF I'M YOUR BIG BROTHER RUDEUS...
OR EVEN A TOTAL STRANGER, LIKE THE MASTER OF DEAD END.
WHAT ...?
AISHA.
YOU'RE STILL LITTLE, BUT YOU'VE HAD A LOT TO DEAL WITH, HAVEN'T YOU?

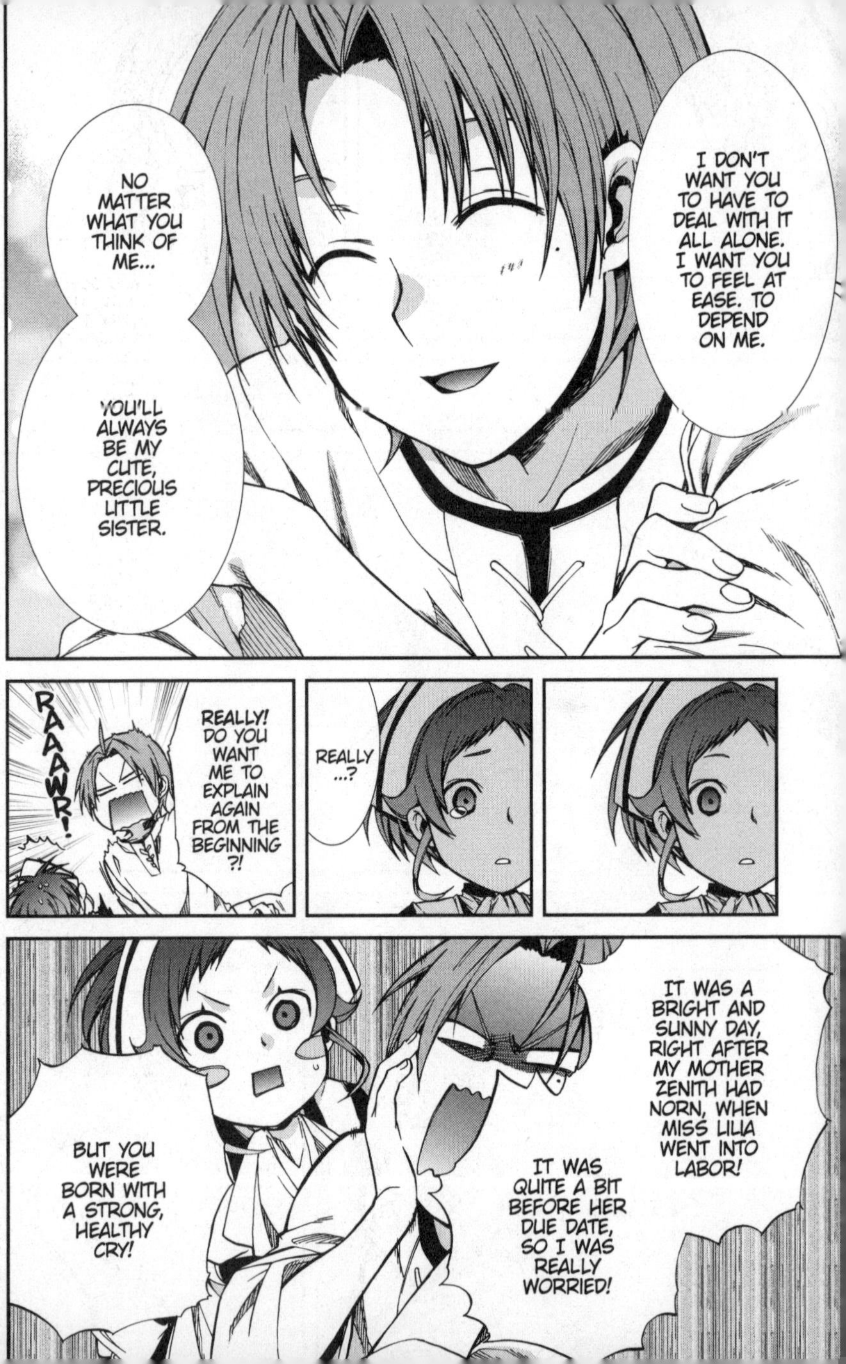
I DON'T WANT YOU TO HAVE TO DEAL WITH IT ALL ALONE. I WANT YOU TO FEEL AT EASE. TO DEPEND ON ME.
NO MATTER WHAT YOU THINK OF ME...
YOU'LL ALWAYS BE MY CUTE, PRECIOUS LITTLE SISTER.
REALLY ...?
RAAAWR!
REALLY! DO YOU WANT ME TO EXPLAIN AGAIN FROM THE BEGINNING?!
IT WAS A BRIGHT AND SUNNY DAY, RIGHT AFTER MY MOTHER ZENITH HAD NORN, WHEN MISS LILIA WENT INTO LABOR!
IT WAS QUITE A BIT BEFORE HER DUE DATE, SO I WAS REALLY WORRIED!
BUT YOU WERE BORN WITH A STRONG, HEALTHY CRY!

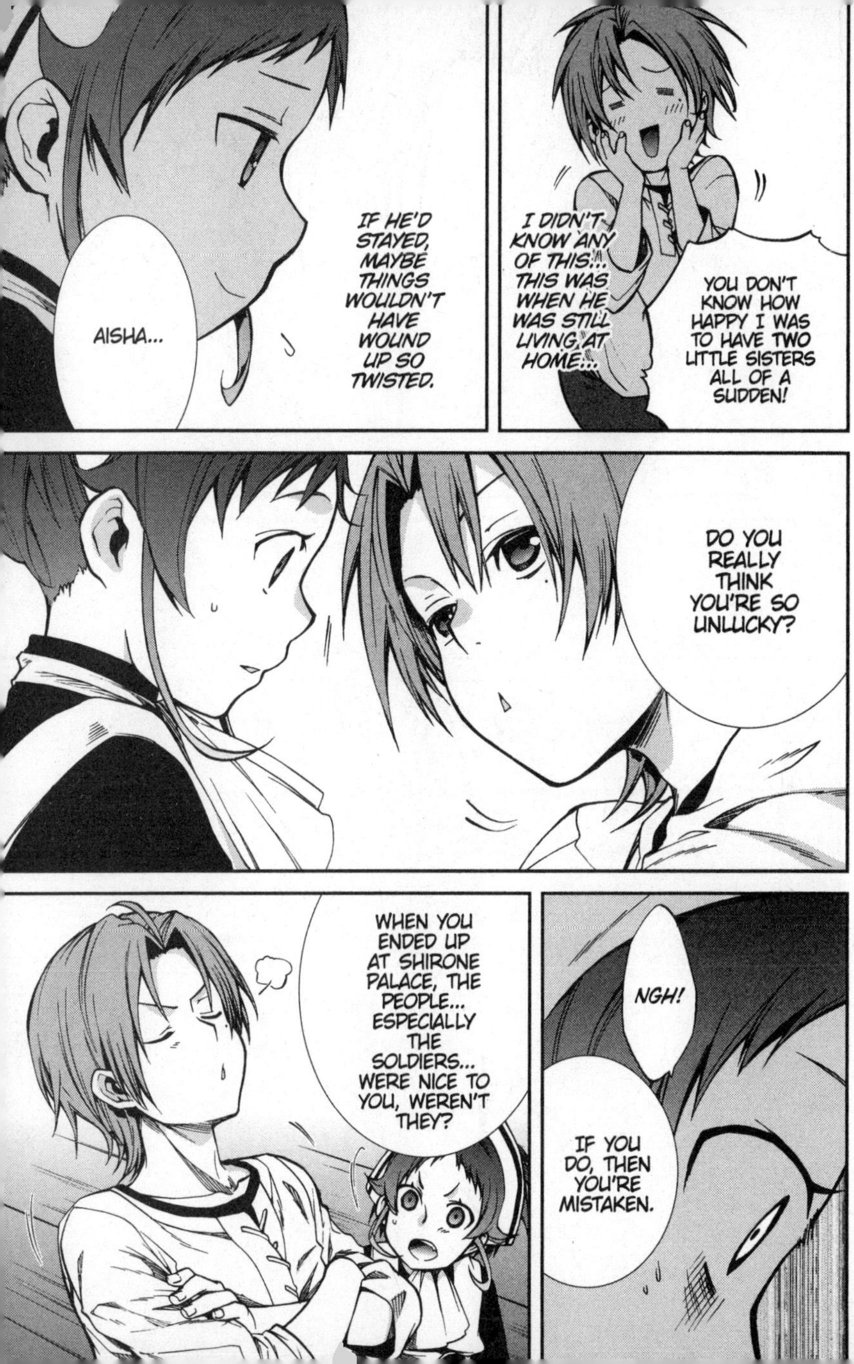
YOU DON'T KNOW HOW HAPPY I WAS TO HAVE TWO LITTLE SISTERS ALL OF A SUDDEN!
I DIDN'T KNOW ANY OF THIS... THIS WAS WHEN HE WAS STILL LIVING AT HOME...
IF HE'D STAYED, MAYBE THINGS WOULDN'T HAVE WOUND UP SO TWISTED.
AISHA...
DO YOU REALLY THINK YOU'RE SO UNLUCKY?
NGH!
IF YOU DO, THEN YOU'RE MISTAKEN.
WHEN YOU ENDED UP AT SHIRONE PALACE, THE PEOPLE... ESPECIALLY THE SOLDIERS... WERE NICE TO YOU, WEREN'T THEY?

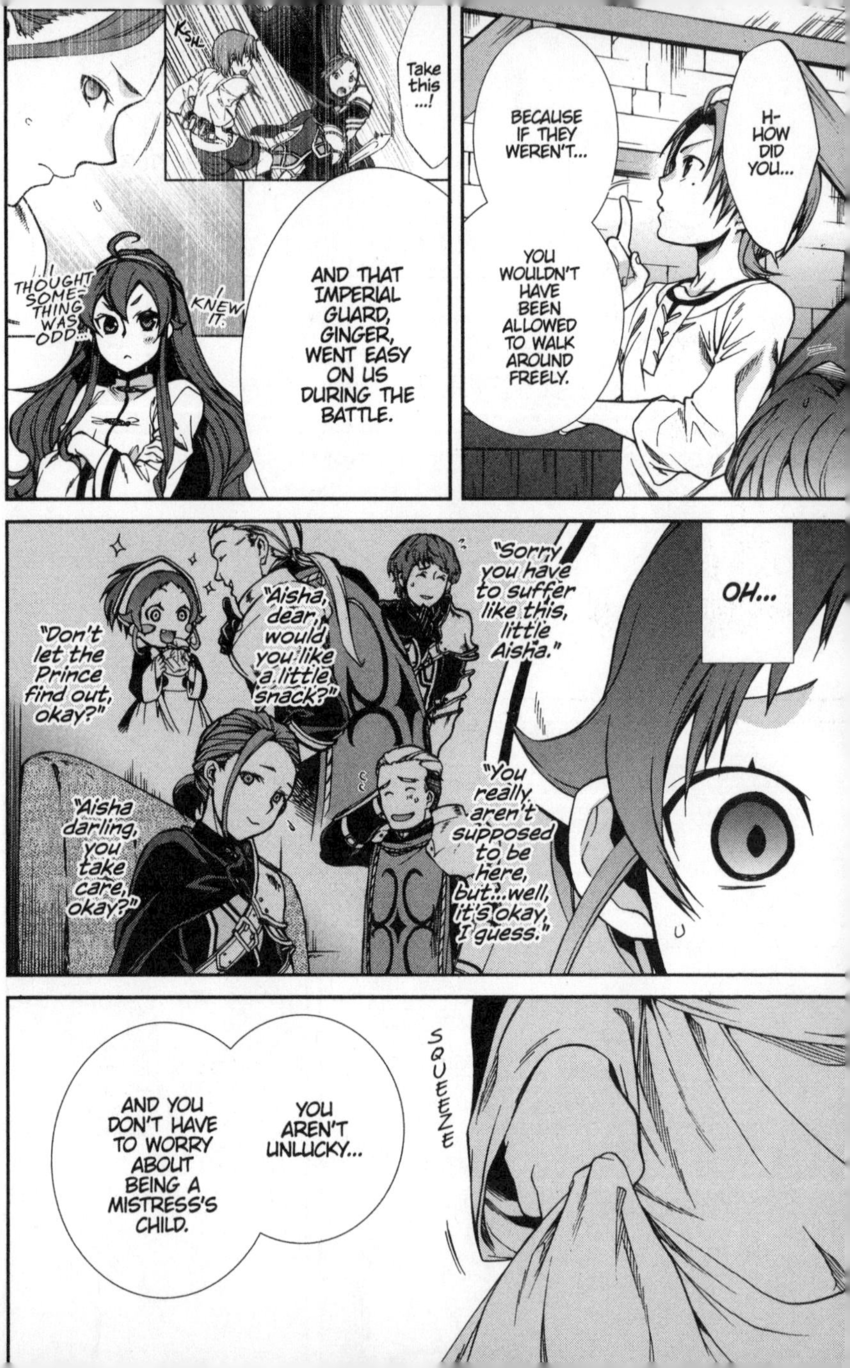
H-HOW DID YOU...
BECAUSE IF THEY WEREN'T...
YOU WOULDN'T HAVE BEEN ALLOWED TO WALK AROUND FREELY.
K-SH-
Take this ...!
AND THAT IMPERIAL GUARD, GINGER, WENT EASY ON US DURING THE BATTLE.
I KNEW IT.
I THOUGHT SOMETHING WAS ODD...
OH...
"Sorry you have to suffer like this, little Aisha."
"Aisha, dear, would you like a little snack?"
"Don't let the Prince find out, okay?"
"You really aren't supposed to be here, but...well, it's okay, I guess."
"Aisha darling, you take care, okay?"
SQUEEZE
YOU AREN'T UNLUCKY...
AND YOU DON'T HAVE TO WORRY ABOUT BEING A MISTRESS'S CHILD.

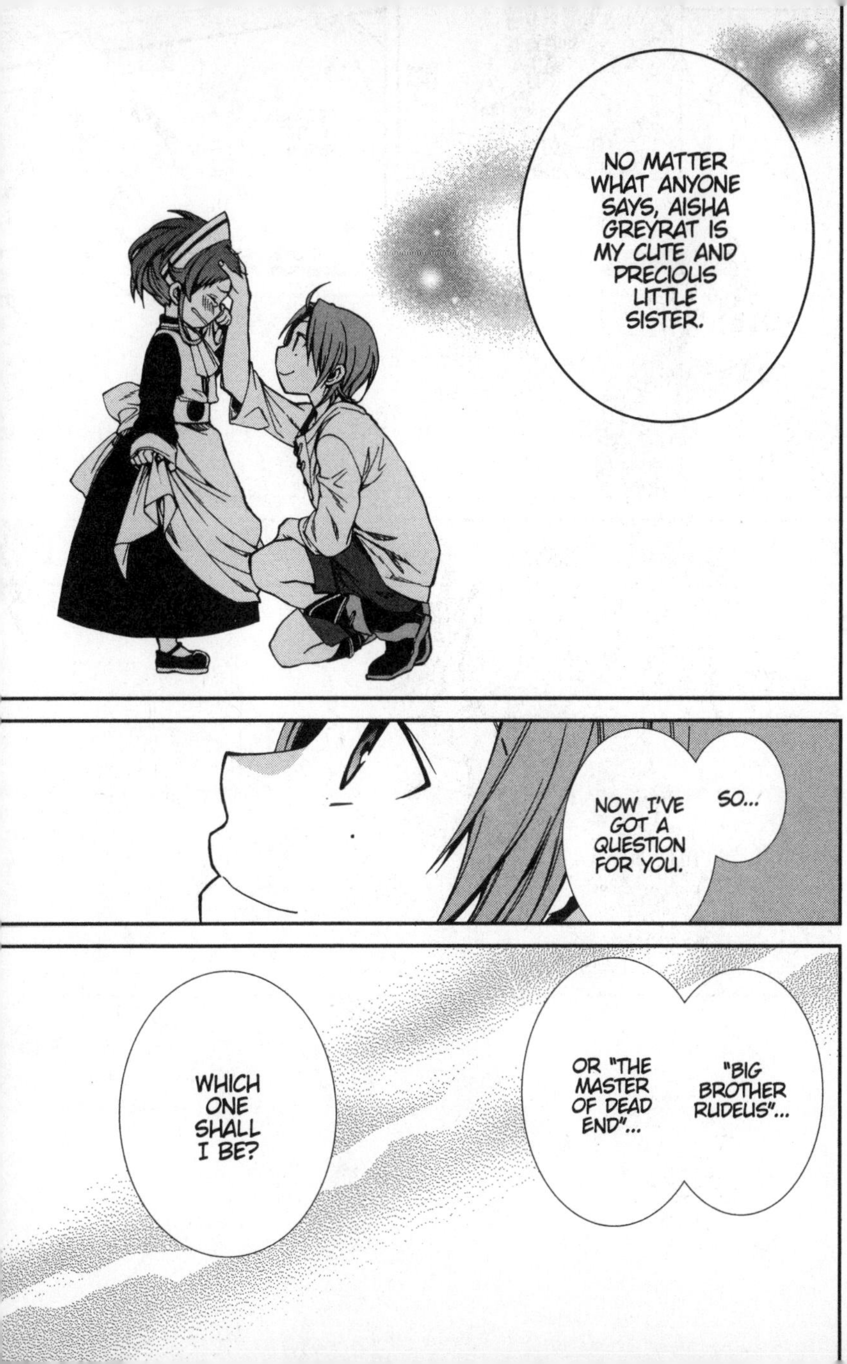
NO MATTER WHAT ANYONE SAYS, AISHA GREYRAT IS MY CUTE AND PRECIOUS LITTLE SISTER.
SO...
NOW I'VE GOT A QUESTION FOR YOU.
"BIG BROTHER RUDEUS"...
OR "THE MASTER OF DEAD END"...
WHICH ONE SHALL I BE?

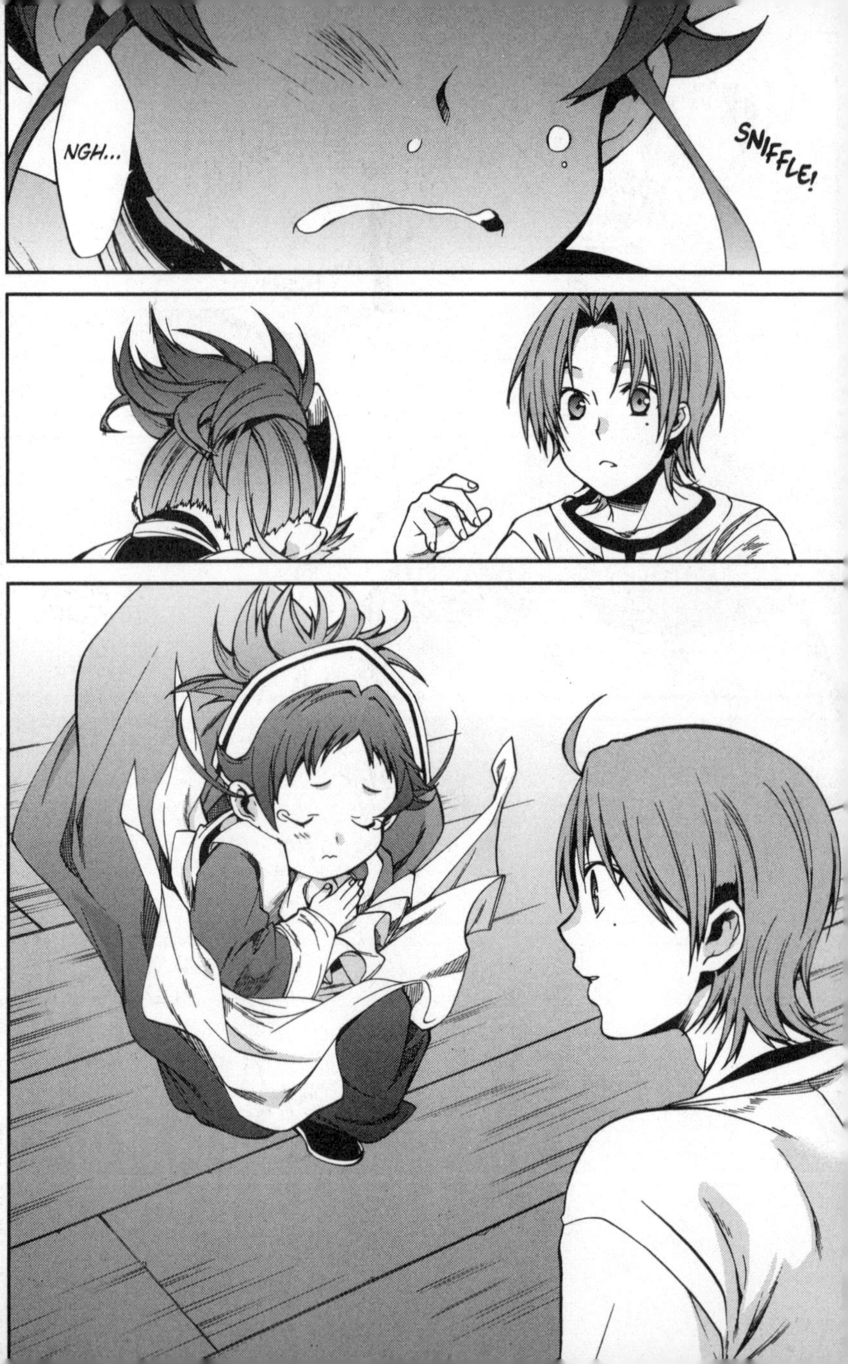
SNIFFLE!
NGH...

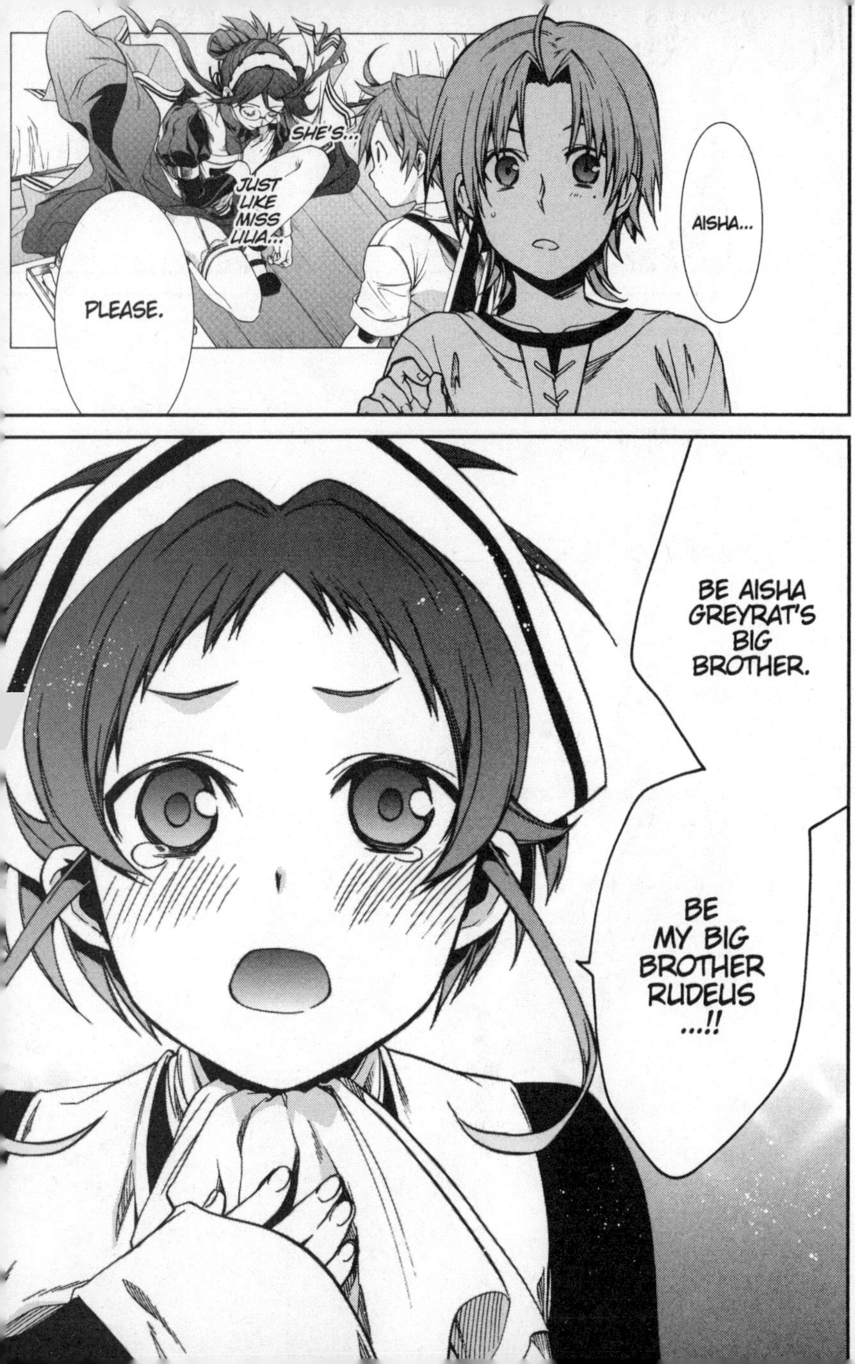
AISHA...
SHE'S...
JUST LIKE MISS LILIA...
PLEASE.
BE AISHA GREYRAT'S BIG BROTHER.
BE MY BIG BROTHER RUDEUS ...!!

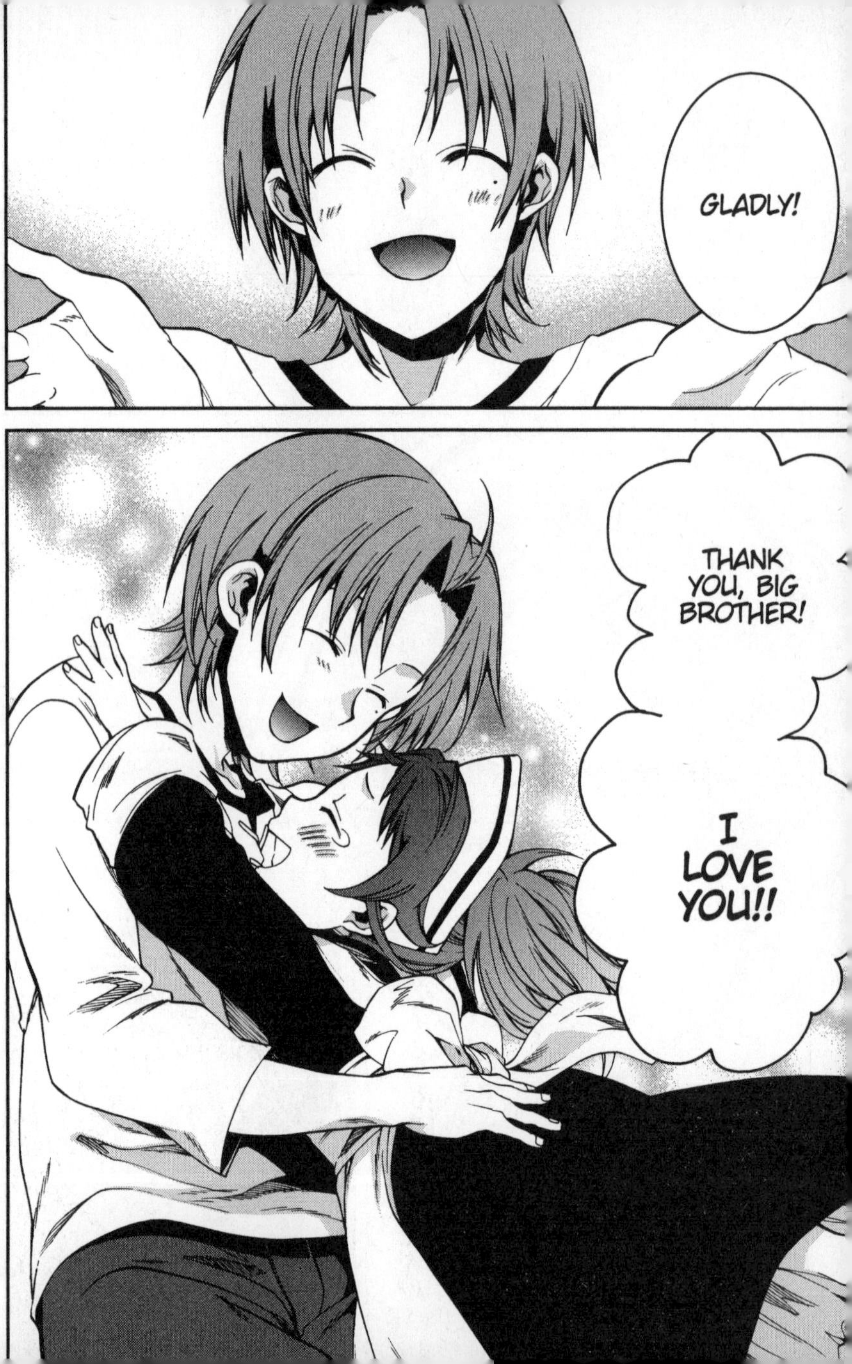
GLADLY!
THANK YOU, BIG BROTHER!
I LOVE YOU!!

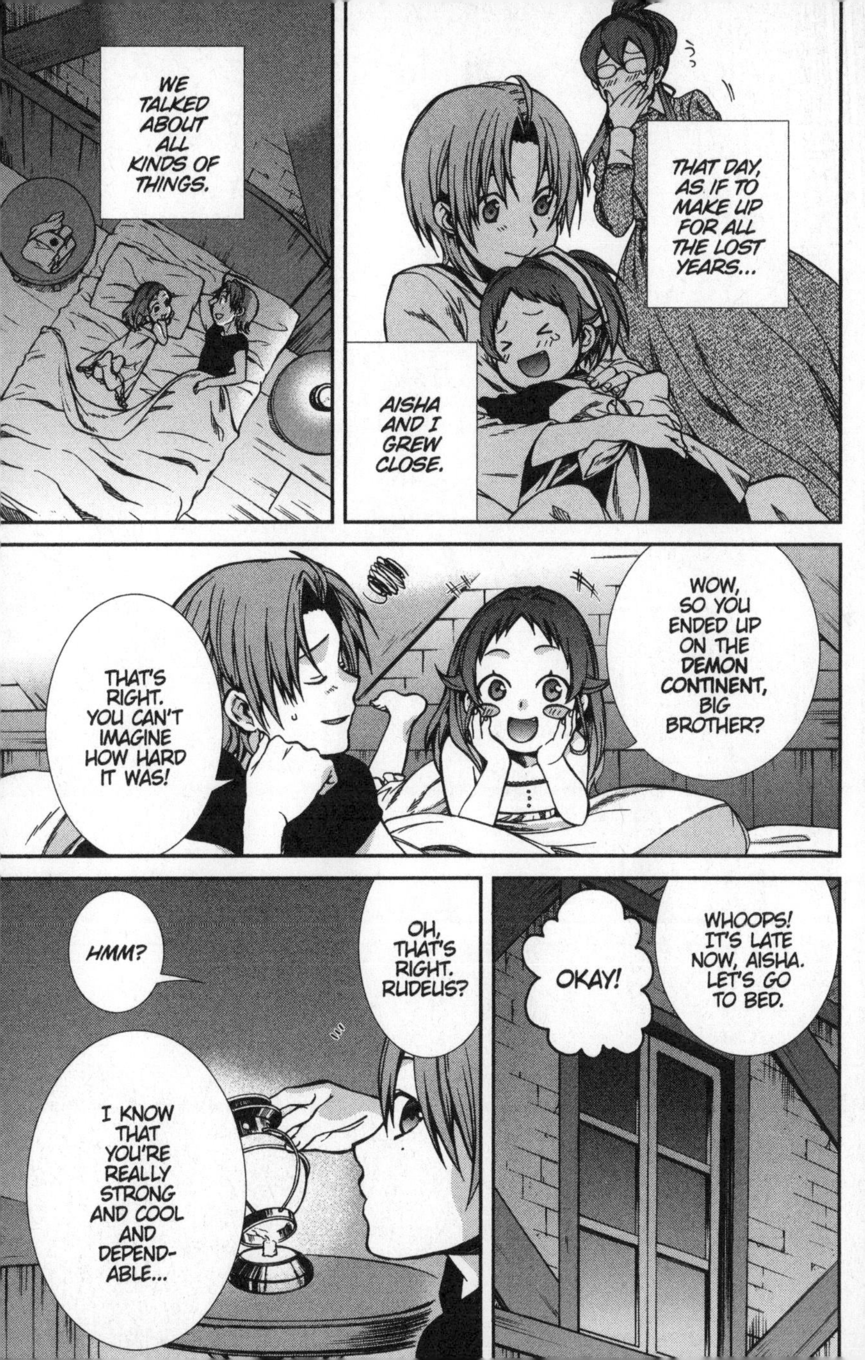
THAT DAY, AS IF TO MAKE UP FOR ALL THE LOST YEARS...
AISHA AND I GREW CLOSE.
WE TALKED ABOUT ALL KINDS OF THINGS.
WOW, SO YOU ENDED UP ON THE DEMON CONTINENT, BIG BROTHER?
THAT'S RIGHT. YOU CAN'T IMAGINE HOW HARD IT WAS!
WHOOPS! IT'S LATE NOW, AISHA. LET'S GO TO BED.
OKAY!
OH, THAT'S RIGHT. RUDEUS?
HMM?
I KNOW THAT YOU'RE REALLY STRONG AND COOL AND DEPEND-ABLE...

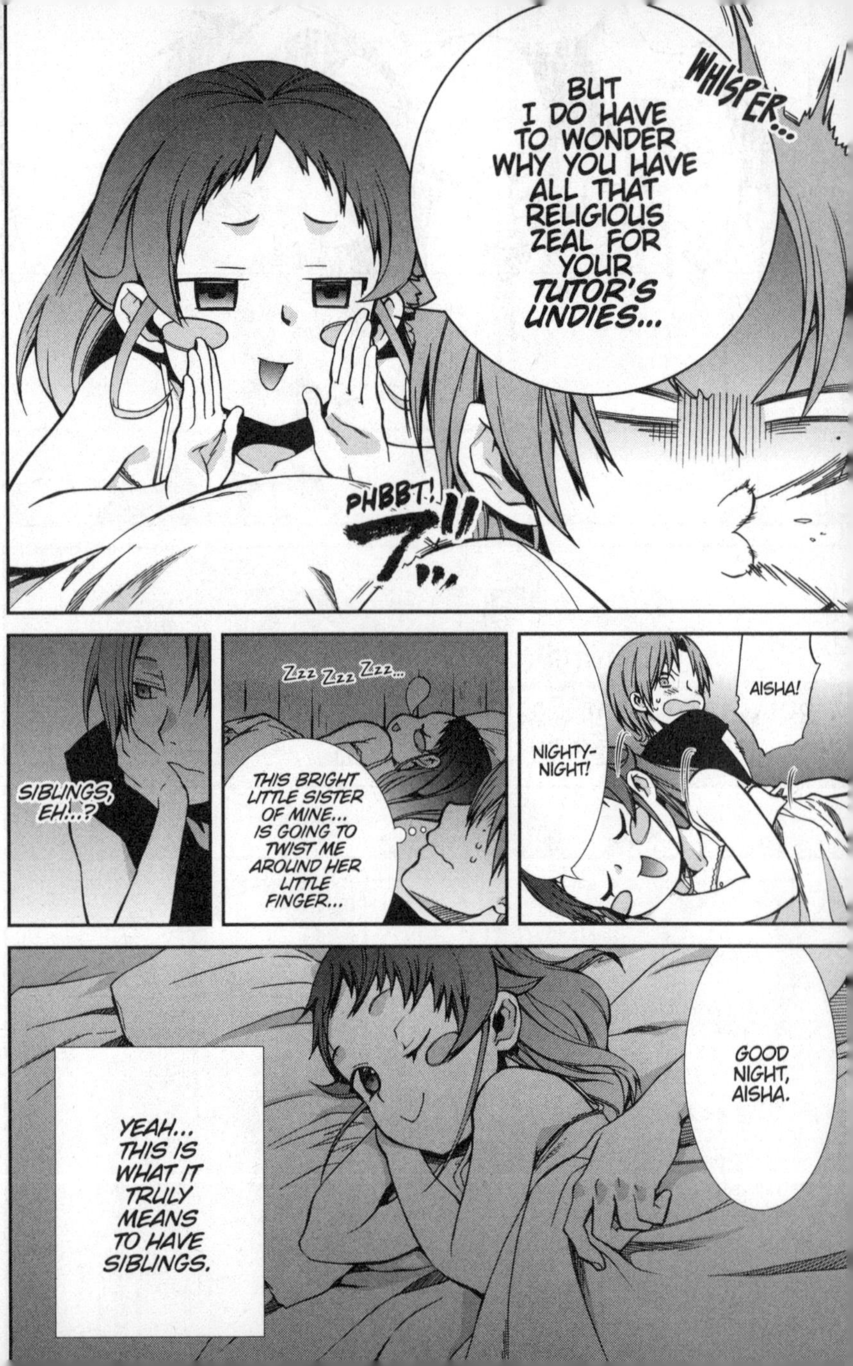
WHISPER...
BUT I DO HAVE TO WONDER WHY YOU HAVE ALL THAT RELIGIOUS ZEAL FOR YOUR TUTOR'S UNDIES...
PHBBT!
AISHA!
NIGHTY-NIGHT!
Zzz Zzz Zzz...
THIS BRIGHT LITTLE SISTER OF MINE... IS GOING TO TWIST ME AROUND HER LITTLE FINGER...
SIBLINGS, EH...?
GOOD NIGHT, AISHA.
YEAH... THIS IS WHAT IT TRULY MEANS TO HAVE SIBLINGS.

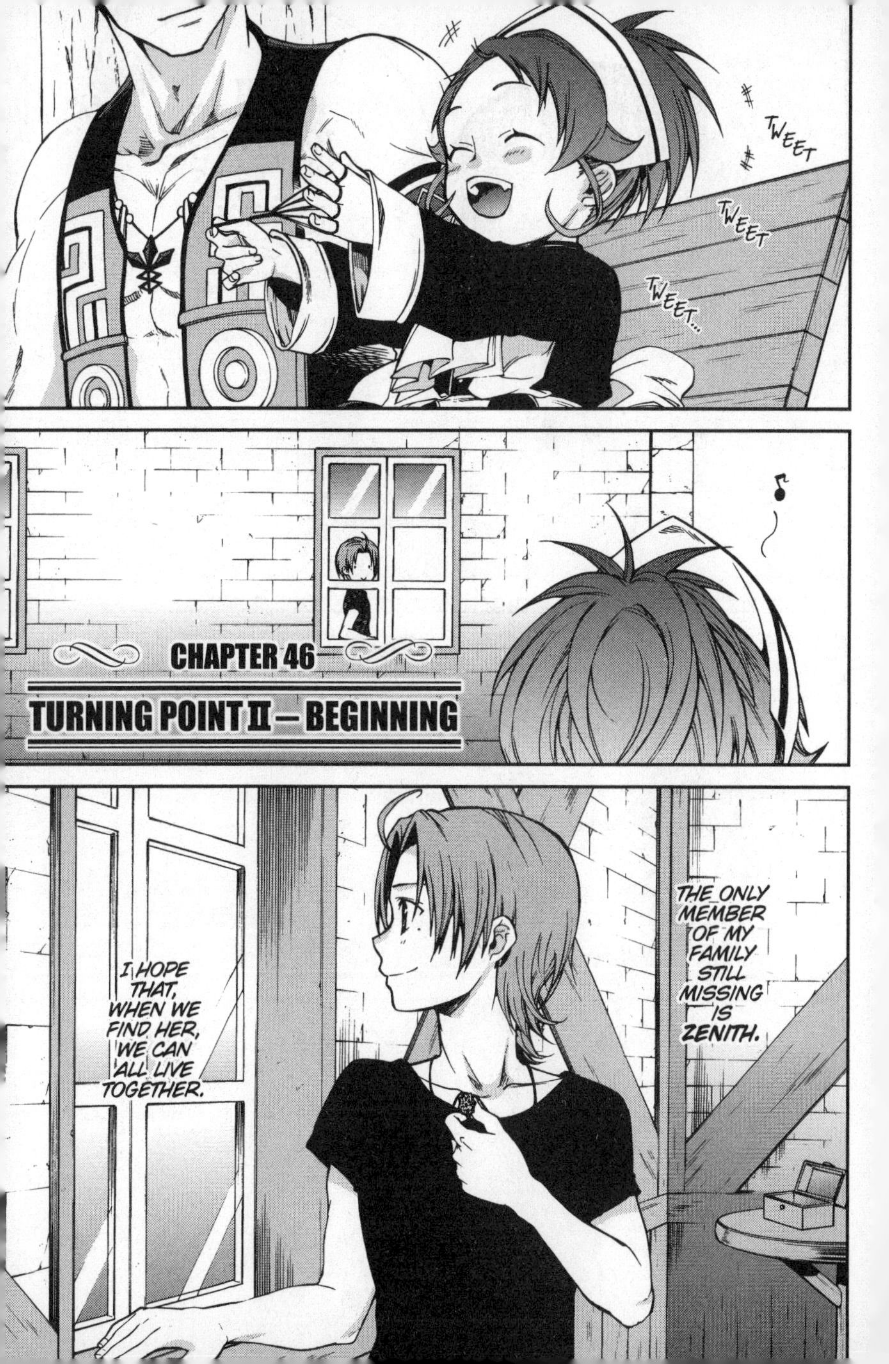
TWEET
TWEET
TWEET...
CHAPTER 46
TURNING POINT II – BEGINNING
THE ONLY MEMBER OF MY FAMILY STILL MISSING IS ZENITH.
I HOPE THAT, WHEN WE FIND HER, WE CAN ALL LIVE TOGETHER.

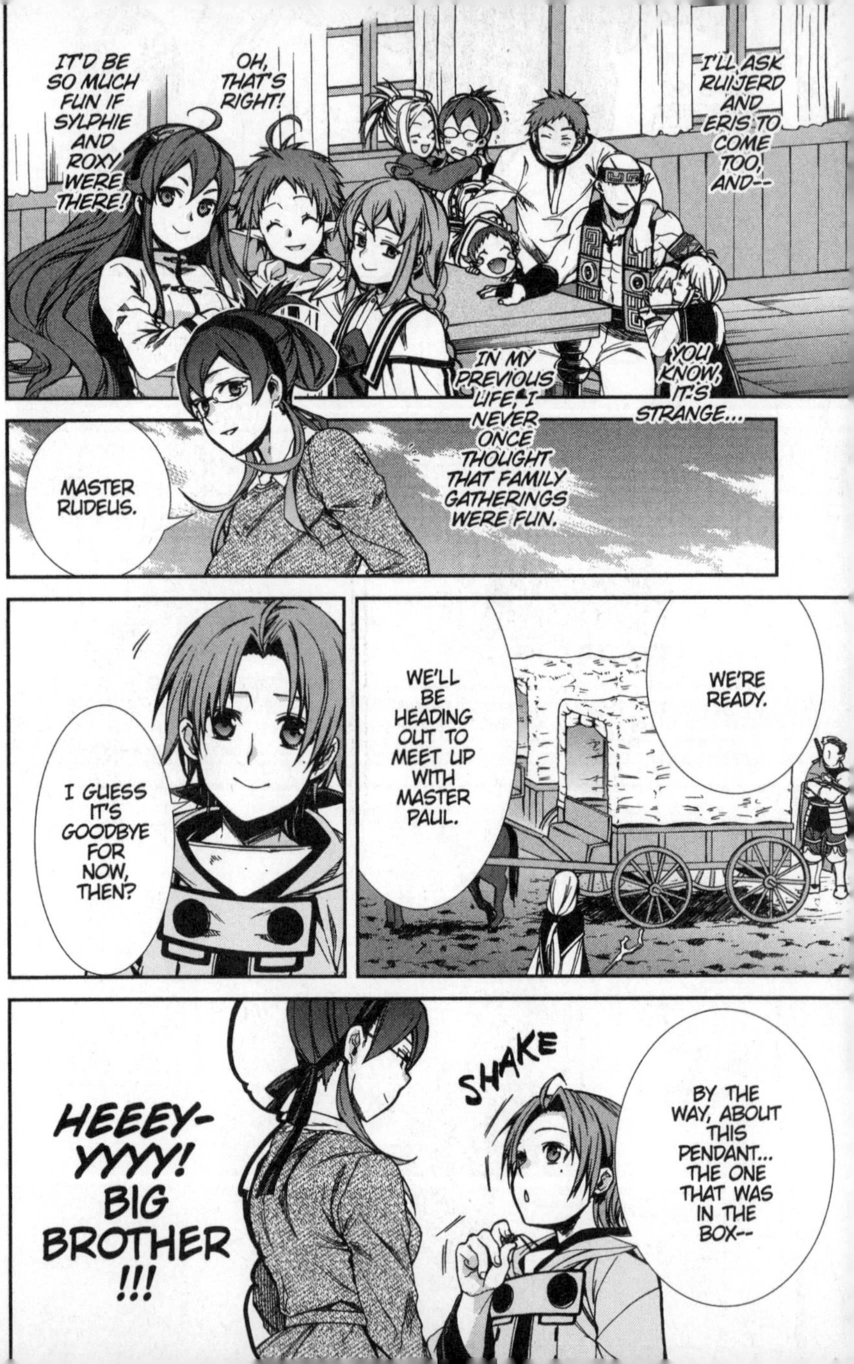
I'LL ASK RUIJERD AND ERIS TO COME TOO, AND--
OH, THAT'S RIGHT!
IT'D BE SO MUCH FUN IF SYLPHIE AND ROXY WERE THERE!
YOU KNOW, IT'S STRANGE...
IN MY PREVIOUS LIFE, I NEVER ONCE THOUGHT THAT FAMILY GATHERINGS WERE FUN.
MASTER RUDEUS.
WE'RE READY.
WE'LL BE HEADING OUT TO MEET UP WITH MASTER PAUL.
I GUESS IT'S GOODBYE FOR NOW, THEN?
BY THE WAY, ABOUT THIS PENDANT... THE ONE THAT WAS IN THE BOX--
SHAKE
HEEEY-YYYY! BIG BROTHER !!!

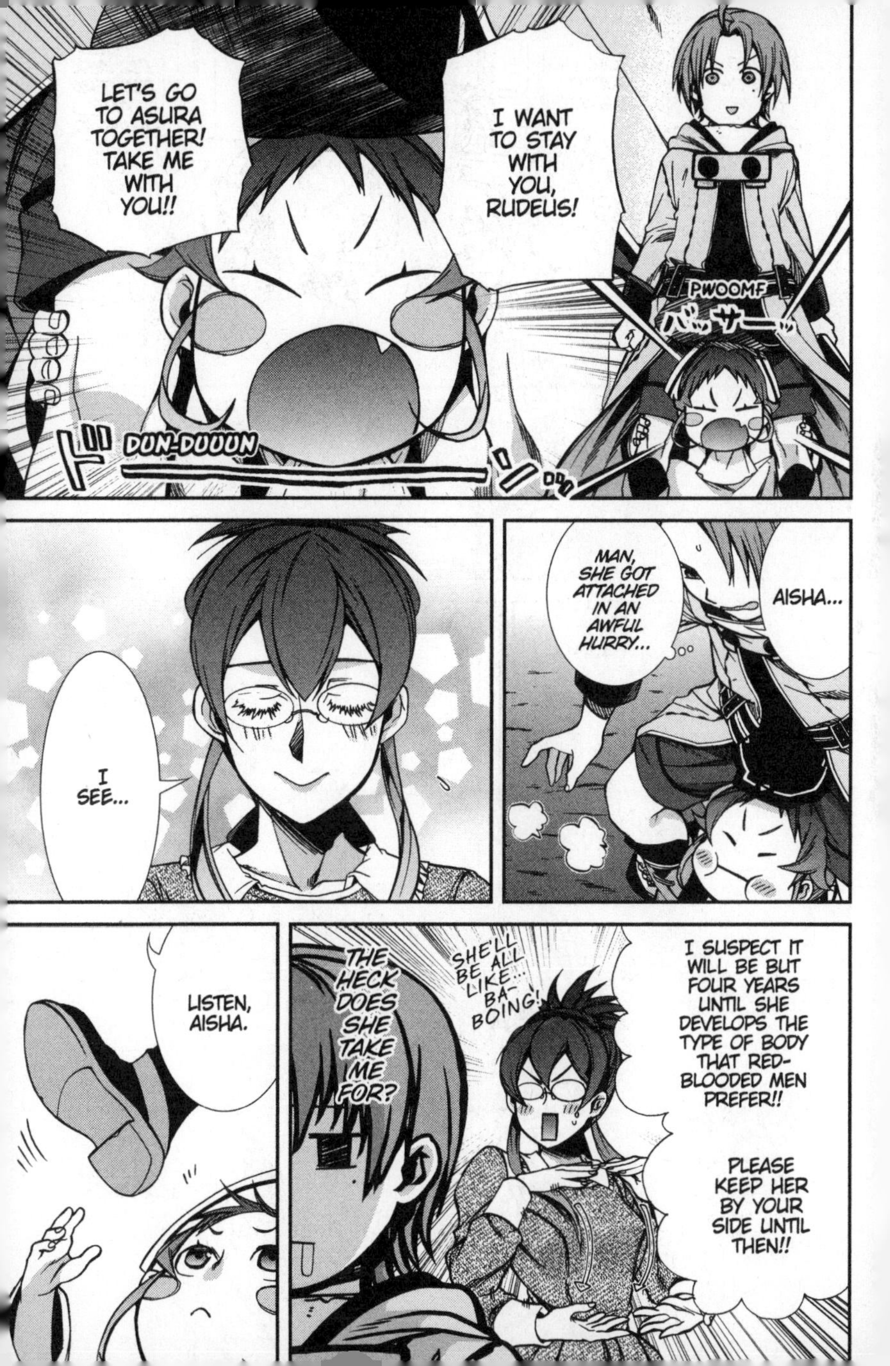

PWOOMF
バッサーッ
I WANT TO STAY WITH YOU, RUDEUS!
LET'S GO TO ASURA TOGETHER! TAKE ME WITH YOU!!
DUN-DUUUN
AISHA...
MAN, SHE GOT ATTACHED IN AN AWFUL HURRY...
I SEE...
I SUSPECT IT WILL BE BUT FOUR YEARS UNTIL SHE DEVELOPS THE TYPE OF BODY THAT RED-BLOODED MEN PREFER!!
PLEASE KEEP HER BY YOUR SIDE UNTIL THEN!!
SHE'LL BE ALL LIKE... BA-BOING!
THE HECK DOES SHE TAKE ME FOR?
LISTEN, AISHA.

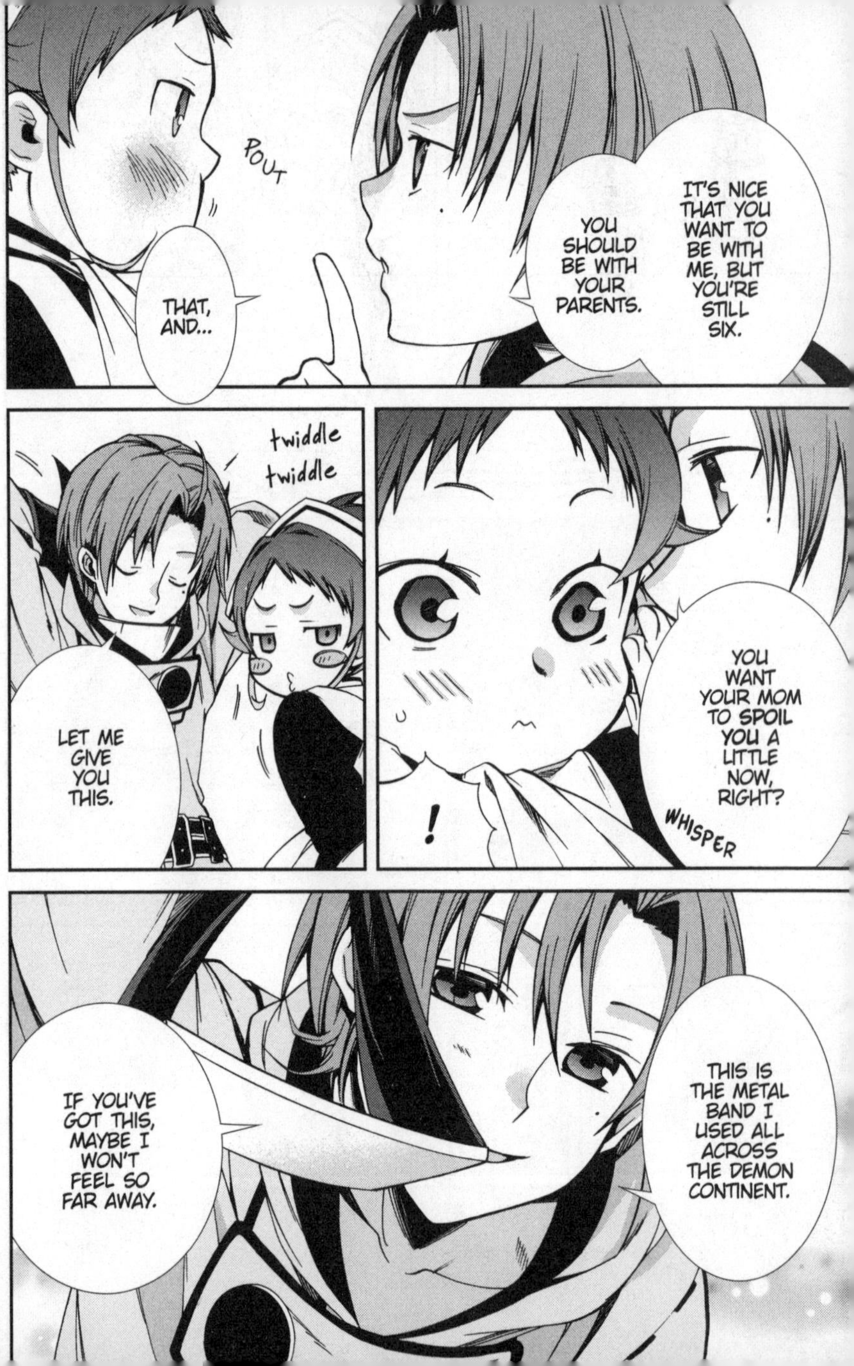
IT'S NICE THAT YOU WANT TO BE WITH ME, BUT YOU'RE STILL SIX.
YOU SHOULD BE WITH YOUR PARENTS.
POUT
THAT, AND...
YOU WANT YOUR MOM TO SPOIL YOU A LITTLE NOW, RIGHT?
WHISPER
!
twiddle twiddle
LET ME GIVE YOU THIS.
THIS IS THE METAL BAND I USED ALL ACROSS THE DEMON CONTINENT.
IF YOU'VE GOT THIS, MAYBE I WON'T FEEL SO FAR AWAY.

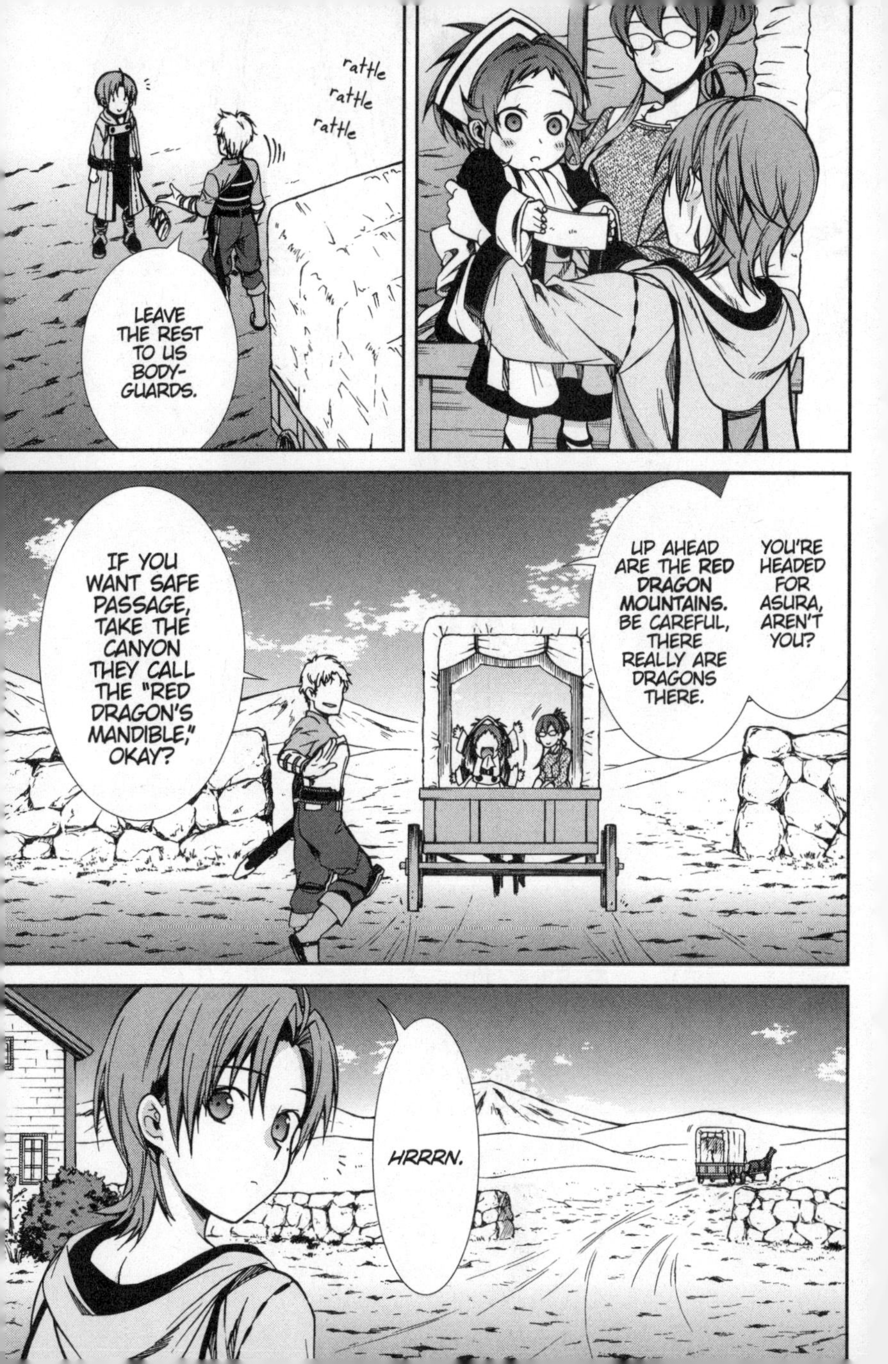
rattle rattle rattle
LEAVE THE REST TO US BODY-GUARDS.
YOU'RE HEADED FOR ASURA, AREN'T YOU?
UP AHEAD ARE THE RED DRAGON MOUNTAINS. BE CAREFUL, THERE REALLY ARE DRAGONS THERE.
IF YOU WANT SAFE PASSAGE, TAKE THE CANYON THEY CALL THE "RED DRAGON'S MANDIBLE," OKAY?
HRRRN.

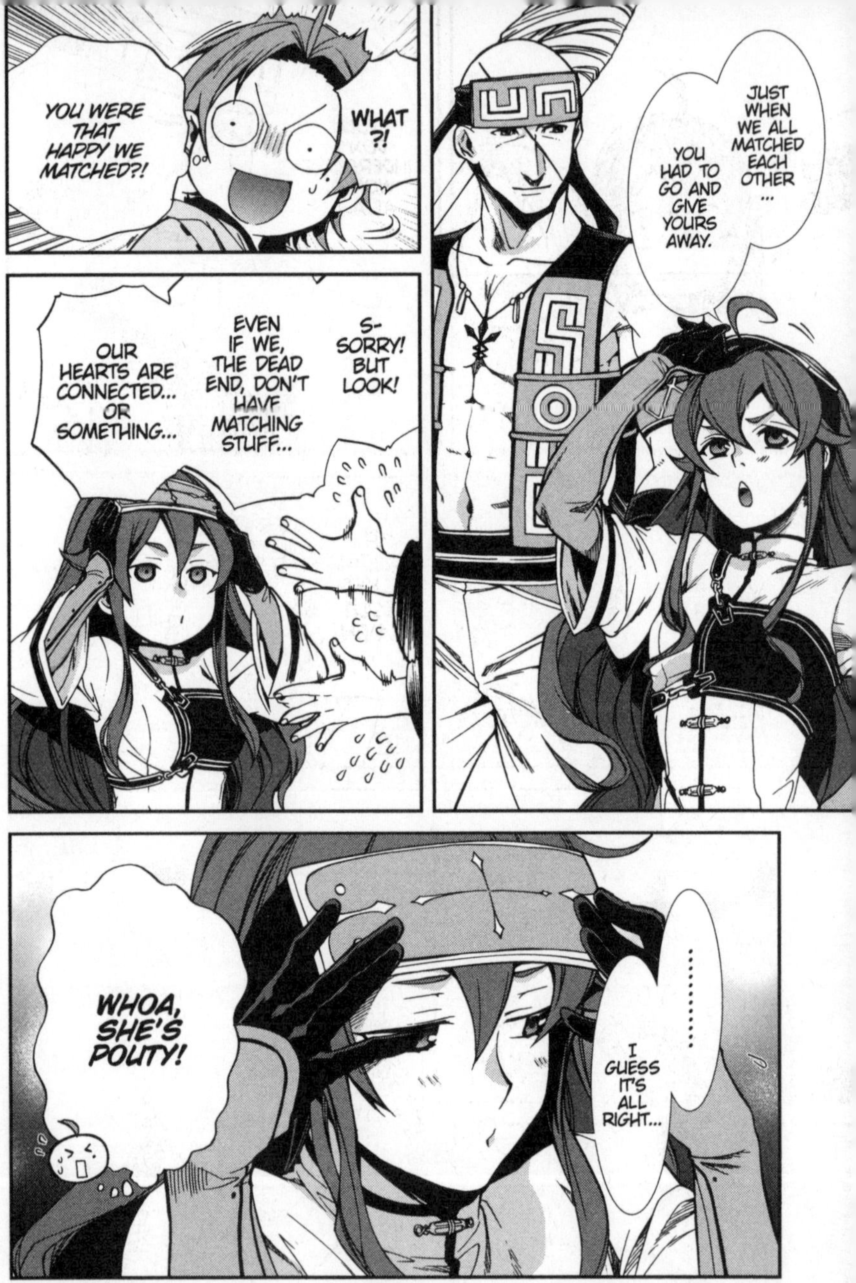
JUST WHEN WE ALL MATCHED EACH OTHER ...
YOU HAD TO GO AND GIVE YOURS AWAY.
WHAT ?!
YOU WERE THAT HAPPY WE MATCHED?!
S- SORRY! BUT LOOK!
EVEN IF WE, THE DEAD END, DON'T HAVE MATCHING STUFF...
OUR HEARTS ARE CONNECTED... OR SOMETHING...
......
I GUESS IT'S ALL RIGHT...
WHOA, SHE'S POUTY!

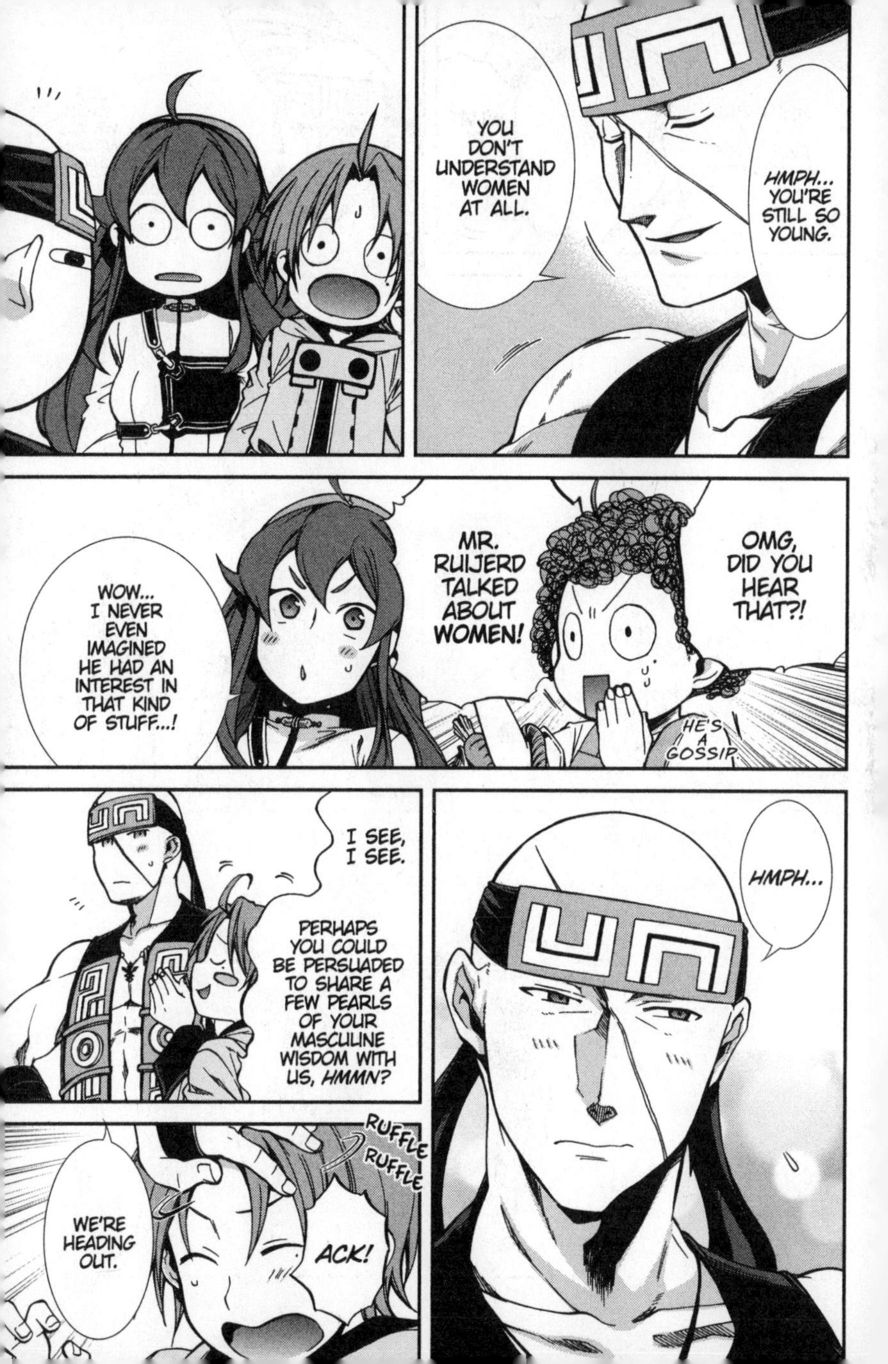
HMPH... YOU'RE STILL SO YOUNG.
YOU DON'T UNDERSTAND WOMEN AT ALL.
OMG, DID YOU HEAR THAT?!
MR. RUIJERD TALKED ABOUT WOMEN!
HE'S A GOSSIP.
WOW... I NEVER EVEN IMAGINED HE HAD AN INTEREST IN THAT KIND OF STUFF...!
HMPH...
I SEE, I SEE.
PERHAPS YOU COULD BE PERSUADED TO SHARE A FEW PEARLS OF YOUR MASCULINE WISDOM WITH US, *HMMN?*
RUFFLE RUFFLE
ACK!
WE'RE HEADING OUT.

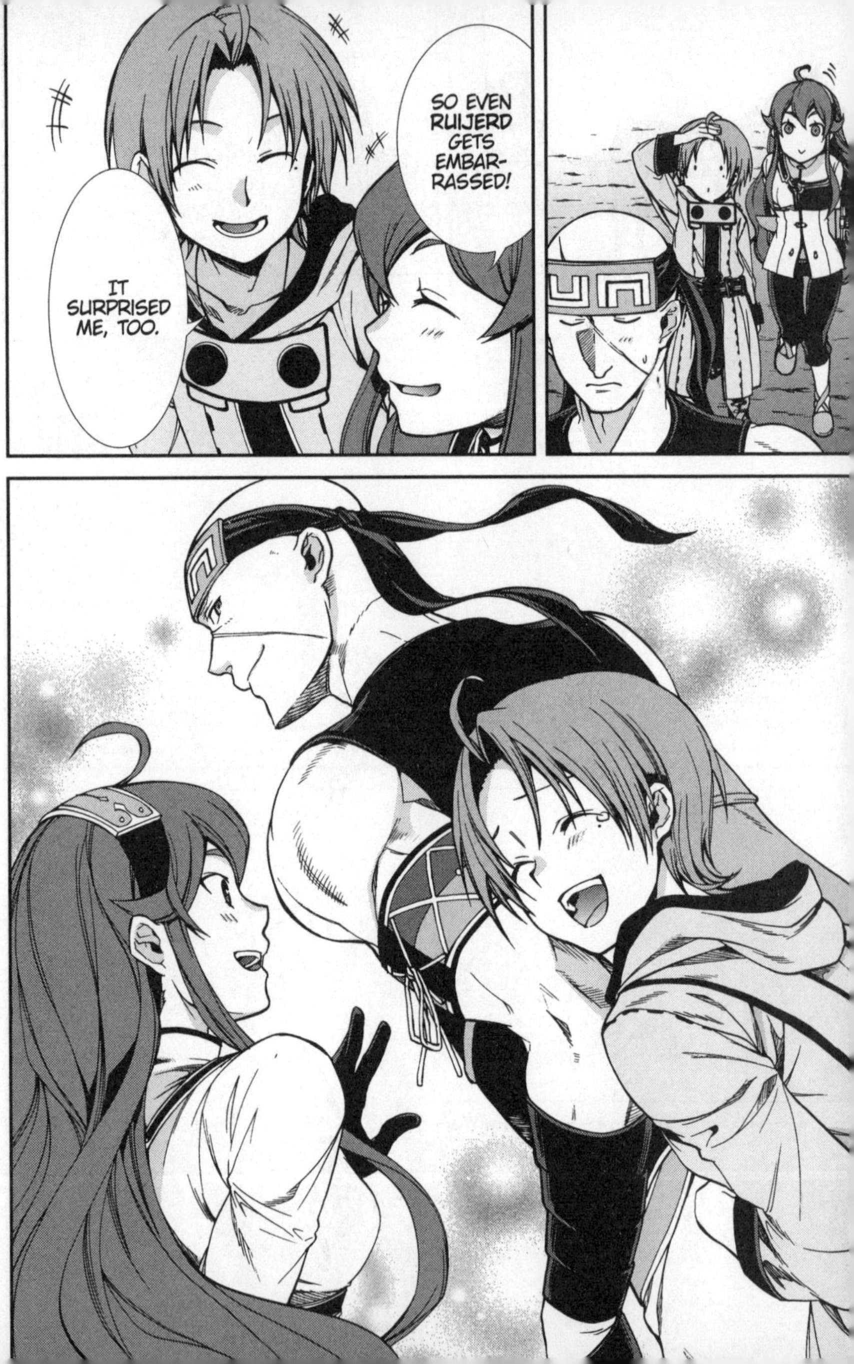
SO EVEN RUIJERD GETS EMBARRASSED!
IT SURPRISED ME, TOO.

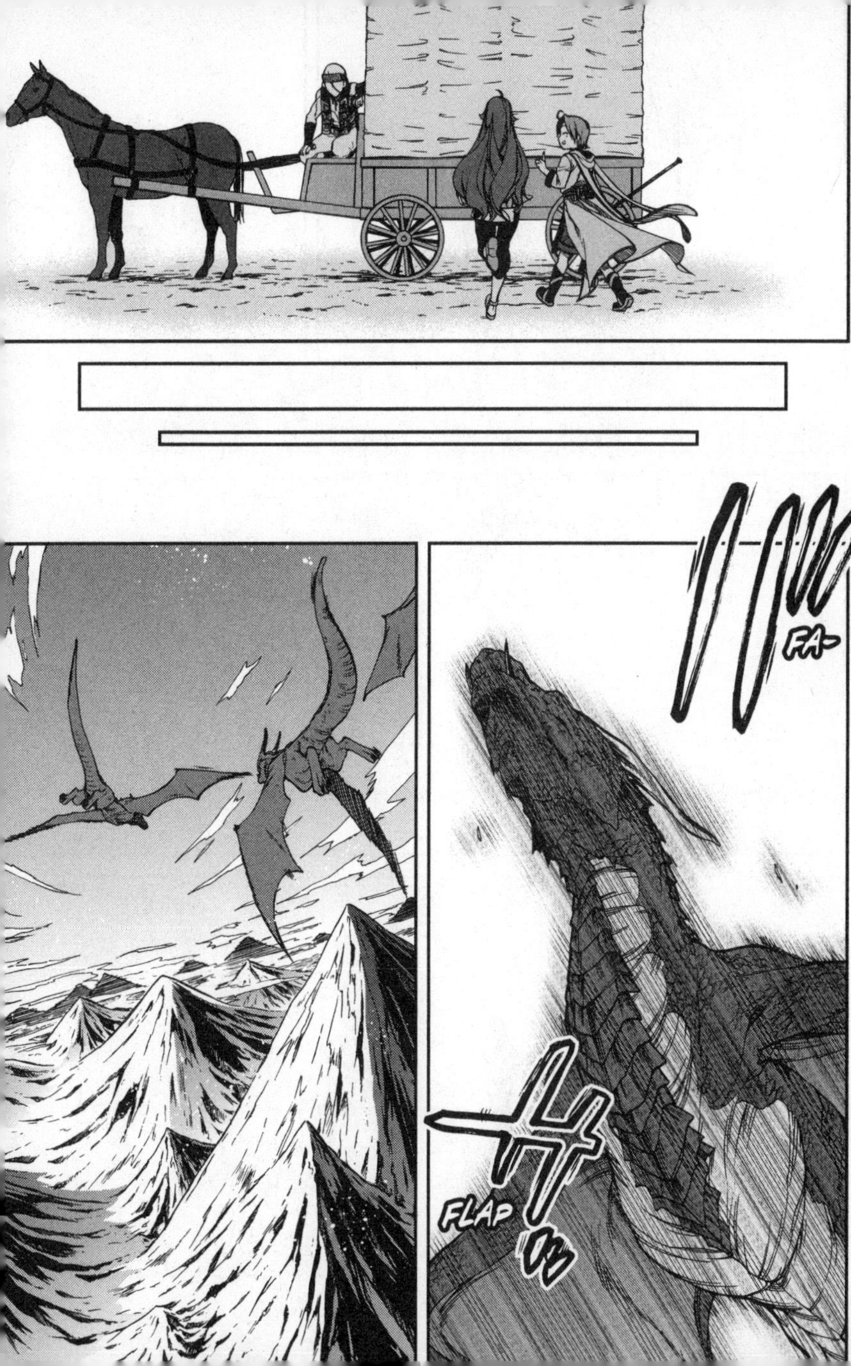
FA-
FLAP

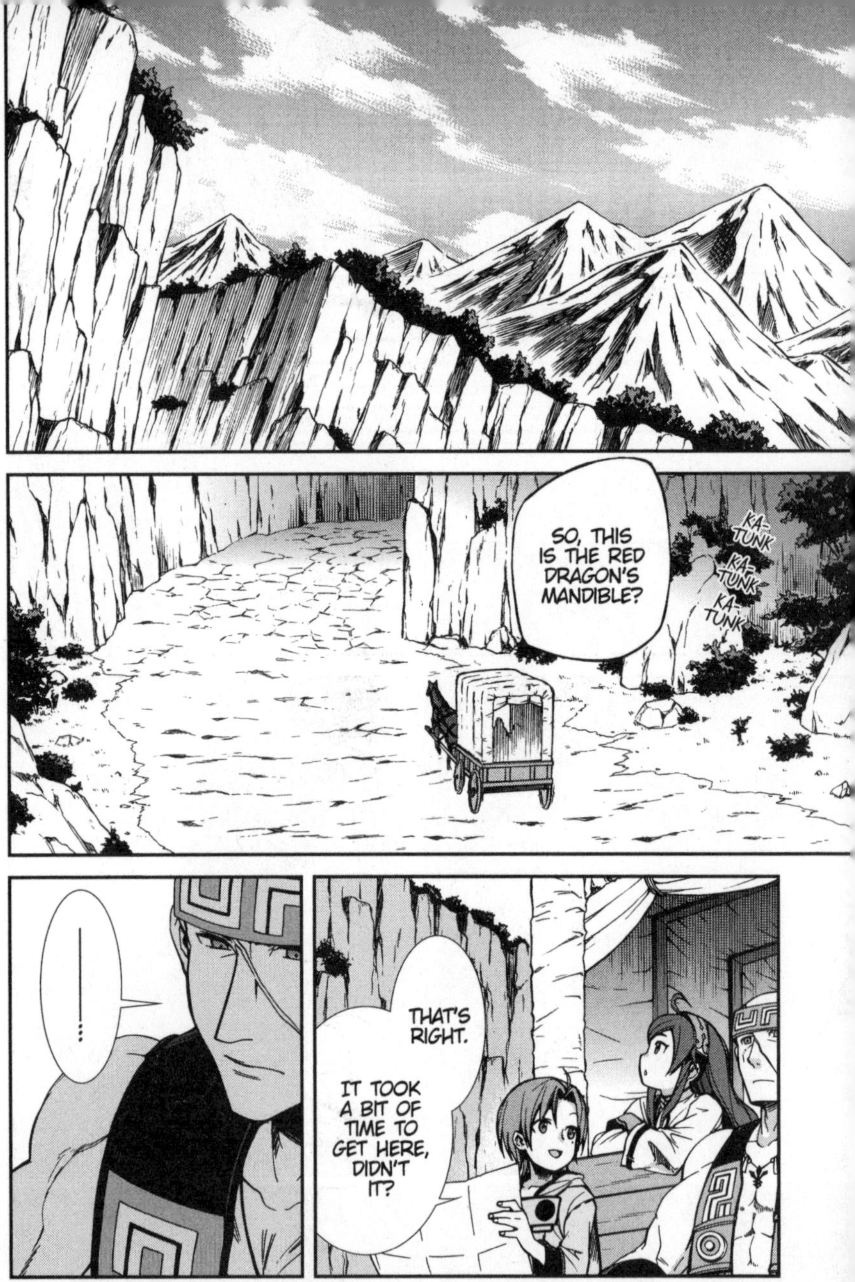
KA-TUNK
KA-TUNK
KA-TUNK
SO, THIS IS THE RED DRAGON'S MANDIBLE?
THAT'S RIGHT.
IT TOOK A BIT OF TIME TO GET HERE, DIDN'T IT?
—......

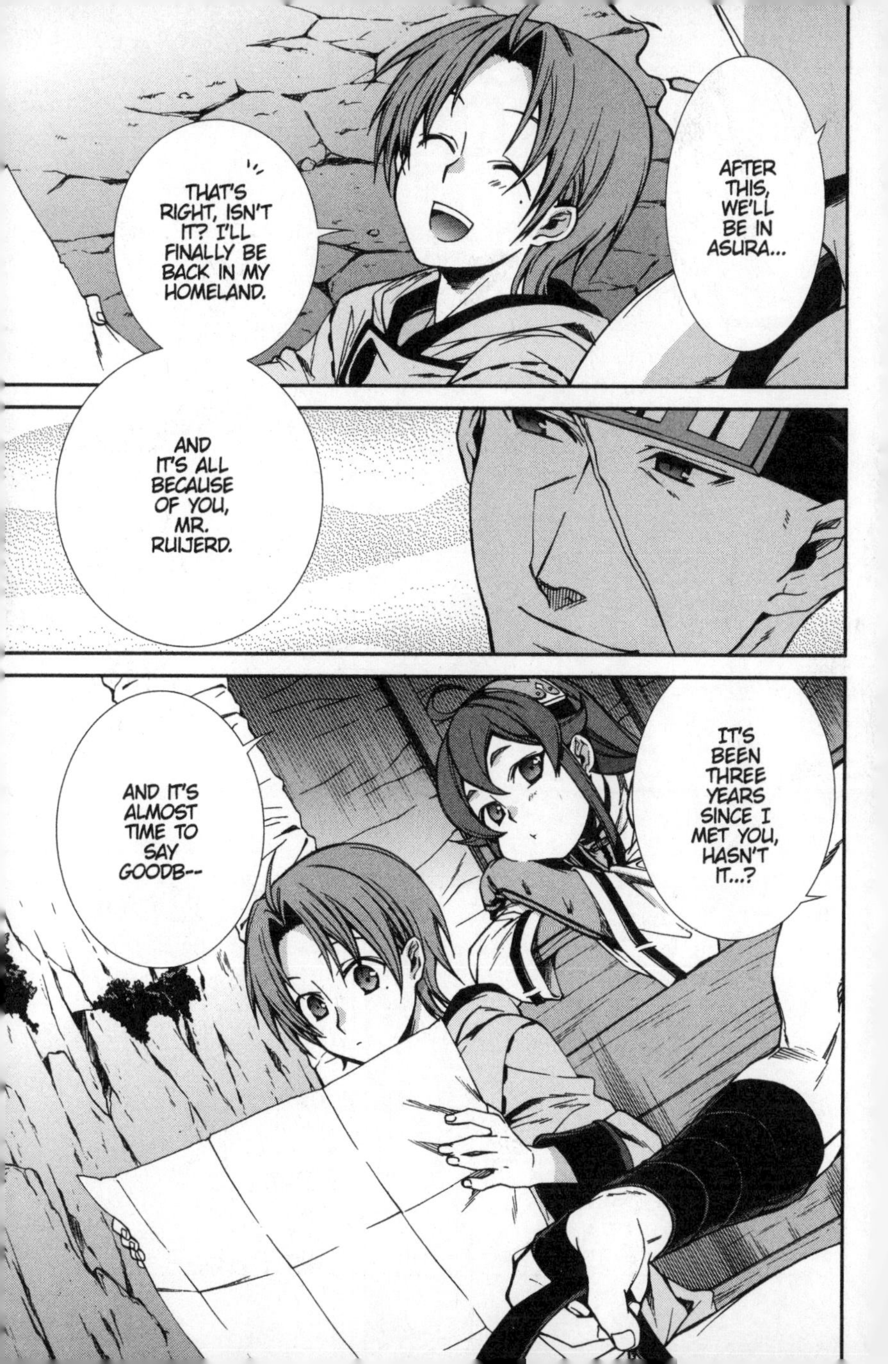
AFTER THIS, WE'LL BE IN ASURA...
THAT'S RIGHT, ISN'T IT? I'LL FINALLY BE BACK IN MY HOMELAND.
AND IT'S ALL BECAUSE OF YOU, MR. RUIJERD.
IT'S BEEN THREE YEARS SINCE I MET YOU, HASN'T IT...?
AND IT'S ALMOST TIME TO SAY GOODB--

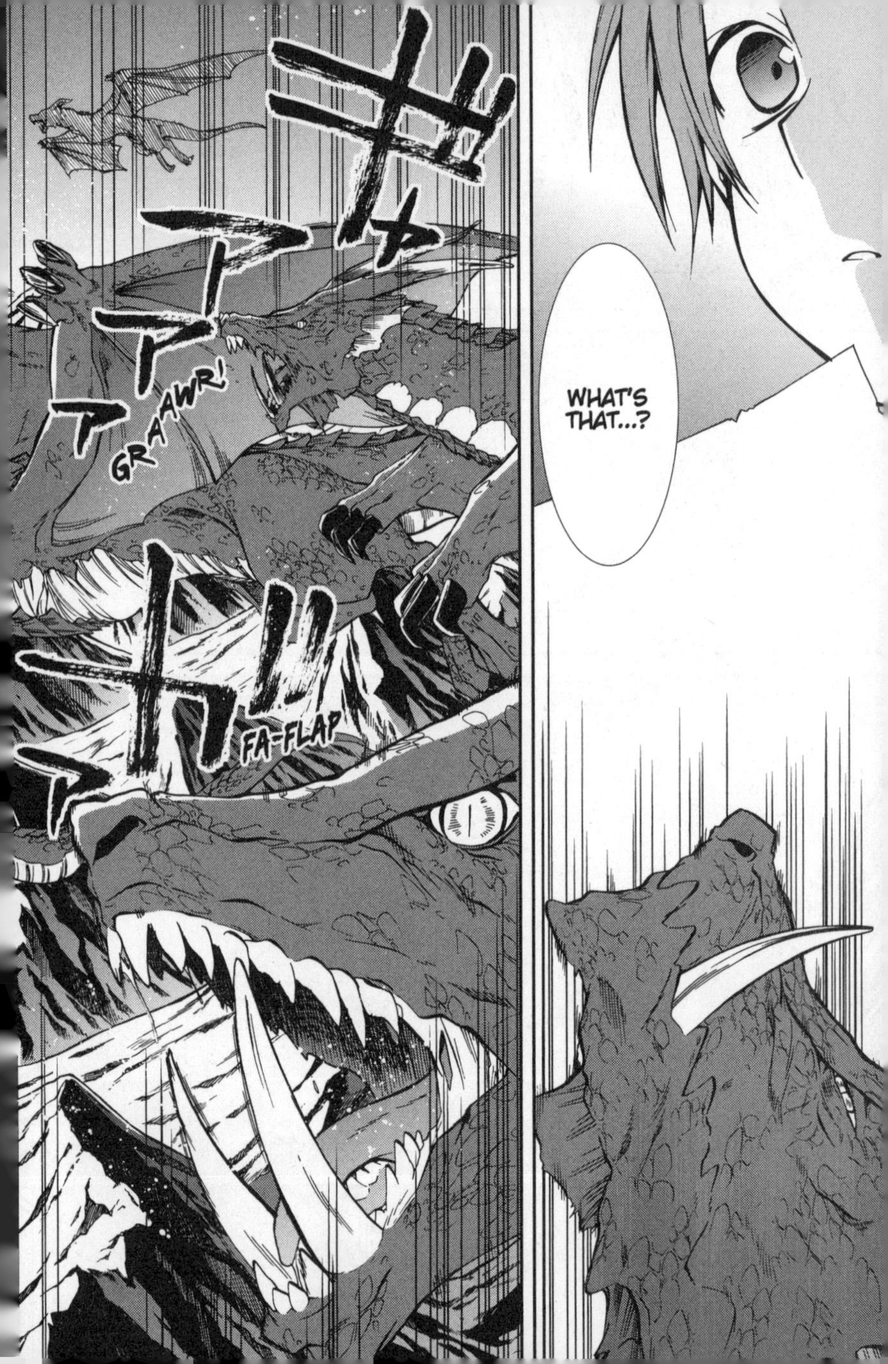
WHAT'S THAT...?
GRAAWR!
FA-FLAP

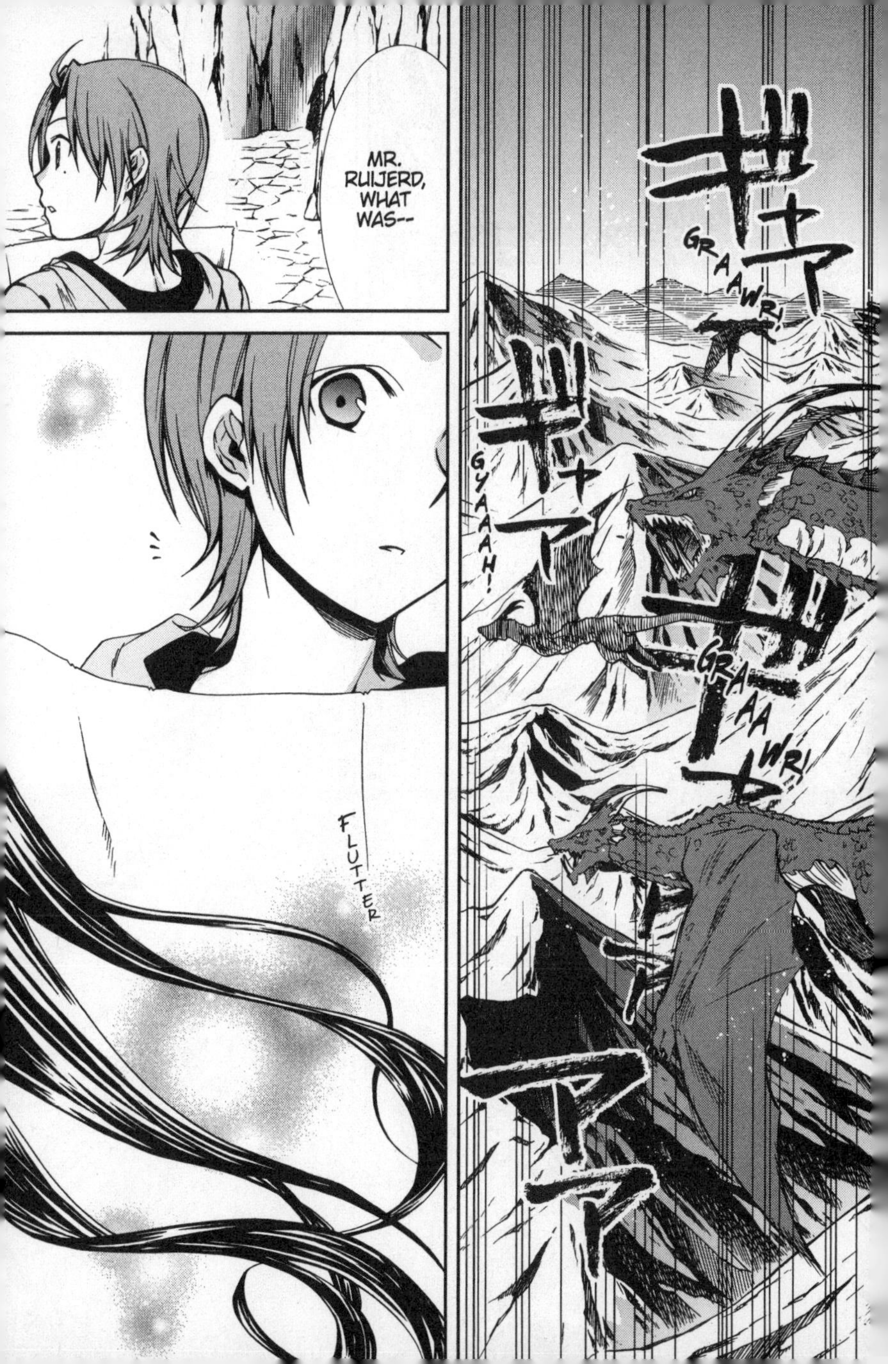
GRAAWR!
GYAAAH!
GRAAAAWR!
MR. RUIJERD, WHAT WAS--
FLUTTER

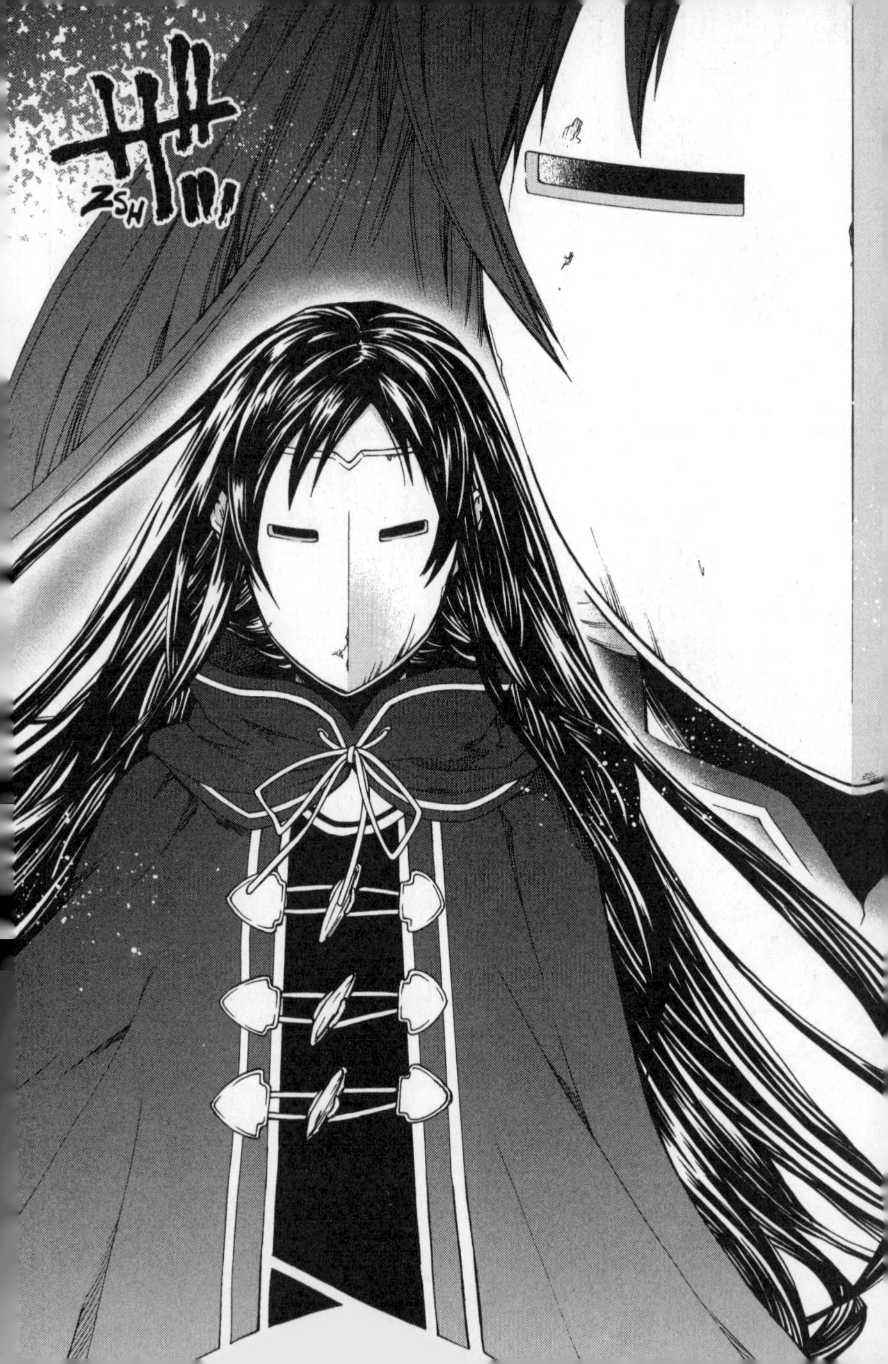
ZSH

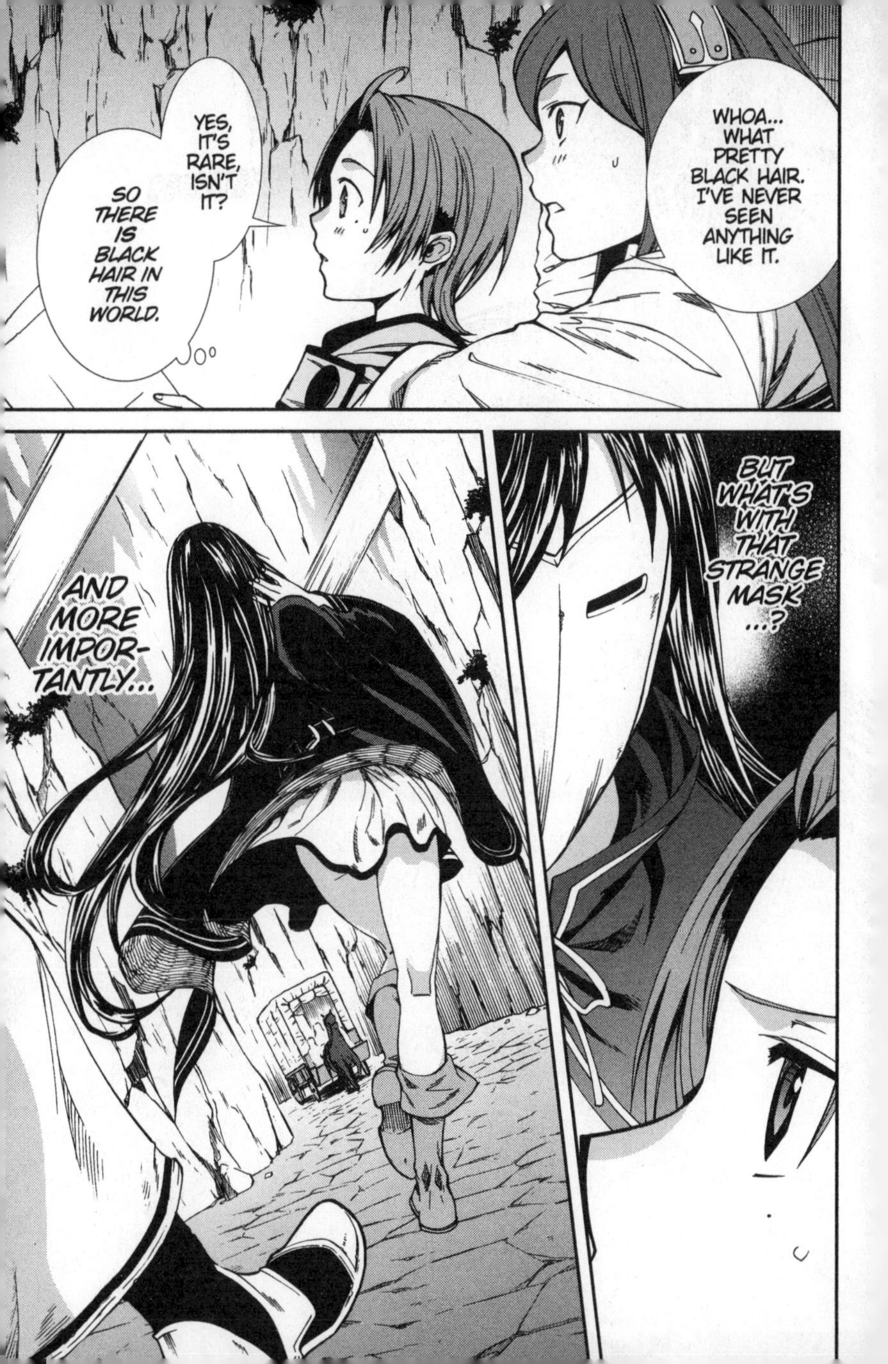
WHOA... WHAT PRETTY BLACK HAIR. I'VE NEVER SEEN ANYTHING LIKE IT.
YES, IT'S RARE, ISN'T IT?
SO THERE IS BLACK HAIR IN THIS WORLD.
BUT WHAT'S WITH THAT STRANGE MASK ...?
AND MORE IMPOR-TANTLY...

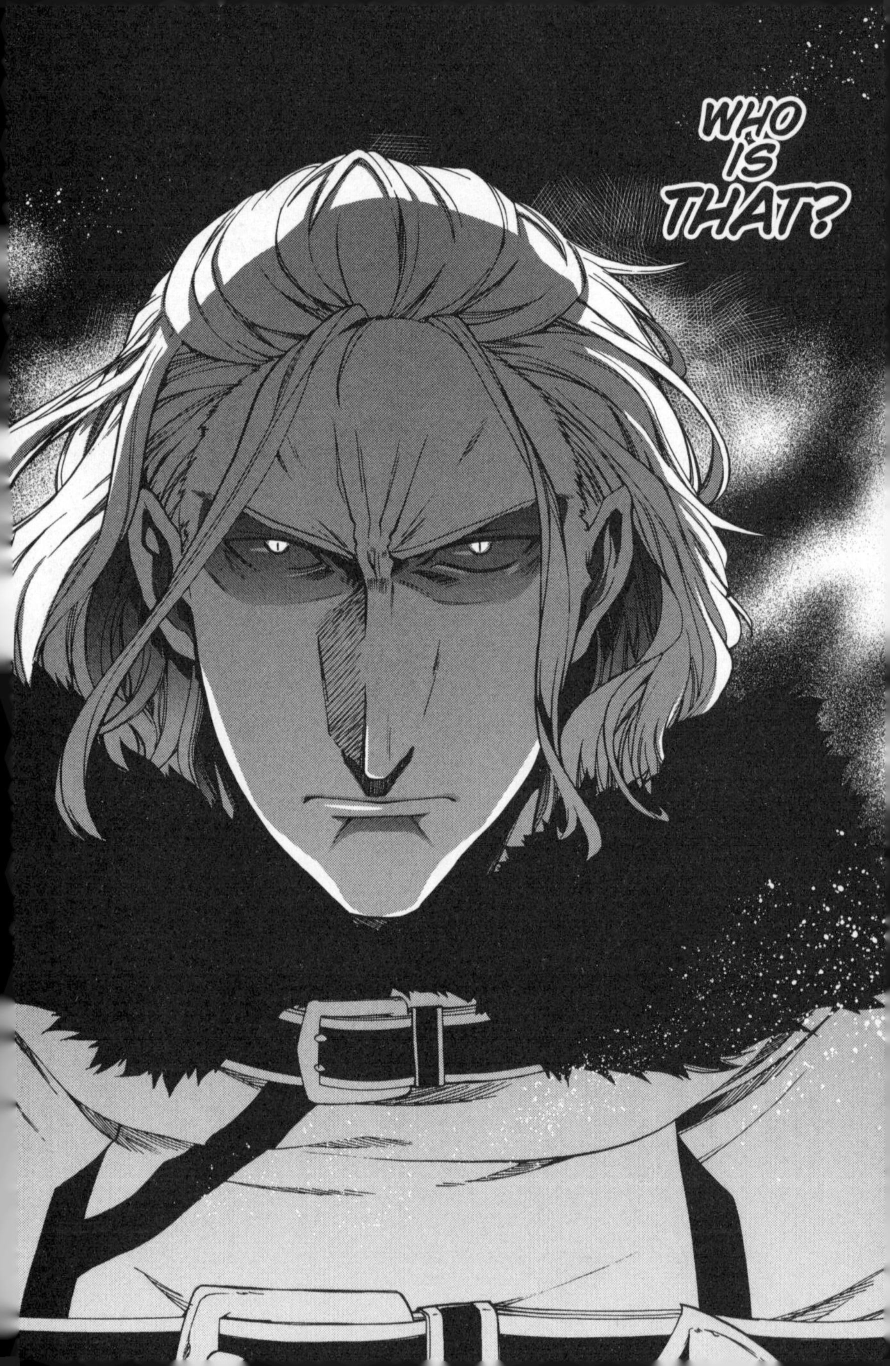
WHO IS THAT?

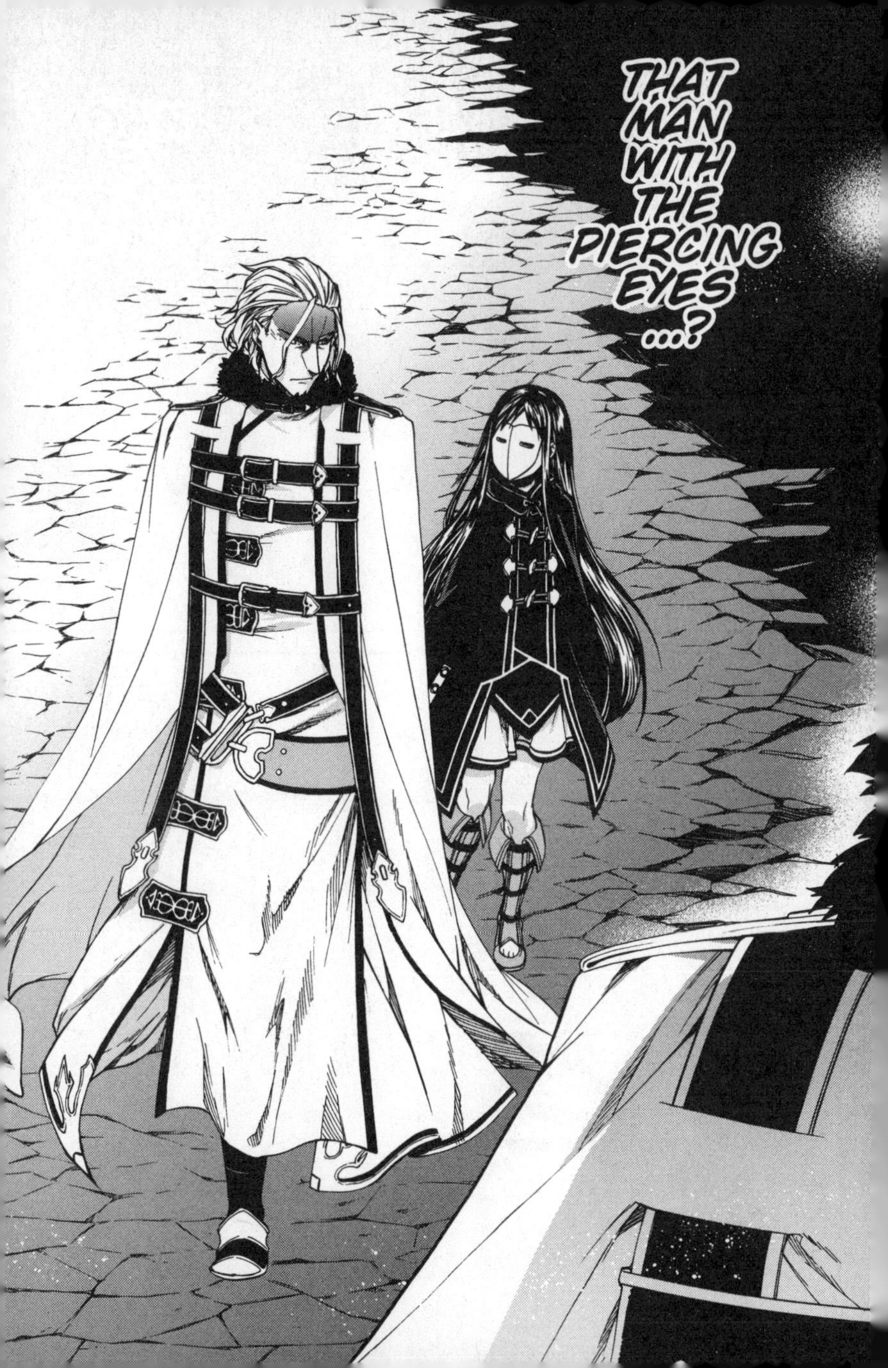
THAT MAN WITH THE PIERCING EYES ...?

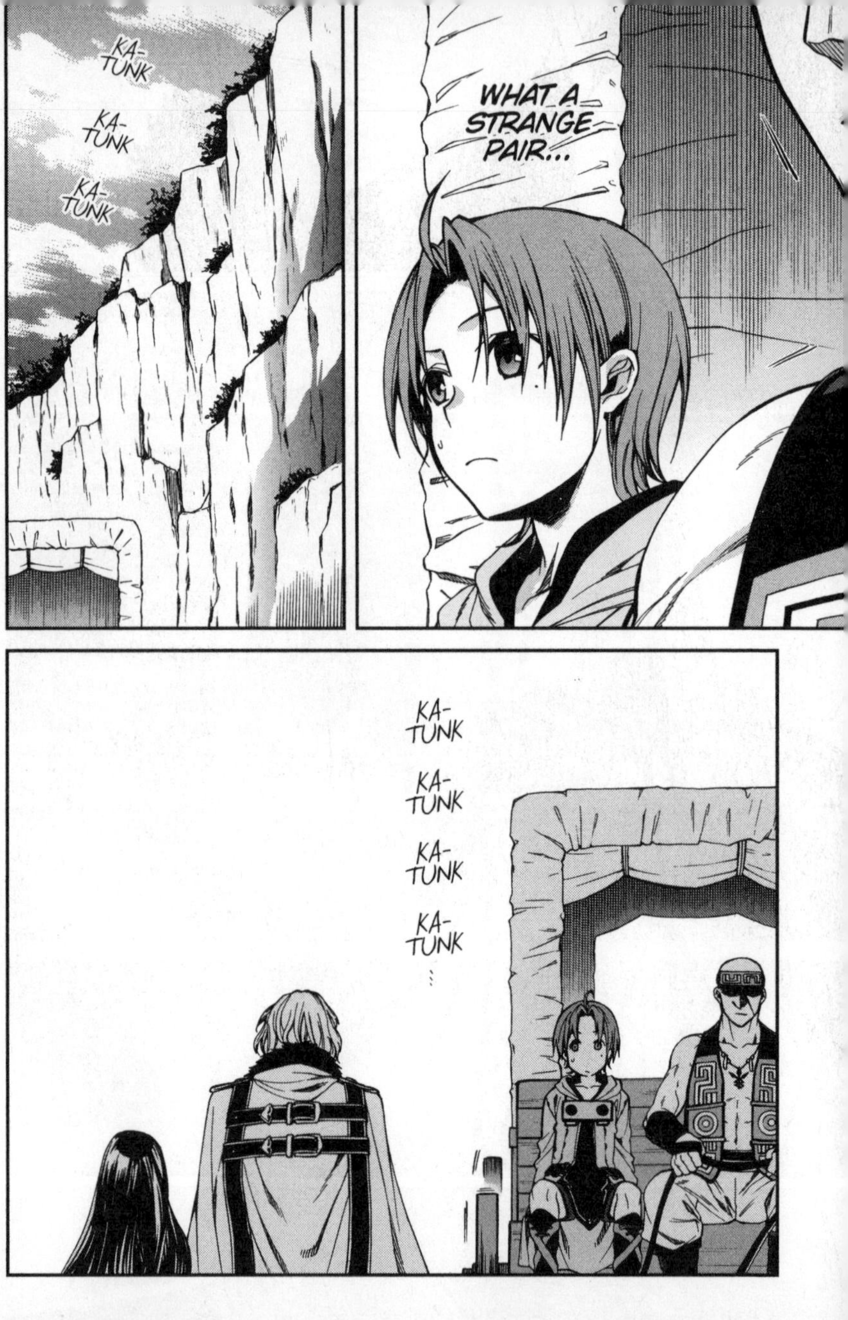
WHAT A STRANGE PAIR...
KA-TUNK
KA-TUNK
KA-TUNK
KA-TUNK
KA-TUNK
KA-TUNK
KA-TUNK
...

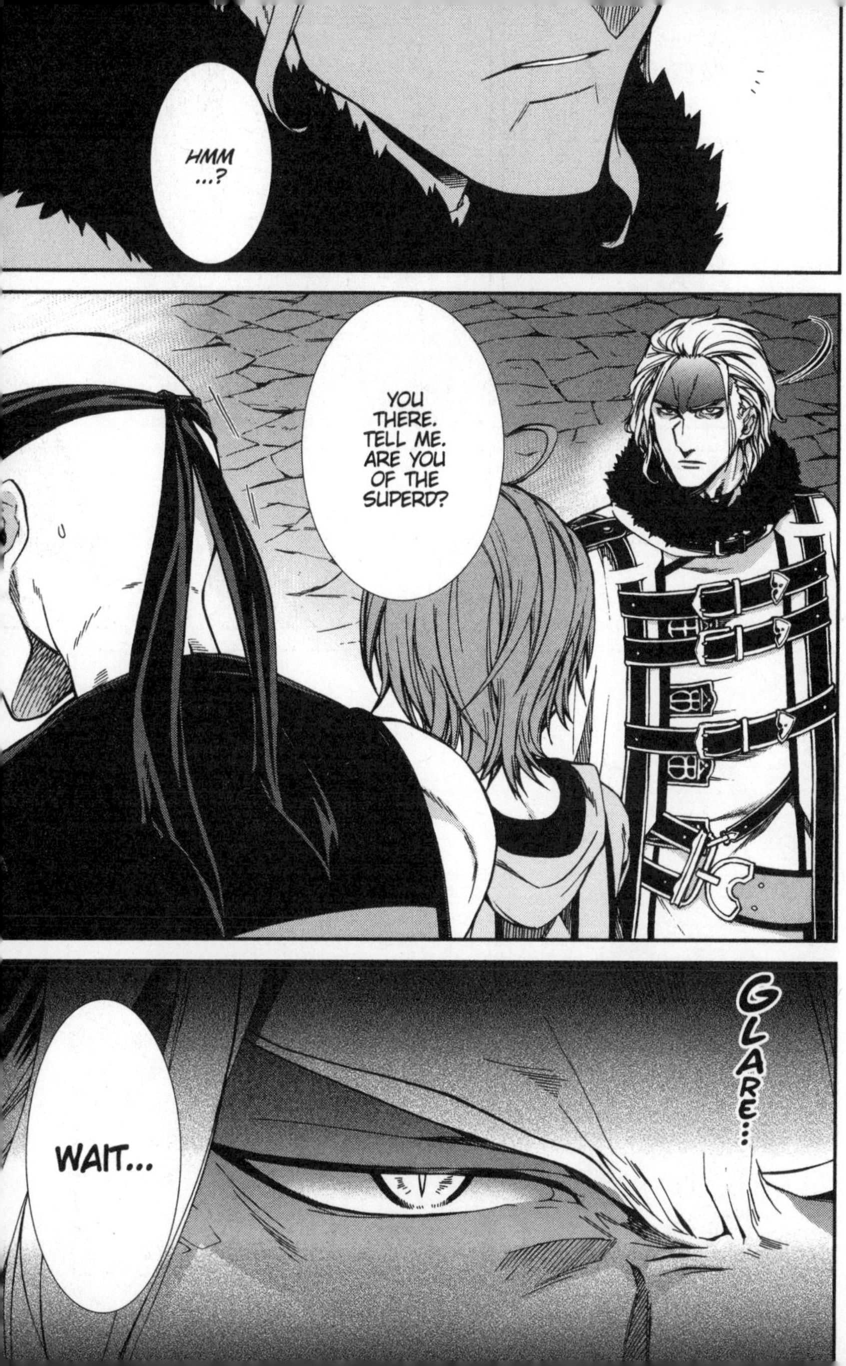
HMM ...?
YOU THERE. TELL ME. ARE YOU OF THE SUPERD?
GLARE...
WAIT...

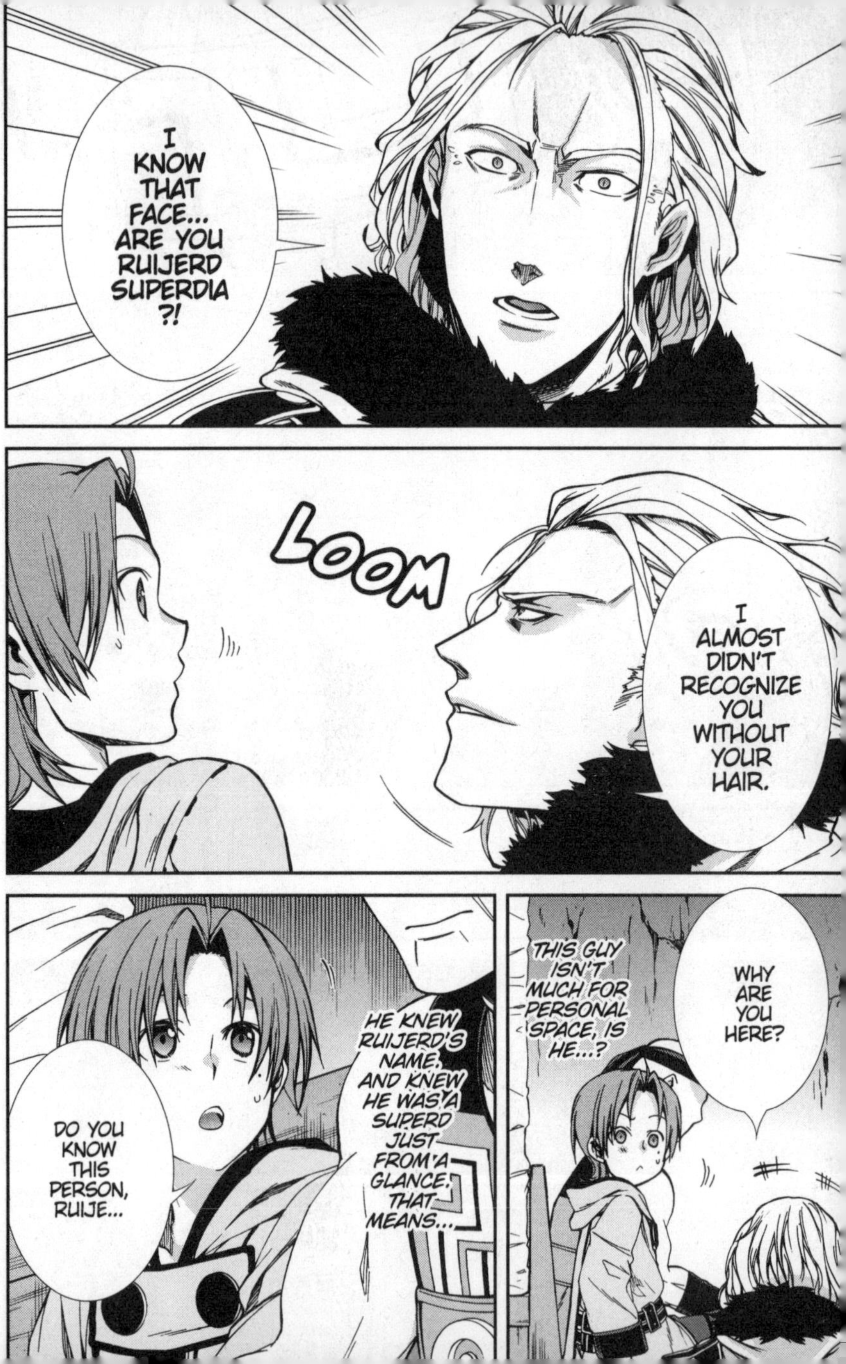
I KNOW THAT FACE... ARE YOU RUIJERD SUPERDIA?!
LOOM
I ALMOST DIDN'T RECOGNIZE YOU WITHOUT YOUR HAIR.
WHY ARE YOU HERE?
THIS GUY ISN'T MUCH FOR PERSONAL SPACE, IS HE...?
HE KNEW RUIJERD'S NAME. AND KNEW HE WAS A SUPERD JUST FROM A GLANCE. THAT MEANS...
DO YOU KNOW THIS PERSON, RUIJE...

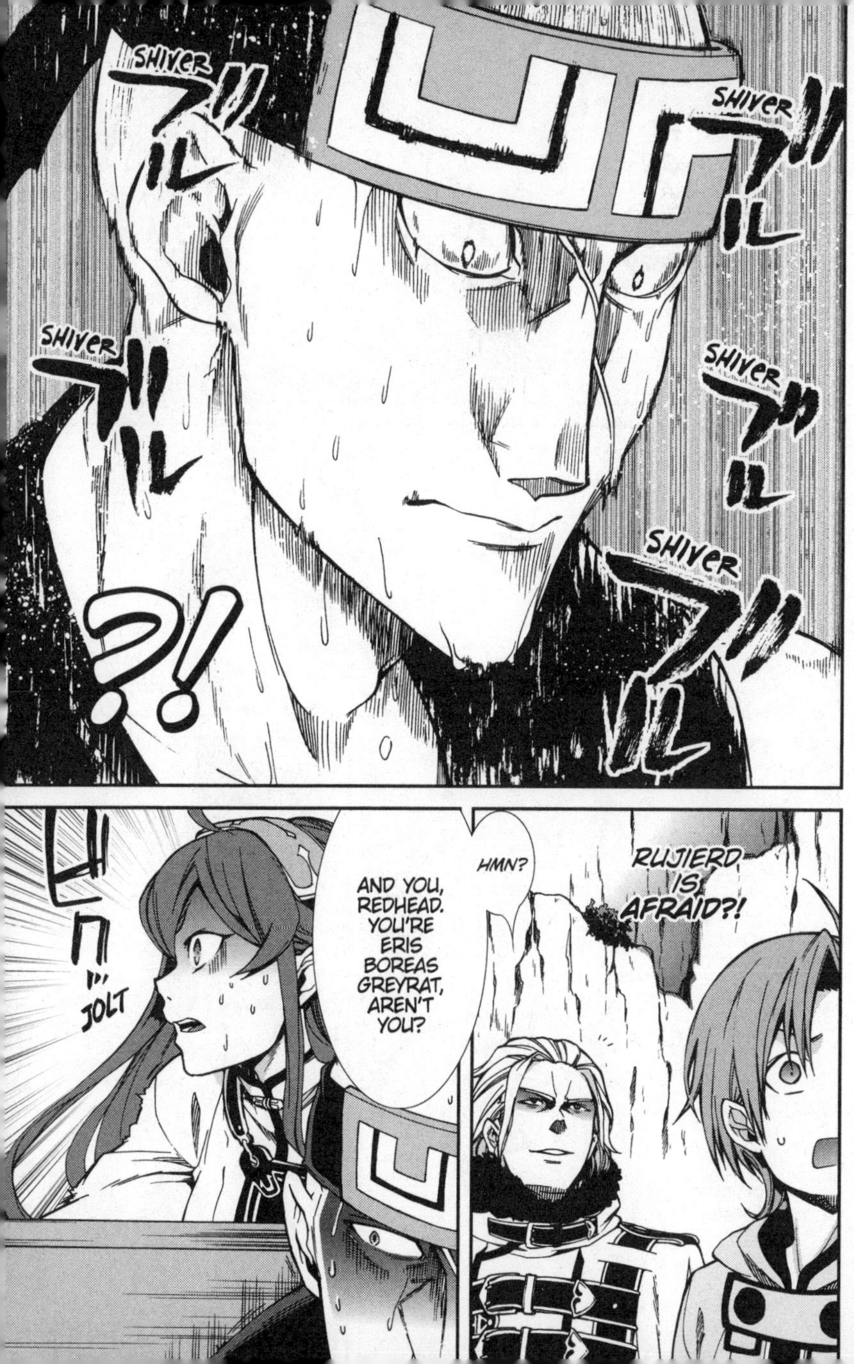
SHIVER
SHIVER
SHIVER
SHIVER
SHIVER
?!
RUJIERD IS AFRAID?!
HMN?
AND YOU, REDHEAD. YOU'RE ERIS BOREAS GREYRAT, AREN'T YOU?
JOLT

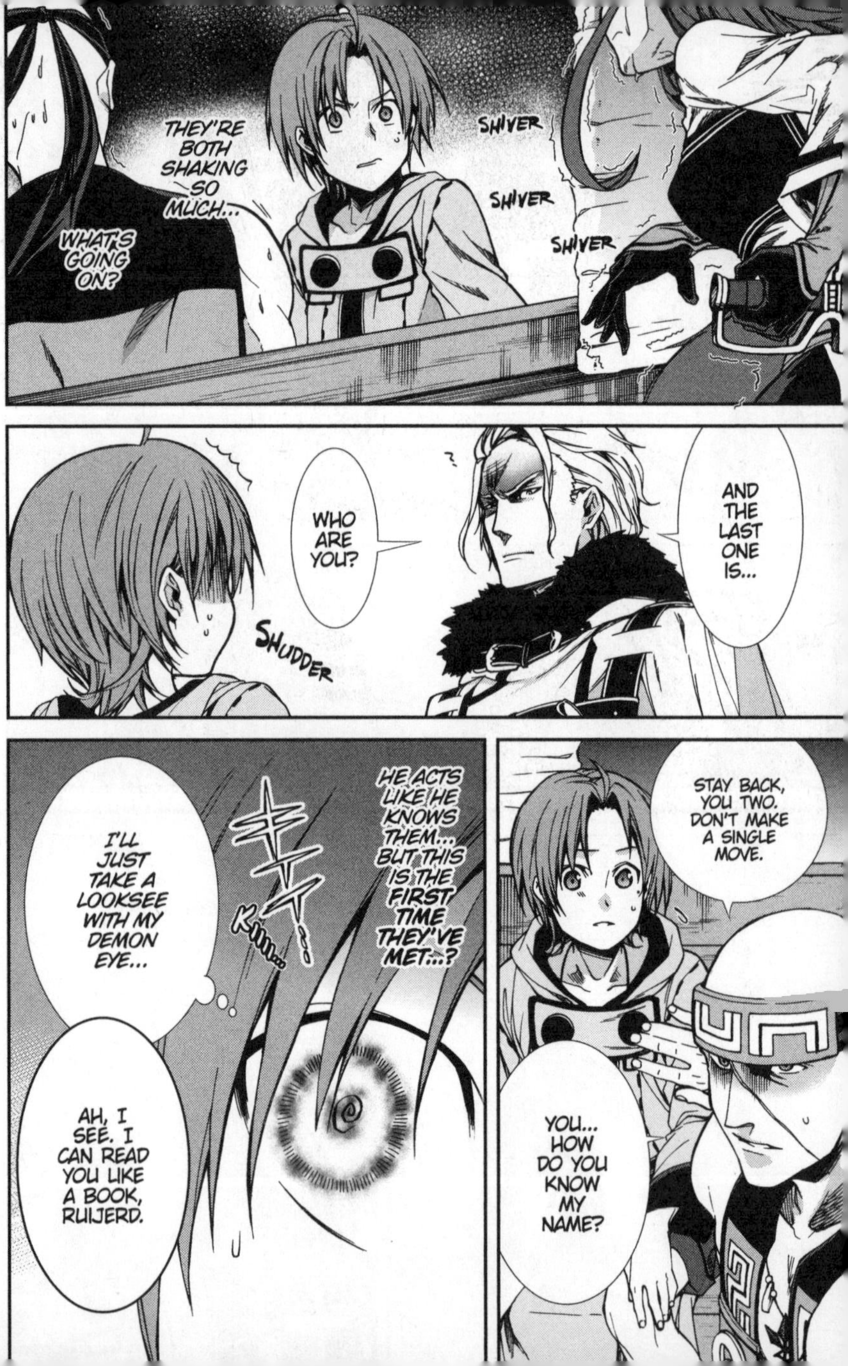
SHIVER
SHIVER
SHIVER
THEY'RE BOTH SHAKING SO MUCH...
WHAT'S GOING ON?
AND THE LAST ONE IS...
WHO ARE YOU?
SHUDDER
STAY BACK, YOU TWO. DON'T MAKE A SINGLE MOVE.
YOU... HOW DO YOU KNOW MY NAME?
HE ACTS LIKE HE KNOWS THEM... BUT THIS IS THE FIRST TIME THEY'VE MET...?
I'LL JUST TAKE A LOOKSEE WITH MY DEMON EYE...
AH, I SEE. I CAN READ YOU LIKE A BOOK, RUIJERD.

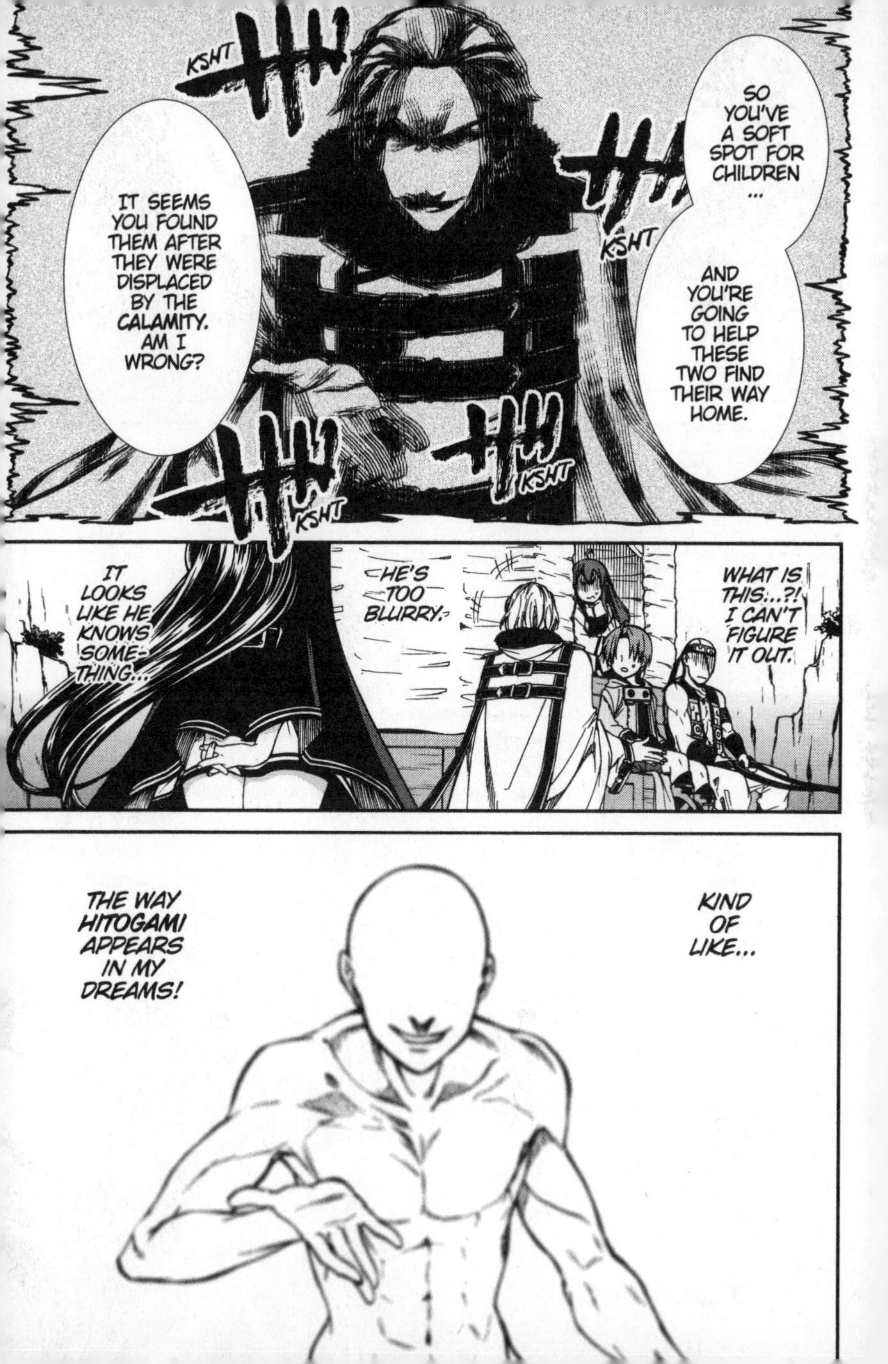
KSHT
SO YOU'VE A SOFT SPOT FOR CHILDREN ...
AND YOU'RE GOING TO HELP THESE TWO FIND THEIR WAY HOME.
KSHT
IT SEEMS YOU FOUND THEM AFTER THEY WERE DISPLACED BY THE CALAMITY. AM I WRONG?
KSHT
KSHT
WHAT IS THIS...?! I CAN'T FIGURE IT OUT.
HE'S TOO BLURRY.
IT LOOKS LIKE HE KNOWS SOME-THING...
KIND OF LIKE...
THE WAY HITOGAMI APPEARS IN MY DREAMS!

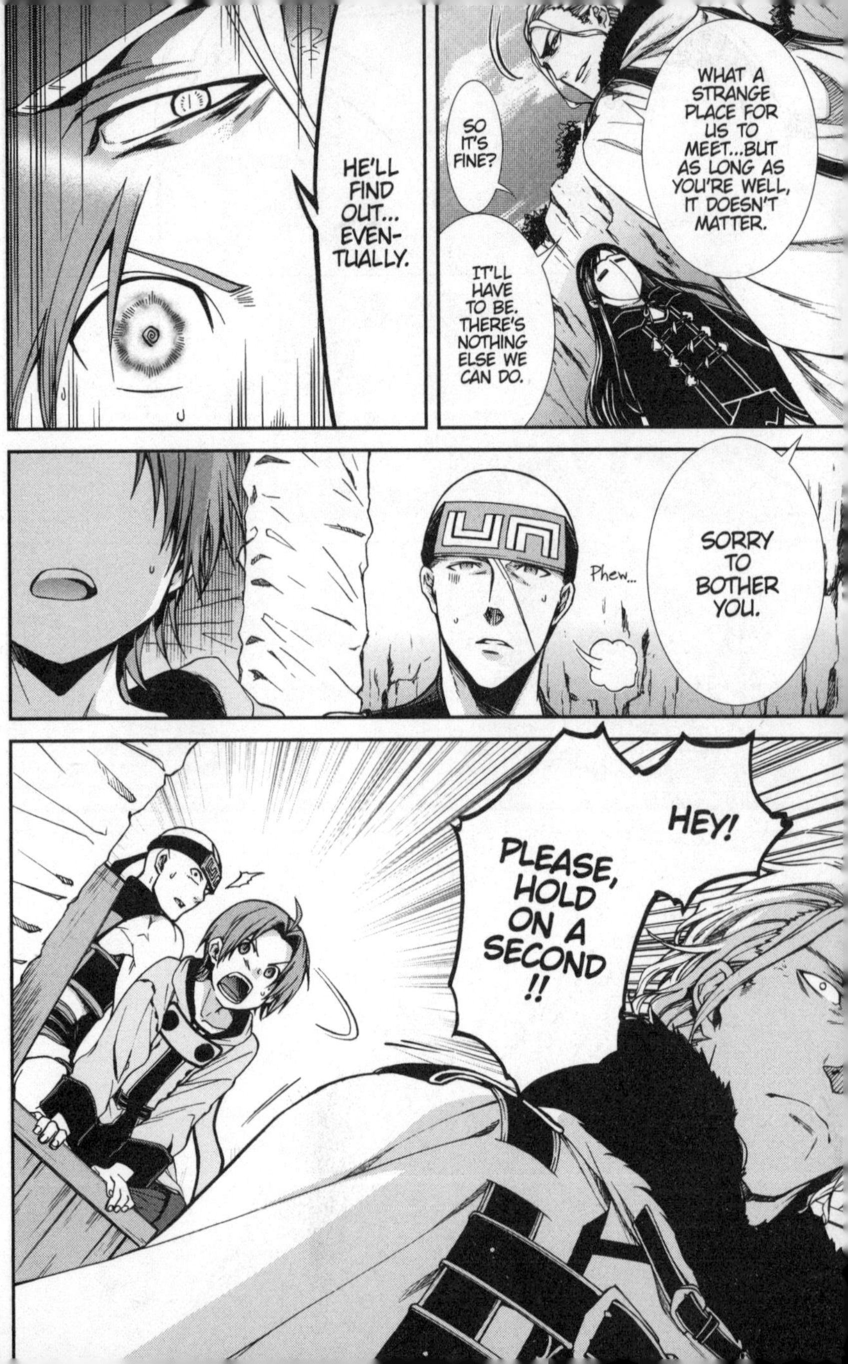
WHAT A STRANGE PLACE FOR US TO MEET...BUT AS LONG AS YOU'RE WELL, IT DOESN'T MATTER.
SO IT'S FINE?
IT'LL HAVE TO BE. THERE'S NOTHING ELSE WE CAN DO.
HE'LL FIND OUT... EVENTUALLY.
SORRY TO BOTHER YOU.
Phew...
HEY!
PLEASE, HOLD ON A SECOND!!

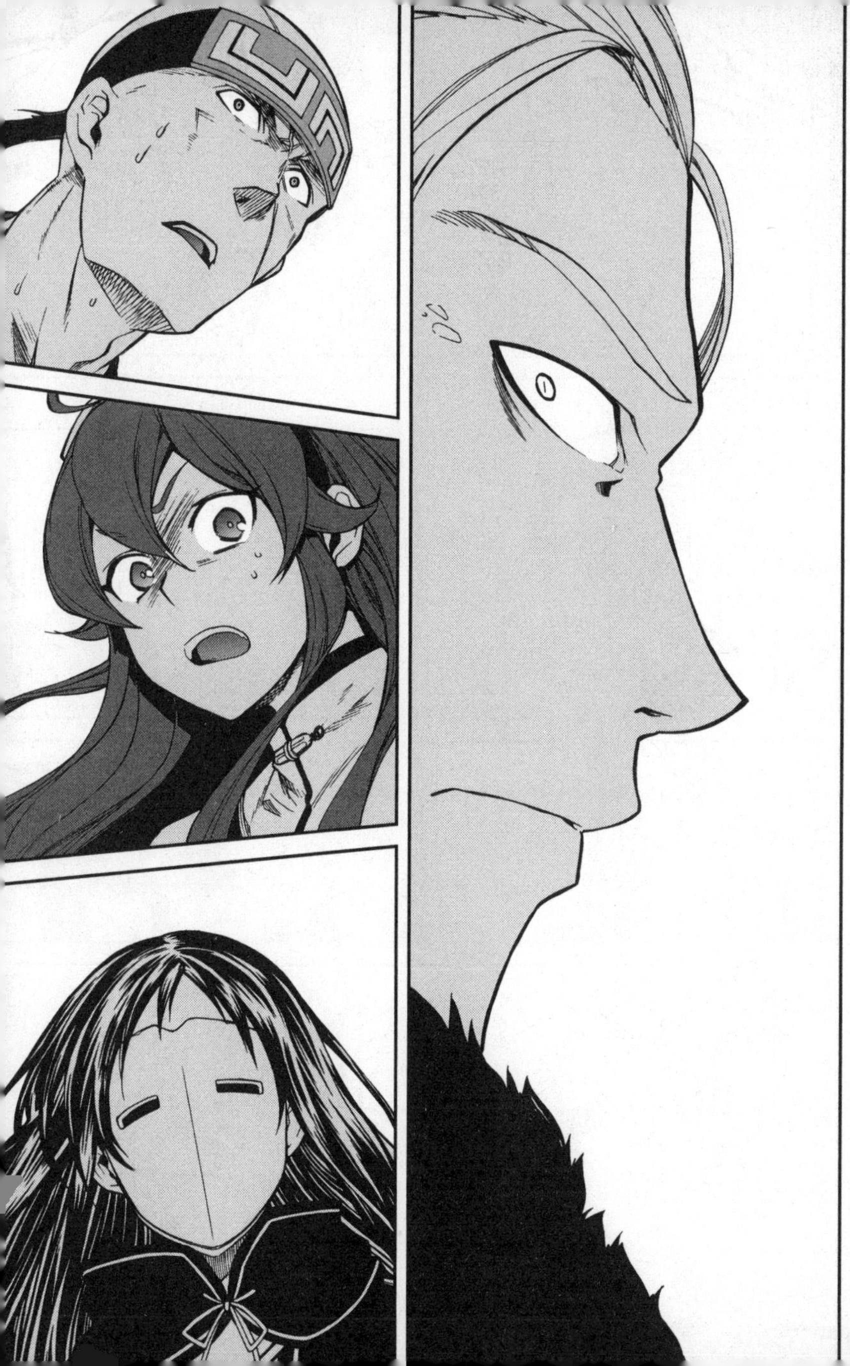

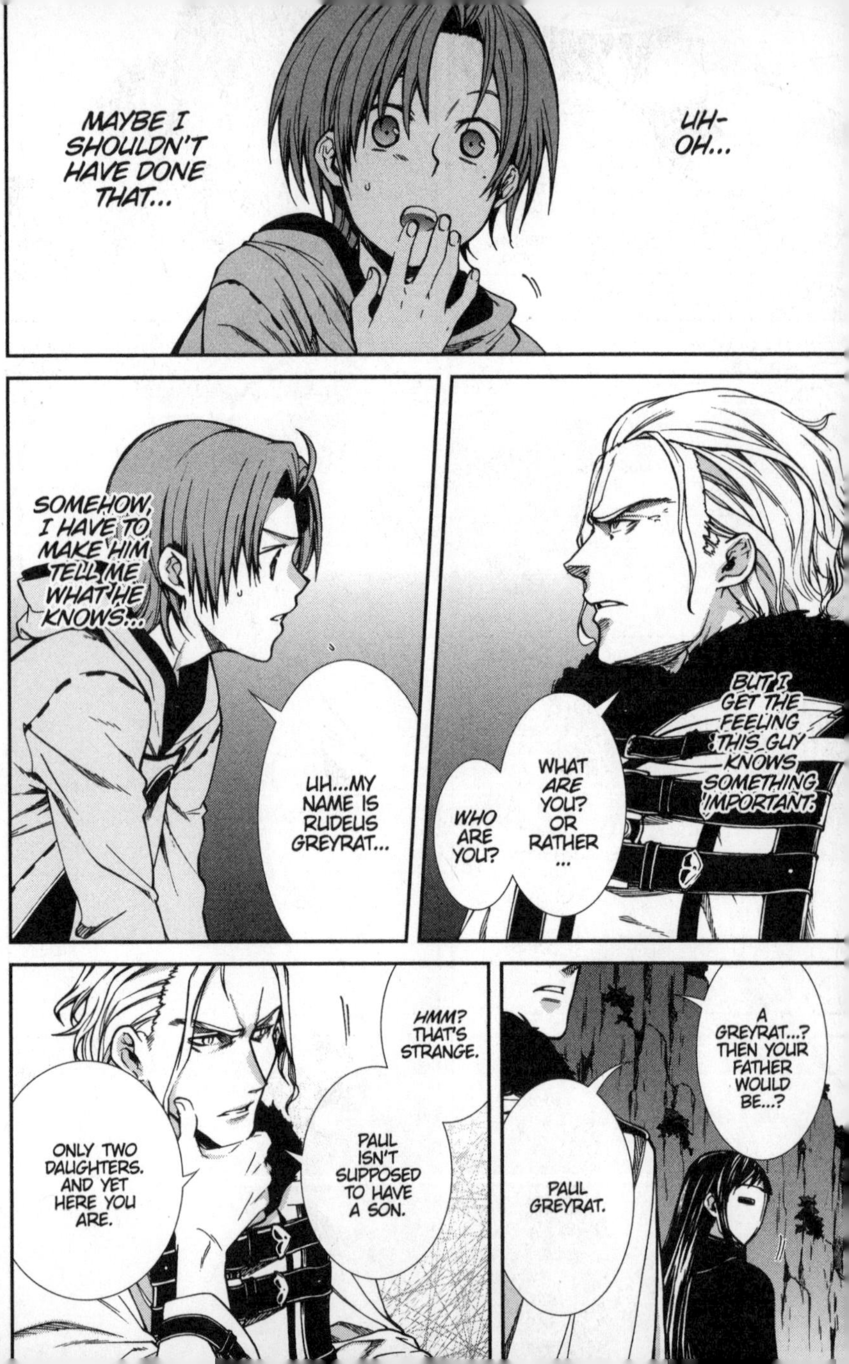
UH-OH...
MAYBE I SHOULDN'T HAVE DONE THAT...
BUT I GET THE FEELING THIS GUY KNOWS SOMETHING IMPORTANT.
WHAT ARE YOU? OR RATHER...
WHO ARE YOU?
UH...MY NAME IS RUDEUS GREYRAT...
SOMEHOW, I HAVE TO MAKE HIM TELL ME WHAT HE KNOWS...
A GREYRAT...? THEN YOUR FATHER WOULD BE...?
PAUL GREYRAT.
HMM? THAT'S STRANGE.
PAUL ISN'T SUPPOSED TO HAVE A SON.
ONLY TWO DAUGHTERS. AND YET HERE YOU ARE.

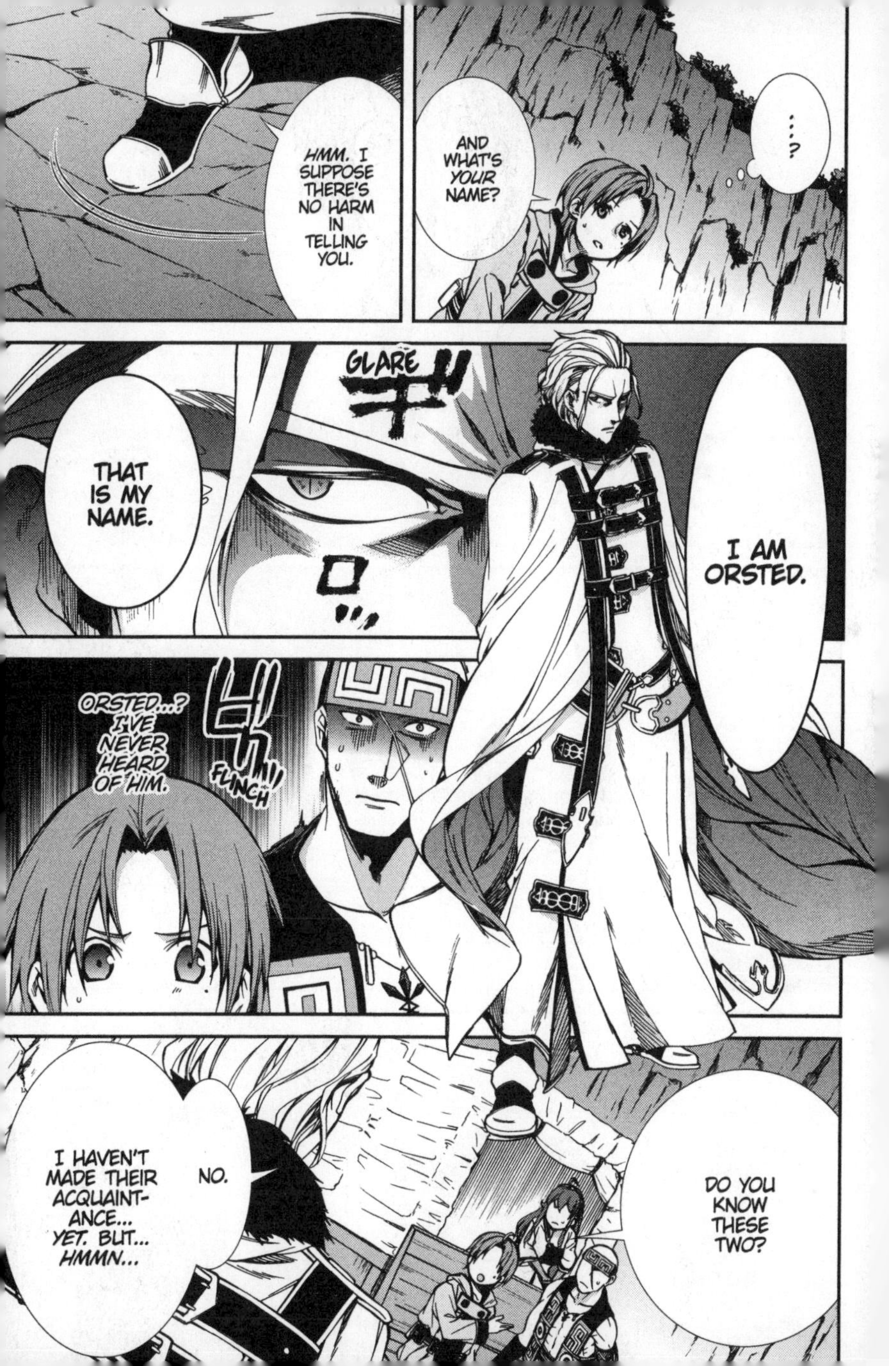
...?
AND WHAT'S YOUR NAME?
HMM. I SUPPOSE THERE'S NO HARM IN TELLING YOU.
I AM ORSTED.
GLARE
THAT IS MY NAME.
FLINCH
ORSTED...? I'VE NEVER HEARD OF HIM.
DO YOU KNOW THESE TWO?
NO.
I HAVEN'T MADE THEIR ACQUAINT-ANCE... YET. BUT... HMMN...

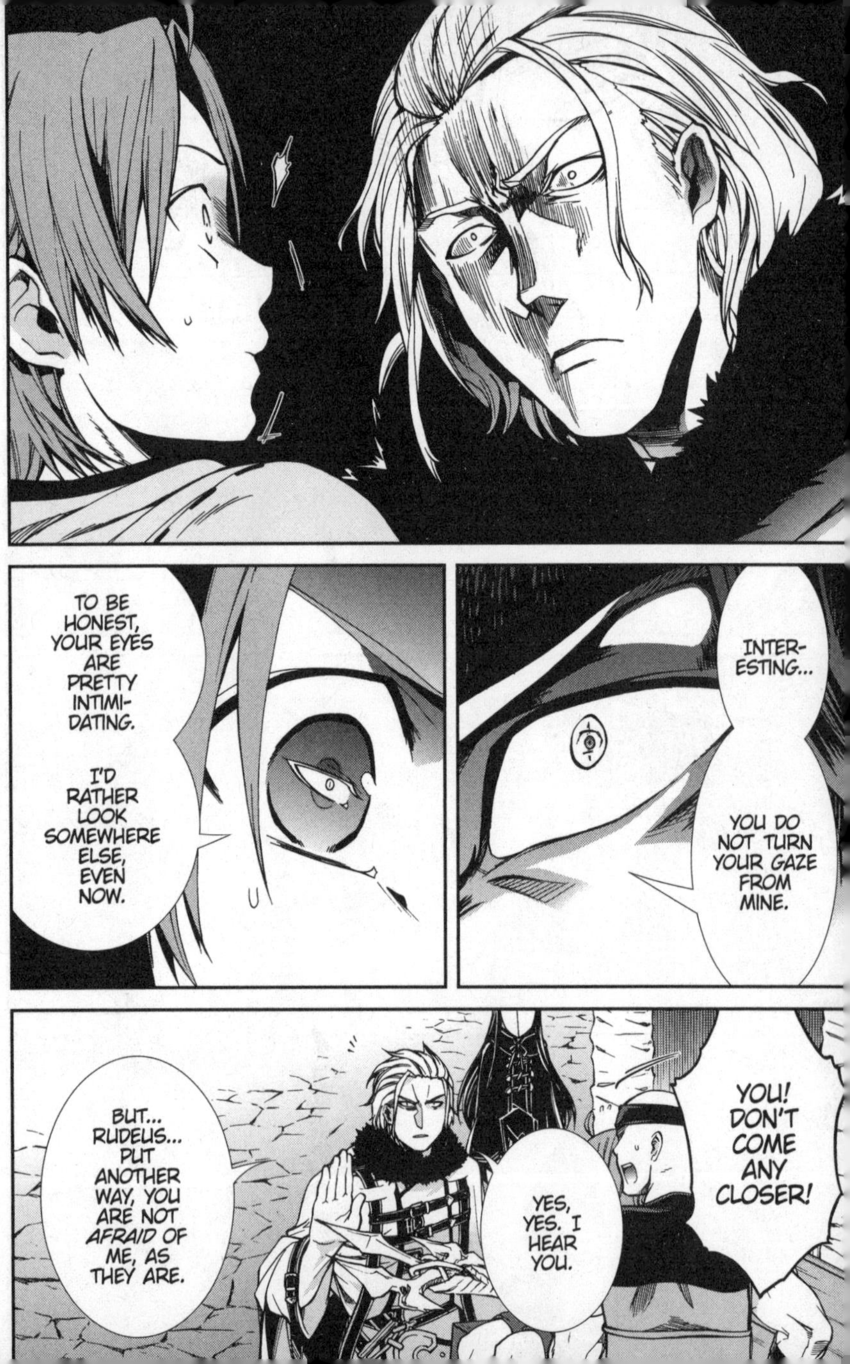
INTER-ESTING...
YOU DO NOT TURN YOUR GAZE FROM MINE.
TO BE HONEST, YOUR EYES ARE PRETTY INTIMI-DATING.
I'D RATHER LOOK SOMEWHERE ELSE, EVEN NOW.
YOU! DON'T COME ANY CLOSER!
YES, YES. I HEAR YOU.
BUT... RUDEUS... PUT ANOTHER WAY, YOU ARE NOT *AFRAID* OF ME, AS THEY ARE.

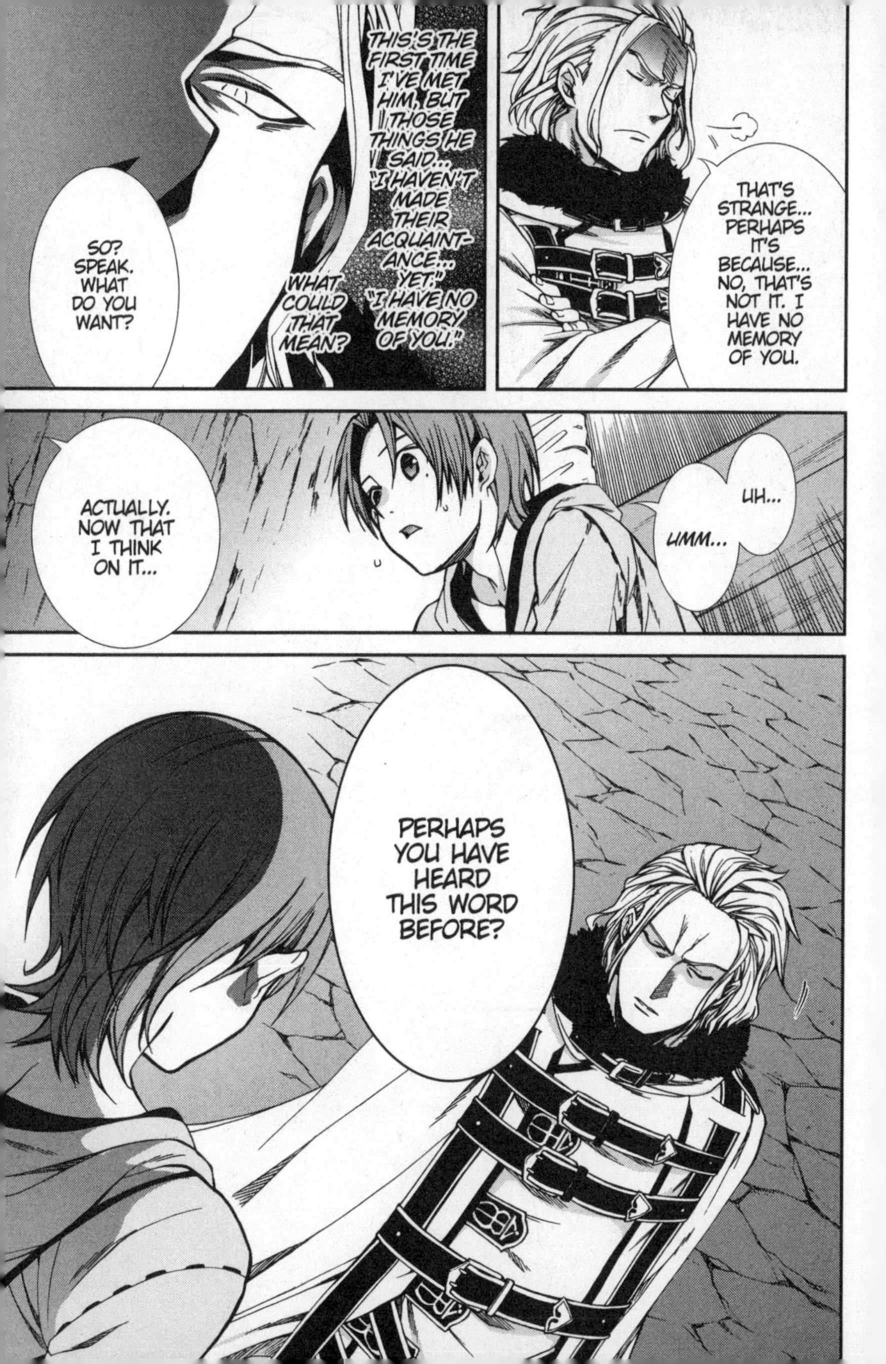
THAT'S STRANGE... PERHAPS IT'S BECAUSE... NO, THAT'S NOT IT. I HAVE NO MEMORY OF YOU.
THIS'S THE FIRST TIME I'VE MET HIM, BUT THOSE THINGS HE SAID... "I HAVEN'T MADE THEIR ACQUAINTANCE... YET." "I HAVE NO MEMORY OF YOU."
WHAT COULD THAT MEAN?
SO? SPEAK. WHAT DO YOU WANT?
UH...
UMM...
ACTUALLY. NOW THAT I THINK ON IT...
PERHAPS YOU HAVE HEARD THIS WORD BEFORE?

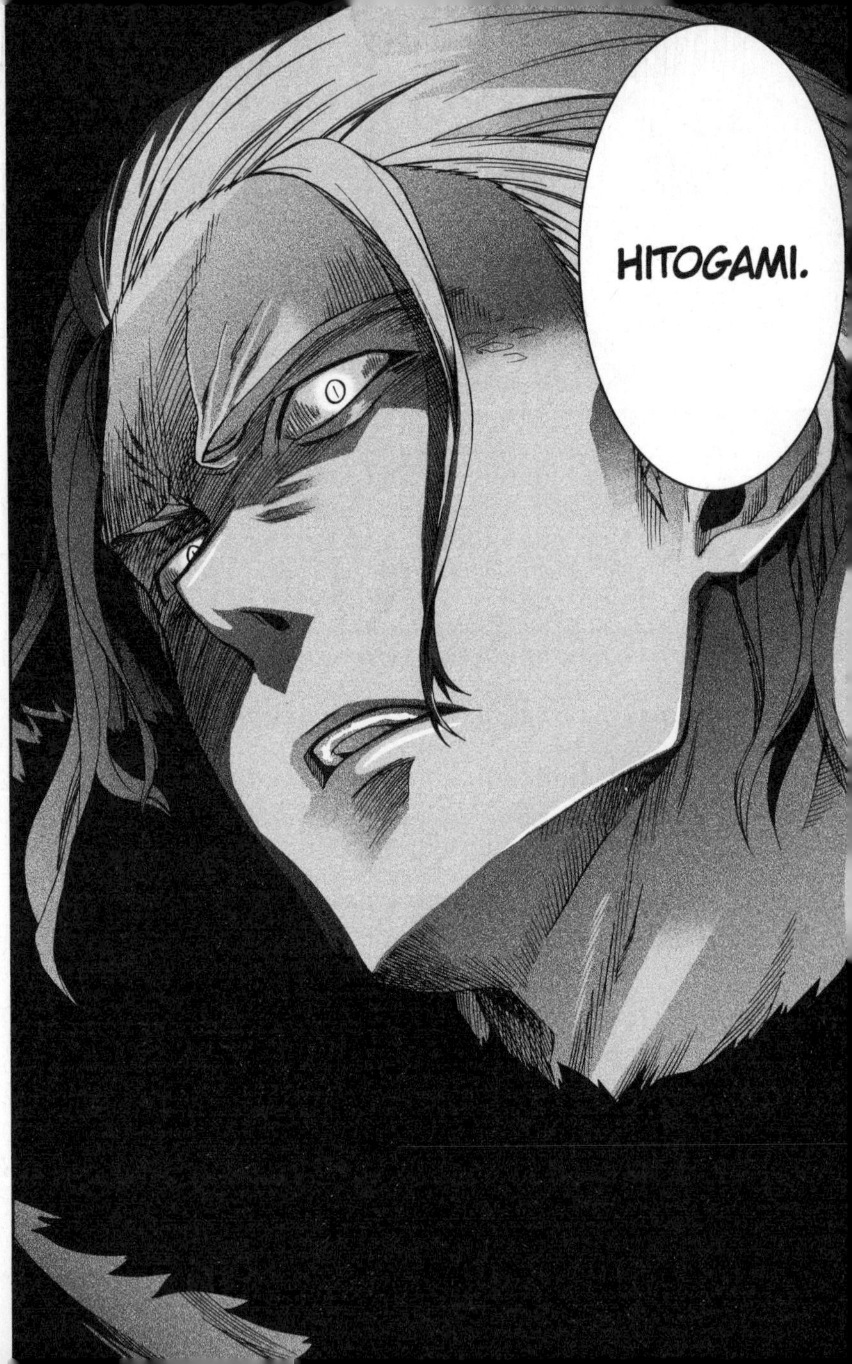
HITOGAMI.

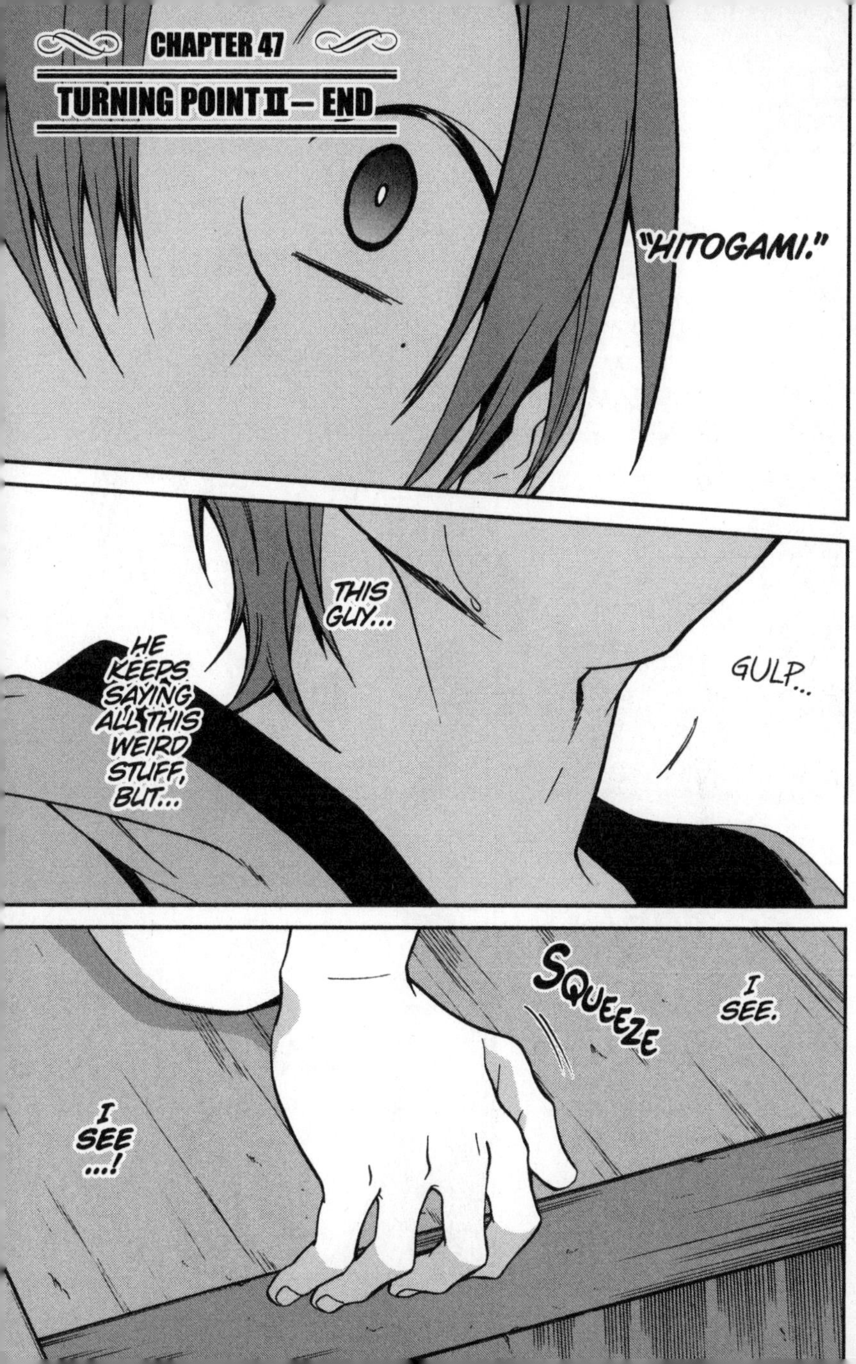
CHAPTER 47
TURNING POINT II — END
"HITOGAMI."
GULP...
THIS GUY...
HE KEEPS SAYING ALL THIS WEIRD STUFF, BUT...
I SEE.
SQUEEZE
I SEE ...!

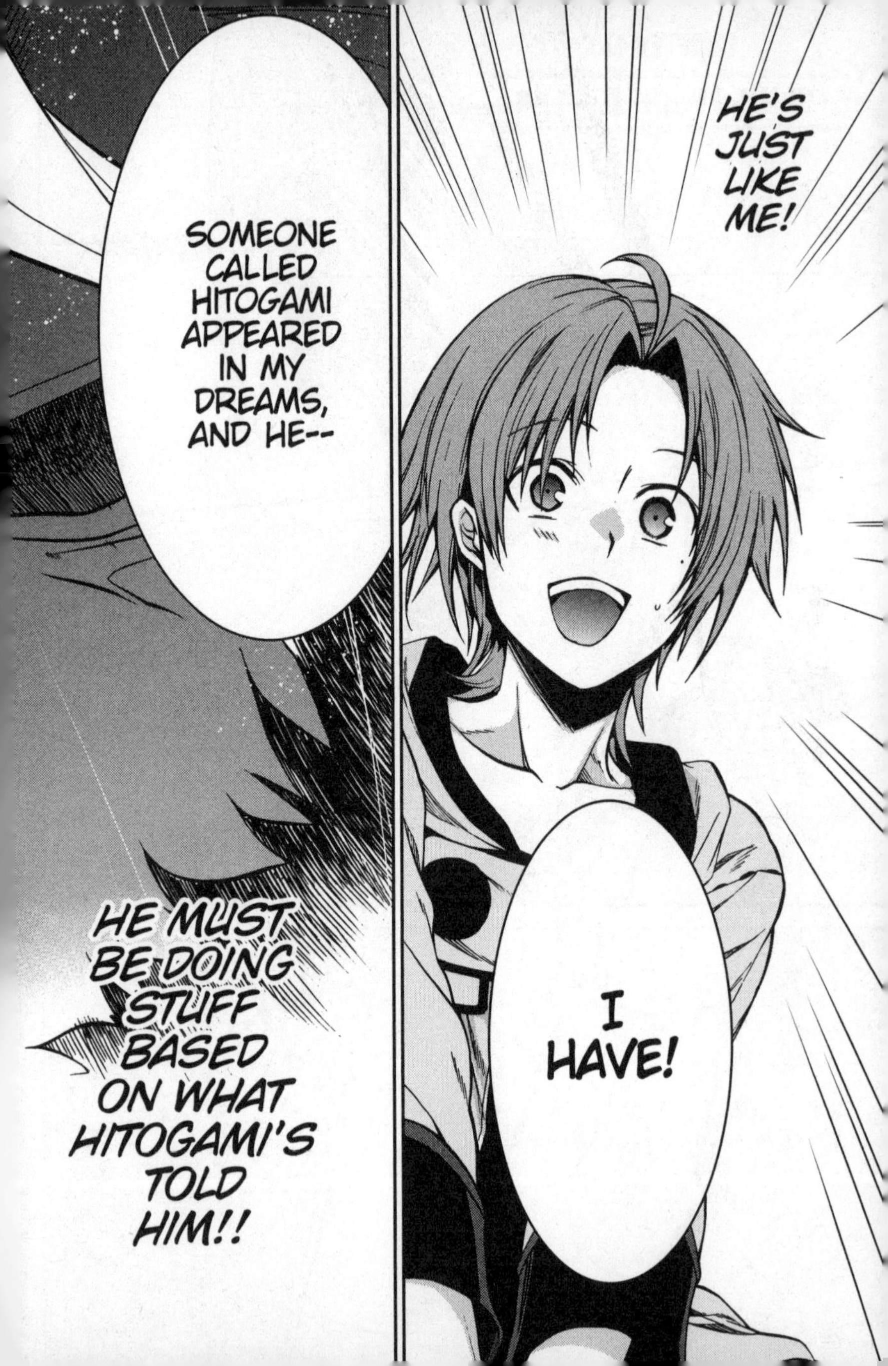
HE'S JUST LIKE ME!
I HAVE!
SOMEONE CALLED HITOGAMI APPEARED IN MY DREAMS, AND HE--
HE MUST BE DOING STUFF BASED ON WHAT HITOGAMI'S TOLD HIM!!

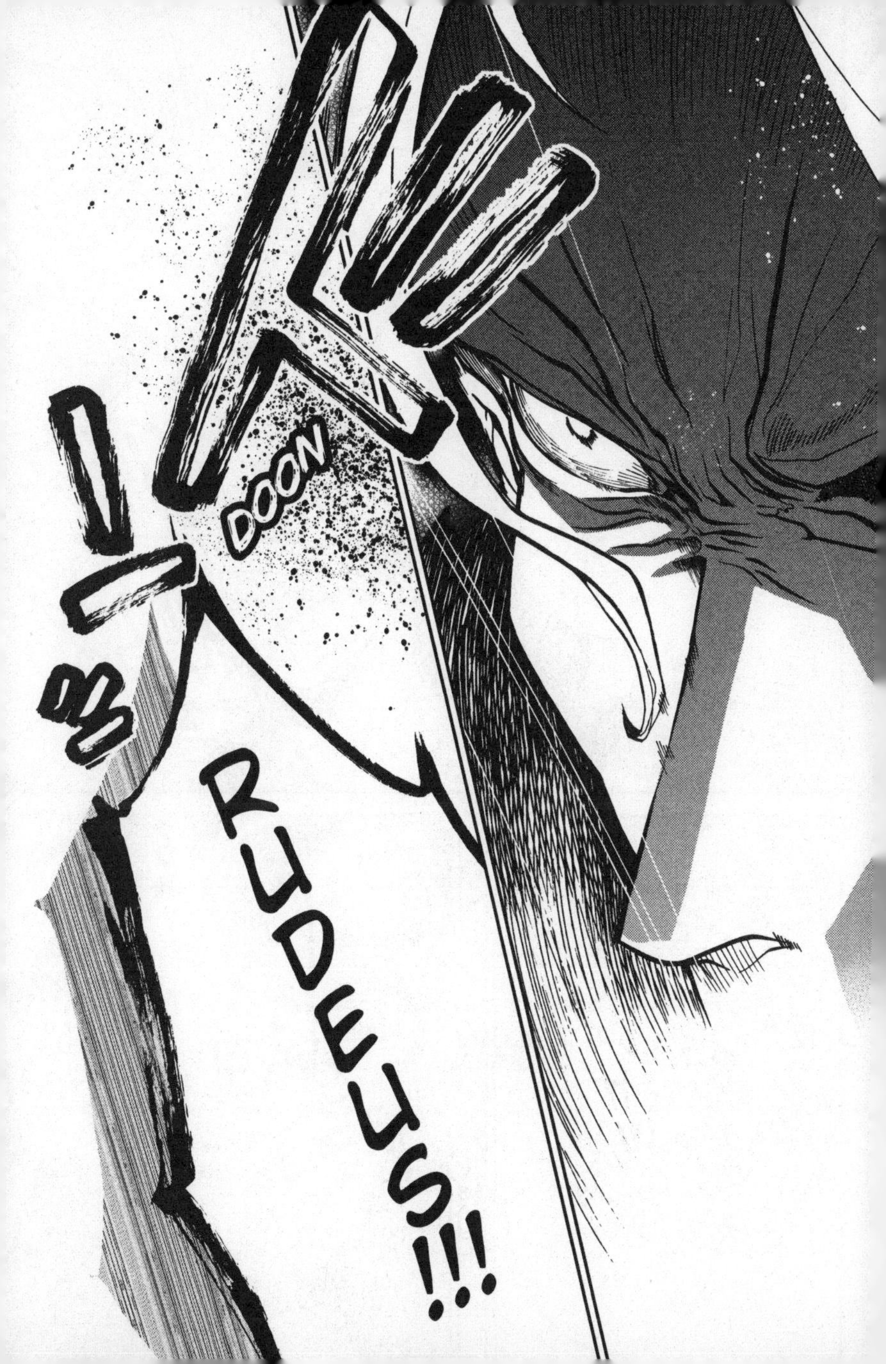
DOON
RUDEUS!!!

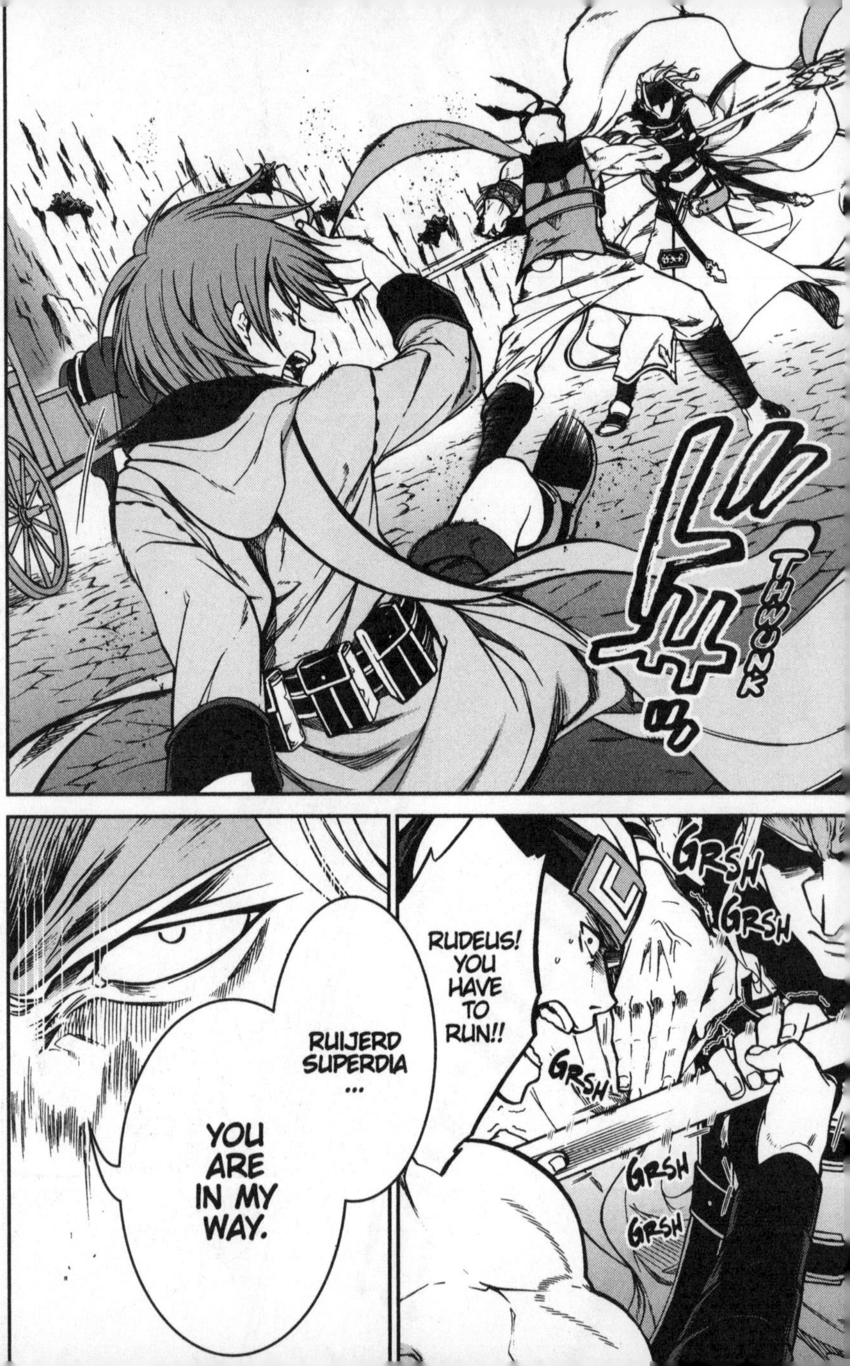
THWUNK
GRSH
GRSH
RUDEUS! YOU HAVE TO RUN!!
GRSH
GRSH
GRSH
RUIJERD SUPERDIA ...
YOU ARE IN MY WAY.

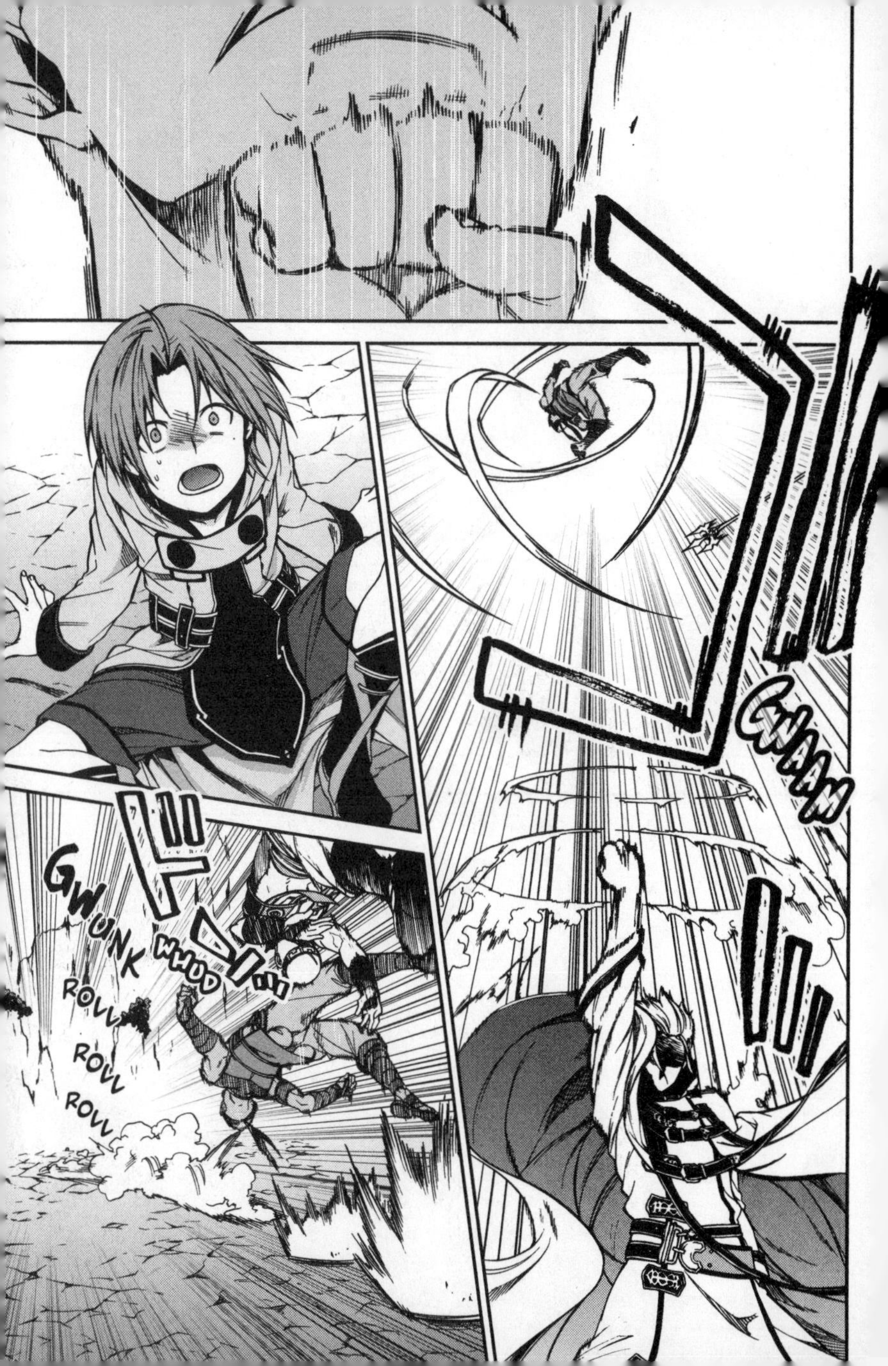
GWAAM
GWUNK
WHUD
ROLL
ROLL
ROLL

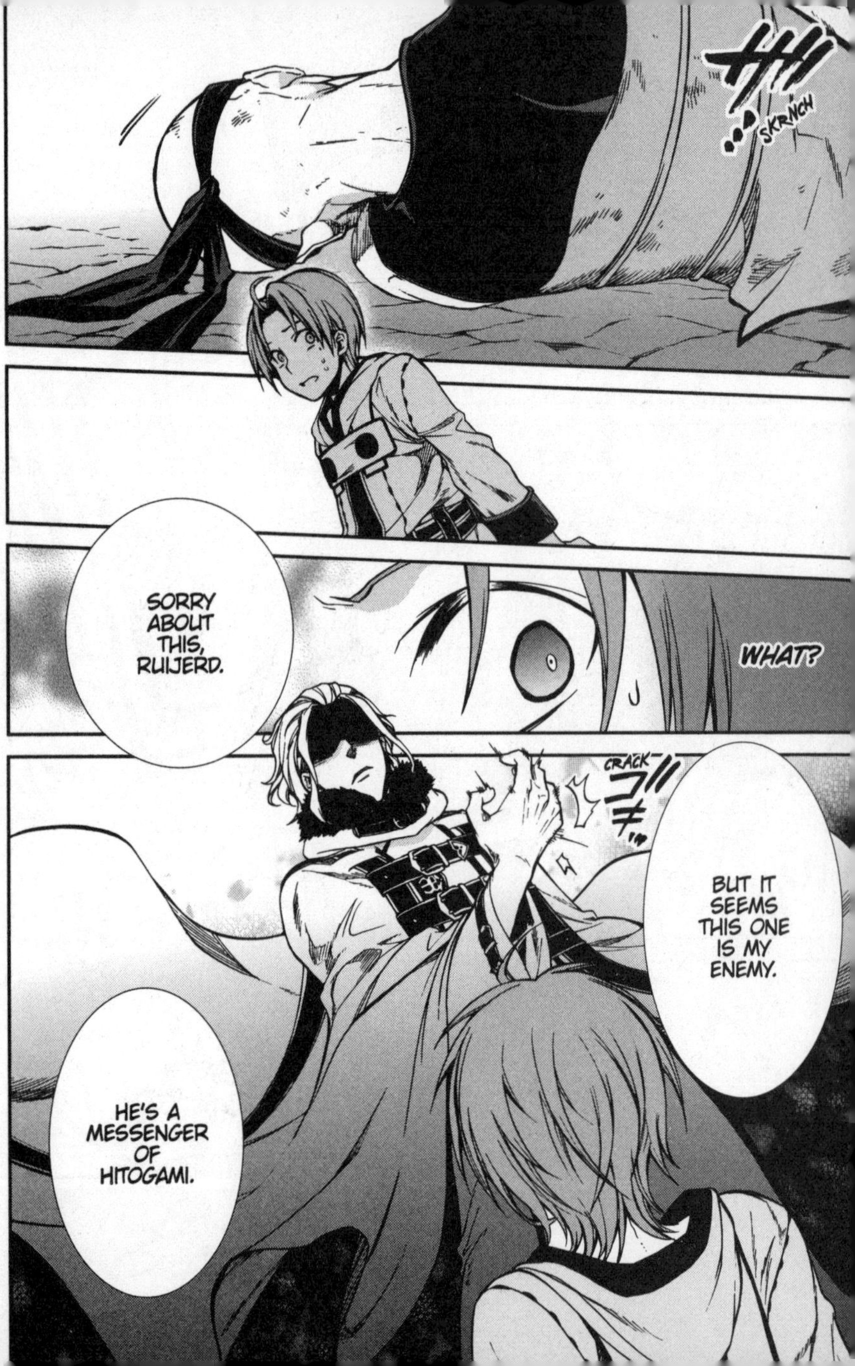

SKRNCH
WHAT?
SORRY ABOUT THIS, RUIJERD.
CRACK
BUT IT SEEMS THIS ONE IS MY ENEMY.
HE'S A MESSENGER OF HITOGAMI.

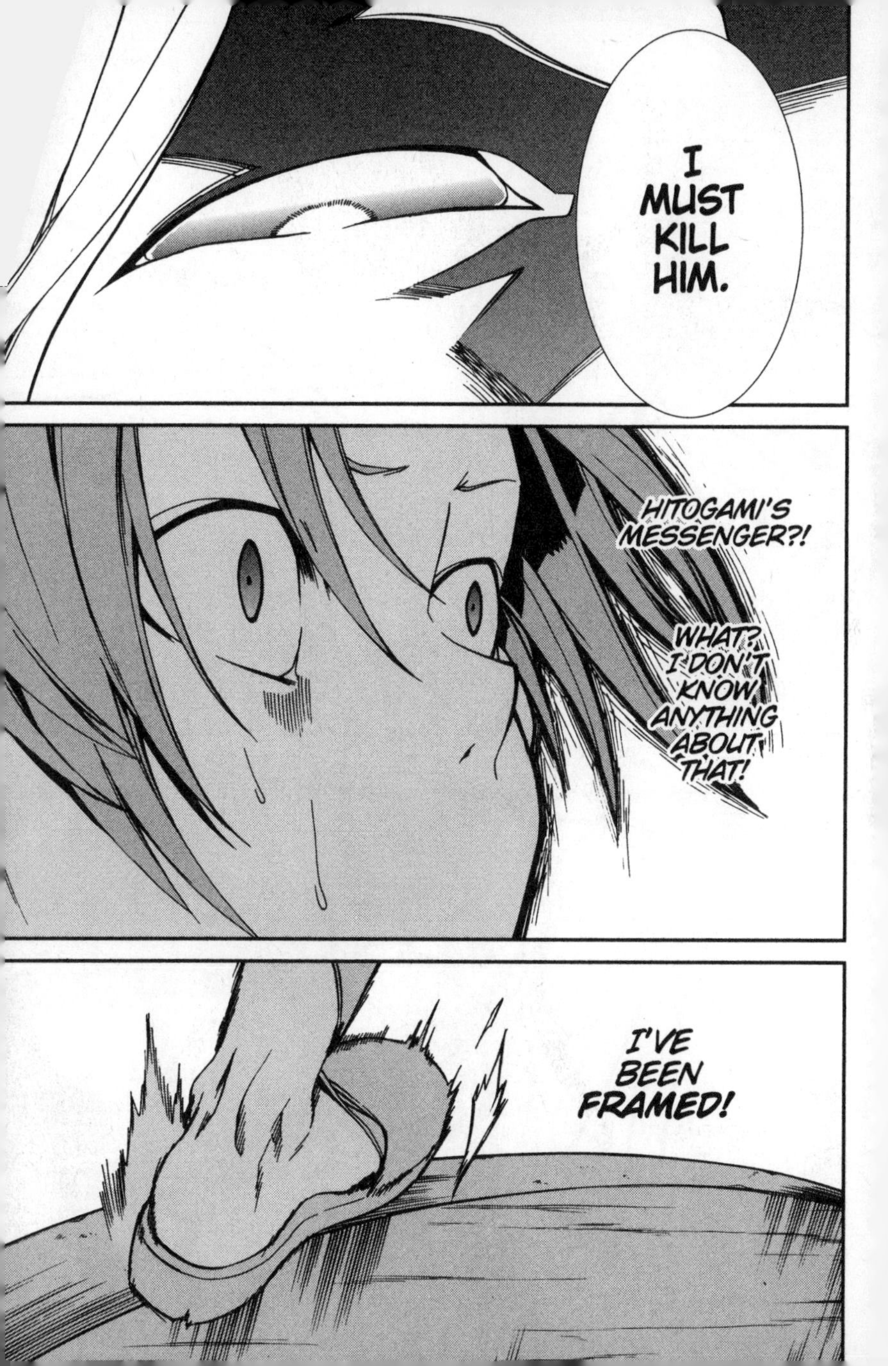
I MUST KILL HIM.
HITOGAMI'S MESSENGER?!
WHAT? I DON'T KNOW ANYTHING ABOUT THAT!
I'VE BEEN FRAMED!

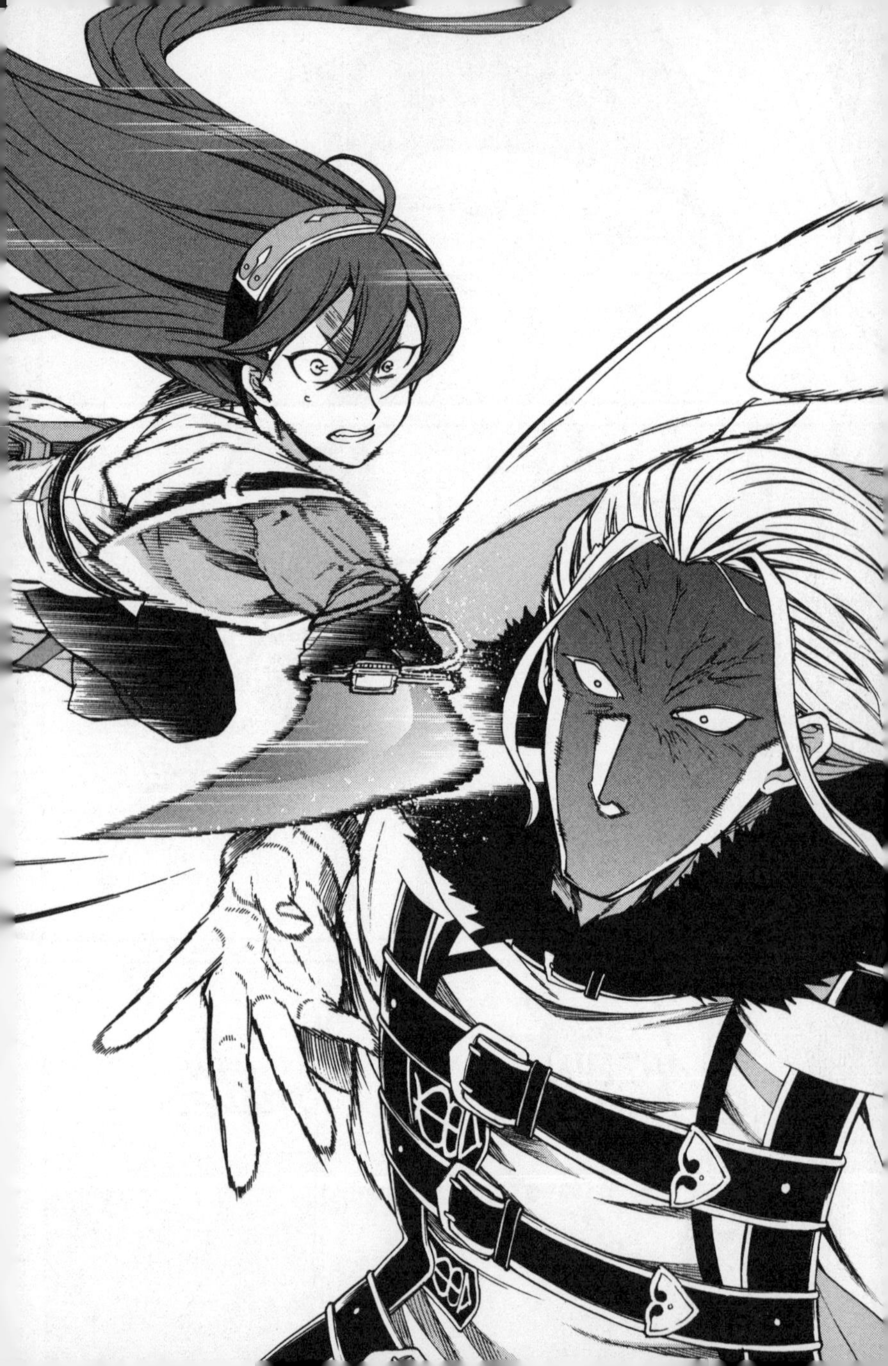

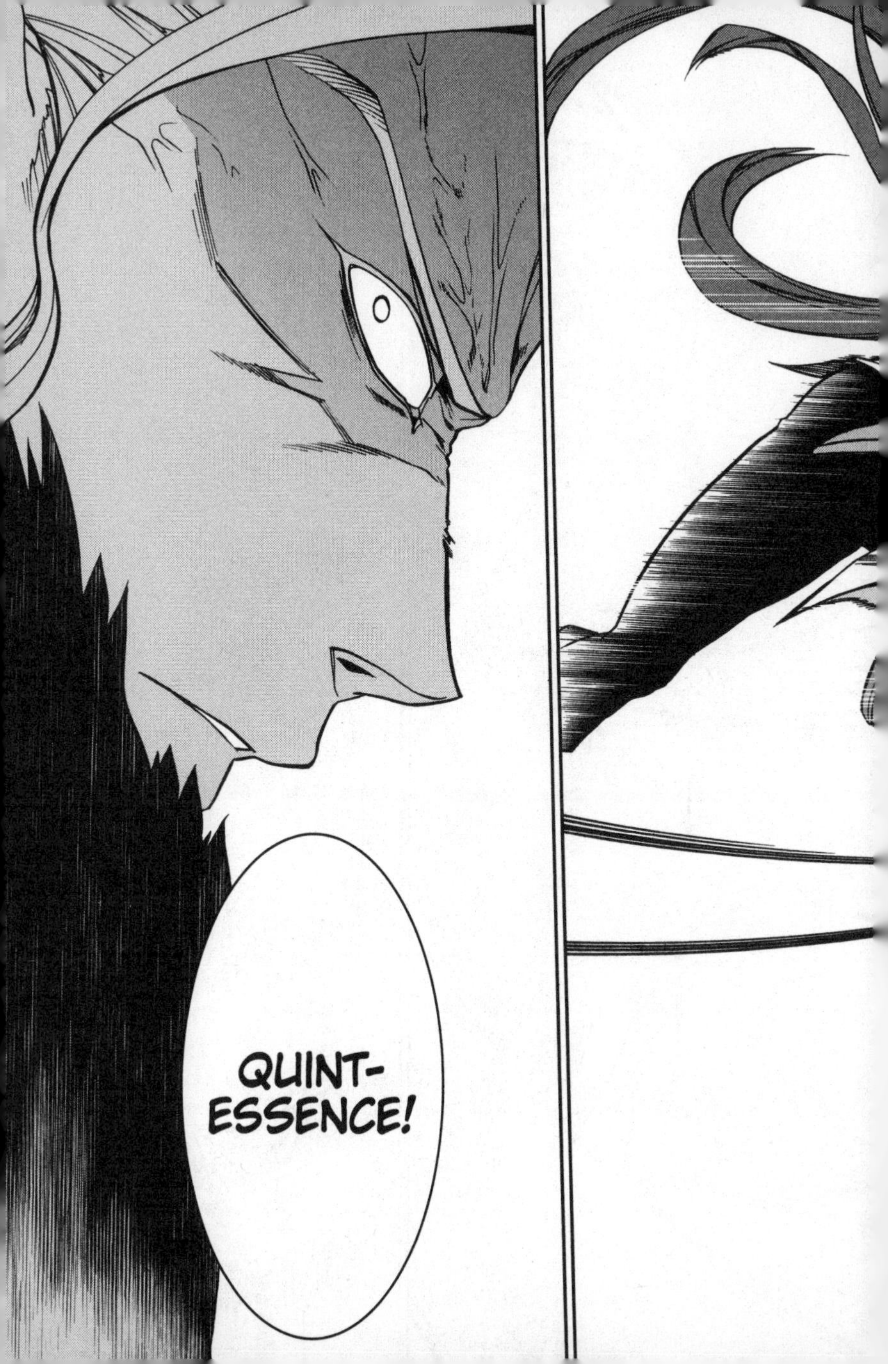
QUINT-ESSENCE!

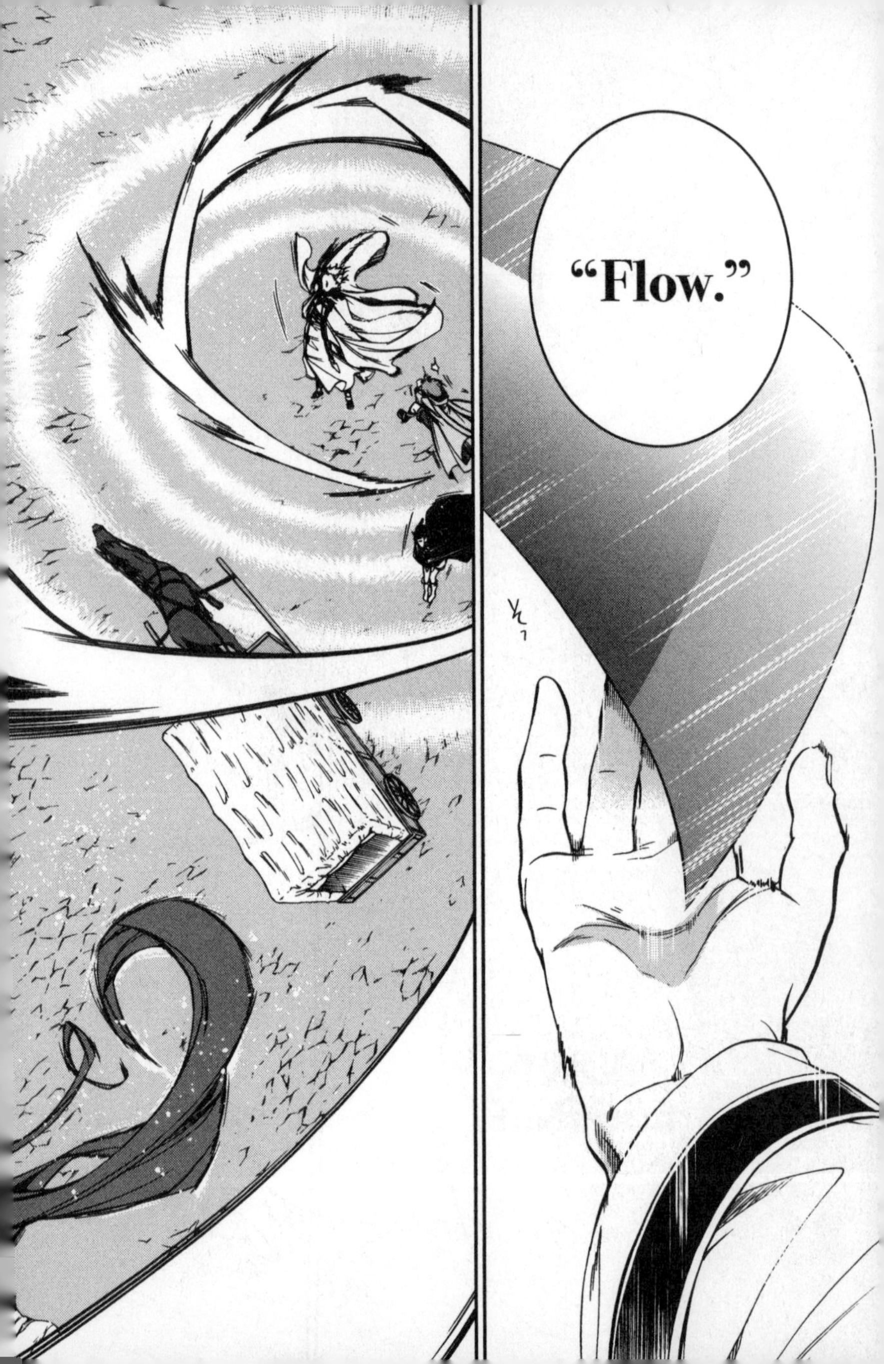
"Flow."

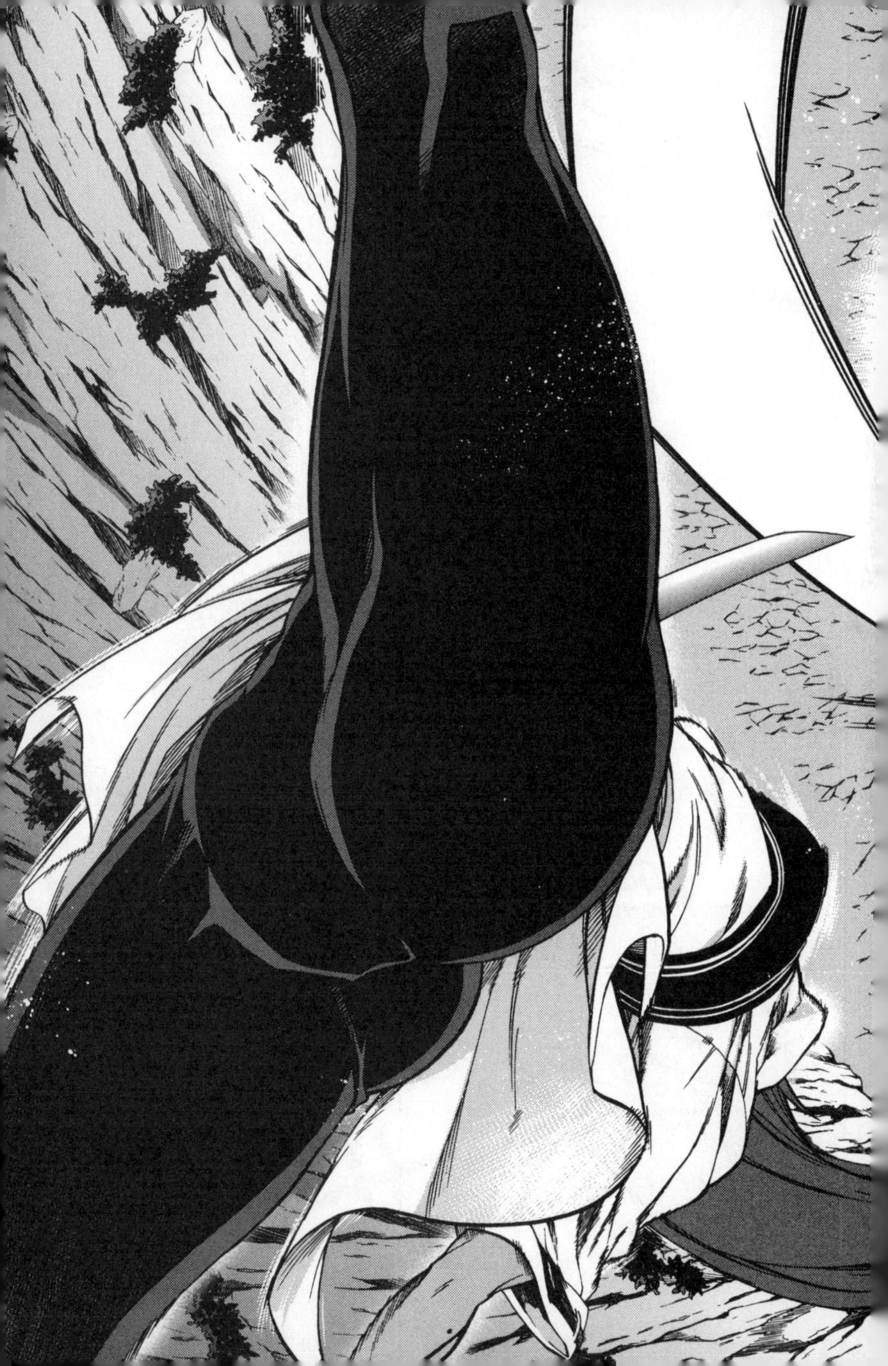

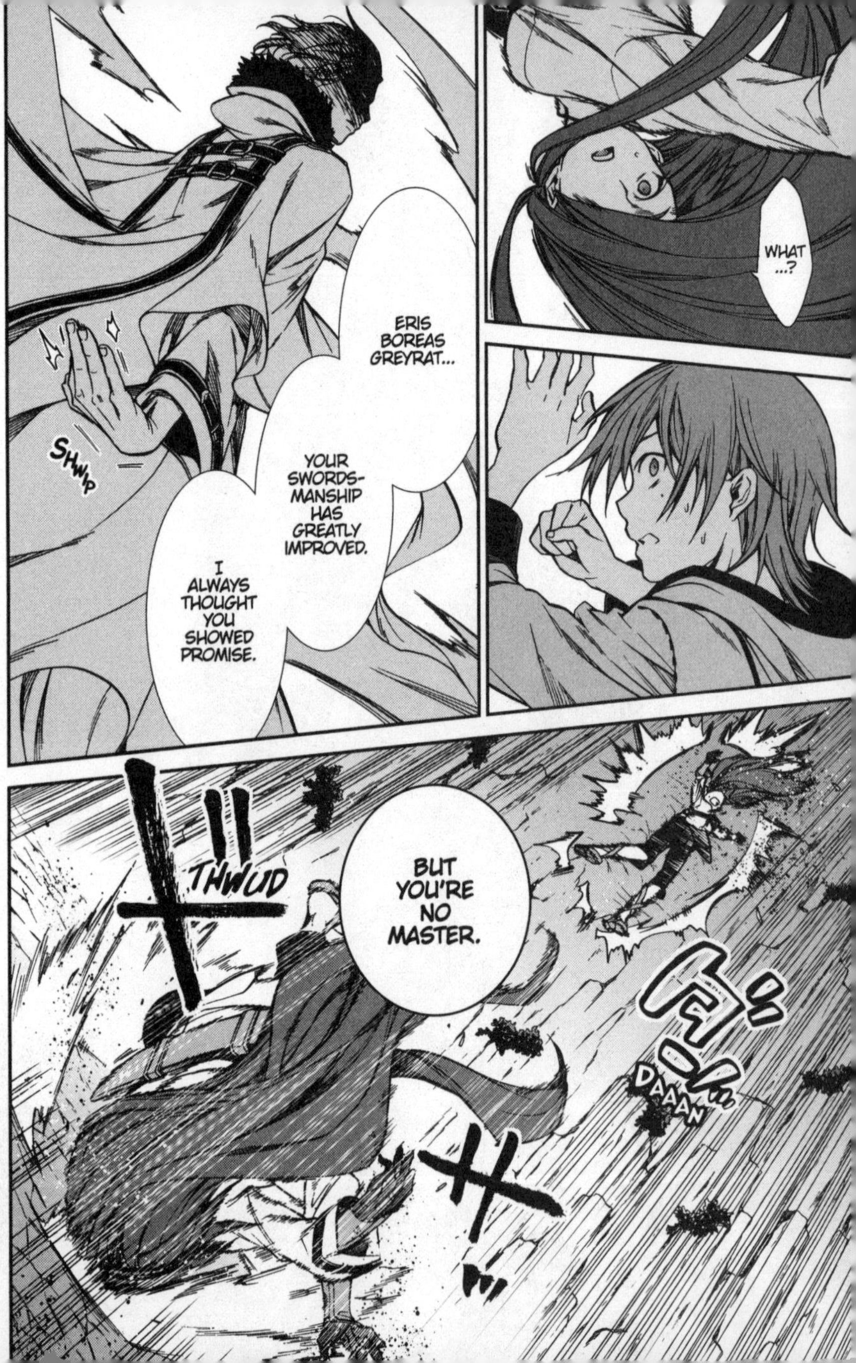
WHAT ...?
ERIS BOREAS GREYRAT...
YOUR SWORDS-MANSHIP HAS GREATLY IMPROVED.
I ALWAYS THOUGHT YOU SHOWED PROMISE.
SHWIP
BUT YOU'RE NO MASTER.
THWUD
DAAAN

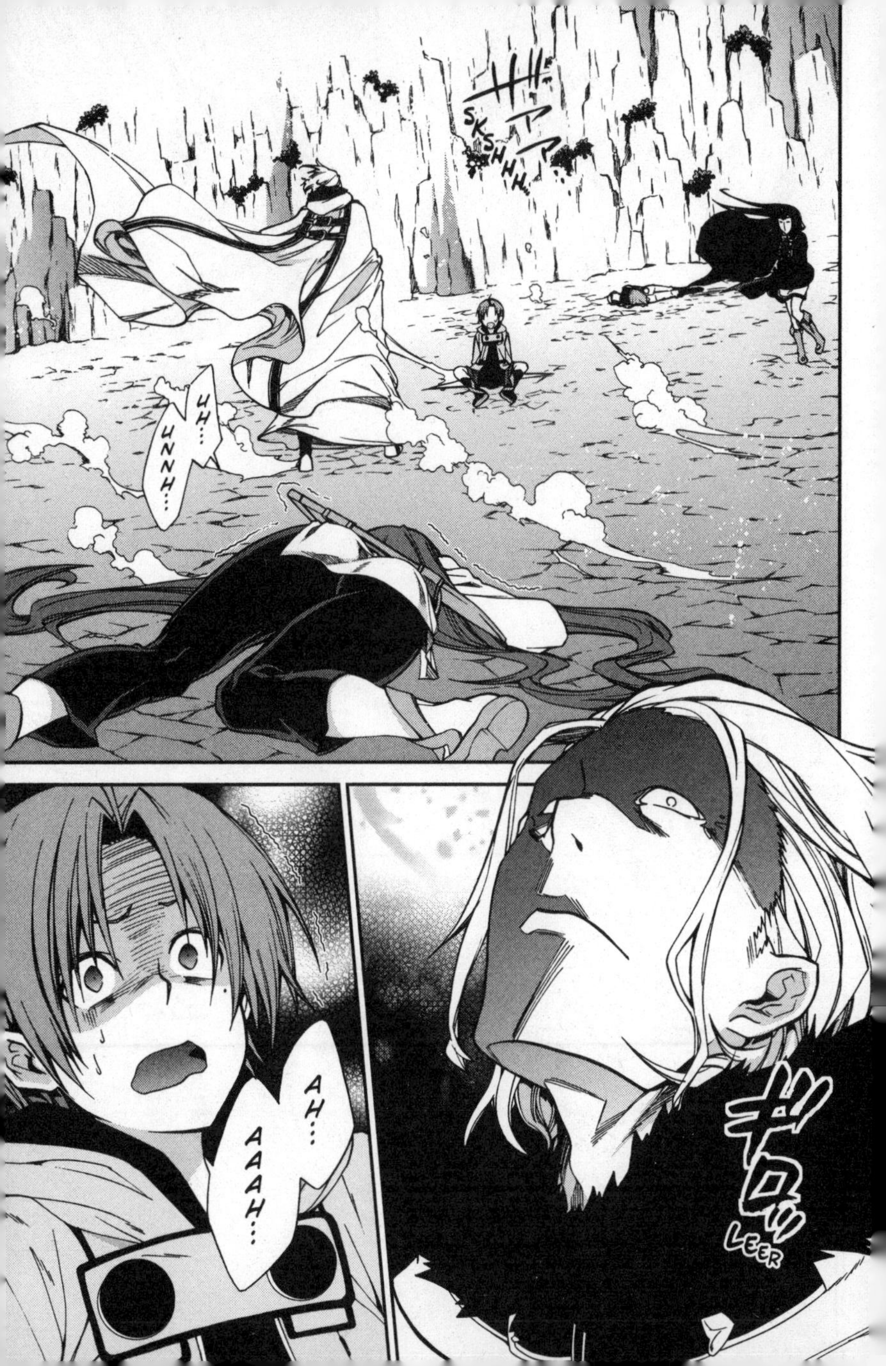
SKSHHH
UH... UNNNH...
ギロッ
LEER
AH... AAAAH...

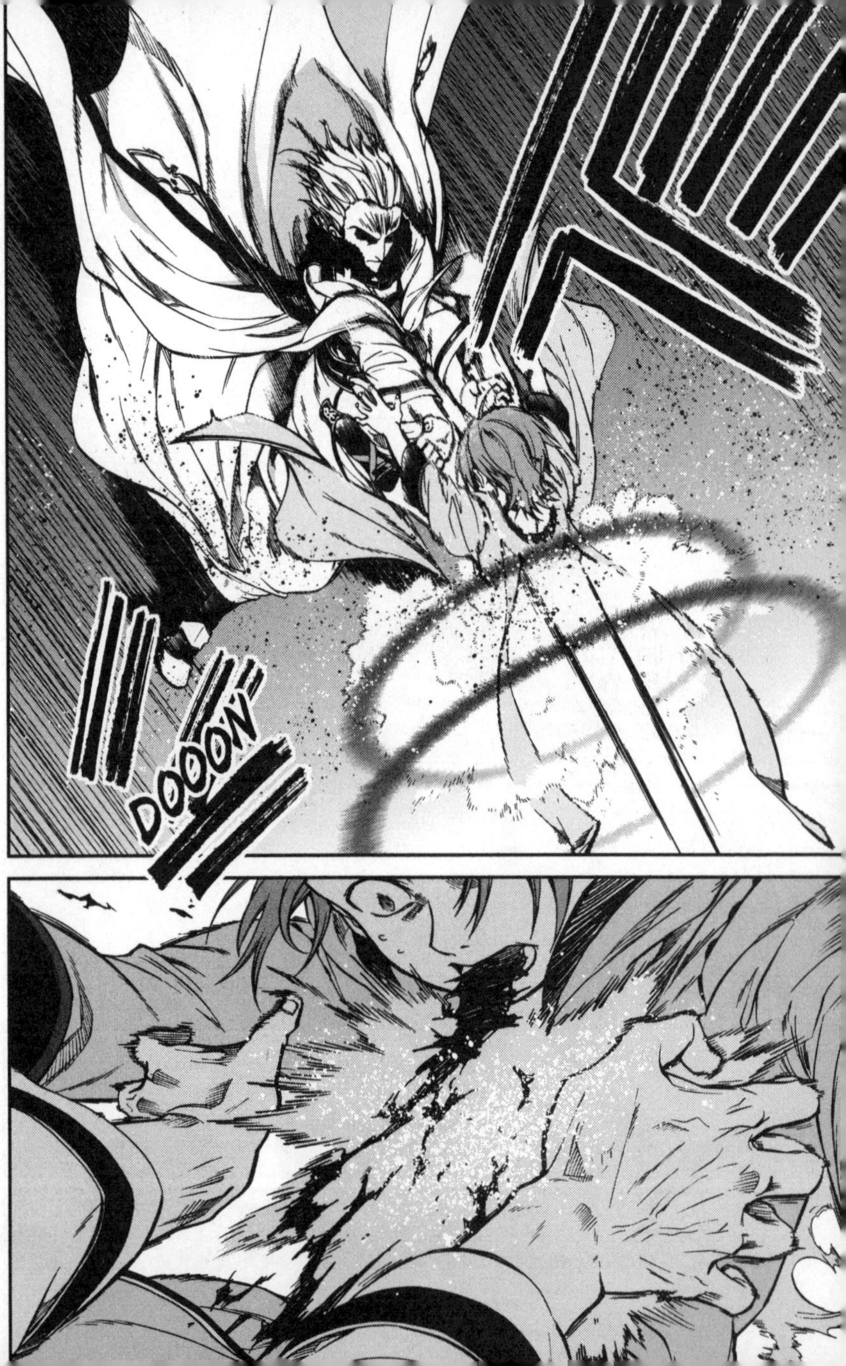
DOOON

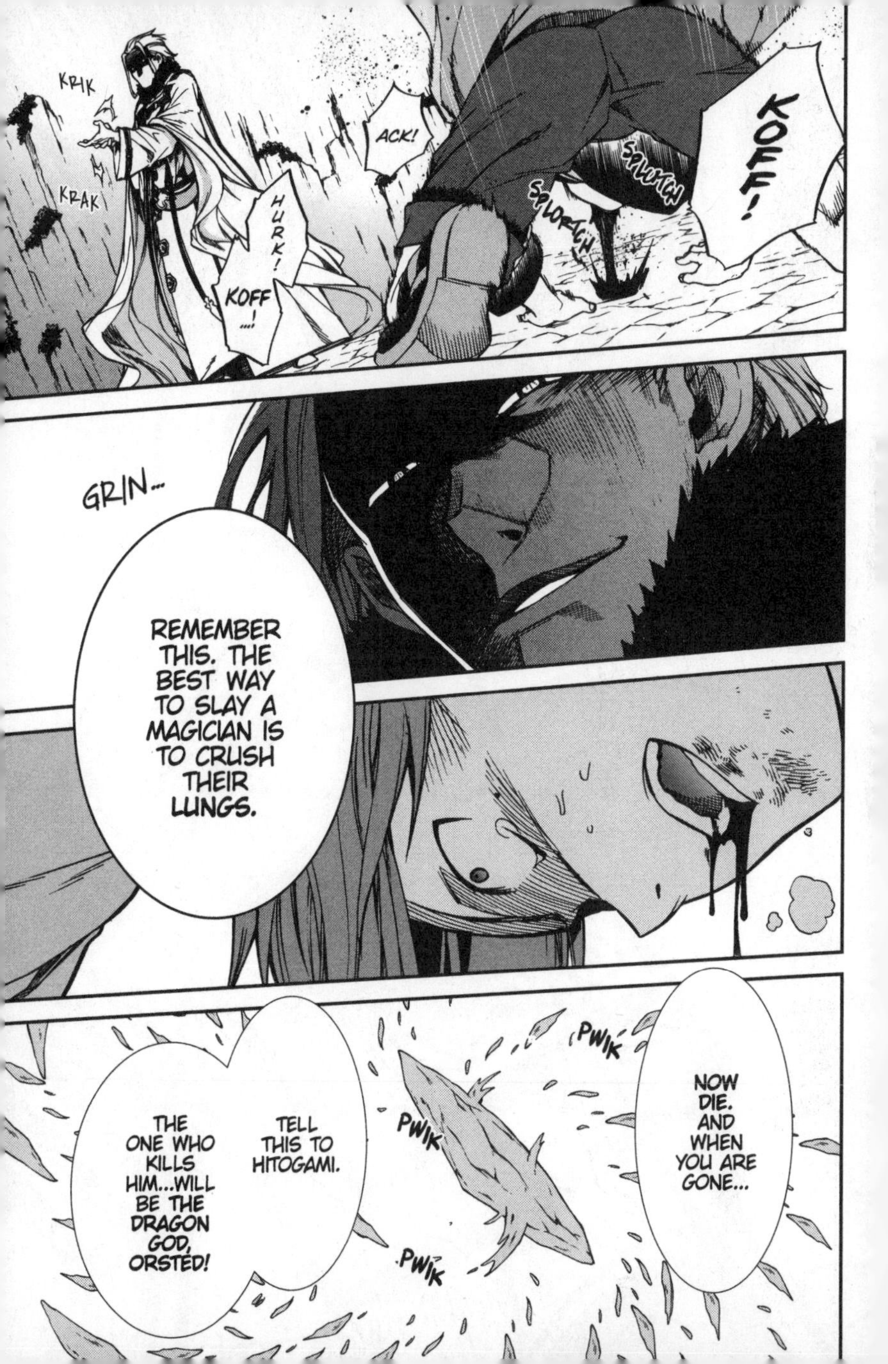
KOFF!
SPLORTCH
SPLORTCH
ACK!
HURK!
KOFF...!
KRIK
KRAK
GRIN...
REMEMBER THIS. THE BEST WAY TO SLAY A MAGICIAN IS TO CRUSH THEIR LUNGS.
PWIK
NOW DIE. AND WHEN YOU ARE GONE...
PWIK
PWIK
TELL THIS TO HITOGAMI.
THE ONE WHO KILLS HIM...WILL BE THE DRAGON GOD, ORSTED!

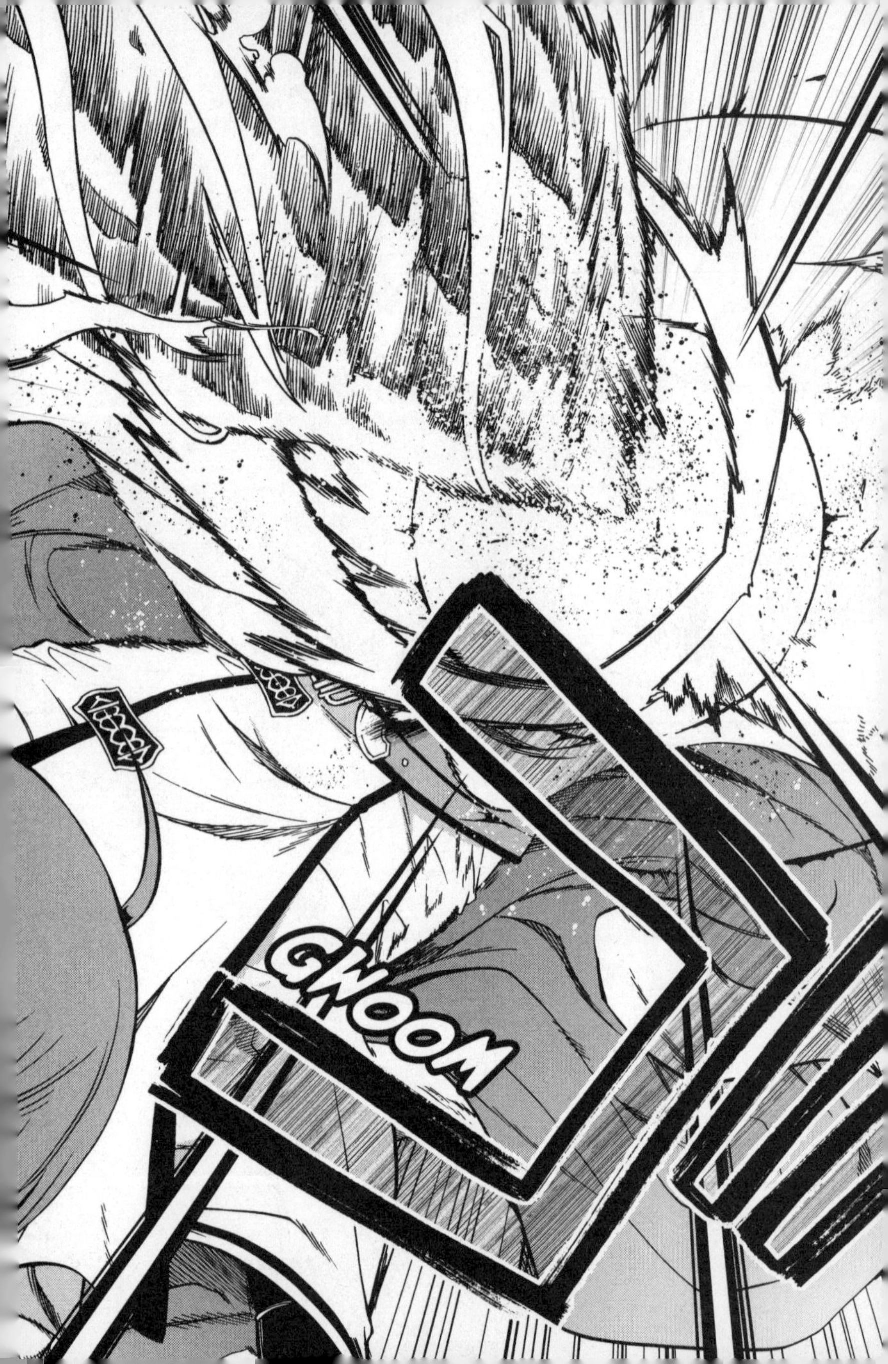
GWOOM

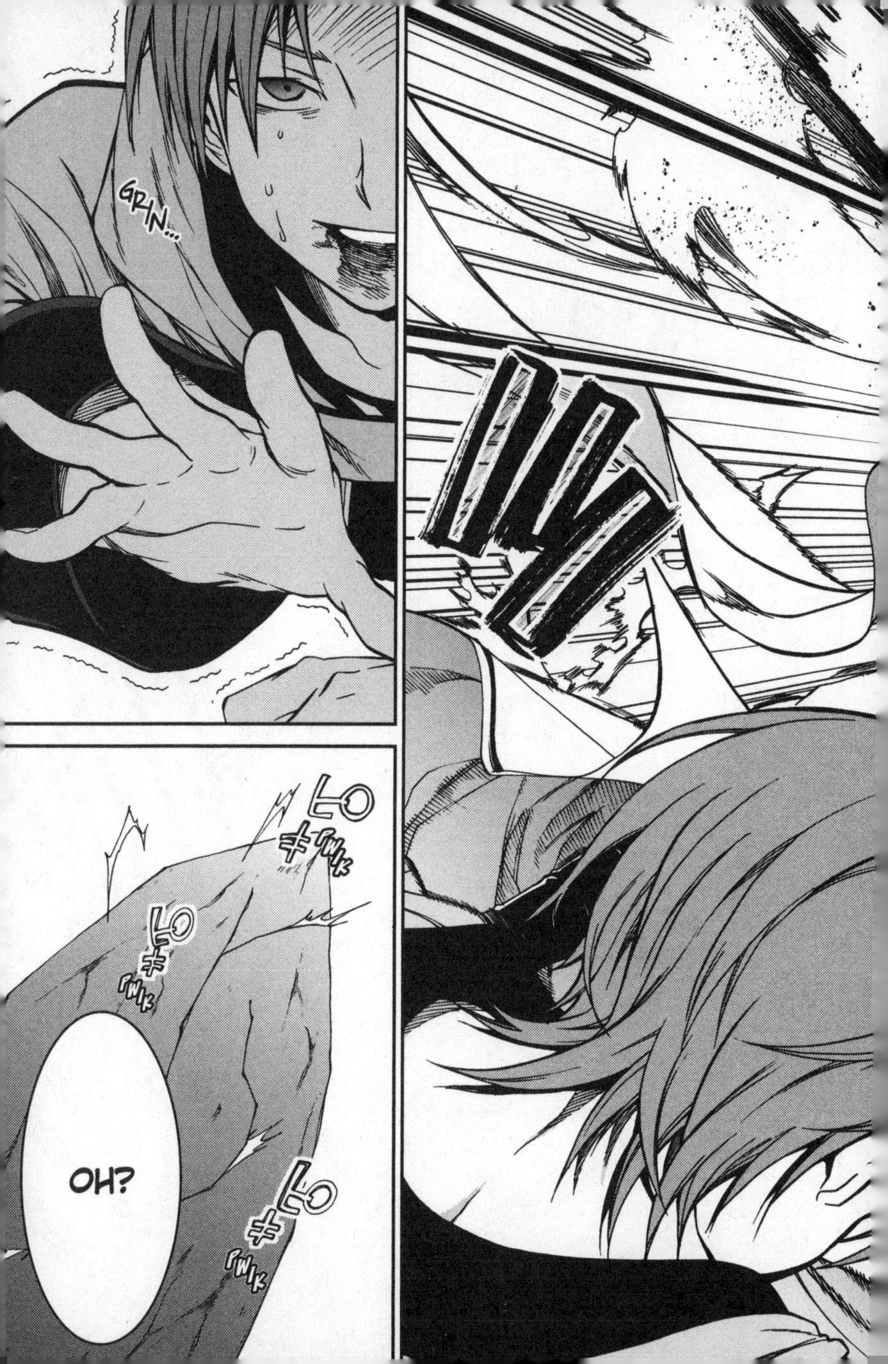
GRIN...
PWIK
PWIK
PWIK
OH?

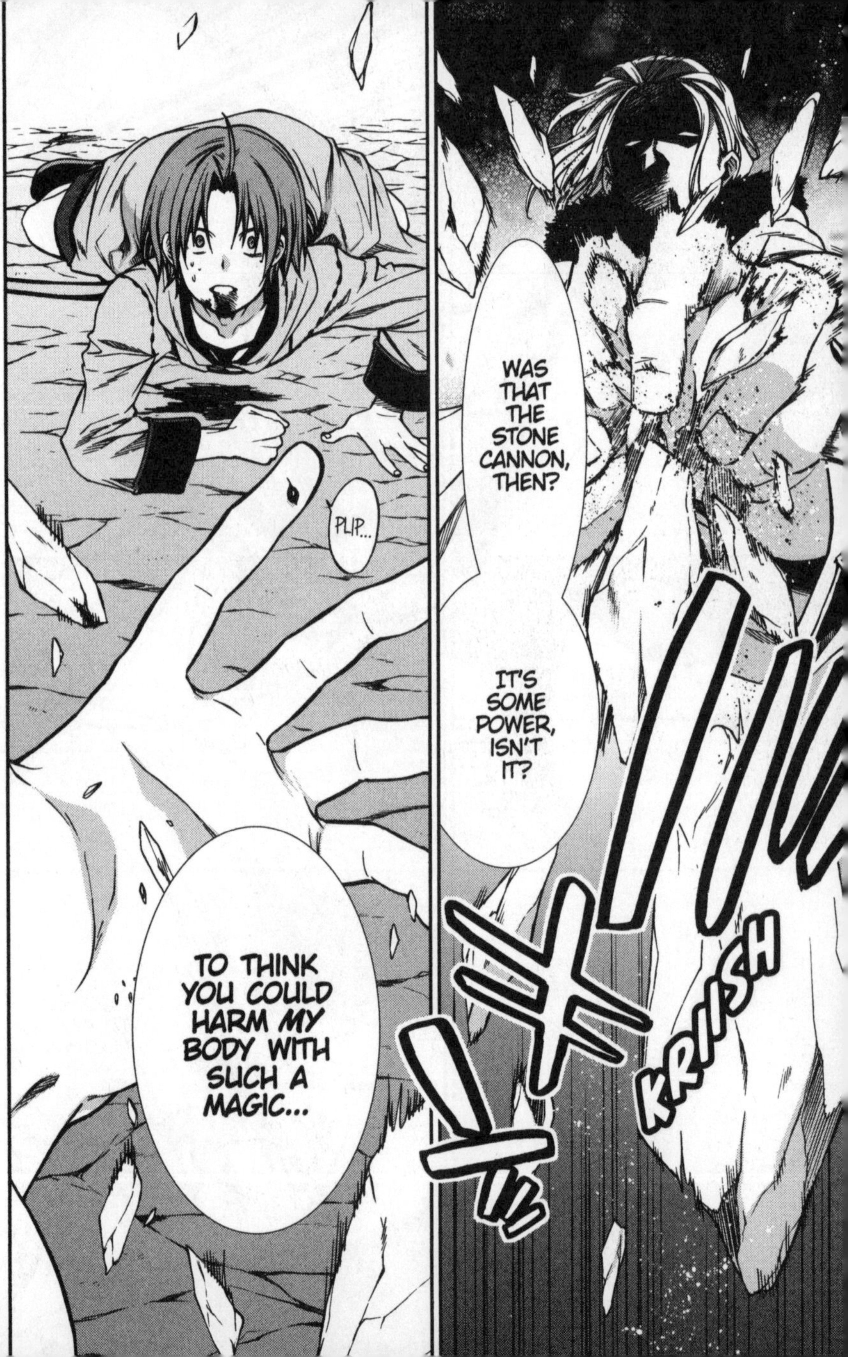
WAS THAT THE STONE CANNON, THEN?
IT'S SOME POWER, ISN'T IT?
KRIISH
PLIP...
TO THINK YOU COULD HARM *MY* BODY WITH SUCH A MAGIC...

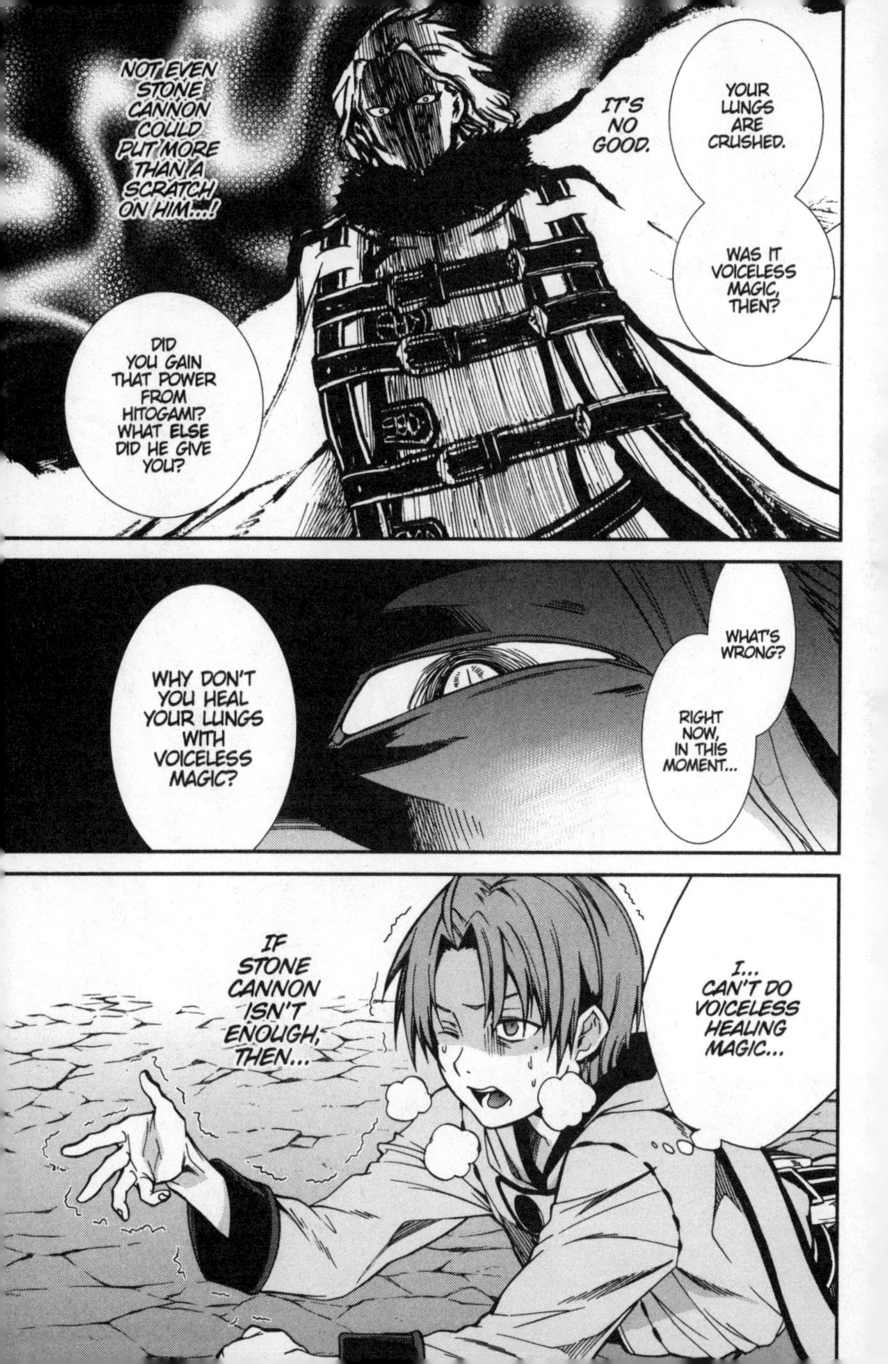
YOUR LUNGS ARE CRUSHED.
IT'S NO GOOD.
WAS IT VOICELESS MAGIC, THEN?
NOT EVEN STONE CANNON COULD PUT MORE THAN A SCRATCH ON HIM...!
DID YOU GAIN THAT POWER FROM HITOGAMI? WHAT ELSE DID HE GIVE YOU?
WHAT'S WRONG?
RIGHT NOW, IN THIS MOMENT...
WHY DON'T YOU HEAL YOUR LUNGS WITH VOICELESS MAGIC?
I... CAN'T DO VOICELESS HEALING MAGIC...
IF STONE CANNON ISN'T ENOUGH, THEN...

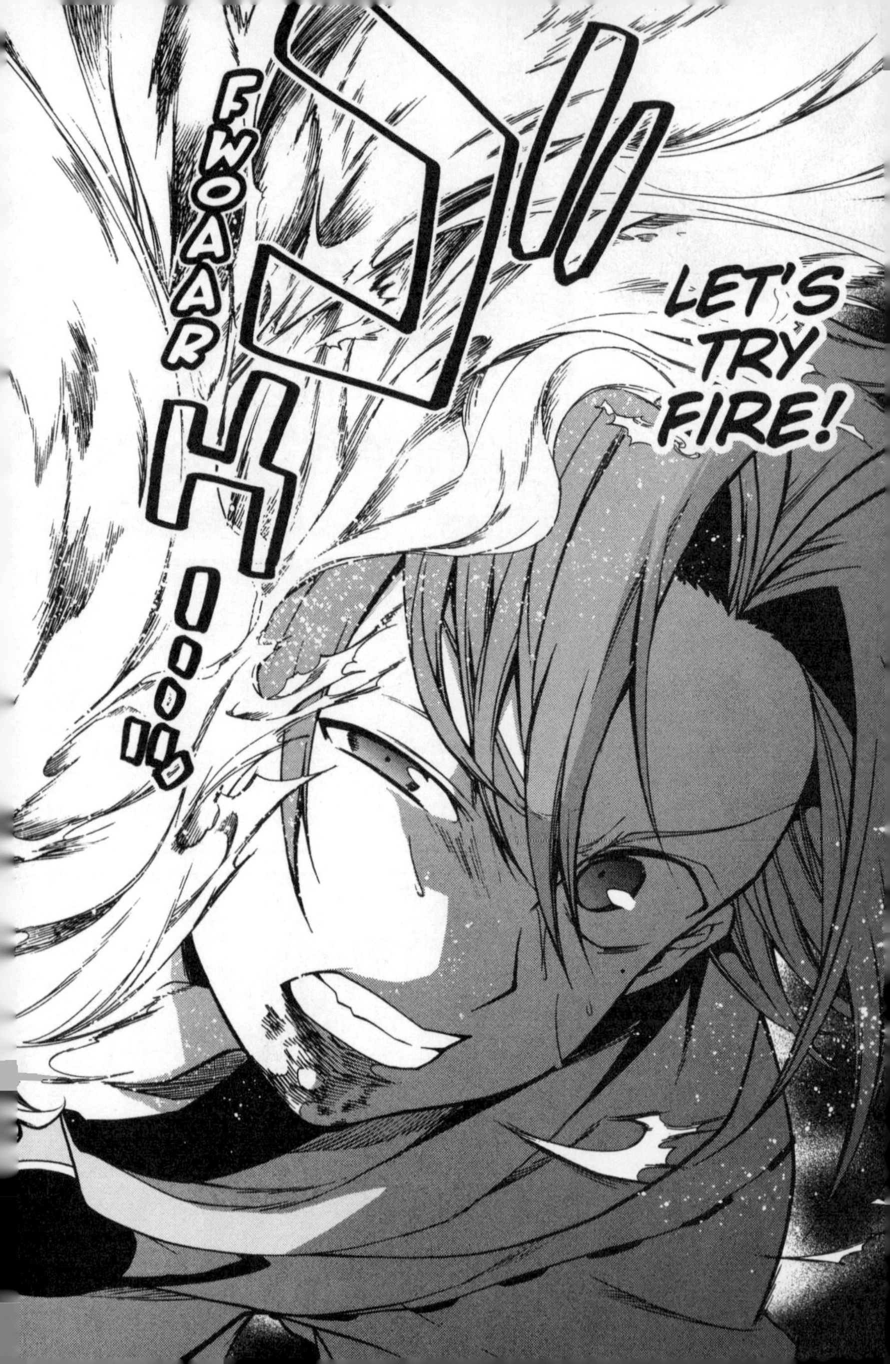
LET'S TRY FIRE!
FWOAAR

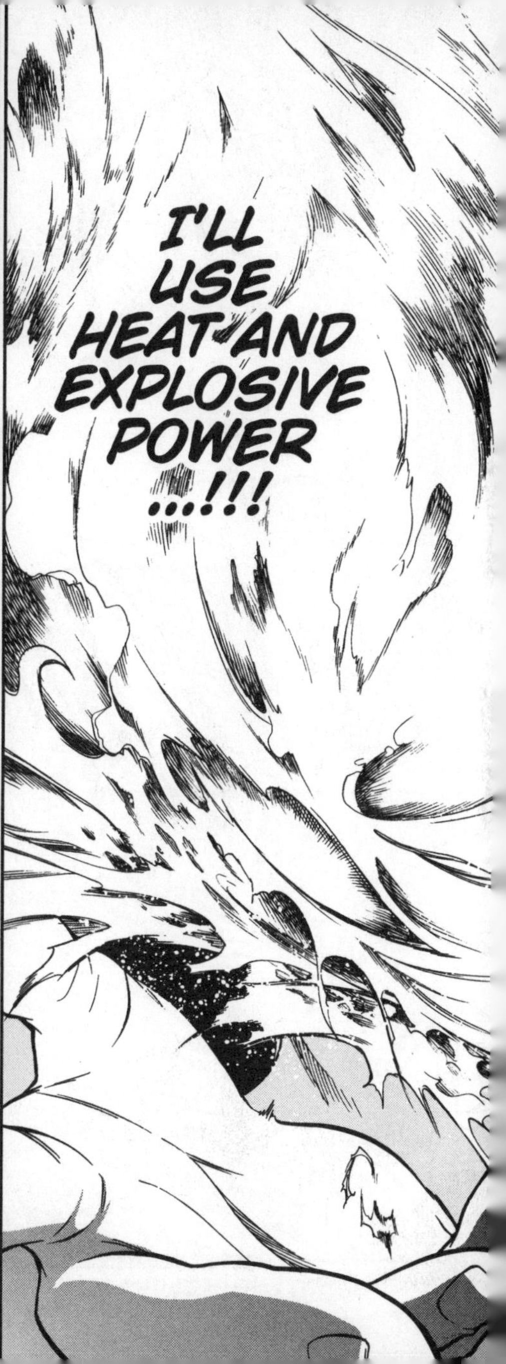
I'LL USE HEAT AND EXPLOSIVE POWER ...!!!
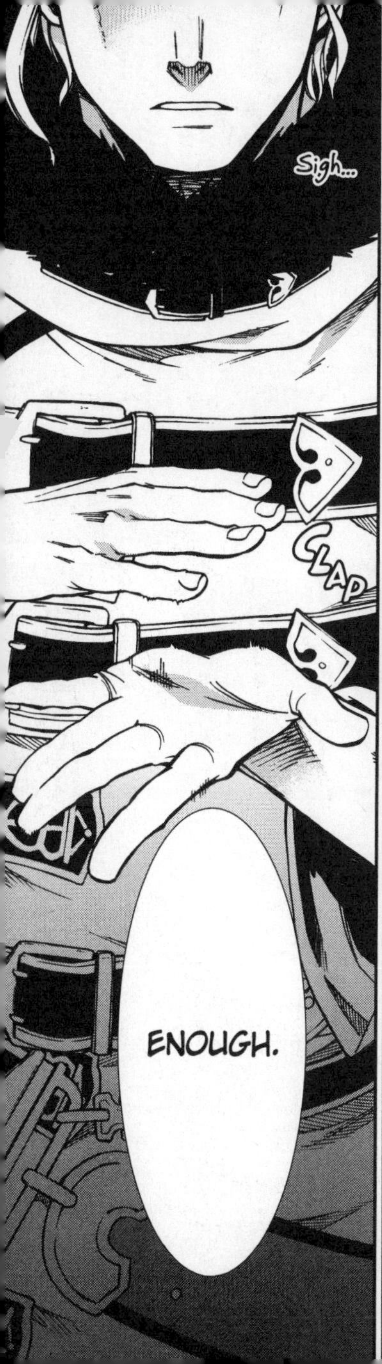
Sigh...
CLAP
ENOUGH.

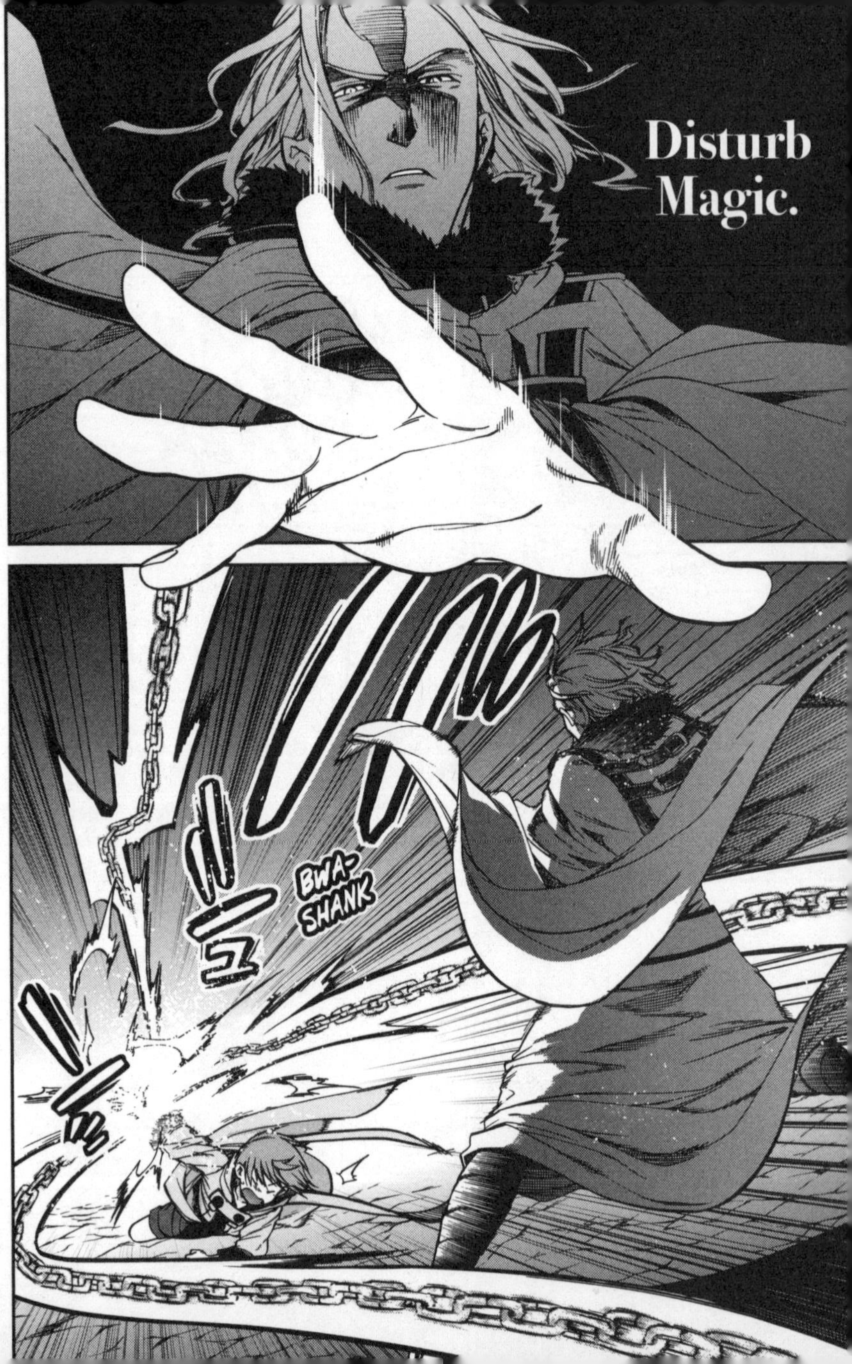
Disturb Magic.
BWA-SHANK

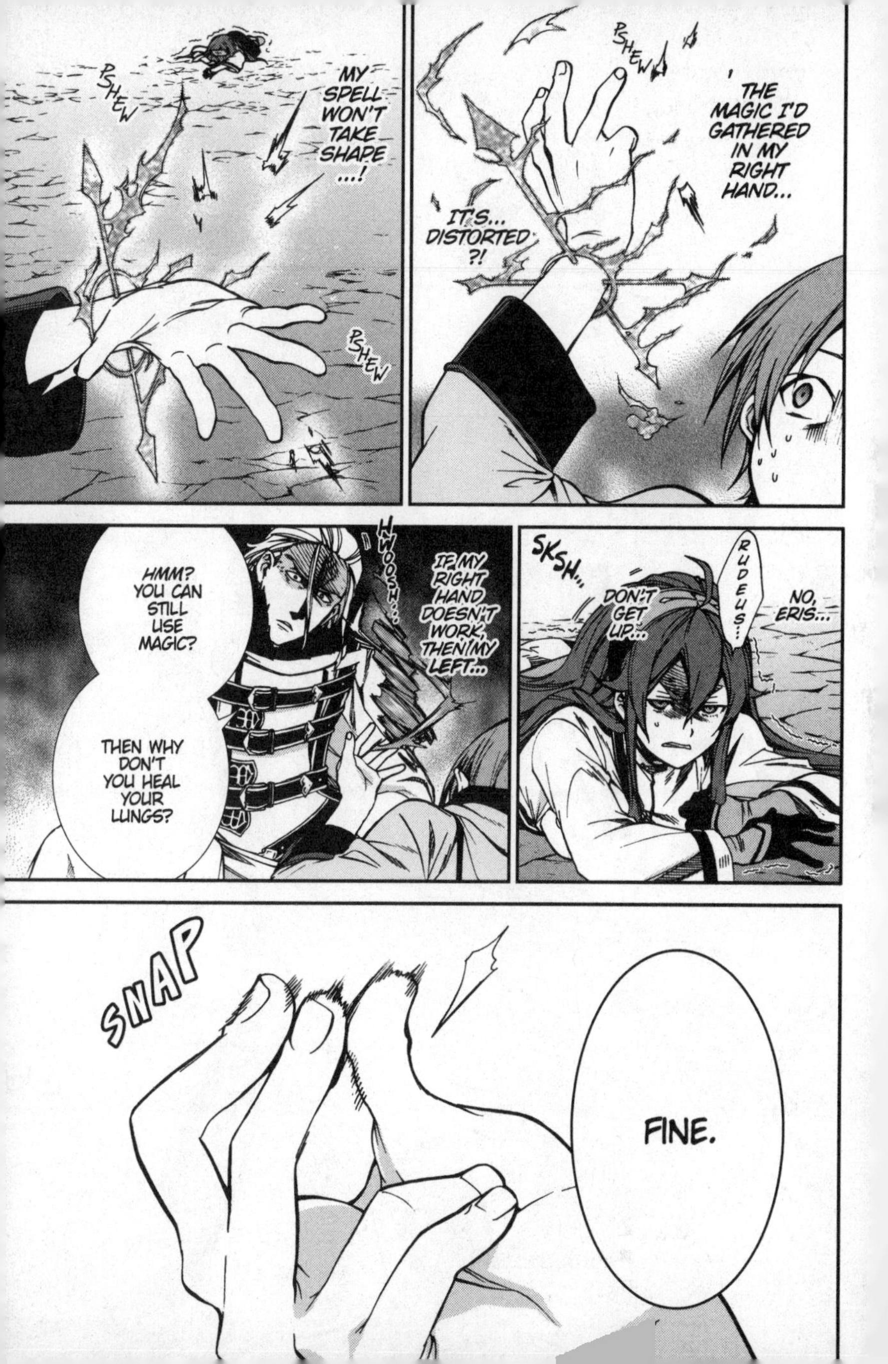
PSHEW
THE MAGIC I'D GATHERED IN MY RIGHT HAND...
IT'S... DISTORTED?!
MY SPELL WON'T TAKE SHAPE...!
PSHEW
PSHEW
SKSH...
RUDEUS...
NO, ERIS...
DON'T GET UP...
HWOOSH...
IF MY RIGHT HAND DOESN'T WORK, THEN MY LEFT...
HMM? YOU CAN STILL USE MAGIC?
THEN WHY DON'T YOU HEAL YOUR LUNGS?
FINE.
SNAP

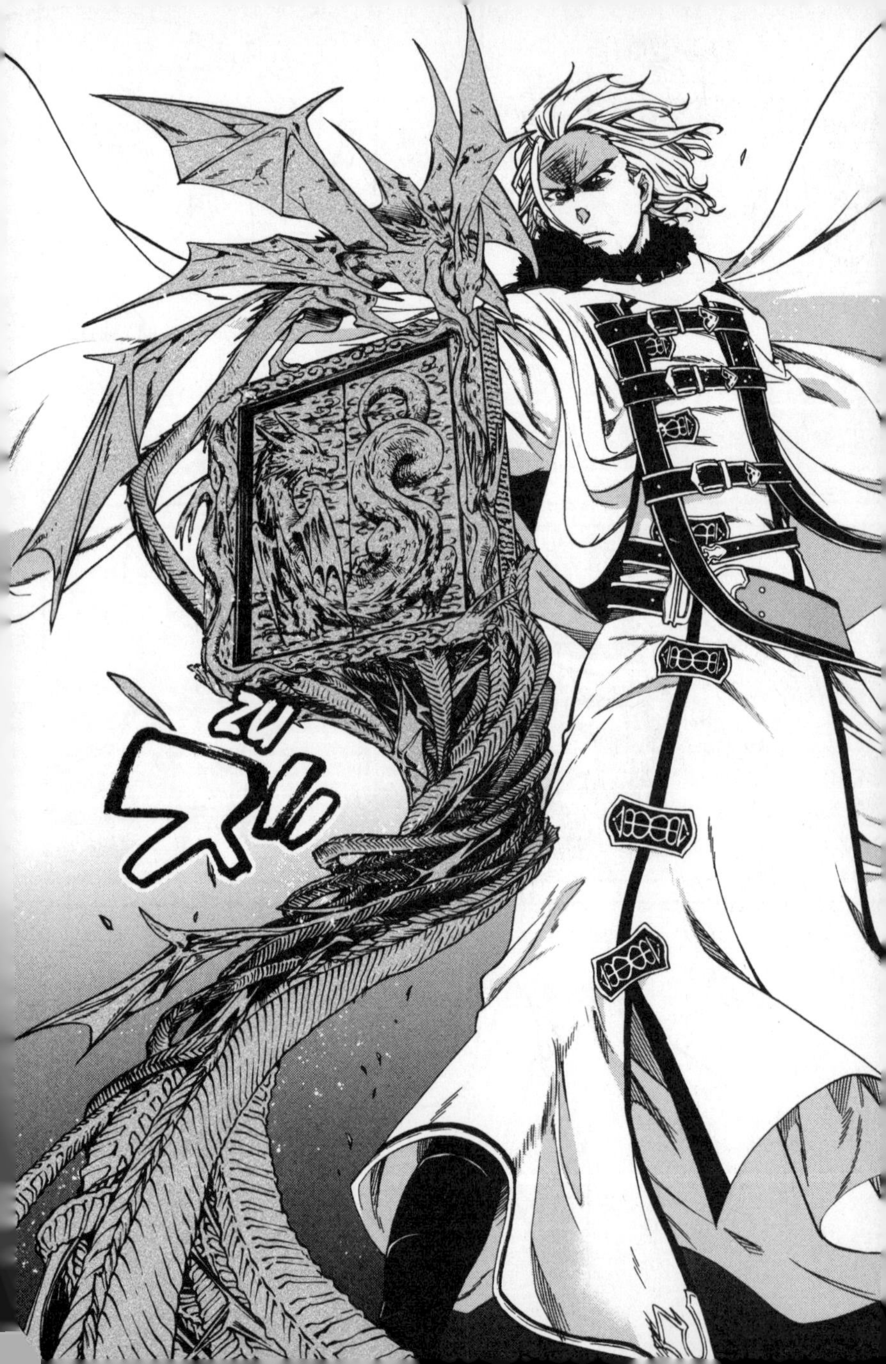
ZU

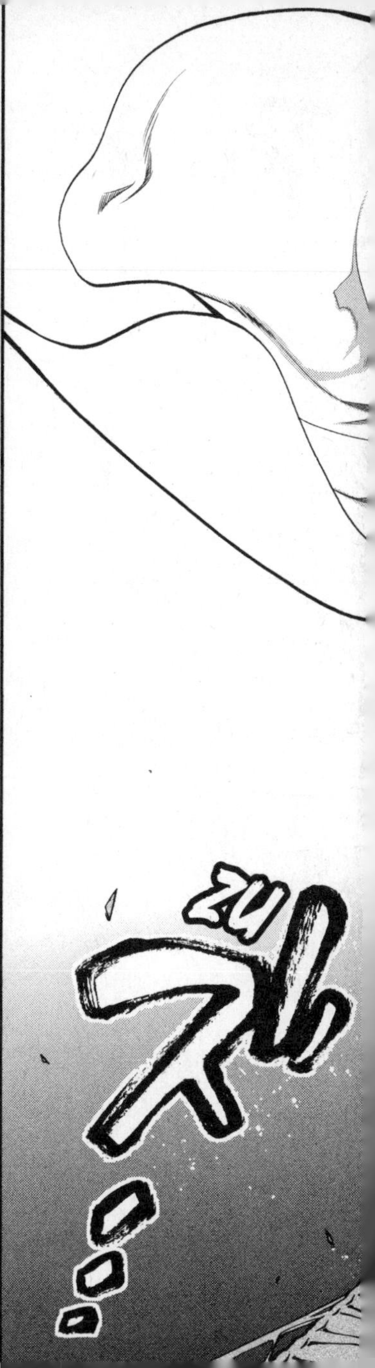
ZU
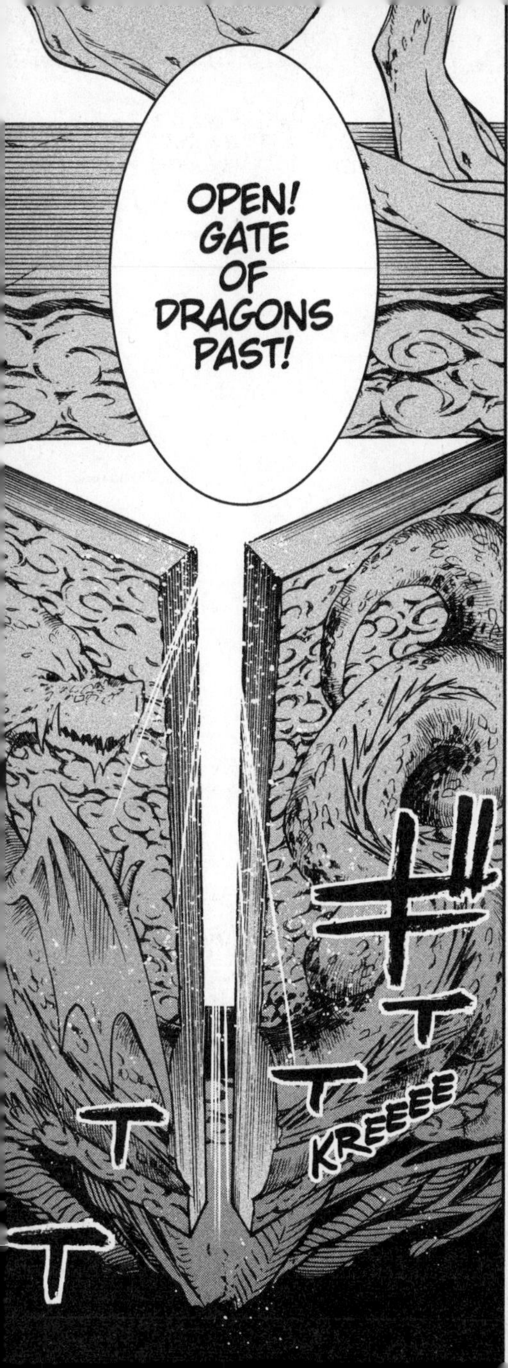
OPEN! GATE OF DRAGONS PAST!
KREEEEE

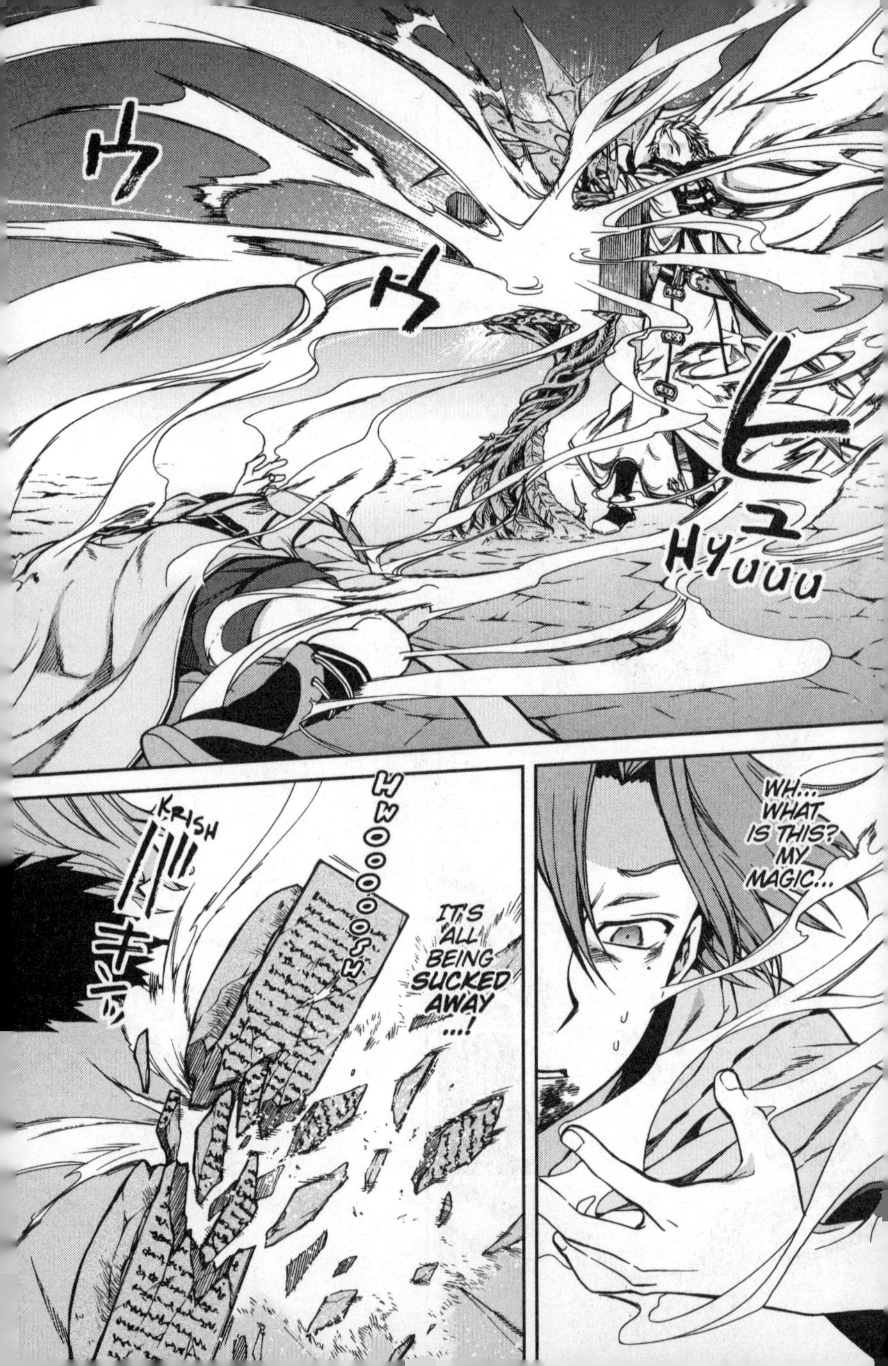
HYUUUU
WH... WHAT IS THIS? MY MAGIC...
IT'S ALL BEING SUCKED AWAY...!
HWOOOOOOSH
KRISH

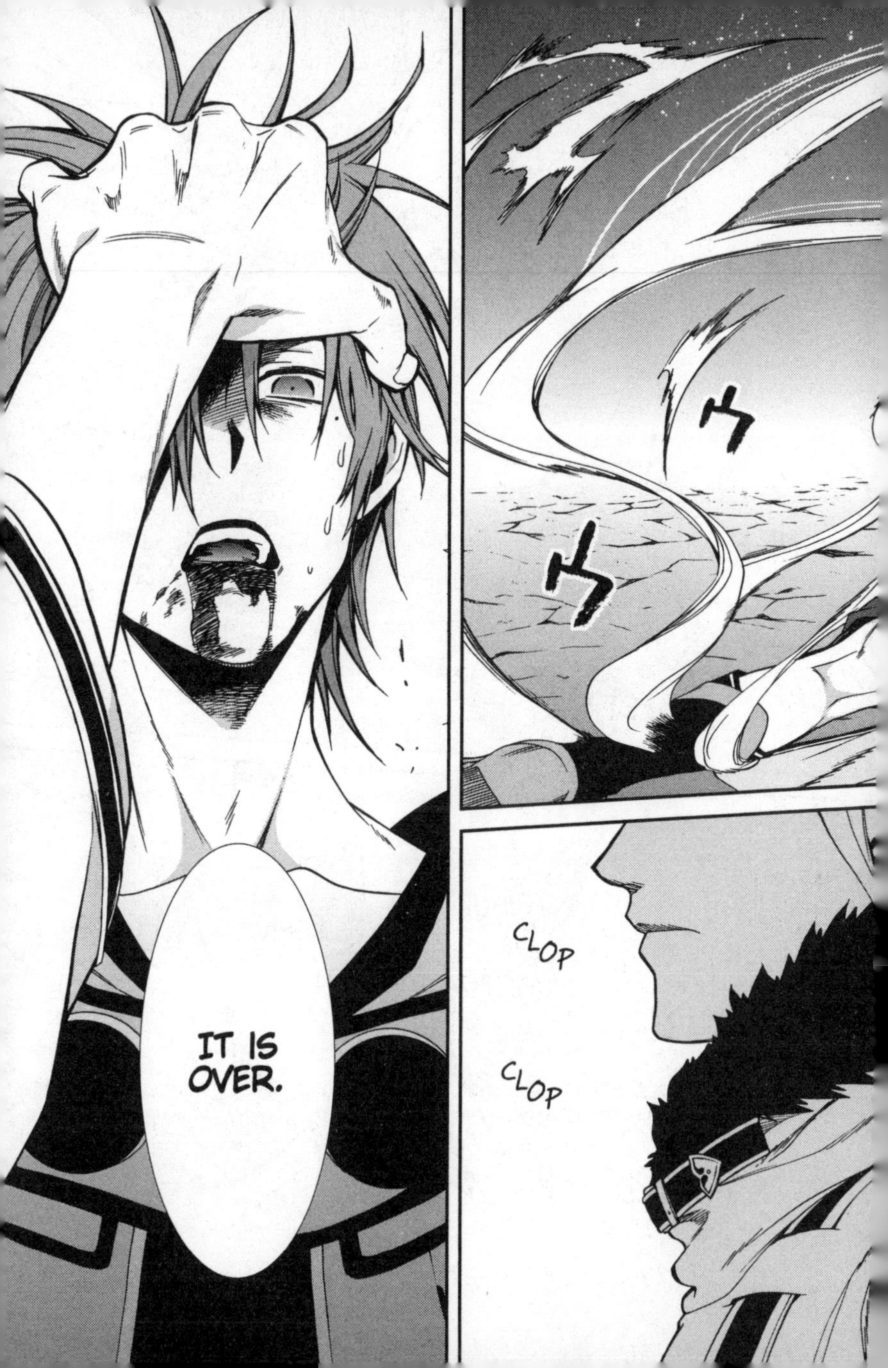
ウ
ウ
CLOP
CLOP
IT IS OVER.

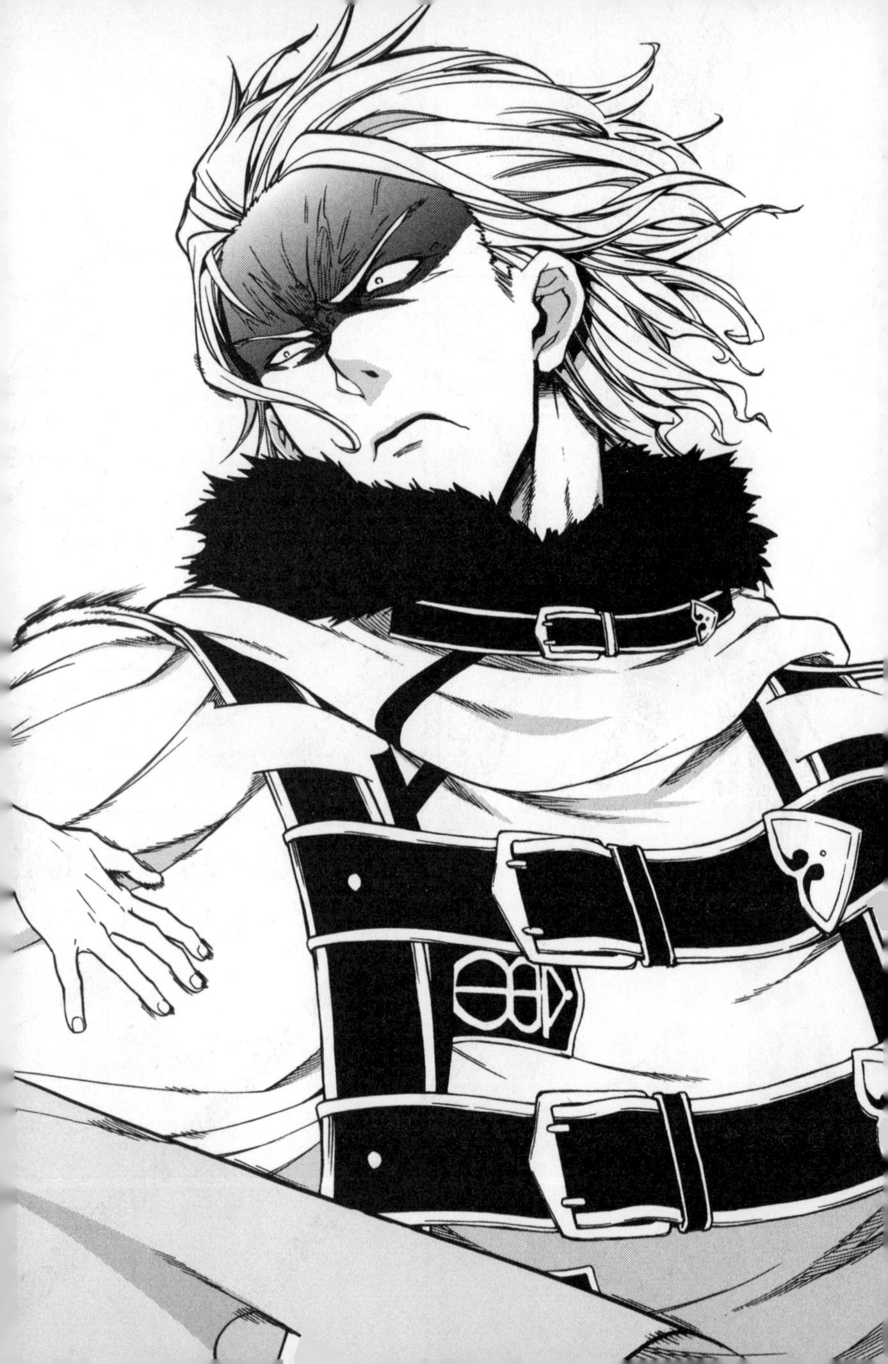

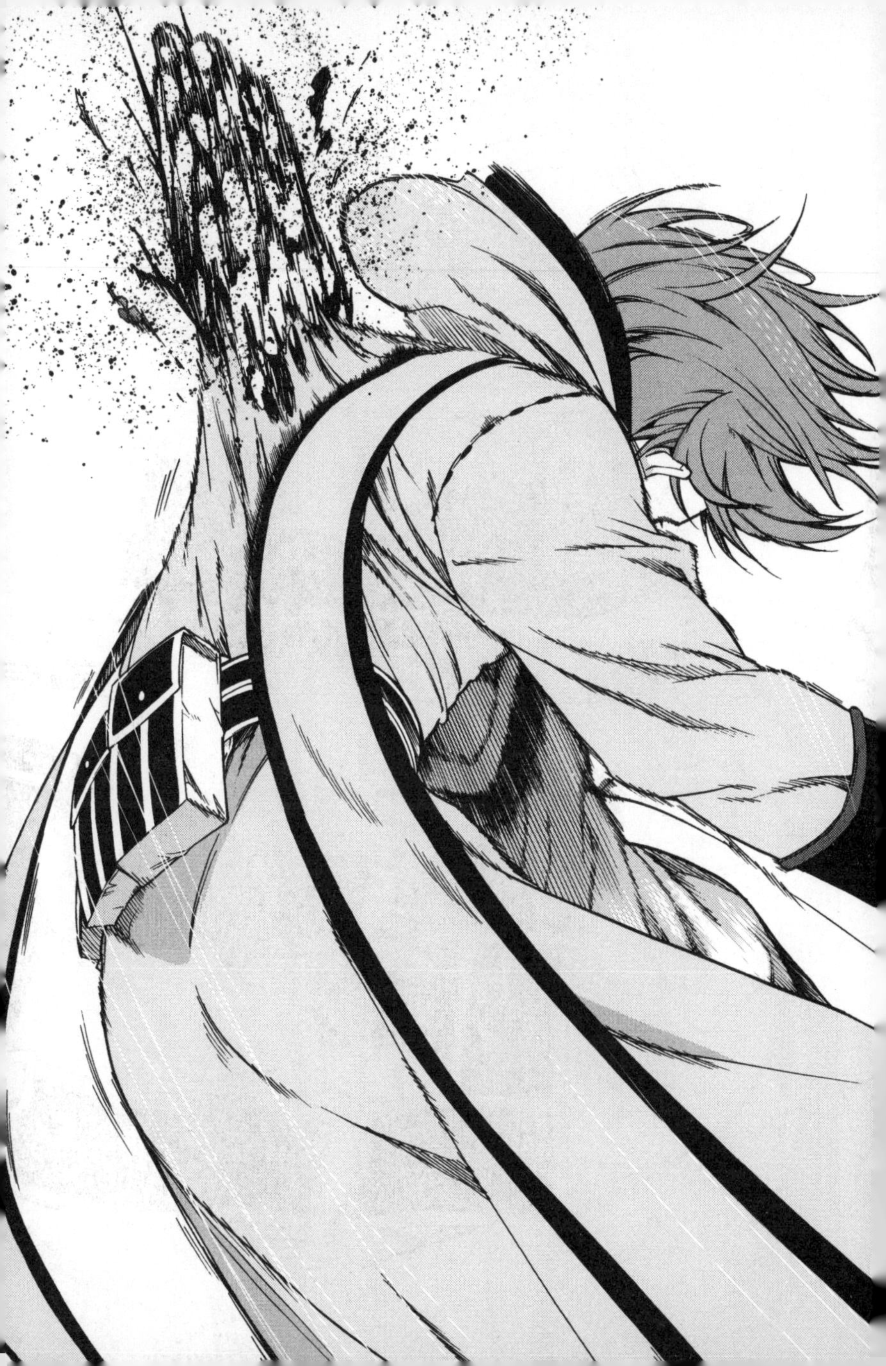

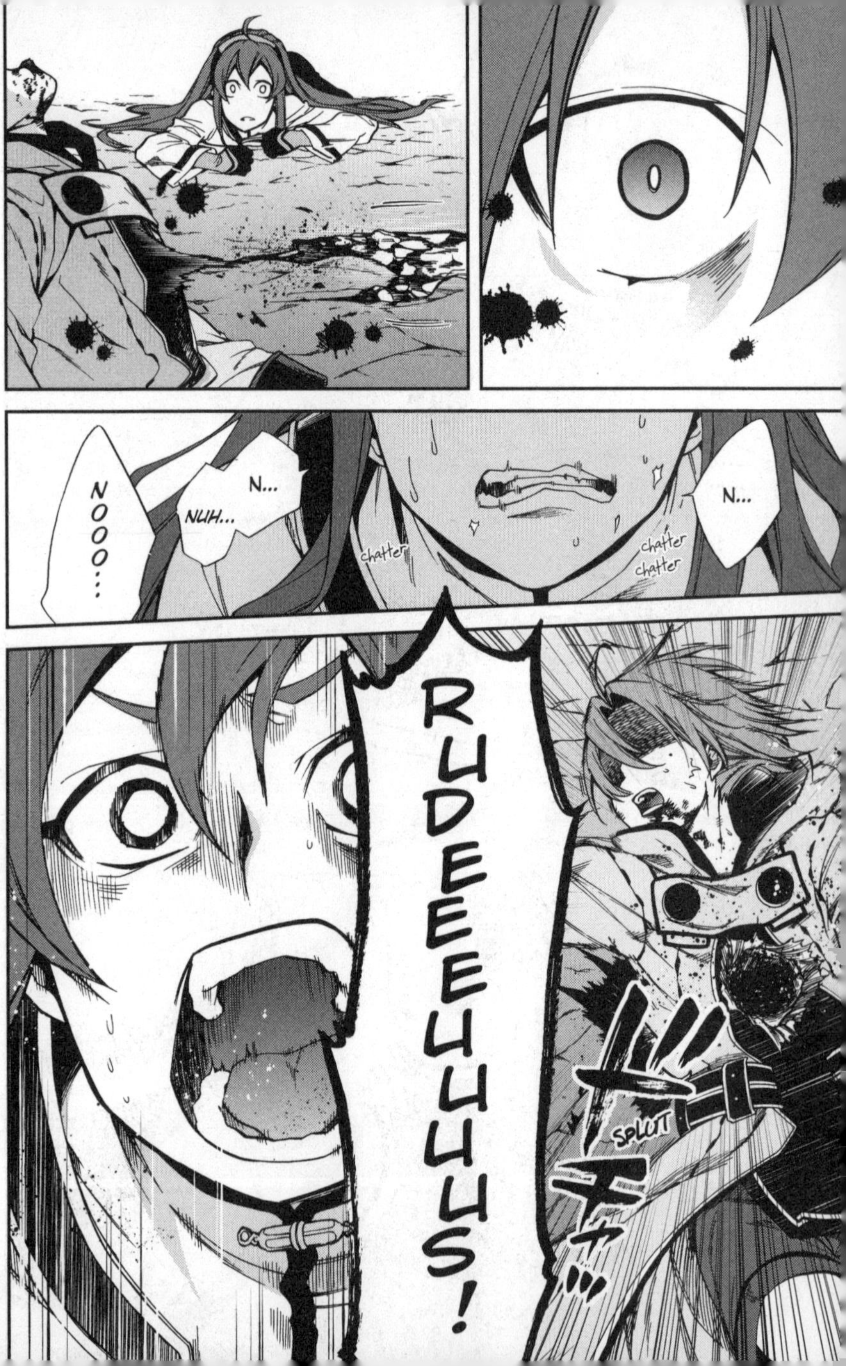
N...
chatter chatter
N... NUH...
chatter
NOOOO...
RUDEEEEUUUUS!
SPLUT

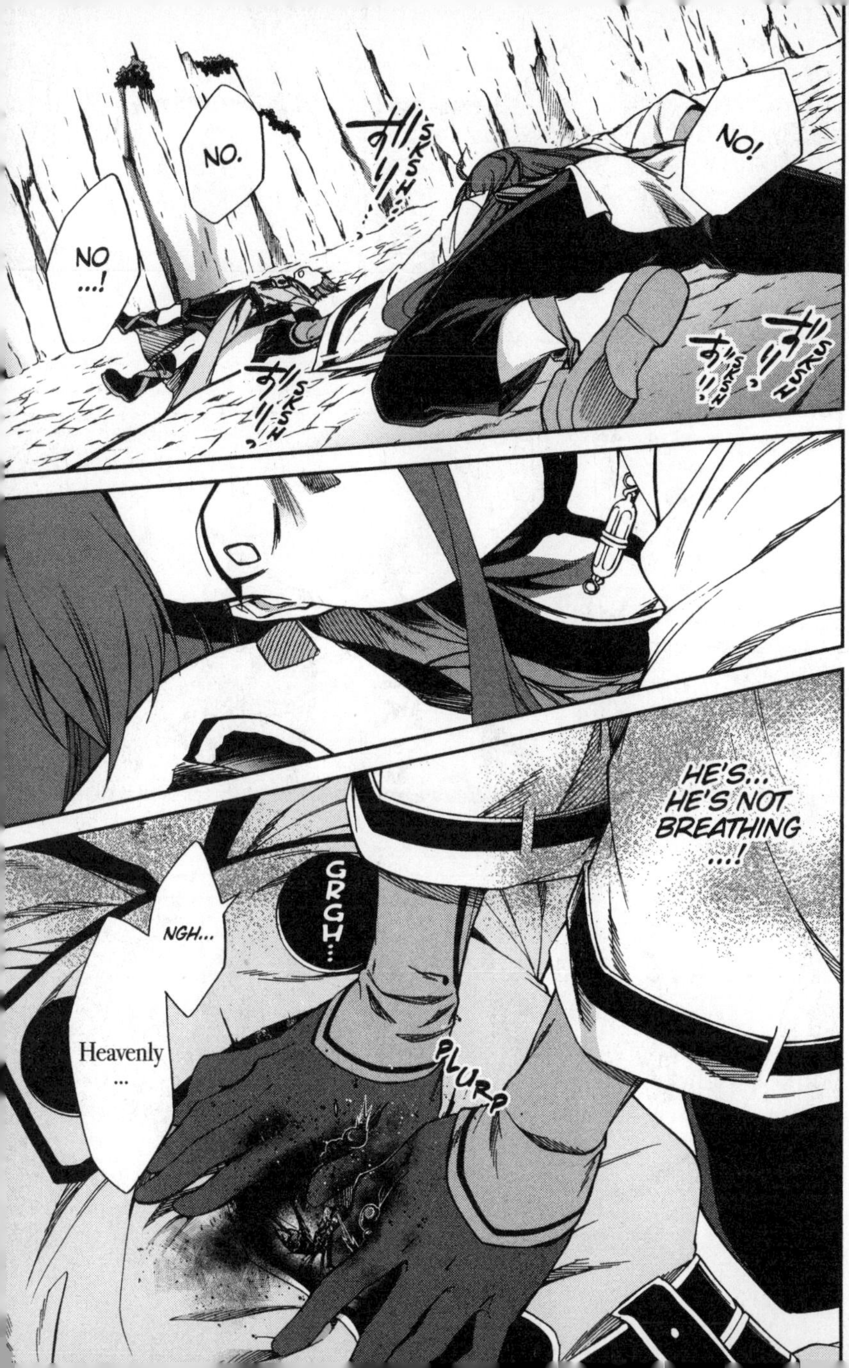
SKSH
SKSH
NO!
NO.
SKSH
NO ...!
SKSH
HE'S... HE'S NOT BREATHING ...!
GRGH...
NGH...
Heavenly ...
PLURP

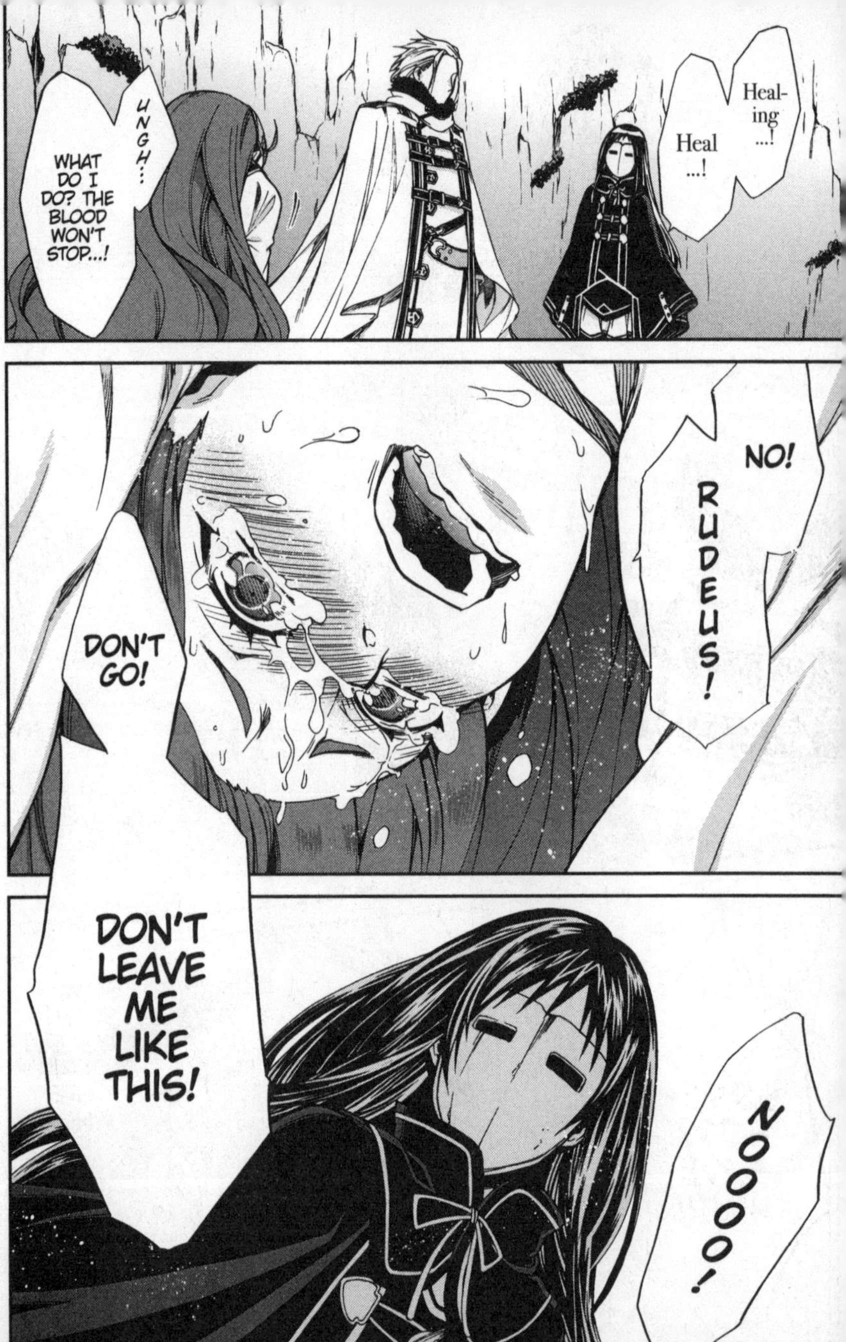
Heal-ing ...!
Heal ...!
UNGH...
WHAT DO I DO? THE BLOOD WON'T STOP...!
NO!
RUDEUS!
DON'T GO!
NOOOOO!
DON'T LEAVE ME LIKE THIS!

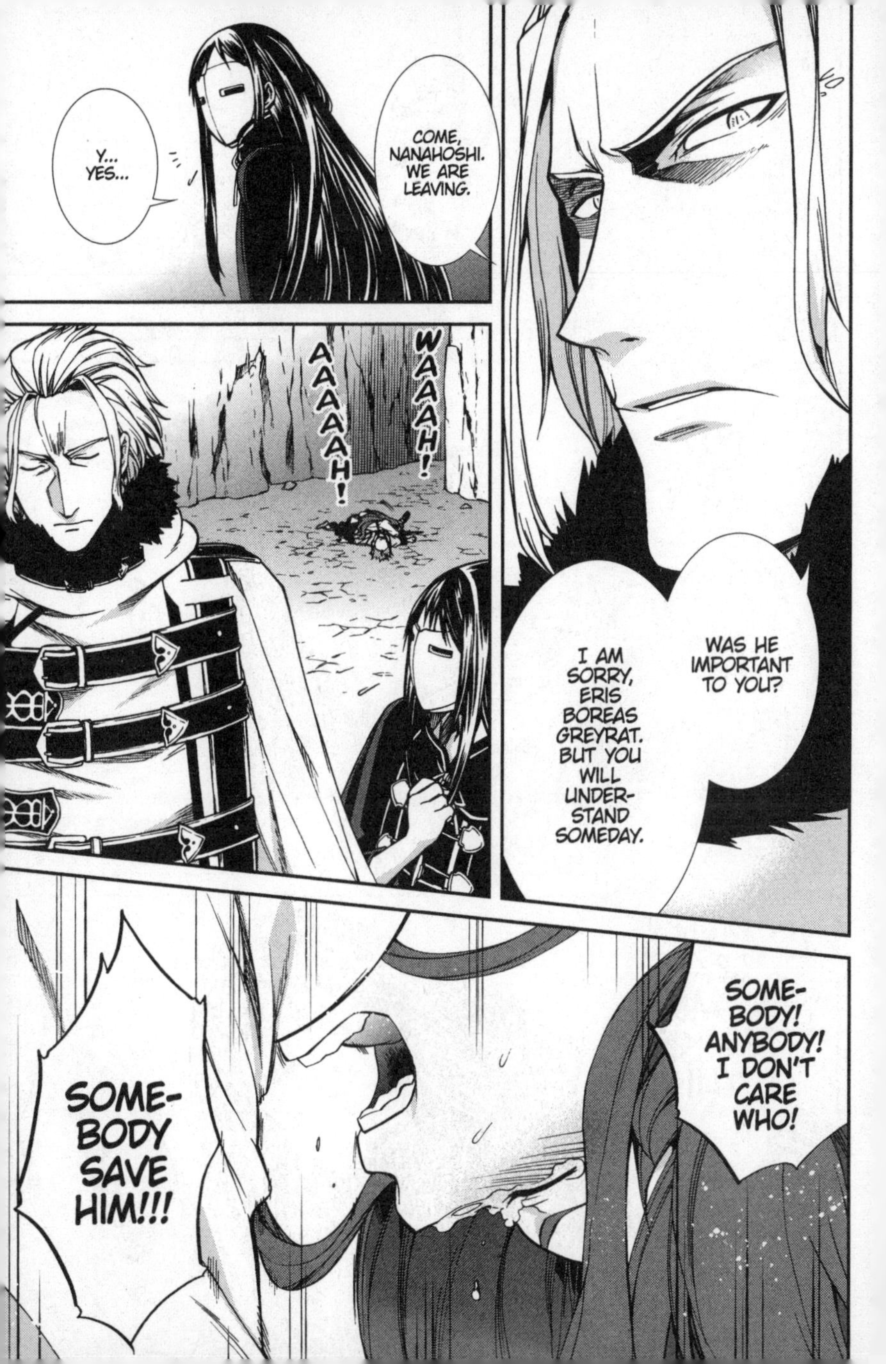

WAS HE IMPORTANT TO YOU?
I AM SORRY, ERIS BOREAS GREYRAT. BUT YOU WILL UNDERSTAND SOMEDAY.
COME, NANAHOSHI. WE ARE LEAVING.
Y... YES...
WAAAAH!
AAAAAH!
SOME-BODY! ANYBODY! I DON'T CARE WHO!
SOME-BODY SAVE HIM!!!

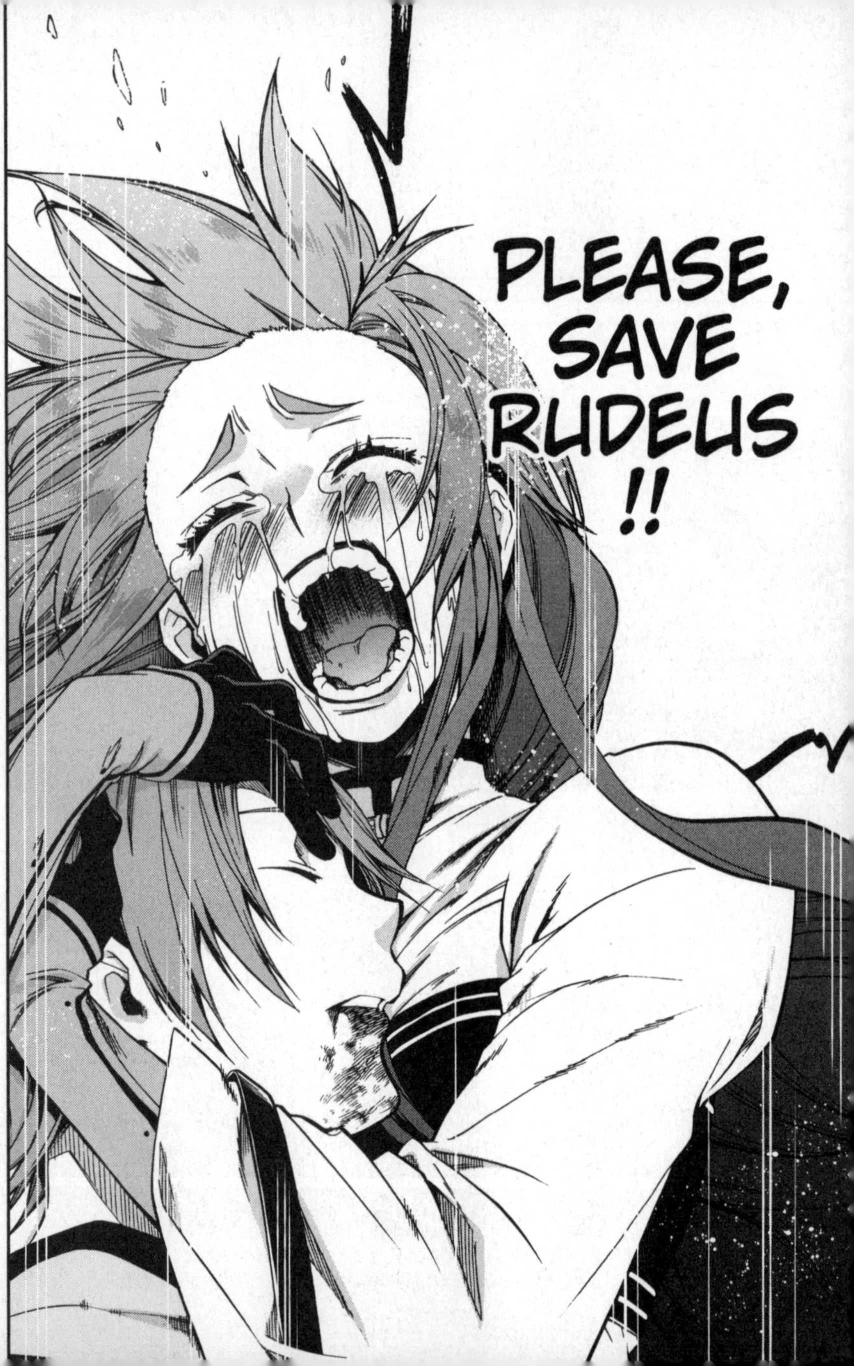
PLEASE, SAVE RUDEUS !!

The story continues in Volume 10!

無職転生

異世界行ったら本気だす

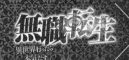

Mushoku Tensei: jobless reincarnation

×

Re:ゼロから始める異世界生活

Re: Life in a different world from zero

Re:ZERO -Starting Life in Another World-

SHORT STORY COLLABORATION:
Mushoku Tensei
X
Re:ZERO
—Starting Life in Another World—

❮❮ Chapter 1 ❯❯

By Nagatsuki Tappei

I was completely at a loss.

"Where am I...?"

I looked right, then left. It didn't matter; I didn't recognize anything. I didn't recognize the town, the faces, or even the feel of the place.

This was definitely an odd situation. A minute ago I'd been inside a mansion, and now all around me was the hustle and bustle of a town I'd never seen before.

There's only one conclusion a person could make.

"I must have teleported."

I snapped my fingers as I said it. That's how I, Natsuki Subaru, rolled.

I guess you could say it was natural. After all, you wouldn't know it to look at me, but this wasn't my first time getting teleported someplace. I'd even experienced being summoned to another world.

It's not like I was going to panic and break down and cry. I wasn't that weak.

"Looks like I have my Summoned-to-Another-World Greed Set with me…"

The plastic bag was just the same as the first day I was summoned: snacks, cup noodles, and in my pocket, a flip-phone. Everything was so much like last time, I could have cried.

"I don't even get a single Excalibur… As if it'd be that easy. Right! I don't have time to be depressed. I have to get back ASAP!"

I closed the flip phone and girded my loins.

Maybe it was my unusual clothes, but I could feel the stab of people's eyes. It bothered me. I had to act, and act now.

I had to get back to the mansion. I made a promise.

"Emilia-tan is waiting for me."

A date with the girl of my dreams. There was no way I'd let anything get in the way of that! I made a vow in my heart, and raced across that unfamiliar town.

"Long story short, you're from another world."

Wow. Seriously.

That was how my conversation with that bland-faced guy went.

He was so average-looking that maybe I should have called him Bystander. But it seemed he was actually some god called Hitogami.

I was pretty surprised to hear him announce himself as a literal god, but I was probably dreaming, so I figured that was just how these things went.

"It's convenient that you're so resilient, Natsuki-kun. Or should I say Subaru-kun?"

If I had to pick one or the other, I'd go with Subaru.

"By the way, Mr. God, is it okay if I ask a few questions? Like why I'm here, in this world?"

"Hmm. That's a good question. To be honest, I don't know the answer myself."

"But you're a god, aren't you?"

"Even gods aren't all-knowing. But hey, I can tell you something that'll help. You do want to go back to the world you came from, don't you?"

"Well…that depends on which world you're talking about."

"The world you were in right before you came here. That one, you know? So, how about it?"

Naturally, I had to answer "yes."

"I made a promise, and I have a bunch of other

reasons to go back. So get me back there ASAP, Mr. God!"

"Well, you know, I'd love to do that, but I told you, didn't I? I can only tell you things. You're the one who has to take action."

I knew it wouldn't be that simple. "So, what do I have to do?"

"Don't get your knickers in a twist. First, why do you think I want to tell you something?"

"Is it because I keep disappearing into different worlds? Have the gods made some kind of mistake?"

"Nah, the Six-Faced World is out of my jurisdiction. I think I've said this before, but do you guys always mistrust gods when this sort of thing happens?"

"'You guys?' Let's put aside the issue of you grouping me together with everyone else...but where I'm from, we don't really see our God screwing up and sending people to other worlds, you know."

"I see. Then for now, let's just drop all our preconceived notions. I'm not like the other gods."

"Got it. By the way, could you explain why you said 'you guys' earlier?"

"Pretty observant, aren't you?"

"More like desperate. Is there someone else here from another world?"

"That answer relates to my previous question. To tell you the truth, I have the power to see people's futures."

"Oh, wow. I guess you are a god."

"And it looks like your future will change because

you're here. And that change isn't too convenient for me. The person I've got my eye on will die."

"Well, that's...that doesn't make me feel too good, either."

"Right? It's a big issue for both of us. To get you back to your old world, you need a certain magical tool. Activating it requires a humongous amount of magical power, you see. You get it now?"

"You mean the person with that humongous amount of magical power is going to die if something doesn't change?"

"Bingo! You catch on quick, don't you? So now that we're on the same page...you understand we have a mutual interest in this, right?"

"I want this person to help me get back to my old world. And you, Hitogami, don't want them to die... That about cover it?"

"Yes. Right now, said person is in the vicinity of the Red Dragon's Mandible... That's south of the town you're in. You should meet up with him there."

"Got it. By the way, what *is* that all-important magical tool?"

"Oh yeah, yeah. I forgot. The tool in question looks like this."

Lo and behold, a vision of the magical tool or whatever-it-was hovered in the sky. It looked kind of like a pendant with a chain attached. The design was so generic that it wasn't going to be easy to find.

"Your dream's almost over. For your sake and mine,

give it all you've got, okay?"

"You make it sound like it's not even your problem. Well, anyway, thanks for your help. I'll do my best. Whoa, whoa, hold on! What about that person I'm supposed to look for?"

"Oh, that's right. Right. His name is—"

"Good morning. I take it you slept well?" So said a middle-aged man with a peacock tattoo on his cheek.

He was wearing a rainbow-colored top, knee-length shorts, and sported a hairstyle that looked like a parabolic antenna—pretty intense.

"Mr. Subaru?"

"Oh, good morning, Mr. Auber. Thank you for letting me stay."

"What? It's nothing. Anyone would do the same," Auber said, out of consideration for me. His smile brimmed with human kindness. Quite the opposite of what you'd expect from him at first glance.

I met him the other day when I was wandering around town with nowhere to go. We hit it off, that's all. And he really liked my tracksuit and flip phone, so he let me sleep here.

Honestly, part of me kind of suspected he was just after my ass, but now that it was morning and my posterior was untouched, I felt bad for thinking that.

Even though I was unfortunate enough to cross worlds, I was still saved by the bonds of our common humanity. I owe people so much.

"And what will you do now, Mr. Subaru? Last night you were troubled, and said you had nowhere to go, but today…"

"Well, I guess you can say that now, I do have somewhere to go. Have you heard of the Red Dragon's Mandible?" I asked timidly, while we had breakfast.

It was Auber's treat. If this Dragon's Mandible was a real place, then I wouldn't have to worry about whether the dream was just a figment of my imagination.

"That is the name of a canyon not far from here. It is near the border in the Red Dragon Mountains. Do you have business there?"

"So it does exist. That's a load off my back. I don't have business at the Mandible, but a town further south. I think a friend of a friend might be there, so…"

"Hmm. I see. Yes, indeed…"

Friend of a friend. That phrase was kind of disrespectful to the god and whoever this other person was, but I decided to let that slide for now.

Auber crossed his arms and nodded. I felt nervous—like maybe he had a problem with what I'd said. But there was never any reason to worry. "You should use a carriage if you're going south of Red Dragon's Mandible. Actually, as it happens, I have some business there as well."

It was obvious Mr. Auber was lying, and badly. He didn't want me to feel indebted to him, but he wanted to take me there. Why?

"Mr. Subaru, you have entertained me with such fascinating stories. I think those tales will perhaps help hone my sword skills. You have saved my future. This is how I would repay you… So please, take it as such."

I thought I was going to cry.

What was with this guy? He looked like…well, you know…but he was such a great guy.

"I appreciate that, Mr. Auber. Seriously, thank you so much."

His words were the words of a swordsman, and I, another swordsman, decided to take them at face value. Although in my case, I only did a little kendo when I was in junior high.

Auber and I got in the carriage and left town, headed south towards Red Dragon's Mandible.

Before we passed through the canyon, I saw some red dragons flying over the peaks. Don't tell anyone, but it made me a little anxious.

"The Red Dragons are the ultimate monsters of the Central Continent. Do not act rashly."

"You couldn't defeat one either, Mr. Auber?"

"I would most likely be defeated by their strength in numbers," answered Auber, adjusting the four swords at his hip.

The ride was uneventful, and we passed the time with small talk until we reached our destination.

"This isn't much, but…"

Auber filled a leather bag with money and handed it

to me. Seriously, I couldn't thank that guy enough.

Of course, he offered to stay until I found that friend of a friend, but I turned him down.

He had already done too much for me. And I learned a lot from him while we were travelling.

I took all that to heart, and decided to do the next part myself.

"Until we meet again, Mr. Subaru. I pray for your good health," said Auber Corvette, the Emperor of the North, as he put his hand to his heart and acknowledged my resolve.

If my wish came true, then I would leave this world. But before that, I hoped I could write him a letter filled with gratitude.

That was what I was thinking when I headed out to find this friend of a friend.

"Now, where are you, Rudeus?"

"Halt," said some brown-haired kid.

He looked old enough to be in elementary school.

He had a kind face and a freckle under his left eye. He was pretty enough that I guessed someday the girls would love him.

The kid held a big staff, standing there at the entrance of an alley.

Thugs around me scattered, and I, on the ground in only my socks and undies, looked up at him in surprise. Everything else had been ripped from me.

"You totally saved me! Thanks! I owe you one! Let me say this again, grazie! Merci beaucoup!"

Undressed and half-naked, I bowed to the boy who saved me.

No, seriously, I legit thought I was going to die.

I parted ways with Auber and flew off feeling like my own man. Like I could really do this. That's when some thugs caught me in a back alley and took everything. Almost my life, too.

My bad luck struck again, and I seriously regretted trying to act like a big man. I never should have asked Auber to go.

"Oh God! Or like, God, I've been saved! But please tell me, in detail, how to save *myself* next time!"

I didn't care how embarrassing I was. Who'd care about that now? They'd already stripped me to my underwear in the middle of town. Living was the most important thing. No more muggings! Please!

"Umm, will you be all right?" said the boy, waiting for an opening in my joyous appreciation of life.

I bowed my head to him again.

"Seriously, you saved me. My name is Natsuki Subaru, and I have no money to thank you with, but let me say it, at least. Maybe a couple thousand times."

"Please don't say it a thousand times. There are a few things I'd like to ask you about, actually. Your appearance, for starters…"

"Oh, this? It might be an unusual look, but it's not anything too nice. Though actually, it's probably the reason they targeted me…"

"It's a tracksuit, right? That, and a bag from a mini-mart, and…" The boy blabbered suddenly, scratching his head. "Oh, damn! I don't even know where to start!"

My brain froze when I figured out what he meant.

The boy took a deep breath.

"Maybe you're from another world, too?"

"I'm Rudeus Greyrat."

"Rudeus! *You're* Rudeus?! The one Hitogami talked about?!"

"Urph."

He made a face, didn't he?!

"It's nothing. It's just…you brought up the name of that shady… So you're mixed up with Hitogami, too?

"He was in my dreams. I get what you mean by shady, but to be honest, he saved me, you know?" I put my hands together in gratitude.

"By that gesture you just made, and your name… you're Japanese, aren't you?"

"Ooh, yes, yes! I'm a Japanese guy who's been summoned to another world. Rudeus, you said 'too,' but you kinda look like a local…"

"In my case, I was reincarnated here. I've been living here since I was a baby."

"So on this day, someone summoned from another world met someone reincarnated from another world…!"

"It's so easy to talk to someone who understands…!

…Oops."

I guessed Rudeus thought he'd said too much, because he covered his mouth. I burst out laughing.

Summoned and reincarnated, we were both doing pretty well.

I guess it was pretty easy for two people from another world to get along. We understood each other's situation. It was almost like we were already best friends.

"So you need my magic and a magical tool to get back to your world…"

"I know it's rude to ask, but it looks like you're doing pretty well for yourself here. Maybe you don't really have time to deal with me…?"

"No, there's no issue with the magic thing. I mean, I just met someone from home, you know? We're on the same team. But I'm thinking that finding this magical tool won't be a walk in the park."

"I can't believe you'll do this for me…just like that!"

"Huh? If you saw someone from Japan in trouble in your world, could you ignore them? You couldn't, right?"

He laughed with a strangely pessimistic expression that didn't match his age.

His words made me think.

I mean, how about it? *Could* I do what Rudeus was doing? After all, I still owed Auber.

If nothing else, I hoped I could at least try to be like Rudeus.

★ ★ ★

I decided to head with him to the Asura Kingdom.

"If we go to Asura, I have friends that will help me out. Plus, there's a lot of people there, so it'll be easier to get some info about that magical tool. We'll just settle in there and find a way to get you home at our leisure."

That was Rudeus's plan, and I had no objections. In fact, the only one who did was the girl who was with him.

"Really, Rudeus, you're too good for your own good! You just keep on making life harder for yourself," said Eris, the pretty redhead, her brows askew.

This lover of his wouldn't sit quietly on the sidelines…or, at least, she was probably a candidate to be his lover someday. She certainly didn't look very happy about me barging in on their journey.

Rudeus talked it over with her, and suddenly I'd become a drifter who needed to get back to his family in Asura. I didn't know anything, couldn't do anything, and had no plans. Rudeus had taken pity on me—that's how he explained it.

"The ends justify the means, right?" said Rudeus.

When he laughed, he looked downright evil. I decided to keep that thought to myself.

Anyway, Eris and Ruijerd—the other person with them—eventually agreed. I was all good to join them on their journey.

Ruijerd was pretty scary-looking, but he was nice to kids, and it looked like he'd decided I was one, too. I guess that's why he was so nice.

That's how I took full advantage of their giving souls.

I even started to think that things would keep going like this: we'd find the magical tool, and I'd be back in no time.

I wish I could curse how dumb I was. When will I ever learn? They say even death can't fix stupid. No one knows that more than me.

No matter how many times I "Return by Death," this part of my personality never goes away.

Once again, we passed the Red Dragon's Mandible—the place I passed through with Auber, but this time from the North side.

We'd just passed that canyon when we met up with him.

"Rudeus, do not move. Eris, Subaru, you, too," warned Ruijerd.

He sounded seriously worried. Eris's face went red and she shook all over.

Rudeus and I had no clue, and scrunched up our faces.

The man was tall with silver hair and golden eyes. I shouldn't talk, but he had an evil gaze.

There wasn't anything more to him, so why are they both acting like that?

"Interesting... You do not turn your gaze from mine," said the man, staring at us.

Real touching that he thought we were brave, but slowly, I started to get a bad feeling about it all. Rudeus seemed worried too.

"That's strange. I have no memory of ever having met you."

I've felt this way before. In that warehouse of stolen stuff, when I was negotiating with the "Bowel Hunter." And back then...things got nasty.

"Tell me. Have heard this word before? *Hitogami.*"

"Yeah."

"Sure have."

Rudeus and I reflexively answered together.

It was a strange feeling of hopelessness and urgency that did it. That was how this guy made us feel. I just wanted to break the silence.

That was a mistake.

"Subaru!"

The voice felt like a blow to my shoulder.

"Ah!"

The man's hand pierced my chest like a spear.

A moment later, my brain registered the pain. Everything turned red. Blood and screams burst out of my throat.

It didn't just hurt. It was heart-rending.

The guy pierced Rudeus's chest too, and he

crumpled to the ground. It was an instantaneous death. At the same time, Rudeus's hand pushed my shoulder. That's why I didn't die right away.

But it was still fatal.

My head struck the hard ground. Hitogami's words belatedly passed through my mind. Rudeus was going to die.

This was it. I knew it.

I'd let it happen.

"…"

Far away, Ruijerd and Eris attacked the guy who'd killed us. They didn't have a chance.

The sounds of their battle reached me, but my eyes couldn't follow. As my world clouded over, I saw something fall from the man's sleeve.

A pendant. A pendant on a chain.

"Wha…?"

I tried to speak, but I couldn't even tell if air or blood came out.

But there was Rudeus's life, and the tool I needed to go back, and that guy was an obstacle between me and them both.

I looked at Rudeus, clinging to this memory.

I was stupid. Because of me, my friend would die with me. Even now, he was fighting death, trying to shield me.

If I had a chance in this world…

If there was a way for me to save my friend, then…

"I…will…save you."

The instant I said that, I lost all consciousness. We died.

Then it began. The loop of another world…in another world.

✦ Chapter 2 ✦

By Rifujin na Magonote

"Good morning. It seems you slept well."

I woke up to see a man with the peacock tattoo on his cheek. He wore a rainbow-colored top, knee-length shorts, and sported a hair style that looked like a parabolic antenna—pretty intense.

"Mr. Subaru?"

"Good morning…Mr. Auber."

I touched my chest with my right hand and wiped the sweat off my forehead with my left. I could feel the echo of my heart beating quickly.

"You do not seem well. Are you sick, perhaps?"

Dream? No, it wasn't a dream. I could still feel That Guy piercing my chest.

So, at that point, it was a "Return by Death," right?

I, Natsuki Subaru, had a special power.

To make a long story short, when I die, my life rewinds to a certain point, so I can redo things.

Even though I called it my power, it wasn't like I could pick where I started over. I'd be hard pressed to say it was convenient.

This time, I didn't know what happened, much less what my goal was. But compared to the other times, it was easy to figure out.

To get back to my old world, I needed that magical tool.

And That Guy had it.

He would kill my friend, Rudeus, who I needed to activate the tool. Rudeus, who was nice to me, who was in a bind in another world, just like I was.

In short, if I could kill That Guy, the crazy one who came out of the blue and killed us while we were traveling, I could get home and Rudeus could stay alive.

He looked really strong, but he was alone. There were a million ways to do it.

We could take a strong bodyguard with us or something, right?

"What will you do now, Mr. Subaru? Last night you were troubled, and said you had nowhere to go, but today…"

"Hrmm, it's about that, but it's hard to explain…"

I raised my head, and there he was. This guy.

The Emperor of the North, Auber Corvette.

In contrast to his strict gaze, he had a cool nickname like "Emperor of the North." I knew someone called a "Sword Saint," and having a nickname like that usually meant you had the skills to back it up.

"Mr. Auber, you're good with swords, right?"

"Well now, as I am still in training, I hesitate to sing

my own praises, but I have indeed been granted the title Emperor of the North. It would not do for me to be overly modest. That is how it stands. Why do you ask?"

"I'm already in your debt for the night and the meal, and I'm embarrassed to say that I have something else to ask of you, but…"

"You want me to kill someone?"

"Yeah, that about sums it up."

"I do not wield this sword lightly."

"Please! The truth is: some guy is after my friend. He's going to kill him! And my friend's a really good guy, who helped me out just because we come from the same place!"

"Hmm… Well, in that case, I suppose it might be all right."

"So it's okay?"

"My teacher once said, 'Do not hold back your sword when indebted to another.' I suppose that applies to cases such as this."

I wanted to cry. Since I'd come to this world, I'd been blessed by fate and the bonds between people.

There was also that crazy guy who assaulted people by the side of the road though, so maybe that evened things out.

"I owe you."

And that's how I got the Emperor of the North, Auber Corvette, to join our party.

"There aren't many details. But to put it bluntly, that guy's going to kill you."

"Seriously? So let me get this straight, you've come here from another world, but originally you're from yet another world. And you've come all this way, with reinforcements, to save my life?! You're such a great guy!"

"Well, admittedly, there's also the bit about me wanting to make it home…"

As usual, Rudeus caught on quickly. After I explained the situation, he figured out the rest.

I suppose it might have been because he was reincarnated and I was summoned, but maybe Rudeus was just a friendly guy. I mean, people were usually more guarded.

"And you believe me? Just like that."

"Well, you know, after you've been reincarnated once…and I've already run into some beings who can see the future, so…"

That brought the hazy outline of Hitogami to mind.

He had a point. If beings like that existed, I guess you'd more easily believe in anything paranormal.

"So, what's the plan?"

"Overwhelm him with numbers, something like that."

Rudeus, Eris, Ruijerd, Auber and me. That was five people.

I was pretty much useless, but the other four, including Rudeus, were incredibly strong.

No matter how strong that man was, if so many super-strong people attacked him, he was going to go down.

"To put it simply, I'll blind him with this, and then everyone will rush in to attack. That's it."

I held my flip phone with a big grin on my face, but Rudeus had a thoughtful look.

"Hmm…"

"Something wrong?"

"No, let's go with that."

All the same, Rudeus seemed to have issues with the plan.

Well, I guess he would, right? From his point of view, That Guy was just a stranger. And it went against his morals to attack a stranger for no reason, even though that stranger would kill him. To be honest, I didn't like it very much either.

"Hey, I can't really explain it, but he's really dangerous. He'll attack you for no reason, all of a sudden. You might not like it, but believe me. Save me."

"No, I believe it. And even if you were lying about that part, it doesn't look like you're lying about wanting to go back to your old world."

He was so kind.

"If you saw someone from Japan in trouble in your world, could you just ignore them? You couldn't, right?"

I'd heard that before, in the previous loop.

No matter how many times I get stuck in this loop, I think Rudeus would always say the same thing.

I just had to repay him for those words.

The Red Dragon's Mandible.

We ran into That Guy again.

The tall man with the silver hair and golden eyes.

As soon as he saw him, Ruijerd shivered with fierce vigilance and Eris grabbed her scabbard. Auber was affected, too. His eyes opened wide and sweat dribbled down his chin.

Only Rudeus and I were immune, so we acted according to the plan.

I stood in front of That Guy as he walked up to us, defenseless.

"Heyyy, you. Do you know what thiiis is?"

I turned on the flash on my flip phone.

Right after that, my arm flew off.

Literally flew off.

The flash didn't even make him blink. He didn't even step back. He just attacked his enemies. Us.

Before I even realized that my arm was gone, Ruijerd jumped on him.

The man caught Ruijerd's spear on the first thrust and punched him in the chin. Ruijerd crumpled to the ground.

Eris and Auber fought on.

It only took one shot for both of them.

Eris didn't even touch the man before she was blown away. Auber's first strike was deflected, and then he got stabbed through the chest.

Then, Rudeus finally used some magic.

He launched a boulder, big enough and fast enough to take off someone's head. It landed with an amazing sound.

But the man wasn't hurt at all.

No, there was the tiniest of injuries where it hit. Just a small wound, like a paper cut.

Right after that, Rudeus died. Stabbed through the chest, just like last time.

"Ah…ah…aaahh…!"

That was when my life ended, too. Just when the man got blurry, his arm was buried in my chest.

"Noooooo!"

Eris's scream echoed.

Why did I underestimate him? Why did I think it'd all work out…?

Why? How…?

Racked with guilt, I heard Auber's last words.

"It can't be…the Dragon God…Orsted…"

So. Now I knew That Guy's name.

★ ★ ★

"Damn…!"

I woke up for the third time, and pounded the bed with my fists.

Why was it so easy? Why did Rudeus just fall down dead like that?!

It had never been that easy, not even once. It was all my fault. I made the wrong decision.

I let Rudeus die again.

Auber, too. I let him die. It's my…

"You don't seem to be in a very good mood. Did you wet the bed?"

I was so absorbed in my self-pity that I didn't even notice Auber standing there.

"Mr. Auber… The Dragon God, Orsted. Do you know him? The one with silver hair and gold eyes."

"Of course! There isn't a swordsman alive who does not know the name. The Dragon God ranks second of the Seven Great Powers of the World. And even the existence of the one who ranks first is uncertain at the moment."

"Can you tell me how strong he is? Like, quantitatively?"

"My teacher was called the 'Northern God,' and ranks seventh among the Seven Great Powers. Descended from the Undying Demon folk, my teacher's body was almost indestructible, almost immortal. A hero who wielded a giant demon sword, itself near as tall as a man. My teacher slayed mountains of gigantic beasts, however…against the Dragon God, even they were helpless as a babe in arms. The battle ended in my teacher's complete and utter defeat. As for other tales…"

The anecdotes about Orsted continued for a while.

And the more I heard, the more dangerous he became.

It was said that he could dodge attacks by reading the future.

It was said he could render attacks he could not dodge invalid.

It was said he'd mastered all the martial arts of this world.

It was said he could smash mountains.

It was said he was so ferocious that even the red dragons avoided crossing his path.

It seemed that all of the "Seven Great Powers of the World" weren't normal, but the top four were said to be in a class of their own.

Why was someone that big wandering around a place like that? What about checks and balances?!

Those anecdotes were enough to drive a person to curse.

Even if I'd been clueless, I cursed myself for trying to take on a monster with one cheap trick.

"But of course, Orsted is quite elusive. Someone you may never meet in your entire life. It is not certain how much of what is said is true."

From what I'd seen, it was all completely true.

Not only did he dodge all attacks, he also countered each one effectively. Auber was definitely skilled, but Eris and Ruijerd must be pretty strong, too. He blew them all away like nothing.

He was probably just as strong as the rumors said.

"Mr. Auber, if you were to fight him, how would you do it? If you couldn't afford to lose."

"Oh dear, dear. Fight? That's not very peaceful, is it?

"No, I'm just curious. I mean, every guy thinks about this stuff, right? How to beat a super-strong guy, that kind of thing."

I didn't know a thing about this world.

So I'd do best to start off by gathering information. Like how the swordsmen fought here, and what kind of decisions they made in battle. Only then could I start thinking about what I should do.

"You're not wrong. If it was me, I'd start by…"

Listening to Auber's ideas, I began to think of another strategy.

"Hmm…"

When I told him my plan, Rudeus raised his voice like he had an idea again.

Yes, again.

"Something wrong?"

"No, let's just go with that."

Same answer, but this time it bothered me a little. I ignored it the last time, but I'd also messed up. This time, I wanted to know.

"No, no. There is something, right? Like the plan's missing something?! Or you're not happy about attacking someone who hasn't done anything?! Say it, please! We're best buds, aren't we?!"

"Since when are we best buds? No, I don't want to die either, you know. You only get one life. I'll fight with all I got."

"I totally agree with you there, but come on, what's eating you?"

"I just thought we could be a little more crazy."

"Crazy?"

"Well, for example..." *Mumble mumble...*

Mumble mumble... "Can you do that? I mean that's..."

The plan Rudeus put forward was wilder than I could have imagined.

Such a pipe dream that my common sense said it was impossible. I would never have come up with it.

But, if something like that were really possible, then then our chances of victory were high.

"That's amazing. What else can you expect from someone who was reincarnated from another world? It's practically cheating, isn't it?"

"Well, I don't know. It's not really cheating, but because I can do all this, I feel like I can make it. Don't you have something, Subaru? Oh yeah, you can predict the future, right?"

"I...well...I can't really explain the details."

It would probably be better to tell Rudeus about "Return by Death," and make our plans accordingly, but there was nothing I could do. Whenever I tried to tell someone, I was assaulted by so much pain that I didn't even want to remember it.

"Oh, that so?"

"Given the situation, I want to tell you everything, you know? I want to tell you, but there's a serious reason why I can't."

"That's okay. If you can't, and it's not because you don't want to, that's just how it is, right? I get it."

"Seriously, I think I'm going to cry."

Someone reincarnated into another world and someone summoned there. Because we had a similar knowledge base, there were some things we didn't have to say. Who could have known how much easier that would make things...

"If you're going to cry, do it when it's all over, brother."

I'm pretty sure Rudeus felt the same way.

The third time began with Rudeus's magic.

First, he made a wall at the entrance to the Red Dragon's Mandible with Earth magic.

He made another behind the unsuspecting Orsted. Having blocked his escape route, calamity ensued. I mean, there's no other way to describe it.

At the top of a cliff, Rudeus handled the various

magic. A fire so explosive, you'd think it was positively nuclear. Unthinkable amounts of water, so much that you'd need Noah's Ark, followed by freezing temperatures that approached absolute zero...and then, for the finale, a sheet of bedrock that fell on Orsted like a blanket.

Nothing could live through that. It was a total calamity.

All that would be left was retrieve the magical tool.

Even though we didn't defeat him mano-a-mano, Orsted had to be seriously injured...

"You're kidding, right...?"

He wasn't hurt at all.

Orsted tossed off the ice and bedrock, completely unharmed. He didn't even have a scratch on him.

The edges of his clothes were just a bit singed. That's all.

"Oh no no no no! R-r-retreat!"

Rudeus lost his cool and ran towards the mountains. That was some good acting...or...huh? Did he seriously lose his cool? Was the next part of the plan going to be okay? Oh well. Here went part two.

"Rudeus! The signal! The signal!"

"Oh, y-yeah!"

Rudeus shot magic into the sky.

It whooshed upwards, made a loud boom and a flash, and disappeared.

"Huh?!"

Orsted stopped. He looked cautiously up at the sky.

We expected him to be more hurt, but he moved so fast. I thought he'd just kill us, but we might just make it.

"What did you do?" Orsted asked.

"I thought," I said. "You know...you, I mean, even the red dragons avoid you. So why would you take a safe road? You took the Red Dragon's mandible, where even the dragon's won't attack!"

Here came the moment of truth. We had no way of knowing how it'd turn out.

But, based on what Auber said, if you flash lights or make loud noises in the area...

"SKREEEEE!"

A gigantic red shadow zoomed in with an ear-piercing shriek. I looked up, and there was a dragon. The ultimate monster of the Central continent. A whole flock of them rushed towards us.

"I see. You did indeed think," said Orsted, like he was supremely bored. "Too bad."

For a split second, he disappeared.

One of the dragons' heads exploded and fell to the ground. Red blood spurted from its body.

After that, the other dragons were visibly shaken.

"With one blow...?"

"Seriously...?"

All we could do was watch. According to the plan, we were supposed defend ourselves from the red dragons and give a signal, at which point Ruijerd and everyone else would go in to finish off Orsted. But we didn't have to. It wouldn't work at all.

All of the red dragons were annihilated in the blink of an eye.

And after that, we died, too.

It happened over and over again.

I think we tried everything.

We even took Auber and Ruijerd's advice and asked for help from the local Adventurer's Guild.

We tried poisoning and trapping him.

But we just couldn't win. Nothing fazed him.

All our plans ended in failure, and our deaths.

But through all of it, no matter what I said, Rudeus helped.

Even when I got stressed and said things I shouldn't have, he said:

"If you saw someone from Japan in trouble in your world, could you just ignore them? You couldn't, right?"

Always with a wry grin, but never like he didn't want to help.

Every time we tried, I wanted Rudeus to live even more.

But I didn't know what to do.

I couldn't find the answer. I didn't know it.

Everything seemed bleak and emotionless. And I kept going through the loop, over and over again.

✦ The Crossover Continues Next Time! ✦

Re:ZERO -Starting Life in Another World- © Tappei Nagatsuki
Illustrations by: Yuka Fujikawa, Character Designs by: Shinichirou Otsuka

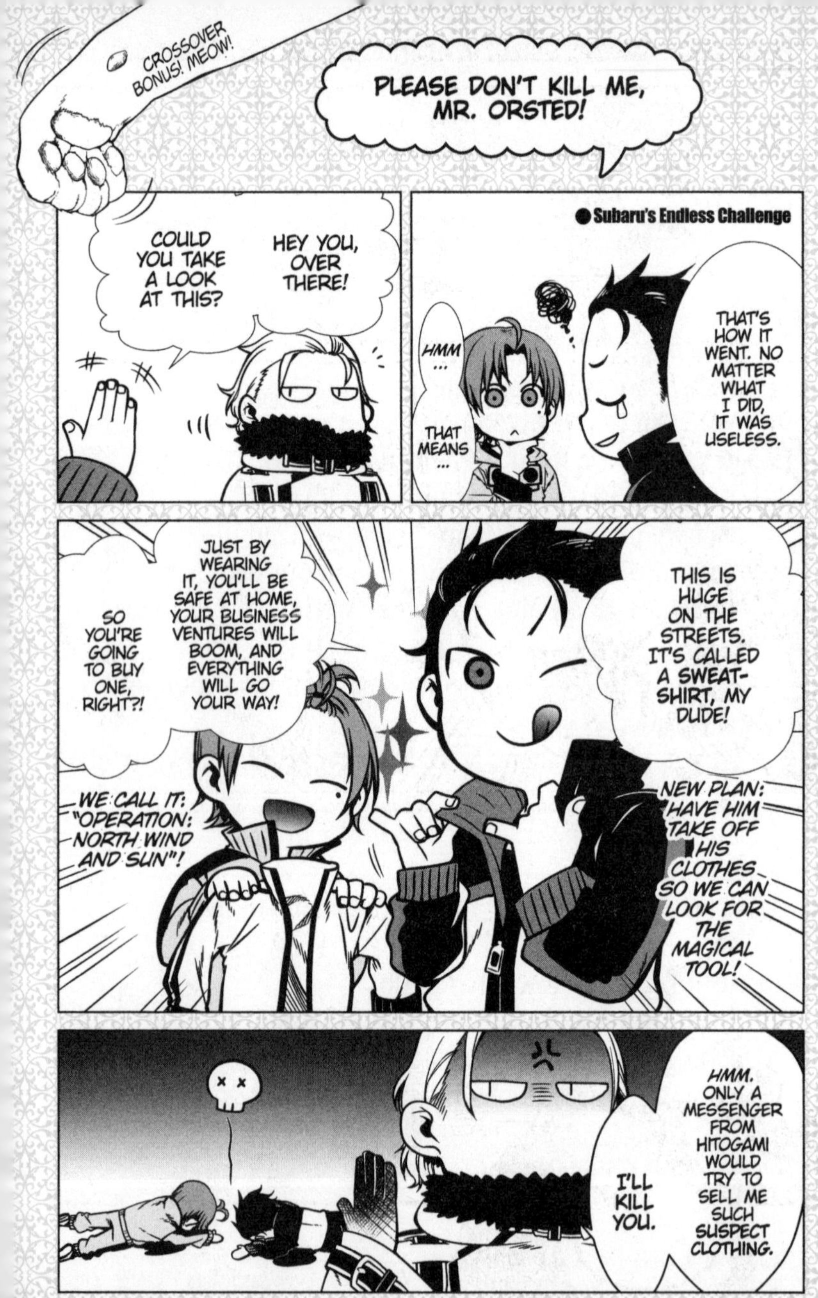
PLEASE DON'T KILL ME, MR. ORSTED!
CROSSOVER BONUS! MEOW!
Subaru's Endless Challenge
THAT'S HOW IT WENT. NO MATTER WHAT I DID, IT WAS USELESS.
HMM...
THAT MEANS...
HEY YOU, OVER THERE!
COULD YOU TAKE A LOOK AT THIS?
THIS IS HUGE ON THE STREETS. IT'S CALLED A SWEAT-SHIRT, MY DUDE!
NEW PLAN: HAVE HIM TAKE OFF HIS CLOTHES SO WE CAN LOOK FOR THE MAGICAL TOOL!
JUST BY WEARING IT, YOU'LL BE SAFE AT HOME, YOUR BUSINESS VENTURES WILL BOOM, AND EVERYTHING WILL GO YOUR WAY!
SO YOU'RE GOING TO BUY ONE, RIGHT?!
WE CALL IT: "OPERATION: NORTH WIND AND SUN"!
HMM. ONLY A MESSENGER FROM HITOGAMI WOULD TRY TO SELL ME SUCH SUSPECT CLOTHING.
I'LL KILL YOU.

Back to the drawing board...

Re:ZERO – Making Dinner in Another World! (Girls' Version)

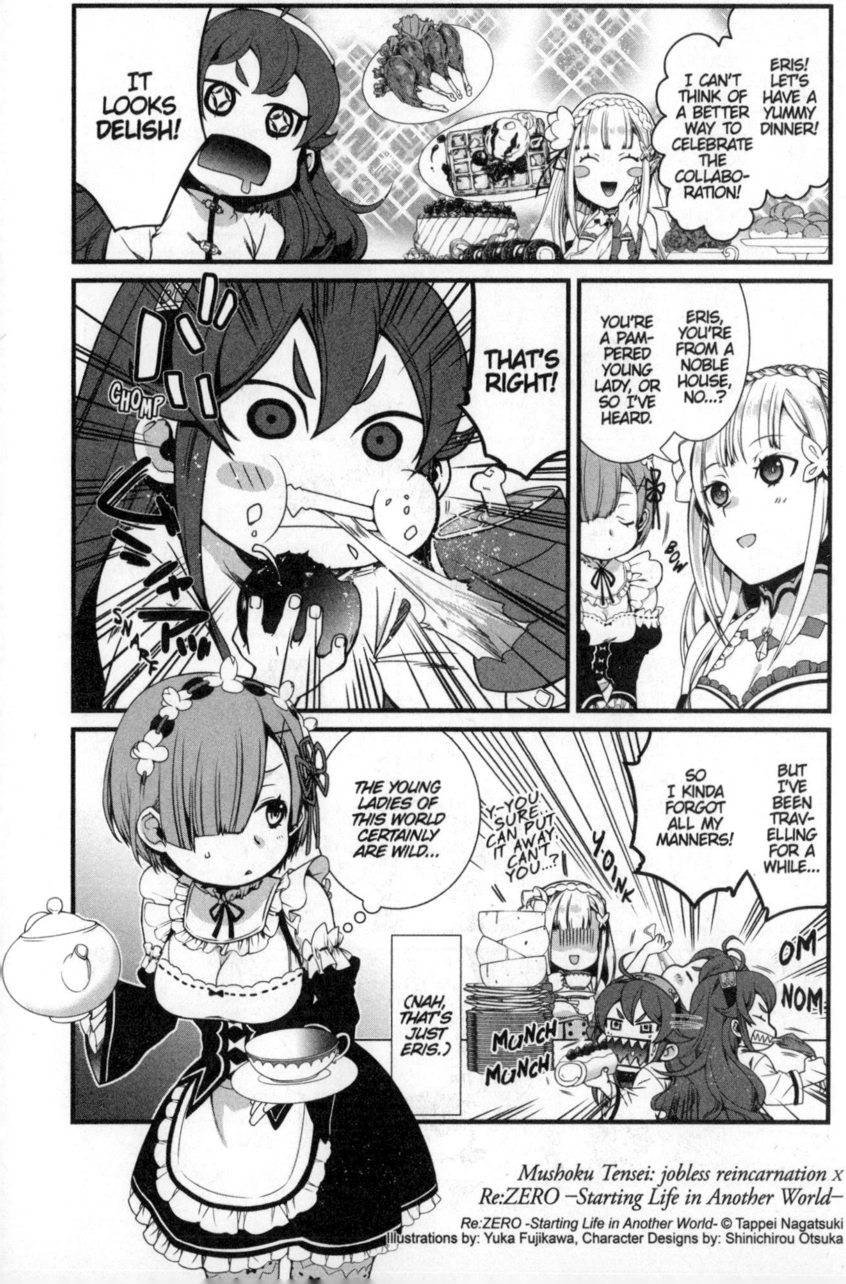
ERIS! LET'S HAVE A YUMMY DINNER!
I CAN'T THINK OF A BETTER WAY TO CELEBRATE THE COLLABO-RATION!
IT LOOKS DELISH!
ERIS, YOU'RE FROM A NOBLE HOUSE, NO...?
YOU'RE A PAM-PERED YOUNG LADY, OR SO I'VE HEARD.
BOW
THAT'S RIGHT!
CHOMP
SNARF
BUT I'VE BEEN TRAV-ELLING FOR A WHILE...
SO I KINDA FORGOT ALL MY MANNERS!
Y-OINK
Y-YOU SURE CAN PUT IT AWAY, CAN'T YOU...?
THE YOUNG LADIES OF THIS WORLD CERTAINLY ARE WILD...
OM NOM
MUNCH MUNCH
(NAH, THAT'S JUST ERIS.)

Mushoku Tensei: jobless reincarnation x
Re:ZERO –Starting Life in Another World–

Illustrations by: Yuka Fujikawa, Character Designs by: Shinichirou Otsuka

Re:ZERO – Making Dinner in Another World! (Boys' Version)

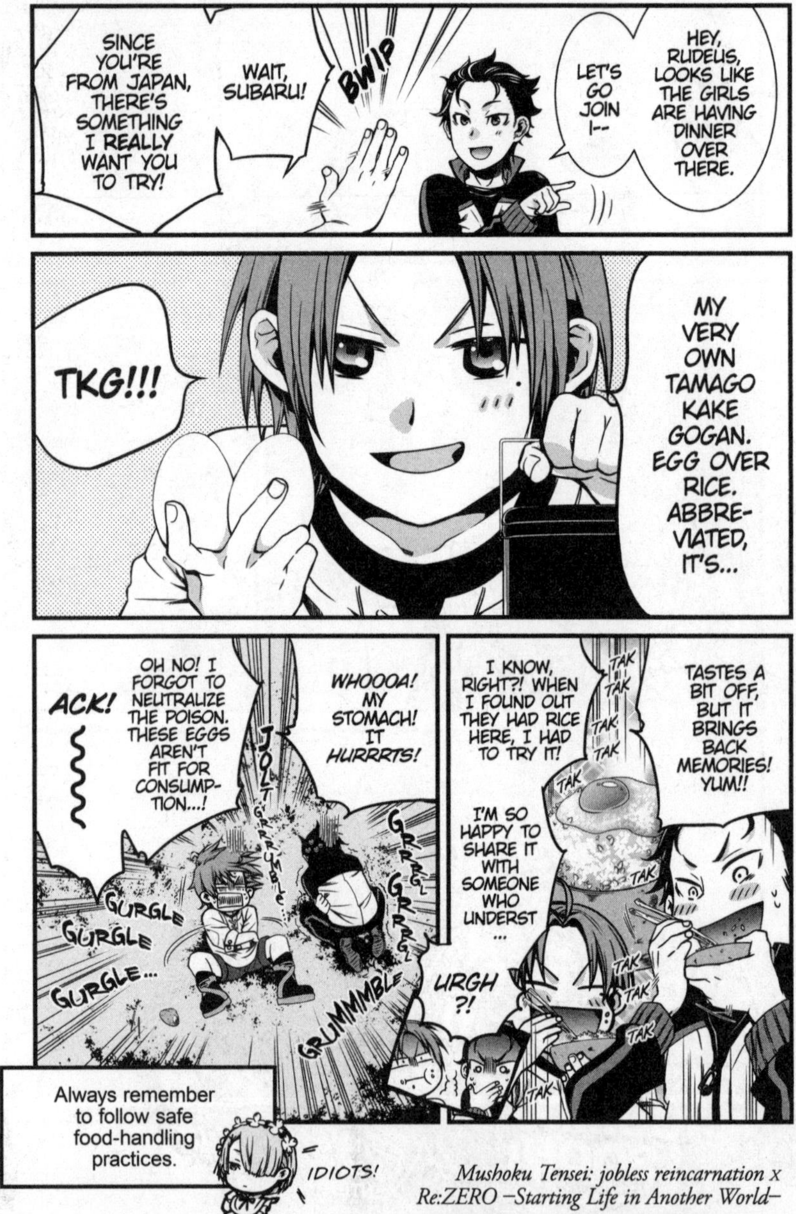

HEY, RUDEUS, LOOKS LIKE THE GIRLS ARE HAVING DINNER OVER THERE.
LET'S GO JOIN I--
BWIP
WAIT, SUBARU!
SINCE YOU'RE FROM JAPAN, THERE'S SOMETHING I REALLY WANT YOU TO TRY!
MY VERY OWN TAMAGO KAKE GOGAN. EGG OVER RICE. ABBRE-VIATED, IT'S...
TKG!!!
TASTES A BIT OFF, BUT IT BRINGS BACK MEMORIES! YUM!!
I KNOW, RIGHT?! WHEN I FOUND OUT THEY HAD RICE HERE, I HAD TO TRY IT!
TAK TAK TAK TAK TAK
I'M SO HAPPY TO SHARE IT WITH SOMEONE WHO UNDERST ...
TAK TAK TAK TAK TAK
URGH ?!
WHOOOA! MY STOMACH! IT HURRRTS!
OH NO! I FORGOT TO NEUTRALIZE THE POISON. THESE EGGS AREN'T FIT FOR CONSUMP-TION...!
ACK!
JOLT
GRRRUMBLE...
GRRRGL GRRRGL
GURGLE GURGLE GURGLE...
GRUMMMBLE
Always remember to follow safe food-handling practices.
IDIOTS!

Mushoku Tensei: jobless reincarnation x
Re:ZERO –Starting Life in Another World–

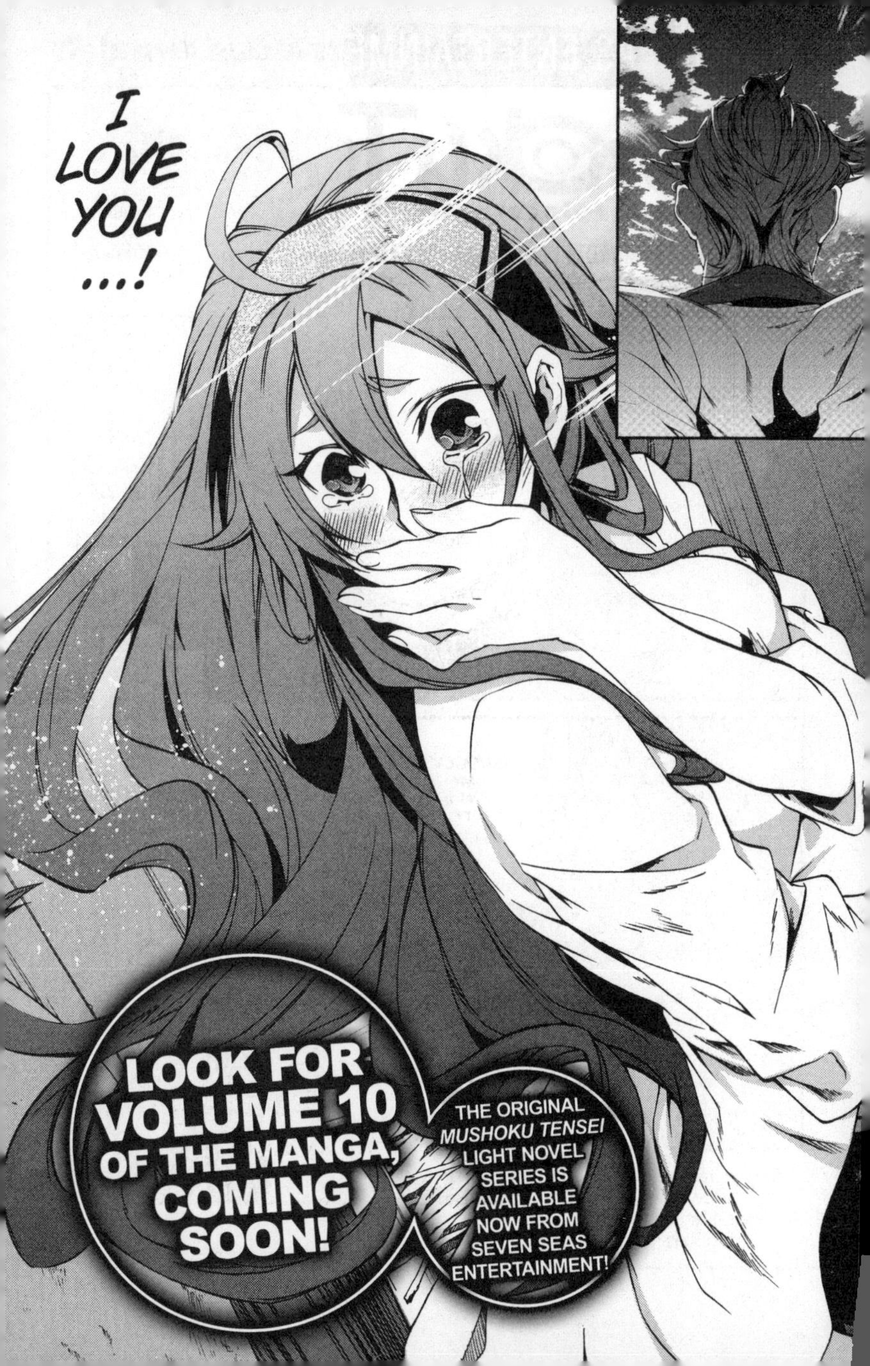
I LOVE YOU ...!
LOOK FOR VOLUME 10 OF THE MANGA, COMING SOON!
THE ORIGINAL *MUSHOKU TENSEI* LIGHT NOVEL SERIES IS AVAILABLE NOW FROM SEVEN SEAS ENTERTAINMENT!

...NT PRESENTS

TENSEI
volume 9

character design by **SHIROTAKA**

TRANSLATION
Beni Axia Conrad

ADAPTATION
Cae Hawksmoor

LETTERING AND RETOUCH
Rai Enril

COVER DESIGN
KC Fabellon

PROOFREADER
Janet Houck
Danielle King

EDITOR
J.P. Sullivan

PRODUCTION MANAGER
Lissa Pattillo

MANAGING EDITOR
Julie Davis

EDITOR-IN-CHIEF
Adam Arnold

PUBLISHER
Jason DeAngelis

MUSHOKU TENSEI: JOBLESS REINCARNATION VOL. 9
©Yuka Fujikawa, Rifujin na Magonote 2018
First published in Japan in 2018 by KADOKAWA CORPORATION, Tokyo.
English translation rights reserved by Seven Seas Entertainment
under the license from KADOKAWA CORPORATION, Tokyo.

Seven Seas press and purchase enquiries can be sent to Marketing Manager
Lianne Sentar at press@gomanga.com. Information regarding the distribution
and purchase of digital editions is available from Digital Manager CK Russell
at digital@gomanga.com.

ISBN: 978-1-64275-119-2

Printed in Canada

First Printing: August 2019

10 9 8 7 6 5 4 3 2 1

FOLLOW US ONLINE: *www.sevenseasentertainment.com*

READING DIRECTIONS

This book reads from *right to left*, Japanese style.
If this is your first time reading manga, you start
reading from the top right panel on each page and
take it from there. If you get lost, just follow the
numbered diagram here. It may seem backwards at
first, but you'll get the hang of it! Have fun!!

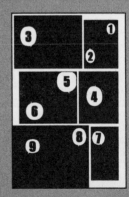
